BASIC
CHESS
OPENINGS

GABOR KALLAI

EVERYMAN CHESS

Everyman Chess, formerly Cadogan Chess, is published by Everyman Publishers, London

First published in 1997 by Gloucester Publishers plc, (formerly Everyman Publishers plc), Northburgh House, 10 Northburgh Street, London, EC1V 0AT

Reprinted 2000

British Library Cataloguing-in-Publication Data
A catalogue record for this book is available from the British Library.

ISBN: 978 1 85744 1130

Distributed in North America by The Globe Pequot Press, P.O Box 480, 246 Goose Lane, Guilford, CT 06437-0480.

All other sales enquiries should be directed to Gloucester Publishers plc, Northburgh House, 10 Northburgh Street, London, EC1V 0AT
tel: 020 7253 7887 fax: 020 7490 3708
email: info@everymanchess.com
website: www.everymanchess.com

To Marika, Oli, Beni and Lili

Advisor: János Szabolcsi

Translator: Zita Rajcsányi

Proofreading: Tim Wall and Alexander Meynell

Typeset by ChessSetter

Printed and bound in the US

Contents

Symbols

+	Check
±	Slight advantage to White
∓	Slight advantage to Black
±	Clear advantage to White
∓	Clear advantage to Black
+−	White wins
−+	Black wins
∞	Unclear position
??	Blunder
?	Weak move
?!	Dubious move
!?	Interesting move
!	Good move
!!	Outstanding move

Contents

Symbols

+	Check
±	Slight advantage to White
∓	Slight advantage to Black
±	Clear advantage to White
∓	Clear advantage to Black
+−	White wins
−+	Black wins
∞	Unclear position
??	Blunder
?	Weak move
?!	Dubious move
!?	Interesting move
!	Good move
!!	Outstanding move

Foreword

Gábor Kállai has undertaken a tremendous task in writing this book. He has composed a handbook that embraces the entire opening theory of chess!

How is this possible, the reader may ask, when even the *Encyclopaedia of Chess Openings*, with its five huge phone book-like volumes fails to do this? Naturally this job can only be done with strict selection. In the first place the book contains the main lines of each opening, taking into account modern fashion. The author explains every opening in detail and gives a diagram at the end of each section, sketching the plans for both sides in the middlegame. These 'plans and counterplans' explanations are tremendous: they not only supply answers to the question 'What happens next?', but also provide us with guidelines for the execution of these ideas. The latter is particularly important as it is no use knowing what our goal is if we do not have the technique to achieve it.

This book is not aimed at grandmasters. It will probably be most useful for players between the rating of 1700 and 2300. But even stronger players may find it useful when, for example, developing a new repertoire, if they want to see the typical possibilities and get a feel of a certain opening. Of course for more detailed preparation, an opening monograph is required. For those who are relatively new to chess I suggest that they thumb through the book from the beginning to the end. It will provide them with a reliable basic grounding in chess openings that will help them to choose a suitable opening to play.

Allow me to provide a short introduction to the author as well. Gábor Kállai has been one of the strongest International Masters in Hungary for a long time. It was a pleasant surprise that, while writing this book, he first made a grandmaster norm in the French Team Championship in 1994 and then repeated this success in a grandmaster tournament in Balatonberény the following year! Thus at the FIDE Congress in Paris he was awarded the Grandmaster title. Besides individual tournaments, he also plays first board for first division teams in France, Hungary and Belgium. He has also been my second several times in world-class tournaments and we have two co-written books that have been published in English. He also publishes chess articles regularly. His writing – as you will see in this book – reflects a search for understanding at every stage of the game.

The author and I hope that you enjoy reading this book and hope that it will help you to create interesting and successful games.

Grandmaster Zoltán Ribli

Publisher's Note: This book is the first volume of a two-part work covering every chess opening. *Basic Chess Openings* deals with all variations in which White's first move is 1 e4.

More Basic Chess Openings is the second volume which completes the series, and covers all other first moves, including 1 d4, 1 c4 and 1 ♘f3.

Introduction

This, the first volume of *Basic Chess Openings*, is entirely concerned with those openings starting with the move 1 e4. The first part deals with the *Open Games*, viz. those openings starting with the moves 1 e4 e5, which are so named because they usually lead to middlegames with an open centre, thanks to the fact that White, utilizing his one-move advantage, often starts a central offensive against Black's e5-pawn at a very early stage. This he can do by d2-d4 (with various piece constellations and perhaps prepared by the pawn move c2-c3) or by f2-f4 (King's Gambit, Vienna Game).

The characteristic of Open Games is a lively tactical battle in which the two players often target the squares f2 and f7, and in this chapter we will come upon gambits and counter-gambits that aim to accelerate one's development to this end. The theory of Open Games is now very well developed, so to play these positions it is not enough to enjoy a complicated fight and possess the ability to cope with tactical variations: one must be familiar not only with the strategic aims of the opening, but also with some very heavily analysed variations. Although it is not easy to keep up-to-date with the latest trends, the reward is worth the effort: colourful and exciting games.

Semi-Open Games are those in which Black does not play 1...e5 in answer to 1 e4. There are several possible strategies. For example, Black may nibble at White's e4-pawn with ...d7-d5, either right away (**Scandinavian Defence**) or prepared by 1...c6 (**Caro-Kann Defence**) or with 1...e6 (**French Defence**). Another idea is to prevent White from gaining further space in the centre with 1...c5. This is the most fashionable variation of all, the **Sicilian Defence**. Among the more unusual strategies, Black has **Alekhine's Defence** – where he lures White's pawns forward in order to undermine them later – and the **Pirc Defence** where Black places his faith in his fianchettoed bishop on g7. The **Nimzowitsch Defence** (1...♘c6) and Black's other first moves are not without some point, but they still do not provide sufficient possibilities against a well-versed opponent.

Centre Gambit

1 e4 e5 2 d4 exd4 3 ♕xd4

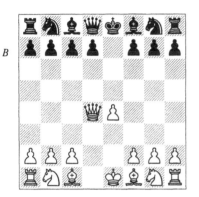

Why is this a gambit? Well, White sacrifices not material but time, making use of the (much too) early development of the queen to castle queenside quickly. Black has nothing to fear if he plays correctly.

3...♘c6 4 ♕e3

On 4 ♕a4 Black develops easily via 4...♘f6 5 ♗g5 ♗e7 6 ♘c3 0-0 7 ♘f3 d6 8 0-0-0 ♗d7!

4...♘f6

An immediate development of the pieces is necessary. Also playable is 4...♗b4+ 5 ♘c3 (5 c3 ♗a5) 5...♘ge7 6 ♗d2 0-0 7 0-0-0 d6 8 ♕g3 ♔h8 9 f4 f5 and the position is level. 4...b6, 4...d6 and 4...♗e7 are chicken's moves but perhaps 4...g6 is acceptable.

5 ♘c3

An interesting idea is 5 c4 to stop Black's freeing manoeuvre ...d7-d5. Sharp and unclear, but not very good, is 5 e5 on account of 5...♘g4 6 ♕e4 d5! (of course taking the pawn on e5 would cost Black a piece to 7 f4) 7 exd6+ ♗e6. Now on 8 dxc7 Black may choose between 8...♕xc7 and 8...♕d1+; he can meet 8 ♗c4 by 8...♘f6 9 ♕e2 ♕xd6 10 ♗xe6 fxe6; while on 8 ♗a6 one can play 8...♕xd6 9 ♗xb7 ♕b4+ 10 ♕xb4 ♘xb4.

5...♗b4

A foolproof alternative is the reply 5...♗e7. On 6 ♕g3 follows 6...♘b4 and White has to give up one of the bishops, while after 6 ♗d2 d5! and 6 ♗c4 ♘b4 7 ♗b3 d5 Black has absolutely nothing to worry about.

6 ♗d2 0-0 7 0-0-0 ♖e8 8 ♗c4

Warding off the threat of ...d7-d5. Note that 8 ♕g3 fails to the response 8...♖xe4!

8...d6 *(D)*

It is risky to snatch the pawn: 8...♗xc3 9 ♗xc3 ♘xe4 (9...♖xe4? 10 ♗xf6 wins) 10 ♕f4 and White has a nice attack. Black can try 8...♘a5 9 ♗d3 d5 but after 10 ♘ge2 c5 11 a3 d4 12 ♕g3 White's threats compensate him for the sacrificed piece: 12...dxc3 (better is 12...♗xc3) 13 ♘xc3 ♗xc3 14 ♗xc3 and Black can hardly deal with the simultaneous threats of 15 ♗b5 and 15 e5 (planning 16 ♗xh7+).

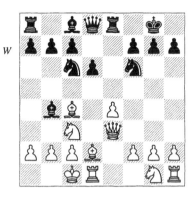

Plans and Counterplans:
White can build up an attack against the black kingside but in the meantime he has to watch out for his e4-pawn. Black neutralizes the strong white bishop with ...♗e6 and opts for the break ...d6-d5. A possible continuation is 9 f3 ♘e5 10 ♗b3 ♗e6 11 ♘d5 with even chances.

Danish Gambit

1 e4 e5 2 d4 exd4 3 c3 dxc3

This reckless gambit, in which White sacrifices two pawns for rapid development and an attack, is rarely seen in tournament practice. The reason is that Black can defend with success – provided, of course, he knows the way!

Declining the gambit by 3...d5 (less good is 3...♕e7 4 cxd4 ♕xe4+ 5 ♗e3 ♘f6 6 ♘c3 ♗b4 7 ♘f3 and White's attack unfolds because of the further tempi Black has to lose with his queen) 4 exd5 ♘f6 (for 4...♕xd5 5 ♘f3 ♘c6 6 cxd4, see the Scotch Gambit) 5 ♗b5+ c6 (5...♗d7 6 ♗c4) 6 dxc6 bxc6 7 ♗c4 ♗c5 8 ♕e2+ ♕e7 9 ♕xe7+ ♔xe7 10 cxd4 ♗xd4 11 ♘f3 leaves White a little ahead. It is better to accept the challenge.

4 ♗c4

4 ♘xc3 ♘c6 5 ♘f3 transposes into the Scotch Gambit.

4...cxb2 5 ♗xb2

White has sacrificed two pawns; in exchange he has both of his bishops nicely developed, ready to attack. Black can parry the attack but the price is one pawn (or perhaps even two).

5...d5

After 5...d6 White has a strong attack: 6 ♘f3 ♘f6 (or 6...♘c6 7 ♘c3 ♗e6 8 ♘d5 with advantage to White) 7 ♕b3 and Black's game is far from attractive. 5...♘f6 6 e5 d5 7 ♗b5+ c6 8 exf6 cxb5 9 fxg7 ♗b4+ 10 ♔f1 ♖g8 11 ♕d3 is good for White.

6 ♗xd5

If 6 exd5 then Black can play 6...♘f6, followed by ...♗d6, and the attack is stopped.

6...♘f6 7 ♗xf7+ ♔xf7 8 ♕xd8 ♗b4+ 9 ♕d2 ♗xd2+ 10 ♘xd2

Plans and Counterplans:
Almost directly from the opening we have arrived at an endgame. The position is even but certainly not a draw! Both sides have a passed pawn and good squares for their pieces. If Black plays ...c7-c5 then White can try to place a knight on d6, while Black, in turn, can obtain the d4 outpost for his knight.

1 e4 e5 2 ♘f3

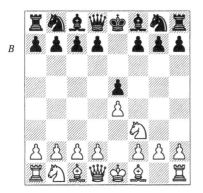

A natural, multi-purpose move which develops a piece, attacks the e5 pawn, prepares for d2-d4 and – after bringing the f1 bishop out – arranges castling. A lot worse is 2 ♘e2, when after 2...♘f6 3 ♘bc3 ♘c6 either 4 d4 exd4 5 ♘xd4 ♗b4! or 4 d3 d5! planning ...♗c5 and ...0-0 or 4 f4?! d5! 5 fxe5 ♘xe4 6 d4 ♗g4! (threatening to play ...♕h4+, ...♗b4, ...f7-f6 or ...♕d7 and ...0-0-0) gives Black an equal game. On 2 ♘f3 Black's alternatives are protecting his e5-pawn or a counter-attack on e4. However, defending by **2...f6?** would put him on the verge of losing at once: 3 ♘xe5! fxe5 (or 3...♕e7 4 ♘f3 ♕xe4+ 5 ♗e2 and ♘c3, 0-0, ♖e1 with a tremendous advantage for White) 4 ♕h5+ ♔e7 (or 4...g6 5 ♕xe5+ winning the h8-rook) 5 ♕xe5+ ♔f7 6 ♗c4+ d5 7 ♗xd5+ ♔g6 8 h4 h5 9 ♗xb7! ♗xb7 10 ♕f5+ ♔h6 11 d4+ and

the show is over. The moral of this is that protection of the e5-pawn must be combined with building up a position with either 2...d6 (Philidor Defence) or 2...♘c6 (Ruy Lopez, Scotch Defence etc.) For an attack on e4 the correct move is 2...♘f6 (Russian Game).

Other possibilities are:

a) 2...d5? 3 exd5 e4 (alternatively 3...♕xd5 4 ♘c3 ♕a5 5 d4!? with a huge lead in development) 4 ♕e2 f5 5 d3 ♘f6 6 dxe4! fxe4 7 ♘c3 ♗b4 8 ♕b5+ c6 9 ♕xb4 exf3 10 ♗g5 cxd5 11 0-0-0 and Black's game falls apart. A similar concept is realized in the Latvian Counter-Gambit:

b) 2...f5?! White's tactical answer is 3 ♗c4!? fxe4 4 ♘xe5 ♕g5 (or 4...d5 5 ♕h5+ g6 6 ♘xg6 ♘f6 7 ♗b5+! – depriving the knight of the c6-square – 7...c6 8 ♕e5+ ♗e7 9 ♘xe7 ♕xe7 10 ♕xe7+ ♔xe7 11 ♗e2 winning a pawn, although White's position is a little passive) 5 d4 ♕xg2 6 ♕h5+ g6 7 ♗f7+ ♔d8 8 ♗xg6 ♕xh1+ 9 ♔e2 and the attack breaks through, for example 9...c6 10 ♘c3 ♘f6 11 ♕h4 ♗e7 12 ♗g5! ♕xa1 13 ♗xf6 ♗xf6 14 ♕xf6+ ♔c7 15 ♘c4! and the lone black king is more and more squeezed by the hostile white pieces. Although this line is very tempting, these days attention has turned to the less risky 3

♘xe5 ♕f6 4 ♘c4! fxe4 5 ♘c3 ♕g6 (or 5...♕e6 6 d3! exd3+ 7 ♘e3 dxc2 8 ♕xc2 c6 9 ♗d3 and 0-0, ♗d2, ♖ae1 breaking Black's resistance) 6 d3 (this is why White did not play 4 d4 instead of 4 ♘c4!) 6...♗b4 (6...exd3 loses beautifully: 7 ♗xd3 ♕xg2 8 ♕h5+ and now on

8...g6 9 ♕e5+ followed by 10 ♗e4 or on 8...♔d8 9 ♗e4! wins) 7 ♗d2 ♗xc3 8 ♗xc3 ♘f6 9 ♗xf6 gxf6 10 dxe4 ♕xe4+ 11 ♘e3 ±. Black's undeveloped position is a wreck while White has an easy attack with ♕h5+, 0-0-0, ♗c4 (♗d3) and ♖he1.

Ponziani Opening

1 e4 e5 2 ♘f3 ♘c6 3 c3

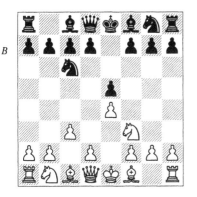

White wants to play d4 and after ...exd4 recapture with the pawn. This, however, is a little too slow, not to mention the fact that the c3-pawn occupies the queen's knight's natural square. Now is the right moment for Black to attack the e4-pawn.

3...♘f6

Another good move is 3...d5 with sharp play, e.g. 4 ♕a4 (after 4 exd5 ♕xd5 Black is okay as the queen cannot be chased away with a tempo) 4...f6 5 ♗b5 ♘e7 6 exd5 ♕xd5 7 d4 and White is more active. Black may instead sacrifice a pawn for development: 4...♘f6 5 ♘xe5 ♗d6! 6 ♘xc6 bxc6. Now taking another pawn would grant Black a decisive development plus, but even after the correct 7 d3! 0-0 8 ♗e2 ♖e8 or 8...♕e8 Black has compensation for the pawn.

4 d4

Should White wish to avoid theoretical lines he can choose 4 d3, then ♘bd2, ♕c2, ♗e2 (or g2-g3, ♗g2), 0-0 and an eventual b2-b4. Of course he cannot hope for any special advantage with this slightly passive setup but altogether it is not bad.

4...♘xe4

Worse is 4...exd4 5 e5.

5 d5

After 5 dxe5 d5 and ...♗c5 Black has a good game.

5...♘b8

Playing it safe. The sacrifice 5...♗c5!? is interesting: 6 dxc6 ♗xf2+ (of course not 6...♘xf2? 7 ♕d5 and White is better) 7 ♔e2 bxc6 8 ♕a4 (to stop ...♗a6+) 8...f5 9 ♘bd2 0-0 10 ♘xe4 fxe4 11 ♕xe4 ♗b6 12 ♔d1! d5 13 ♕xe5 ♗f5! with an unclear position. A good attacking player would never avoid such a position where the enemy king is stuck in the middle. White, a piece ahead, may hope to win in the long run ... if he can survive the immediate storm!

6 ♗d3

After 6 ♘xe5 ♗c5 7 ♕g4 0-0 8 ♕xe4 d6 9 ♗d3 f5 10 ♕c4 b5! 11 ♕xb5 ♕e7 12 0-0 dxe5 13 ♗g5 ♕d6 Black has compensation for the pawn.

6...♘c5 7 ♘xe5 ♘xd3+ 8 ♘xd3 d6 9 0-0 ♗e7 10 ♕f3 0-0

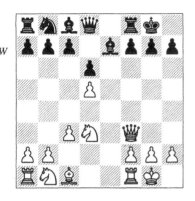

Plans and Counterplans:
The position is even with a peaceful, positional character. White must try to transfer his minor pieces to the kingside for an attack and may occupy the e-file with his rooks. Black develops his knight to f6 or f8 and activates his queenside with a well-prepared ...c7-c5 and ...b7-b5.

Scotch Game

1 e4 e5 2 ♘f3 ♘c6 3 d4

White, in similar fashion to the Sicilian Defence, does not make a preparatory move but starts the central fight right away. He can achieve a slight spatial plus in the centre, but Black can fight for equality with quick piece play and often the counter-thrust ...d7-d5.

3...exd4

3...d5? fails to the simple 4 ♘xe5! ♘xe5 5 dxe5 dxe4 6 ♕xd8+ ♔xd8 7 ♘c3 ♗b4 8 ♗d2 ± followed by 0-0-0, ♗c4 (♗b5), ♖he1.

4 ♘xd4

In order to accelerate his development, White can attempt the Scotch Gambit, the two forms of which are the following:

a) 4 ♗c4 ♗c5 (not 4...♗b4+ 5 c3 dxc3 6 0-0 d6 – 6...cxb2? 7 ♗xb2 ♘f6 8 e5! – 7 a3! ♗a5 8 b4 ♗b6 9 ♕b3 ♕f6 10 ♘xc3 ♘ge7 11 ♗b2 0-0 12 ♘d5 ♕g6 13 a4! with a tremendous advantage to White) 5 c3 dxc3 6 ♘xc3 (an even game is reached after 6 ♗xf7+ ♔xf7 7 ♕d5+ ♔f8 8 ♕xc5+ ♕e7, and now 9 ♕xc3!? ♕xe4+ 10 ♗e3 d5 ∞ or 9 ♕xe7+ ♘gxe7 10 ♘xc3 d5! and ...♘c6-b4 =) 6...d6 7 ♗g5 ♘ge7 8 ♘d5 and White bears down unpleasantly on the black centre, for example on 8...0-0 9 0-0 ♗e6 10 ♘f6+! ♔h8 (after 10...gxf6 11 ♗xf6, 12 ♕d2 followed by ♕g5 or ♕h6 is unavoidable), then 11 ♖c1

and ♘h4, ♕h5 with a forceful attack. Also 8...f6 9 ♗xf6!? gxf6 10 ♘xf6+ ♔f8 11 ♕c1! is promising for White. If Black does not want to defend, then on 5 c3, instead of 5...dxc3, a good alternative is to take on the Italian Game with 5...♘f6!?

b) 4 c3 d5!? (also good is 4...dxc3 and now after 5 ♘xc3, 5...♗b4 6 ♗c4 d6 7 ♕b3 ♗xc3+ 8 bxc3 ♕d7 9 ♕c2 ♘f6 and ...0-0 is better for Black, or on 5 ♗c4 d6 6 ♘xc3 ♘f6 7 ♕b3 ♕d7 8 ♗g5 ♘e5 9 ♗b5 c6 10 f4 ♘eg4 11 h3 cxb5 12 hxg4 b4!? 13 ♘d5 b6 14 ♘xf6+ gxf6 15 ♖xh7 ♖xh7 16 ♘xh7 ♗e7 when the g4-pawn is hanging and the threats are ...♗b7, ...0-0-0 or even ...d7-d5!?) 5 exd5 ♕xd5 6 cxd4 ♗g4 7 ♘c3 ♗b4 8 ♗e2 ♗xf3 9 ♗xf3 ♕c4 with mutual chances. The moral is: a Scotsman should not sacrifice! Let us get back to 4 ♘xd4!

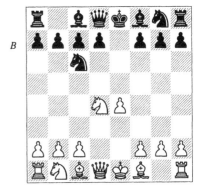

B

Black's main continuations are:
4...♘f6 (section I) and **4...♗c5**
(section II). It is also worth mentioning a few other options. For
example:
  a) 4...d5? 5 ♘xc6 bxc6 6 exd5
♕xd5 (6...cxd5 7 ♗b5+ +−) 7 ♗d3!
± ♕xg2? 8 ♕e2+ ♗e7 9 ♗e4 followed by ♗xc6+ +−.
  b) 4...♘xd4? 5 ♕xd4 ♕f6 6 e5
♕b6 7 ♗e3 ±.
  c) 4...♕f6 5 ♘b5! ♗c5 6 ♕e2
♗b6 7 ♘1c3 ♘ge7 8 ♗e3 ♗a5 9
0-0-0 a6! 10 ♘d5 ♘xd5 11 exd5
axb5 12 dxc6 bxc6 (12...♕xc6 13
b4! ♗xb4 14 ♗c5+ wins a bishop)
13 ♗d4+ ♕e6 14 ♕xe6+ fxe6 15
♗xg7 ♖g8 16 ♗h6 ∞ and in this
unusual endgame White's plan is
17 ♗d3. Black's pieces are discon-
nected from the kingside; he needs
to mobilize his centre.
  d) 4...♕h4!? A unique move,
the idea of which is that White
has trouble defending his pawn
on e4. But a serious drawback is
that it abandons protection of the
pawn on c7. A strong suggestion
for White is 5 ♘c3!? (after 5
♘xc6?! ♕xe4+ 6 ♗e2 dxc6 White
has nothing for the pawn and on
5 ♘b5 Black plays 5...♗b4+! 6
♘1c3 ♗a5! 7 ♗d3 a6 8 ♘a3 b5
with even chances) 5...♗b4 6 ♗e2
♕xe4 7 ♘b5 ♗xc3+ (7...♕xg2 8
♗f3 and ♘xc7+ +− or 7...♘f6 8
0-0! ♗xc3 9 ♘xc3 ♕d4 10 ♗d3 0-0
11 ♘b5 ♕b6 12 ♗e3 ♕a5 13 c3
♘d5 14 b4 ♘xe3 15 ♗xh7+! and
whatever Black's reply 16 ♕h5+
wins) 8 bxc3 ♔d8 9 0-0 ♘f6 10

♗e3 ♖e8 11 ♖e1 and with his king
stuck in the middle and the queenside undeveloped, Black is far
behind. For example: 11...a6? 12
♘d6! cxd6 13 ♗f3 and the black
queen has no good options in view
of the threat of mate, or 11...♕e5
12 ♕c1! d6 13 ♕a3 followed by
♖ad1, c4-c5 initiating a strong attack against the black king. If
Black accepts that a pawn is not
sufficient to warrant undertak-
ing risks in the opening, then instead of 6...♕xe4 he can consider
6...♘f6!?, for example 7 0-0 (7
♘db5? ♘xe4) 7...d6! 8 ♘db5 ♗a5
followed by ...a6 and ...0-0.

I. 1 e4 e5 2 ♘f3 ♘c6 3 d4 exd4 4 ♘xd4 ♘f6 5 ♘xc6

White prepares e4-e5 which, if
played at once, would be a blunder: 5 e5? ♘xe5 6 ♕e2 ♕e7 7 ♘f5
♕b4+ and now on 8 ♘c3 d6 or 8
c3 ♕e4 Black maintains the extra
pawn.

5...bxc6 6 e5
  Or 6 ♗d3 d5! 7 exd5 cxd5 8 0-0
♗e7 9 ♘c3 0-0 10 ♗g5 c6 followed
by ...♖b8 with a pleasant game for
Black.

6...♕e7
  This is better than 6...♘d5?! 7
c4! ♗b4+ 8 ♗d2 ♗xd2+ 9 ♕xd2
♘e7 10 ♘c3 0-0 11 0-0-0 ± (the c8-
bishop is stuck) or 6...♘e4 7 ♕f3!
♕h4 (7...♘g5 8 ♕g3 ♘e6 9 ♗d3
d5 10 0-0 g6 11 ♘d2 f5 12 ♘b3
♗g7 13 f4 0-0 14 ♕f2! ± followed
by ♗e3 and White's control of the

dark squares d4 and c5 paralyses Black) 8 g3! ♘g5 9 ♕e2 ♕e4 10 ♗xg5! ♕xh1 11 ♘c3 ± and White is threatening to trap the black queen with 0-0-0, f2-f4 (f2-f3), ♗f4, ♗g2, ♖h1, while the journey ♘c3-e4-d6 may also be unpleasant. On 11...♕h2 12 ♕f3! followed by 0-0-0, ♗d3 (c4), ♖h1 is a good plan.

7 ♕e2 ♘d5

After 7...♘g8 8 b3! the bishop on c1 is threatening to emerge with effcect on a3.

8 c4

On 8 ♘d2, 8...♗b7 is possible: 9 c4 ♘f4!? 10 ♕e3 ♘e6 11 ♘b3 (otherwise Black can play 11...♕c5) 11...a5!? ∞ with the idea of ...a5-a4, ...♗a6.

8...♘b6

8...♗a6!? offers good prospects as well:

a) 9 ♘d2 g6! 10 b3 (10 ♘e4 ♕b4+! 11 ♕d2 ♗xc4 ∓) 10...♗g7 11 ♗b2 ♘b4! 12 ♘f3 c5 13 g3 0-0 14 ♗g2 d5! and Black has seized the initiative. In this variation we have seen everything that is important for Black! First a quick ...g7-g6, ...♗g7 and ...0-0, then away with the knight from d5 and play ...d7-d5. White is not developed enough to keep his opponent at bay.

b) 9 g3 g6! 10 ♗g2 ♗g7 11 0-0 0-0 12 ♘d2 ♘b6 13 f4 d5! ∓ and White is in trouble on c4.

c) 9 b3!? g6! 10 f4 (or 10 ♗a3 ♕g5 11 g3 ♘c3!? 12 ♘xc3 ♗xa3 13 ♘e4 ♕e7 14 ♘f6+ ♔f8 followed by ...♗b4+ and ...d7-d6, ...♗c3

threatening to snuff out the pawn on e5) 10...f6!? 11 ♗a3 ♕f7 12 ♕d2 ♘e7! 13 ♕a5 and now Black makes a fantastic sacrifice with 13...fxe5!? 14 ♕xa6 ♕xf4 15 ♘d2 (15 ♕a5 ♕h4+! wins one of the rooks!) 15...♕d4! 16 ♖c1 ♘f5! 17 ♗xf8 ♖xf8 18 ♕a5 0-0-0! 19 ♕c3 ♖de8, threatening ...♘f5-e3, with serious compensation for the piece. The plan 10 f4 had to be prepared by 9 b3 since after the immediate 9 f4 ♕b4+! White has no good interposition.

9 ♘d2

On 9 b3 Black follows the usual plan that works well on nearly every occasion: 9...g6 followed by ...♗g7, ...0-0 and ...d7-d5. But the nowadays abandoned 9 ♘c3 is interesting, e.g. 9...♗a6 10 ♕e4 0-0-0 11 c5 ♗xf1 12 cxb6 ♗a6 13 bxc7 ♔xc7 14 ♗d2!? and now White can play either 0-0-0 or b4-b5!?

9...♗b7

Of course now 9...g6? is bad in view of 10 ♘e4 ♗g7 11 ♗g5! ♕xe5 12 ♗f6! and wins. On the other hand, 9...♕e6 is playable, with the idea of ...♗b4 and ...0-0.

10 b3

White prepares to castle queenside and at the same time strengthens e5.

10...a5!

Apparently a strong move. Besides it is always a pleasure when a pawn that would become weak in a future endgame, plays the main role in the middlegame!

11 a4

Not 11 ♗b2 a4 12 ♕e3 axb3 13 axb3 ♖xa1+ 14 ♗xa1 ♕a3 and the black pieces invade along the path of the a-pawn.

11...♕e6 12 ♗b2 ♗b4 13 0-0-0 0-0-0!

Preparing an immediate ...d7-d5, while the king is not badly placed on the queenside either.

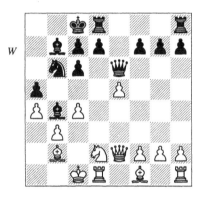

W

Plans and Counterplans:

Black is preparing for ...d7-d5 and White needs to be careful as his kingside is undeveloped, while his king is not bomb-proof either. For example **14 f4?** d5 15 exd6 ♕xd6 and Black takes over with ...♗a3 and ...♖he8. Better is **14 ♘f3!?** ♕h6+!? 15 ♕e3 (15 ♔b1 d5 ∞) 15...♕xe3+ 16 fxe3 ♖de8 17 ♗d3!? with mutual chances.

II. 1 e4 e5 2 ♘f3 ♘c6 3 d4 cxd4 4 ♘xd4 ♗c5

Black intends to develop his pieces by means of ...♕f6, ...d7-d6, ...♘ge7 and ...0-0. In the meantime he would be delighted to chase away the well-placed knight on d4.

5 ♗e3!?

The knight cannot be protected with 5 c3? owing to 5...♕e7! 6 f3 ♗xd4 7 cxd4 ♕b4+ winning the pawn on d4, while if the knight moves Black can obtain equality with precise play:

a) 5 ♘f3? ♘f6 threatening ...♘g4, ...♘xe4 and ...d7-d5, while 6 ♗g5? fails to 6...♗xf2+ 7 ♔xf2 ♘xe4+ and 8...♕xg5.

b) 5 ♘b3 ♗b6! (it is better not to exchange this bishop with 5...♗b4+ 6 ♗d2! as from b6 it will first attack f2 and then, after White castles kingside, it will pin the f-pawn, preventing f2-f4) 6 a4 a6!? (6...a5 would hand White the b5-square. The difference between 6...a6 and 6...a5 is so tiny that it is worth imitating the play of a world-class positional player – in the present case, Karpov. He considers it important to control the squares near his forces) 7 ♘c3 ♕f6 8 ♕e2 ♘ge7 9 ♘d5 ♘xd5 10 exd5+ ♘e7 11 a5 ♗a7 12 h4 h6! 13 ♗d2 d6 14 ♗c3 ♕f4 and now after 15 ♗xg7, 15...♖g8, followed by ...♗d7 and ...0-0-0, offers Black counterplay.

c) 5 ♘f5 d5!? 6 ♘xg7+ ♔f8 7 ♘h5 ♕h4 8 ♘g3 ♘f6 9 ♗e2! (9...♘g4 must be prevented) and now Black can choose between the lines 9...♘e5 10 ♘c3 ♘eg4 11 ♗xg4 ♘xg4 12 ♕xd5 ♗xf2+ 13 ♔e2 ♖g8!? and 9...♘xe4 10 0-0 ♗e6 11 ♘xe4 dxe4 12 ♗e3 ♗d6 13 g3 ♖g8. In both cases he has some initiative for the pawn.

d) 5 ♘xc6 ♕f6!? (or 5...bxc6 6 ♗d3 ♘e7 7 0-0 0-0 8 ♘d2!, when if Black plays 8...d6 then White answers ♕e2, ♘b3, ♗e3, a2-a4 and forces the exchange of the strong bishop on the diagonal a7-g1, and if 8...d5 then 9 ♕h5! is dangerous: besides attacking the pawn on h7, the queen is also threatening horizontally along the fifth rank) 6 ♕d2 (on 6 f4, 6...♕xc6 7 ♘c3 ♘f6 strikes at the white pawn centre, while 6 ♕e2 bxc6 followed by ...d7-d6, ...a7-a5, ...♗a6 and ...♘ge7 yields Black pleasant play. Finally, on 6 ♕f3 good is 6...♕xf3 7 gxf3 bxc6!? and ...d7-d6, ...♘ge7, ...♗e6, ...♖b8 and ...a7-a5 with a queenside initiative or 6...dxc6!? with a quick ...♗e6 and ...0-0-0 to follow) 6...dxc6 7 ♘c3 ♗e6 8 ♘a4 (on 8 ♗d3, 8...0-0-0 is possible) 8...♖d8 9 ♗d3 ♗d4 10 0-0 (10 c3 ♗xf2+ 11 ♕xf2 ♖xd3) 10...a6! vacating a square for the bishop after which Black can complete his development by ...♘e7 and ...0-0, although White can make life more difficult for Black here with 11 ♕a5!?

5...♕f6 6 c3

White should not allow his pawns to become ravaged, as for example after 6 ♘b5?! ♗xe3 7 fxe3 ♕h4+! 8 g3 ♕d8 9 ♕g4 ♔f8 10 ♕f4 d6 11 ♘1c3 a6 12 ♘d4 ♘e5, although here he has an advantage in development to counterbalance his inferior pawn structure. Black can think of artificial castling via ...♘f6, ...h7-h6, ...g7-g6, ...♔g7 while White may concentrate his forces on the open f-file.

6...♘ge7 7 ♗c4!?

It is important both to develop and to hinder Black's explosive move ...d7-d5.

7...0-0

The other popular continuation is 7...♘e5. Then after 8 ♗e2 (8 ♗b3 d6 9 f4? ♘g4! demonstrates the need to withdraw the bishop to e2 in order to control the g4-square) 8...♕g6 9 0-0 Black has to abstain from 9...♕xe4?!: 10 b4 ♗b6 (10...♗xd4 11 cxd4 and ♘c3 ±) 11 c4 d6 12 ♘c3 ±, threatening to assail the pawn on c7 with ♘cb5! So instead of 9...♕xe4, it is advisable to play 9...d6!?, which prevents White's 10 ♘f5 while at the same time preparing ...♗c8-h3. A characteristic example of this double-edged position is 10 f4! ♕xe4 11 ♗f2 ♗xd4 12 cxd4 ♘g6 13 g3 0-0 14 ♘c3 ♕f5 15 ♗f3! ∞ and White has obtained sufficient positional compensation for the pawn (the bishop pair, a spatial advantage and an attack on the black queenside)

8 0-0 ♗b6

8...d6?! is wrong here due to 9 ♘xc6 ♘xc6 10 ♗xc5 dxc5 11 f4! and White controls the centre.

9 ♘a3!?

On the passive 9 ♔h1 Black's answer is 9...♖d8! followed by ...d7-d5. Black can also achieve active play on 9 ♗b3: 9...♘a5! 10 ♗c2 ♘c4 11 ♗c1 d6 and ...♘c6 ∞. Interesting is 9 ♘c2!?, refusing to live with the bishop on b6, e.g. 9...d6 10 ♗xb6 axb6 11 f4 ± or 9...♕g6 10 ♗xb6 axb6 11 ♘d2 ♔h8 12 ♘e3. Therefore Black has to act more aggressively, meeting 9 ♘c2!? with 9...♘e5! 10 ♗e2 ♘5g6! 11 ♗xb6 axb6 12 ♘e3 ♘f4! and the knight manoeuvres have created counter-chances.

9...d6 *(D)*

White gains time after 9...♕g6 10 ♕d2 ♕xe4 11 ♖ae1 ♕g6 12 ♗d3 ♕h5 13 ♘xc6! ♘xc6 14 ♘b5!, regaining the pawn on c7 with a superior position.

Plans and Counterplans:

Black is preparing for ...♕g6, so White should lead the game along a tactical path with an offensive against the pawn on c7: 10 ♘db5!? a6 11 ♘xd6! ♗xe3 12 ♘xc8 and now Black has the choice between 12...♖axc8 13 fxe3 ♕g5 14 ♕f3 ♘e5 15 ♕f4 ♕h5 (when White is a pawn up but his advantage is only

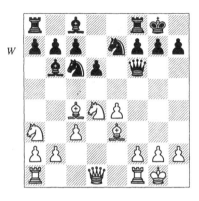

an isolated doubled e-pawn) or the pawn sacrifice 12...♗c5!? 13 ♘xe7+ ♕xe7 14 b4 ♗d6 (when Black threatens 15...a5, 15...♕xe4 and 15...♕e5, and although the position has become complicated, the chances are balanced).

White failed to develop entirely smoothly in the opening as Black attacked his d4-knight which White had to protect, having no better options, with c2-c3. However, then the knight on b1 had difficulties joining the game. This slight disharmony was enough for Black to achieve a good position with natural moves.

Four Knights Defence

1 e4 e5 2 ♘f3 ♘c6 3 ♘c3

Recently we have seen a revival of this opening, thanks partly to the Latvian-born superstar Alexei Shirov who has a liking for spine-tingling complexities. It is best for Black to follow the symmetry of development since he is worse after both 3...♗c5 4 ♘xe5! ♘xe5 (4...♗xf2+ 5 ♔xf2 ♘xe5 6 d4 ±) 5 d4 ♗d6 6 dxe5 ♗xe5 7 ♗d3 in view of the threatened f2-f4, and 3...g6 4 d4! exd4 5 ♘xd4 (nothing is gained by 5 ♘d5 ♗g7 6 ♗g5 ♘ce7! 7 ♘xd4 c6! 8 ♘xe7 ♘xe7 9 ♕d2 h6 10 ♗h4 d5! =) 5...♗g7 6 ♗e3 ♘f6 7 ♘xc6 bxc6 8 e5! ♘g8 9 ♗d4.

3...♘f6

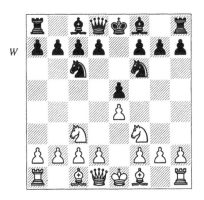

Now White can determine the character of the middlegame. He can play 4 d4 in similar fashion to the Scotch Game (section I: Open Variation) or he can go 4 ♗b5, keeping the centre closed (section II: Spanish-like).

I. 1 e4 e5 2 ♘f3 ♘c6 3 ♘c3 ♘f6 4 d4 (Open Variation)

4...exd4

It is simpler to clear the air in the centre than to undertake the complications of 4...♗b4 5 ♘xe5 ♘xe4 (5...♕e7 6 ♕d3! ♘xe5 7 dxe5 ♕xe5 8 ♗d2 followed by 0-0-0 and f2-f4 is favourable for White) 6 ♕g4 ♘xc3 7 ♕xg7 ♖f8 8 a3 ♗a5 9 ♘xc6 dxc6 10 ♕xe5+ ♕e7 11 ♕xe7+ ♔xe7 12 ♗d2 ♗f5 13 bxc3! ♗xc2 14 c4! where White has a central and spatial advantage.

5 ♘xd4

On the tricky 5 ♘d5!?, 5...♘xe4 6 ♕e2 f5 7 ♘g5! or 5...♘xd5 6 exd5 ♘b4 7 ♘xd4 ♘xd5 8 ♘f5! would be to White's taste, but 5...♗e7! 6 ♗f4 d6 7 ♘xd4 ♘xd5 8 exd5 ♘xd4 9 ♕xd4 ♗f6 10 ♗b5+ ♗d7 11 ♕e3+ ♕e7 ensures Black equality.

5...♗b4 6 ♘xc6

There is no other satisfactory way to protect the pawn on e4, and 6 ♗g5 fails to 6...h6! 7 ♗xf6 (or 7 ♗h4 g5! and 8...♘xe4 ∓) 7...♕xf6 8 ♘e2 0-0 9 a3 ♗c5 ∓.

6...bxc6 7 ♗d3 d5!? 8 exd5

8 e5? is no good, as 8...♘g4 9 ♗f4 f6! picks up the pawn.

8...cxd5

Also conceivable is 8...♕e7+ 9 ♕e2 cxd5.

9 0-0 0-0 10 ♗g5 c6

10...♗xc3 is too much of a simplification, as after 11 bxc3 White stands better: his bishop pair is strong, while the ugly queenside pawns are impossible to attack and obstruct the black queenside just as much as if they were 'good-looking'. Besides, White is even threatening the double attack 12 ♗xf6 ♕xf6 13 ♕h5! (h7, d5). On 10...♗e6, White can play 11 ♘e2 and then ♘d4.

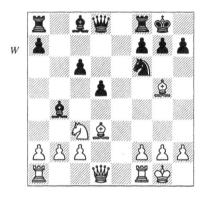

Plans and Counterplans:
White gets nothing after **11 ♕f3** since 11...♗e6 12 ♗xf6 ♕xf6 13 ♕xf6 gxf6 is no better for him. The critical plan is **11 ♘a4!?** and an attack on the d5-pawn via c2-c4, or the blockade of the black c- and d-pawns. Black's most precise answer is 11...h6 12 ♗h4 ♖e8! 13 c4! ♗d6!? 14 cxd5 (14 ♖c1 ♗f4 15 ♖c2 ♕d6!?) 14...cxd5 15 ♘c3 ♗e5! with serious counterplay (after 16 ♘xd5? ♕xd5 17 ♗xf6 ♗b7!

Black wins a piece). We should note that instead of 13...♗d6!?, 13...d4? is a positional blunder as the black pawn has not much to say on d4 while White can comfortably build up his game against the weakened c- and d-pawns with a2-a3, b2-b4, ♕f3 and ♖fd1. The strength of the blockaded passed pawn on the d-file is always determined by concrete factors in the position. In the present case – since the black pieces are unable to support it with active play – the pawn would end up as a weakness.

II. 1 e4 e5 2 ♘f3 ♘c6 3 ♘c3 ♘f6 4 ♗b5 (Spanish-like)

White, just as he does in the Spanish (Ruy Lopez), develops swiftly, castles and attacks the pawn on e5 by putting pressure on the c6-knight.

4...♗b4

Black can also deviate from the symmetry:

a) 4...♗c5 5 0-0 0-0 (or 5...d6 6 d4! exd4 7 ♘xd4 ♗d7 8 ♘f5! ♗xf5 9 exf5 ±. White is threatening to play ♖e1+, ♗g5 and ♘a4) 6 ♘xe5! ♘xe5 7 d4 ♗d6 8 f4! ♘c6 9 e5 ♗e7 10 d5! ♘b4 11 exf6 ♗xf6 12 a3 ♗xc3 13 bxc3 ♘xd5! 14 ♕xd5 c6 15 ♕d3 cxb5 16 f5! and the white attack on the kingside starts to take shape.

b) 4...♘d4!? 5 ♗a4 (5 ♘xd4 exd4 6 e5 dxc3 7 exf6 ♕xf6 8 dxc3 ♕e5+ 9 ♕e2 ♕xe2+ 10 ♗xe2 d5

and ...c7-c6 =) 5...c6!? (5...♗c5!? is
an exciting sacrifice, for example
6 ♘xe5 0-0 7 ♘d3 ♗b6 8 e5! – 8 0-0?
d5! 9 ♘xd5 ♘xd5 10 exd5 ♕xd5
11 ♘f4 ♕g5! followed by ...♗g4
with a tremendous attack for
Black – 8...♘e8 9 ♘d5! d6 10 ♘e3
dxe5 11 ♘xe5 ♕g5 12 ♘5c4 f5!
13 f4!! ♕xf4 14 c3 ♘e6 15 d4 and
White gains the advantage from
the complications) 6 ♘xe5 (on 6
d3, 6...b5 7 ♗b3 ♘xb3 8 axb3 d6 is
equal, while on 6 0-0 either 6...b5
7 ♗b3 ♘xb3 followed by ...d7-d6
or 6...♕a5!? 7 ♖e1 d6 is playable
for Black) 6...d5!? (6...d6!? comes
into consideration as well: 7 ♘f3
♗g4 8 d3 d5 ∞) 7 d3! ♗d6 8 f4
dxe4 9 dxe4 ♗xe5 10 fxe5 ♘g4 11
0-0 0-0 and, utilizing his bishop
pair in an open position, White
can pester Black with 12 h3 ♘xe5
13 ♗e3!

5 0-0
It is no use being greedy with 5
♗xc6 dxc6 6 ♘xe5 as Black easily
equalizes with 6...♗xc3 7 bxc3
♘xe4 8 ♕e2 ♕d5! and then ...0-0.

5...0-0
5...d6? is a mistake, since White
is on top after 6 ♘d5! ♗c5 7 d4!
exd4 8 ♘xd4.

6 d3
Not 6 ♗xc6 dxc6 7 d3 ♗d6 8
♗g5 h6 9 ♗h4 c5 10 ♘d5 g5! 11
♘xf6+ ♕xf6 and Black takes control on the kingside (∓).

6...d6
Black is worse in the variation
6...♗xc3?! 7 bxc3 d5 8 exd5 ♕xd5
9 c4 ♕d6 10 ♗xc6 bxc6 11 ♗b2

♖e8 12 ♕e1! ♗g4 13 ♘xe5 ♘d7 14
f4 f6 15 ♕g3 ±.

7 ♗g5!
Now Black needs to be ex-
tremely careful! The threats are 8
♘d5 and 8 ♗xf6 ♕xf6 9 ♘d5 followed by ♗xc6 and ♘xb4 bagging
a piece.

7...♗xc3!
The only way to prevent the
move ♘c3-d5. A horrifying example of blindly maintaining the
symmetry is 7...♗g4?! 8 ♘d5 ♘d4
9 ♘xb4 ♘xb5 10 ♘d5 ♘d4 11 ♕d2
♕d7? 12 ♗xf6 ♗xf3 13 ♘e7+!
♔h8 14 ♗xg7+! ♔xg7 15 ♕g5+
♔h8 16 ♕f6 mate!

8 bxc3 ♕e7!?
Black prepares the manoeuvre
...♘d8-e6 with which he hopes to
eliminate the unpleasant pin of
the bishop on g5. Note that the
pin cannot be immediately bro-
ken with 8...h6?! 9 ♗h4 g5, as after 10 ♘xg5! hxg5 11 ♗xg5 it
becomes permanent and White
will be winning after f2-f4.

9 ♖e1
White plans d3-d4, gaining space
in the centre and opening the way
home for his bishop on b5. 9 ♘d2
prepares the opening of the f-file,
but this can be thwarted by 9...h6!
10 ♗h4 ♘d8, e.g. 11 f4? exf4 12
♖xf4 g5 –+.

9...♘d8 10 d4 ♘e6
A worthy attempt is 10...♗g4!?
11 h3 ♗h5 (11...♗xf3 12 ♕xf3
♘e6 13 ♗e3 c5!? ∞) 12 g4 ♗g6 13
d5 c6 14 ♗f1 cxd5 15 exd5 ♕c7
with an unclear position.

11 &c1

The bishop gets stuck on the kingside after 11 &h4 ♘f4! followed by ...h7-h6.

11...♖d8

11...c5 used to be the recommended line, when after 12 dxe5 dxe5 13 &c4 ♖d8 14 &d5 ♘c7 15 c4 &g4 16 h3 ♘cxd5 17 cxd5 &xf3 18 ♕xf3 ♘e8!, followed by ...♘d6, Black tried to compensate for White's passed d5-pawn with his good blockading knight.

12 a4!?

Less enticing is 12 &f1!?, although it is still hard for Black to come up with a plan. For instance the gallop ...♘f6-d7-f8-g6-f4 can be rendered useless by g2-g3. But perhaps he can play 12...c5!? 13 d5 ♘f8 and ...h7-h6, ...g7-g5, ...♘g6, ...&g4 to follow up with a kingside initiative, naturally only because the centre is closed!

12...c5!?

White is better in the line 12...♘f8 13 ♘h4! c6 14 &d3 h6 15 ♕f3 ♖e8 16 ♘f5 &xf5 17 ♕xf5 as the bishop pair and possession of

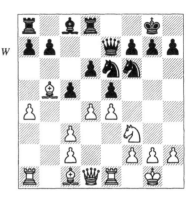

the centre grant him a lasting initiative.

Plans and Counterplans:

White's dilemma is whether he should open the centre (to make use of the bishop pair) or close it (to ensure a permanent spatial plus). Here is an example of each option: **13 dxe5** dxe5 14 ♕e2 ♕c7!? 15 &c4 ♖e8 16 ♘h4 ♘f4 with mutual chances or **13 &f1!?** ♘f8 14 d5 ♘g6 15 ♘d2 b6 16 ♘c4 &d7 17 g3 h6 with a tough fight in which White's game is a little more attractive due to his spatial advantage.

Two Knights Defence

1 e4 e5 2 ♘f3 ♘c6 3 ♗c4

This quick development of the kingside is very natural, as after castling the rook on h1 will have important duties on e1, while the c4-bishop keeps an eye on Black's Achilles' heel, the f7-pawn. The humble 3 ♗e2 cannot be recommended. Black achieves easy play with 3...♘f6 4 d3 d5 (also possible is 4...g6 and then ...♗g7, ...d7-d6 and ...0-0) 5 ♘bd2 ♗c5 6 0-0 0-0 7 c3 a5! (Without this move Black is in trouble because b2-b4 and then perhaps b4-b5 gains space on the queenside while at the same time sending the black pieces into disarray!) 8 ♕c2 ♕e7 and the position is equal.

3...♘f6!?

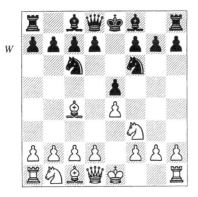

The Two Knights Defence is not an opening for the timid! Black does not chicken out of the attack on his f7-pawn but develops in a way that attacks the e4-pawn and prepares the counter-thrust ...d7-d5. Such risky lines should only be undertaken with a thorough knowledge and analysis of the consequences! (Alternatives to 3...♘f6 are considered in the next chapter, 'The Italian Game'.)

White has two active continuations which turn the position upside down: **4 d4** (I. Violent central attack) and **4 ♘g5** (II. Attack on the f7-pawn). Tournament practice has also seen the quieter **4 d3**. Then Black should avoid immediately opening up the e-file with 4...d5? 5 exd5 ♘xd5 6 0-0 ♗g4 7 ♖e1 ♗e7 (7...f6? 8 ♘xe5! ♗xd1 9 ♘xc6+ +−) 8 h3! ♗h5 9 g4 ♗g6 10 ♘xe5 ±, but simple equality is granted by 4...♗e7 5 0-0 0-0 6 c3 d6 7 ♗b3 ♘a5 8 ♗c2 c5 9 ♖e1 ♘c6 and after ...♖e8, ...h7-h6, ...♗f8 Black can opt for ...d7-d5.

I. 1 e4 e5 2 ♘f3 ♘c6 3 ♗c4 ♘f6 4 d4 (Violent central attack)

4...exd4

4...♘xd4? is wrong: 5 ♗xf7+! ♔xf7 6 ♘xe5+ followed by ♕xd4 +−. Also bad is 4...♘xe4, as after 5 dxe5 White threatens 6 ♕d5.

5 0-0

5 ♘g5 is ineffective, as Black can easily guard his f7-pawn from

attack: 5...♘e5 6 ♗b3 h6 7 f4 hxg5 8 fxe5 ♘xe4 9 ♕xd4 (9 0-0 d5! 10 exd6 ♕xd6 11 ♗xf7+ ♔d8 and suddenly it is the white king that has become vulnerable!) 9...♘c5 10 ♘c3 d6 followed by ...♘xb3 and Black has the more harmonious game, or 5...d5!? 6 exd5 ♕e7+ 7 ♕e2 ♘b4!? giving Black excellent counter-chances.

On 5 ♘xd4 ♘xe4 6 ♗xf7+ ♔xf7 7 ♕h5+ g6 8 ♕d5+ ♔g7 9 ♘xc6 bxc6 10 ♕xe4, Black has an unusual option: 10...♕e8!!, when 11 ♕xe8 ♗b4+ and 12...♖xe8 puts Black on top in the queenless middlegame in view of his bishop pair and development advantage.

The most important alternative to 5 0-0 is 5 e5!?, when Black can play:

a) 5...♘g4 6 ♕e2 ♕e7 7 ♗f4 f6 (or 7...d6 8 exd6 cxd6!?) 8 exf6 ♘xf6 9 ♘bd2 ∞ and White regains the pawn with ♘b3-♘bxd4.

b) 5...d5!? (this central counterthrust is almost always effective against e4-e5!) 6 ♗b5 ♘e4 7 ♘xd4 ♗d7 8 ♗xc6 bxc6 9 0-0 ♗c5!? 10 f3 ♘g5 11 f4 ♘e4 12 ♗e3 ♗b6 13 ♘d2 ♘xd2 14 ♕xd2 c5 15 ♘f3 d4 16 ♗f2 ♗c6 with mutual chances, White's plan is f4-f5 while Black is ahead in the centre.

c) 5...♘e4!? 6 ♕e2 (or 6 0-0 d5 7 exd6 ♘xd6 =) 6...♘c5 7 0-0 ♘e6! 8 ♖d1 d5 9 ♗b5! ♗c5 10 c3 ♗d7 11 ♗xc6 ♗xc6 12 cxd4 ♗b6 13 ♘c3 0-0 leads to an interesting, nearly balanced position.

5...♘xe4

Black takes on even more risk in the Max Lange Attack: 5...♗c5 6 e5 d5 (note that again the answer to e4-e5 is ...d7-d5!) 7 exf6 dxc4 8 ♖e1+ ♗e6. Now after 9 fxg7 ♖g8 10 ♗g5 ♗e7! 11 ♗xe7 ♔xe7! Black is on top. Correct is 9 ♘g5! ♕d5 10 ♘c3! ♕f5 11 ♘ce4 (after 11 g4? ♕g6 12 ♘ce4 ♗b6 13 f4 0-0-0 14 f5 ♗xf5 15 gxf5 ♕xf5 Black obtains more than sufficient compensation for a piece: three pawns and a forceful attack!) 11...0-0-0 12 g4 ♕e5 13 ♘xe6 fxe6 14 fxg7 ♖hg8 15 ♗h6 d3! with total chaos.

6 ♖e1

Black cannot answer 6 ♘c3 with 6...dxc3 owing to 7 ♗xf7+! ♔xf7 8 ♕d5+ ♔e8 9 ♖e1 ♗e7 10 ♖xe4 d6 11 ♗g5 cxb2 12 ♖ae1, but instead he can play 6...♘xc3! 7 bxc3 d5 8 ♗b5 ♗e7 9 ♘xd4 ♗d7, when he is 'peacefully' ahead.

6...d5 7 ♗xd5!?

No better is 7 ♘c3: 7...dxc3! 8 ♗xd5 ♗e6! 9 ♗xe4 ♗b4 10 b3 ♕xd1 11 ♖xd1 ♗d7 with ...0-0-0 to follow and Black is a pawn up.

7...♕xd5 8 ♘c3 ♕a5 9 ♘xe4 ♗e6 *(D)*

Weaker is 9...♗e7: 10 ♗g5! 0-0 11 ♗xe7 ♘xe7 12 ♕xd4, and now White's development and spatial advantage is clear. The main point of 9...♗e6 is to prepare ...0-0-0.

Plans and Counterplans:

White has shattered Black's centre with the tactical blows 7 ♗xd5 and 8 ♘c3, but he is still a pawn

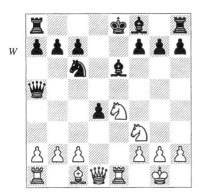

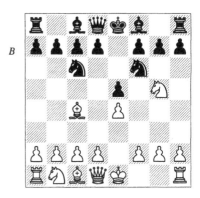

down, which Black may not have to give back after ...0-0-0! **10 ♗g5** is pointless, as after 10...h6 11 ♗h4 ♗b4 12 ♖e2 g5 Black is still able to castle. However, the pawn can be regained with **10 ♘eg5**: 10...0-0-0 11 ♘xe6 fxe6 12 ♖xe6 ♗d6 and now 13 ♕e2 ♕h5 14 ♕e4 ♖de8 and 13 ♗g5 ♖de8 14 ♕e2 ♔d7 15 ♖e1 ♕xe1+! 16 ♘xe1 ♖xe6 17 ♕g4 ♖he8 lead to more or less even endgames. One attempt to improve White's play is **10 ♗d2**, but then it turns out that Black can calmly choose between 10...♕f5 11 ♗g5 h6 12 ♗h4 ♗c5, 10...♕d5 11 ♗g5 ♗d6 12 ♗f6 0-0 13 ♘xd4 ♘xd4 14 ♕xd4 ♕xd4 15 ♗xd4 ♖fd8 and finally 10...♗b4 11 ♘xd4! ♘xd4 12 c3 ♗e7 13 cxd4 ♕d5 14 ♗b4!? ♗xb4 15 ♕a4+ ♕c6! 16 ♕xb4 0-0-0. In none of these cases are his chances any worse.

II. 1 e4 e5 2 ♘f3 ♘c6 3 ♗c4 ♘f6 4 ♘g5!? (Attack on the f7-pawn)

Has Black overlooked the attack on his pawn at f7? No.

4...d5!

This central counter-thrust is the point of Black's play. This move has been so successful that it has almost completely removed the daring and perhaps really too risky 4...♗c5!?, the Wilkes-Barre (Traxler) Gambit from tournament practice. However, it is worth seeing a small selection from the theory of this gambit:

a) 5 d4 d5! (a splendid idea, opening the way for the bishop on c8 and at the same time shutting down that of the bishop on c4) 6 ♗xd5 (neither 6 exd5 ♘xd4 7 d6 0-0 nor 6 dxc5 dxc4 7 ♕xd8+ ♘xd8 cause Black any problems) 6...♘xd4 7 ♗xf7+!? (after 7 ♘xf7 ♕e7 8 ♘xh8 ♗g4! 9 f3 – on 9 ♕d2 or 9 ♕d3 Black plays 9...♘xd5 10 exd5 ♗f5 – 9...♘xd5 10 fxg4 ♕h4+ 11 g3 ♕h3 followed by 12...♕g2 and Black is winning!) 7...♔e7 8 ♗c4 b5 9 ♗d3 ♖f8 10 ♗e3 h6 11 ♘f3 ♗g4 and Black has sufficient initiative for the pawn.

b) 5 ♘xf7 ♗xf2+! 6 ♔f1 (6 ♔xf2 ♘xe4+ 7 ♔g1 ♕h4 8 g3 ♘xg3 gives Black a promising attack) 6...Qe7 7 Nxh8 d5 8 exd5 Bg4 (analysts consider 8...Nd4 to be playable as well) 9 Be2 Bxe2+ 10 Kxe2! (after 10 Qxe2 Nd4! 11 Qxf2 0-0-0 and then ...Rf8 Black maintains a dangerous attack) 10...Nd4+ 11 Kxf2 Ne4+ 12 Ke3 Qg5+ 13 Kxe4 Qxg2+ 14 Kd3 Qh3+ 15 Ke4 Qg2+ with a draw by repetition.

c) 5 Bxf7+!? (White is undeveloped, so it is logical that by grabbing less material he has more realistic chances of an advantage) 5...Ke7 6 Bd5!? (6 Bb3!? Rf8 7 d3 d6 8 Be3!? also comes into consideration) 6...Rf8!? (on 6...d6 7 c3! Qe8!? 8 d4 exd4 9 Bxc6 Qxc6 10 cxd4 Bb4+ 11 Bd2 Nxe4 12 0-0! ±, White's king is sheltered while its black counterpart is stuck the middle) 7 0-0 d6 and now on 8 h3, 8...Qe8 followed by ...Qg6 is Black's plan, while on 8 c3!?, 8...h6 is possible with a sharp, unclear game.

5 exd5 Na5!
Other possibilities are:

a) 5...Bg4? 6 Nxf7! Qe7 7 d6 cxd6 8 f3 Rg8 9 Nxd6+ Qxd6 10 fxg4 Rh8 11 d3 ±.

b) 5...b5 6 Bf1! (not 6 Bxb5? Qxd5 7 Be2 Bb7 ∞) 6...Nxd5? (for 6...Nd4 see the following line with 5...Nd4) 7 Bxb5 Bb7 8 d4! ±. White has an extra pawn and a better position.

c) 5...Nd4 6 c3! b5 7 Bf1! Nxd5 8 cxd4!? (after 8 Ne4 Qh4 9 Ng3 Bb7!? 10 cxd4 0-0-0 11 d3

Nf4 12 Bxf4 exf4 13 Qh5 Qe7+ 14 Ne2 g5!? 15 Nd2 Rxd4 16 0-0-0! White has an extra piece though Black is not entirely without compensation) 8...Qxg5 9 Bxb5+ Kd8 10 0-0 Bb7 11 Qf3 Rb8 12 Nc3! exd4 (but not 12...Nxc3 13 dxc3 Qxc1? 14 Qxf7 +-) 13 d3 Qf6 14 Qg4! Bc8 15 Qh5 Ne7 16 Ne4 and at last White gets on top.

d) 5...Nxd5? (an unsound but frequently played move, so White must be prepared) 6 d4! (6 Nxf7?! is not convincing: 6...Kxf7 7 Qf3+ Ke6 8 Nc3 Nb4! 9 Qe4 c6 10 a3 Na6 11 d4 Nc7, and White has no clearly advantageous continuation, just a piece less) 6...exd4 (alternatively, 6...Bb4+ 7 c3 Be7 8 Nxf7! Kxf7 9 Qf3+ Ke6 10 Qe4 ±, threatening f2-f4, while 6...Be7 7 Nxf7! Kxf7 8 Qf3+ Ke6 9 Nc3 Nb4 10 Qe4 c6 11 a3 Na6 12 Qxe5+ Kf7 13 Nxd5 cxd5 14 Bxd5+ Kf8 15 0-0 is also better for White) 7 0-0 Be6 8 Re1 Qd7 9 Nxf7! Kxf7 10 Qf3+ Kg8 11 Rxe6! and Black has to resign.

6 Bb5+
The artificial 6 d3 h6 7 Nf3 e4 8 Qe2 Nxc4 9 dxc4 Bc5 and 10...0-0 favours Black, whose natural follow-up moves are ...Bg4 and ...c7-c6.

6...c6! 7 dxc6 bxc6 8 Be2
White is in trouble after 8 Bd3? Nd5 9 Ne4 f5 10 Ng3 Nf4 11 Bf1 Bc5 ∓ or 8 Ba4 h6 9 Nf3 e4 10 Qe2 Be6 11 Ne5 Qd4! 12 Bxc6+ Nxc6 13 Nxc6 Qd5! 14 Qa6 Bc8 15 Qa4 Bd7 -+. However, Black

has a more difficult task after 8 ♕f3!?, when 8...cxb5?! is insufficient: 9 ♕xa8 ♕d7 10 ♕f3 ♗b7 11 ♕e2 ♗xg2 12 ♖g1 ♗c6 13 d3 followed by ♘c3, ♗d2 and 0-0-0 ±. Instead of 8...cxb5?!, he should play 8...♖b8!? 9 ♗d3 (9 ♗xc6+ ♘xc6 10 ♕xc6+ ♘d7 ∓. White has a fatal lack of development and is threatened by ...♕xg5, ...♖b6 ...♗b7 and ...e5-e4, after the withdrawal of the knight from g5) 9...h6 10 ♘e4 ♘d5 11 ♘g3 (11 b3 g6 12 ♕g3 ♗g7 13 ♗a3 ♘b4! blocks the a3-f8 diagonal) 11...g6 12 0-0 ♗g7 13 ♘c3 0-0 ∓. The clumsiness of the white pieces will be exposed by ...f7-f5 and ...e5-e4 or ...♖b4 followed by ...♗g4 or ...♖f4. Another typical attack against the knight on g3 is ...h6-h5-h4.

8...h6

The knight must be attacked immediately, as after, for instance, 8...♗c5? 9 d3! h6, 10 ♘e4! is possible.

9 ♘f3

9 ♘h3!? seems totally bizarre, but it is not! White has a lot of trouble with this knight in any case, so he would gladly trade it for the bishop on c8. Another advantage of 9 ♘h3 compared to 9 ♘f3 is that Black's move ...e5-e4 does not win a tempo. However, Black still has several ways of reaching an unclear, mutually challenging position. In the lines 9...♗c5 10 0-0 0-0 11 d3 ♘d5 ∞ and 9...♗d6 10 d3 0-0 11 ♘c3 ♘d5 12 ♗d2 ♖b8 ∞, ...♗xh3 is always

in the air. The threat is stronger than the execution in this case, as after the immediate 9...♗xh3?! 10 gxh3 ♕d5 11 ♗f3 e4 12 ♘c3 ♕e5 13 ♗g2 ♗d6 14 ♕e2 0-0 15 d3! exd3 16 ♕xe5 ♗xe5 17 cxd3 White is somewhat better in the endgame.

9...e4 10 ♘e5

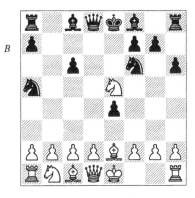

Plans and Counterplans:

Black develops by attacking the knight on e5. His ultimate goal is an attack on the white kingside, for which he is well organized due to the pawn on e4 and active piece play. White would like to develop his queenside pieces some time, and if it were his turn again, he would most probably play d2-d4 in order to facilitate ♘c3, ♗e3, 0-0, ♕d2 and ♖ad1. Then he would be in control owing to his pawn advantage and Black's poorly positioned knight on a5. Let us see how things turn out in concrete lines!

a) 10...♕d4 11 f4 (11 ♘g4 ♗xg4 12 ♗xg4 ♗c5 13 0-0 0-0 ∓. Black is threatening 14...e3! or

14...♕e5 and then ...♗d6) 11...♗c5 12 ♖f1 ♗d6 13 c3 ♕b6 14 ♕a4! 0-0 15 b4! ♘b7 16 ♕xc6, and White has sprung to life. He has restricted the black pieces and has won yet another pawn.

b) 10...♗d6!? Now Black obtains a dangerous initiative if the knight moves: 11 ♘c4?! ♘xc4 12 ♗xc4 ♘g4 13 ♕e2 0-0 14 h3 ♕h4 ∓, threatening 15...♘xf2 followed by ...♗g3 (15 0-0 is answered by 15...♘e5 and ...♗xh3) or 11 ♘g4?! ♘xg4 12 ♗xg4 ♕h4! 13 ♗xc8 ♖xc8 14 ♕e2 0-0 15 ♘c3 ♖ce8 16 b3 e3! 17 dxe3 ♗b4 18 ♗d2 ♕f6 19 ♕d3 ♖d8 and Black wins the c3-knight. So White has to choose between two pawn moves to protect the knight:

b1) 11 f4 exf3 (also playable is 11...♕c7: 12 0-0 0-0 13 ♘c3 ♗f5 14 a3 ♘d5 15 b4 ♘b7 16 ♗b2 ♖ae8 ∞) 12 ♘xf3 0-0 13 d4 c5 14 0-0 ♖e8 =. Black will follow up with ...♗b7, when he has active play for the pawn and the white king position is weak due to the missing f2-pawn.

b2) 11 d4 exd3! (not 11...♕c7 this time due to 12 ♗d2! ♗xe5 13 dxe5 ♕xe5 14 ♗c3! ±. Black has regained the pawn but lost his activity) 12 ♘xd3 ♕c7 13 b3! (13 h3?! 0-0 14 0-0 ♗f5 15 ♘d2 ♖fe8 16 a3 ♖ad8 with complete compensation for the pawn) 13...0-0 14 ♗b2 and now based on the lines 14...♘d5 15 ♘c3 ♘f4 16 ♘xf4 ♗xf4, 14...♘e4 15 ♘d2 ♗f5 16 ♘xe4 ♗xe4 or 14...♗f5!? 15 ♗xf6? (better is 15 ♘d2) 15...gxf6 16 ♘c3 ♖ad8 17 ♕d2 ♖fe8, Black achieves full compensation.

It is worth noting how Black disrupted White's impetus with a pawn sacrifice after 4 ♘g5 and obtained an advantage in development. By the end of the opening the game has reached a dynamic balance: Black has offset White's extra pawn with active piece play and pressure along the e- and d-files.

Italian Game

1 e4 e5 2 ♘f3 ♘c6 3 ♗c4

What can Black do if he does not want to enter the tactical complexities of the Two Knights Defence? Should he opt for 3...♘d4?! and base his play on the trap 4 ♘xe5? ♕g5! 5 ♘xf7? ♕xg2 6 ♖f1 ♕xe4+ 7 ♗e2 ♘f3 mate(!)? No, 3...♘d4?! is positionally refuted by the line 4 ♘xd4! exd4 5 c3! dxc3 6 ♘xc3 d6 7 d4 ±. So should Black prefer the solid 3...♗e7 (the Hungarian Defence)? Now that is a better idea, only it produces a slightly passive position: 4 d4 d6 5 ♘c3 (White can create a centre characteristic of closed openings with 5 d5!? ♘b8 6 ♗d3 ♘f6 7 c4 with a typical King's Indian plan: ♘c3, h2-h3 and then playing for c4-c5 after the preparatory b2-b4 or ♗e3 with an initiative on the queenside) 5...♘f6 6 h3 0-0 7 0-0 exd4 (Black is not well enough prepared for 7...♘xe4?!: 8 ♘xe4 d5 9 ♗xd5! ♕xd5 10 ♘c3 ♕d6 11 dxe5! ♘xe5 12 ♘xe5 ♕xe5 13 ♖e1 ♕d6 14 ♘d5 followed by ♗f4 and Black's position is uncomfortable) 8 ♘xd4 ♘xd4 9 ♕xd4 c6 10 a4 ± with ♗e3 and ♖ad1 to follow, when White has permanent pressure.

Instead of playing for tricks or being overly cautious, the player who wishes to avoid the Two Knights Defence should opt for a plan whereby the pieces can develop and create effective counterplay. For these requirements the **Italian Game**, typified by **3...♗c5!?**, is a perfect solution.

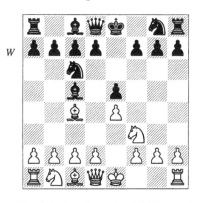

Black intends to build his position with ...♘f6 (when ♘f3-g5 is harmless, as Black can comfortably defend the pawn on f7 by castling), followed by ...0-0, ...d7-d6 and ...♗g4. Meanwhile, his c5-bishop stops White's central thrust d2-d4. Of course White has some ideas, too: he can control the type of middlegame that ensues and the speed at which it is reached. There are three basic plans:

I. With a closed centre, i.e. without d2-d4.
II. Möller Attack: c2-c3 and d2-d4.
III. Accelerated development: The Evans Gambit (4 b4!?).

I. With a closed centre

1 e4 e5 2 ♘f3 ♘c6 3 ♗c4 ♗c5 4 c3

The position is equal after 4 d3 ♘f6 5 ♘c3 d6 6 ♗g5 ♗e6!? (or 6...h6 7 ♗xf6 ♕xf6 8 ♘d5 ♕d8 9 c3 and now 9...0-0 10 b4 ♗b6 11 a4 a5 12 ♘xb6 cxb6 13 bxa5 ♘xa5 14 ♗d5 ♕c7 or 9...♘e7 10 d4 ♘xd5 11 dxc5 ♘f4 both offer good chances of equality) 7 ♘d5 ♗xd5 8 ♗xd5 h6! 9 ♗xf6 ♕xf6. The situation is similar in the line 4 0-0 d6 5 d3 ♘f6 6 ♗g5 h6 where 7 ♗h4? is a mistake in view of 7...g5! 8 ♗g3 ♗e6, when Black is threatening to exploit the poor placement of the bishop on g3 with ...h6-h5-h4 and at the same time initiate a kingside attack.

4...♘f6

Besides this natural move we should become acquainted with two distinctive strategies:

a) 4...d6 5 d4 exd4 6 cxd4 ♗b6! (after 6...♗b4+ 7 ♗d2 ♗xd2+ 8 ♕xd2 ♘f6 9 d5! ♘e7 10 ♘c3, the plan 0-0, ♘d4 and f2-f4 grants White the initiative) 7 ♘c3 ♘f6 8 ♗e3 ♗g4 9 ♗b5 0-0 and Black has handed over the centre in order to attack the d4- and e4-pawns with his pieces. Later on he can consider the moves ...♕e7 and ...♗xf3.

b) 4...♕e7 5 d4 ♗b6 (5...exd4 6 0-0! dxc3 7 ♘xc3 d6 8 ♘d5 and due to the threat of b2-b4, Black can only obtain the silver medal in this game) 6 0-0 d6 7 h3 ♘f6 8

♖e1 and now instead of the reflex action 8...0-0 Black can continue 8...h6!? 9 a4 a6 10 ♗e3 and prepare a kingside initiative by means of 10...g5!

5 d3

For 5 d4 see section II, while on 5 b4 ♗b6 6 d3 d6 7 a4 Black equalizes with 7...a5! 8 b5 ♘e7 9 0-0 0-0 10 ♗b3 ♘g6 11 ♘bd2 c6 12 bxc6 bxc6 13 d4 ♖e8.

5...d6

5...d5? is no good: 6 exd5 ♘xd5 7 0-0 0-0 8 ♖e1 ♖e8 9 b4! and after 10 ♕b3 White wins at least the pawn on e5.

6 0-0 0-0 7 ♘bd2

7 b4 ♗b6 8 a4 a5 9 b5 ♘e7 10 ♘bd2 ♘g6 11 ♗a3 ♘h5!? 12 d4 (not 12 ♘xe5?? ♘xe5 13 ♕xh5 ♗g4 −+) 12...♘hf4 13 ♖e1 ♗g4 yields Black strong kingside play which cannot be forcefully prevented by his opponent: 14 h3? ♗xh3! 15 gxh3 ♘xh3+ 16 ♔h2 ♘xf2 17 ♕e2 ♘g4+ 18 ♔g3 ♘f4 19 ♕f1 ♕f6! with a storm of an attack. Note also that 7 ♗g5 can be answered by 7...h6 8 ♗h4 a6 9 ♗b3 ♕e7 10 ♘bd2 ♗e6.

7...a6!?

An important detail, vacating the a7-square for the bishop on c5 and hoping to catch the bishop on c4 with 8...♘a5.

8 ♗b3! ♗a7!?

Perhaps the most precise move, sheltering the bishop and waiting to see the enemy plan before deciding how to react. At the same time this move permits Black to regroup by 9...♘e7 10 d4 (the bishop on c5 was rescued from this tempo!) 10...♘g6.

9 h3

On 9 ♖e1 Black can continue 9...♘g4 10 ♖e2 ♔h8 11 h3 ♘h6 (how good that on move 8 Black did not play ...h7-h6 instead of ...♗a7!?), followed by ...f7-f5. Black acts promptly on 9 ♘c4: 9...♗e6 10 ♗g5 h6 11 ♗h4 ♗xc4! 12 ♗xc4 ♘a5 13 ♘d2 ♕e7 14 ♔h1 ♘xc4 15 ♘xc4 ♕e6! =, and the tension generated by the bishop on h4 has been nullified.

9...h6 10 ♖e1 ♘h5

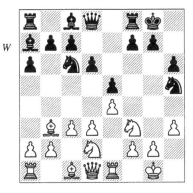

Plans and Counterplans:
Here Black has already shown his hand: he wants to annoy White on the kingside with ...♘f4 followed by ...♕f6. White would first like to force Black to retreat and then carefully make progress in the centre, gladly exchanging the active bishop on a7 if possible. Depending on how White decides to move his knight from d2, play might continue:

a) 11 ♘f1 (not 11 ♘xe5? ♘xe5 12 ♕xh5 ♘xd3 ∓) 11...♕f6 12 ♗e3 ♘f4 13 ♗xa7 ♖xa7 14 ♔h2 ♘e7 15 ♘e3 ♖a8.

b) 11 ♘c4!? ♕f6 12 ♘e3 ♘f4 13 ♘d5 ♘xd5 14 ♗xd5 ♗e6.

In both cases the game is a dour fight (with all sixteen pawns on the board!), with mutual chances.

II. 1 e4 e5 2 ♘f3 ♘c6 3 ♗c4 ♗c5 4 c3 ♘f6 5 d4 (Möller Attack)

5...exd4

5...♗b6? would be a bad mistake: 6 dxe5 ♘xe4 7 ♕d5! +−.

6 cxd4 ♗b4+

On 6...♗b6 the white centre pawns get going: 7 d5 ♘e7 8 e5 ♘g4 9 d6! ♘xf2 10 ♕b3 ♘xh1 11 ♗xf7+ ♔f8 12 ♗g5 +−

7 ♘c3!?

A brave pawn sacrifice. 7 ♗d2 does not promise anything more than equality: 7...♗xd2+ 8 ♘bxd2 d5! 9 exd5 ♘xd5 10 ♕b3 ♘ce7 11 0-0 0-0 12 ♖fe1 c6 13 a4 ♕b6 =. On 7 ♔f1? simplest is 7...d5! 8 exd5 ♘xd5 9 ♘c3 ♗e6 followed by ...0-0 and Black is on top in view of the poor placement of the king on f1.

7...♘xe4

Not 7...d5?! 8 exd5 ♘xd5 9 0-0 ♗e6 10 ♗g5! ♗e7 11 ♗xd5 ♗xd5 12 ♘xd5 ♕xd5 13 ♗xe7 ♘xe7 14 ♖e1 ±.

8 0-0 ♗xc3!

The only way! After 8...♘xc3? 9 bxc3 ♗xc3 (9...♗e7 10 d5 ♘a5 11 d6! cxd6 12 ♗xf7+ ♔xf7 13 ♕d5+

♔f8 14 ♘g5 ♕e8 15 ♕xa5 h6 16 ♕f5+ ±) 10 ♗a3! d5 (10...d6 11 ♖c1 ♗a5 12 ♕a4 a6 13 ♗d5 ♗b6 14 ♖xc6 ♗d7 15 ♖e1+ ♔f8 16 ♖xd6! +−) 11 ♗b5 ♗xa1 12 ♖e1+ ♗e6 13 ♕a4 ♖b8 14 ♘e5 Black's position is in its last throes.

9 d5!

Forced, since on 9 bxc3 d5 10 ♗a3 dxc4 11 ♖e1 ♗e6! 12 ♖xe4 ♕d5 13 ♕e2 0-0-0 White is in serious trouble.

9...♗f6!

It is worth keeping the bishop to provide protection for the king. Another idea is 9...♘e5!? 10 bxc3 ♘xc4 11 ♕d4 0-0 12 ♕xe4 ♘d6 13 ♕d3 ♘e8, although after 14 ♗g5 or 14 ♘g5 ♘f6 15 d6 White can no longer lose.

10 ♖e1 ♘e7

On 10...0-0 White has a strong attack: 11 ♖xe4 ♘a5 12 ♗d3 d6 13 g4 c5 14 g5 ♗e7 15 ♗d2 b6 16 ♕e2 ♗f5 17 ♖e1! ±.

11 ♖xe4 d6

Black is hamstrung after 11...0-0 12 d6! cxd6 (if 12...♘g6, then 13 ♕b3 cxd6 14 ♗d2 followed by ♖ae1 and ♗xf7+) 13 ♗g5!? ♘g6 14 ♕d5! and it is hard for him to make a move. White is planning ♖ae1 and ♖e8.

12 ♗g5

The strongest black defender has to be exchanged. 12 g4 0-0 13 g5 ♗e5 14 ♘xe5 dxe5 15 ♖xe5 ♘g6 is clearly and securely better for Black, due to the scattered white pawns.

12...♗xg5 13 ♘xg5 h6!?

After 13...0-0 analysts have demonstrated that the game ends in perpetual check: 14 ♘xh7 ♔xh7 15 ♕h5+ ♔g8 16 ♖h4 f5!? (or 16...f6 17 g4! ♖e8 18 ♗d3 ♔f8 19 ♕h8+ ♘g8 20 ♗h7 ♔f7 21 ♗g6+! ♔f8 22 ♗h7 with a draw by repetition) 17 ♖h3!? f4! 18 ♕h7+ ♔f7 19 ♕h5+ is one of the variations.

14 ♕e2!?

Black is close to victory after 14 ♗b5+? ♗d7 15 ♕e2 ♗xb5 16 ♕xb5+ ♕d7 17 ♕e2 (17 ♕xd7+ ♔xd7 18 ♘xf7 ♖f8 19 ♖f4 ♔e8 −+ or 17 ♕xb7 0-0 18 ♖ae1 ♘g6 19 ♘f3 ♖fb8 ∓) 17...♔f8 18 ♘xf7 (or 18 ♘f3 ♘xd5) 18...♔xf7 19 ♖e1 ♘g8! 20 ♖e6 ♔f8 21 f4 ♘f6 22 ♖e7 ♖e8! −+.

14...hxg5 15 ♖e1 ♗e6 16 dxe6 f6

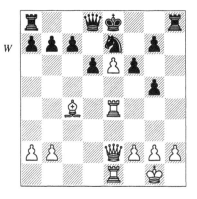

Plans and Counterplans:

White plans to invade the black camp with his major pieces, but Black can hinder this and hope to reach a favourable queenless endgame. Play might continue: 17 ♖e3 d5!? 18 ♖h3 ♖xh3 19 gxh3 g6! 20 ♕f3 ♕d6 21 ♕xf6 ♕f4 22 ♕h8+ ♕f8 23 ♕d4 ♕f4 24 ♕h8+ ♕f8 with a draw or, instead of 17...d5, 17...♔f8!? 18 ♖h3 ♖xh3 19 gxh3 g6 20 ♕f3 ♔g7 21 ♕xb7 ♕c8 22 ♕f3 ♖b8 23 ♗b3 ♕b7 24 ♕c3?! ♕b4, and although the situation is unclear, Black's chances seem to be more concrete.

III. Accelerated development: The Evans Gambit

1 e4 e5 2 ♘f3 ♘c6 3 ♗c4 ♗c5 4 b4!?

Sacrificing a pawn to speed up his plan of c2-c3 and d2-d4.

4...♗xb4

4...♗b6 is also quite playable: 5 a4 a6 6 ♘c3 ♘f6 7 ♘d5 ♘xd5 8 exd5 e4! 9 dxc6 exf3 10 ♕xf3 ♕e7+ and 11...dxc6 =.

5 c3 ♗c5!?

5...♗e7 is more passive, as after 6 d4!, 7 ♕b3 is threatened, while after 5...♗a5. the bishop is somewhat out of play: 6 d4! d6 (6...exd4 7 0-0 dxc3 8 ♕b3 ♕f6 9 e5 ♕g6 10 ♘xc3 ♘ge7 11 ♗a3! 0-0 12 ♖ad1 and Black is tied up) 7 ♕b3 ♕d7 8 dxe5 dxe5 9 ♗a3! ♗b6 10 ♘bd2 ♘h6 11 0-0 f6 12 ♖ad1 ♘a5 13 ♕b4 ♘xc4 14 ♘xc4 ♕e6. For a long time this line was assessed as '∓', but then a Cuban player continued 15 ♖d5! and it turned out that Black's game is critical in view of the threats 16 ♘fxe5 and 16 ♖fd1!

6 d4 exd4 7 0-0!?

Offering another pawn, though this one cannot be accepted. On 7 cxd4, 7...♗b4+ fails, as after 8 ♔f1! White is threatening 9 ♕b3 and d4-d5. So Black should play 7...♗b6 8 0-0 d6 transposing to the main line.

7...d6!

Not 7...dxc3? 8 ♗xf7+ ♔xf7 9 ♕d5+ ♔f8 10 ♕xc5+ d6 11 ♕xc3, after which White has shattered the black position for a mere pawn.

8 cxd4 ♗b6 9 ♘c3 ♗g4! 10 ♗b5!

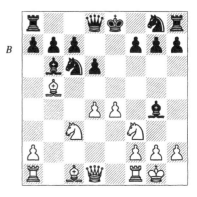

Plans and Counterplans:

The threat of d4-d5 should not be thwarted by the retreat **10...♗d7** as after 11 e5! ♘ge7 12 ♗g5! Black is even more pinned down, while **10...♗xf3?** 11 gxf3 would also strengthen the white centre. That leaves us with **10...♔f8!** After both 11 ♗e3 ♘ge7 12 a4 a5 13 ♗c4 ♗h5! ∞ (the threat was 14 ♗xf7) and 11 ♗xc6 bxc6 12 ♗a3 ♗xf3 13 gxf3 ♕g5+ 14 ♔h1 ♘e7 ∞, White has enough for the pawn (the king is on f8!). However, as he has no concrete threats, his opponent cannot complain.

Spanish (Ruy Lopez) Opening

1 e4 e5 2 ♘f3 ♘c6 3 ♗b5

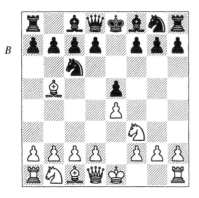

This move was already the subject of rigorous examination by the Spaniards Lucena and Lopez five hundred years ago, so it deserves to be known as the 'Spanish'.

The point of White's 3 ♗b5 is not to play the simple 4 ♗xc6 dxc6 5 ♘xe5, as Black would then easily regain the pawn with 5...♕d4, but to develop a long-lasting strategic initiative based upon:

- quick kingside development and immediate castling, after which White's king is sheltered and his rook joins the central fight from e1.
- pressure exerted by the white light-squared bishop on the c6-knight, strengthening his influence on the important d4- and e5-squares.

- after first developing and building up his position, the d2-d4 advance. In the meantime he tries to clamp down on Black's counterplay or to meet it effectively.

Black, according to his style and temperament, can direct the fight into a quiet, positional struggle, in which the pawn structure is changing every minute, or into a tactical minefield in which the position is no less exciting than in the sharpest lines of the King's Gambit! After White's third move Black's play can follow two main tracks:

I. Black avoids 3...a6.
II. On the way to the Main Line: systems with 3...a6.

I. Black avoids 3...a6

We will see in section II that Black risks nothing with the move 3...a6, and even obtains extra chances to mobilize his queenside. However, there are a few lines that can only be undertaken if the white bishop is still on b5 so that Black can attack it at an important juncture. Among these systems it is worth investigating the **Berlin Variation** (3...♘f6), section A, and the **Jänisch (or**

Schliemann) Gambit (3...f5), section B, in detail. Besides these lines Black has several other options, which can be dealt with in a nutshell:

a) 3...♗b4?! 4 c3 ♗a5 5 ♘a3! ♗b6 6 ♘c4 d6 7 a4! a6 8 ♘xb6 cxb6 9 ♗c4 is clearly better for White.

b) 3...g6 4 c3!? (the other option is 4 d4 exd4 5 ♗g5!? ♗e7 6 ♗xe7 ♘gxe7 7 ♘xd4 d5! and Black equalizes) 4...d6 5 d4 ♗d7 6 0-0 ♗g7 7 ♕b3!? (also good is 7 dxe5 dxe5 8 ♗g5! and on 8...♘ge7 9 ♕c1, while 8...f6 9 ♗e3 is also slightly better for White) 7...♘a5 (the threat was 8 ♗xc6 ♗xc6 9 d5 and White would win the b7-pawn) 8 ♕a4 c6 9 ♗e2 b5 10 ♕c2 ♘e7 11 ♗e3 0-0 12 dxe5 dxe5 13 a4!, and in this position Black faces serious problems on the queenside.

c) 3...♗c5 4 c3 f5!? (4...♘f6 5 d4 ♗b6 6 ♗xc6!? bxc6 7 ♘xe5 0-0 8 0-0!? ♘xe4 9 ♖e1 ♘d6 10 ♗f4 ±. The black pieces are hard to develop, while White can consider a kingside attack with ♘d2, ♕h5 and ♖e3) 5 d4! fxe4 6 ♗xc6 dxc6 7 ♘xe5 ♗d6 8 ♕h5+ g6 9 ♕e2 (Black gains too many tempi after 9 ♘xg6 ♘f6 10 ♕h6 ♖g8 11 ♘e5 ♕e7! 12 ♗g5 ♗xe5 13 dxe5 ♘g4! 14 ♕h5+ ♕f7 and the complications lead to an equal endgame) 9...♕h4 10 ♘d2 ♗xe5 11 dxe5 ♗f5 12 h3 0-0-0 13 g4! e3 (13...♗e6 14 ♘xe4 ±, threatening 15 ♗g5) 14 ♕xe3 ♗e6 15 ♕xa7 ♗xg4 16 ♕a8+!

♔d7 17 ♕a4 ♘f6, when a seemingly unclear position is turned to White's favour with 18 ♕f4!! ♖de8 19 0-0! ♕xh3 20 exf6 +−. If Black wants to play ...♗f8-c5 then he should first play 3...♘f6 4 0-0 and only then 4...♗c5 – see section A below.

d) 3...♘ge7 4 ♘c3!? (4 c3!? a6 5 ♗a4 d6 6 d4 also comes into consideration, when the game transposes into the Improved Steinitz Variation – see section II. Also playable is 4 d4 exd4 5 ♘xd4 g6 6 ♘xc6!? ♘xc6 7 ♗xc6 bxc6 8 ♕d4! f6 9 ♘c3 ♗g7 10 ♕c4!?) 4...♘g6 (White obtains a strong initiative after 4...g6 5 d4 exd4 6 ♘d5! ♗g7 7 ♗g5 h6 8 ♗f6 ♗xf6 9 ♘xf6+ ♔f8 10 ♘xd4 ♗g7 11 ♕d2!, as he has the murderous threat of 12 ♕c3!) 5 d4 exd4 6 ♘xd4 ♗c5 7 ♗e3 ♗xd4 8 ♗xd4 0-0 9 ♗e3 d6 10 0-0 and White, with his bishop pair and spatial plus, enjoys a clear advantage.

e) 3...♘d4. Black establishes a knight on d4, thus thwarting White's plan of d2-d4. White's simplest answer is to capture: 4 ♘xd4 exd4 5 0-0 ♗c5 (5...c6 6 ♗a4!? ♘f6 7 d3 d5 8 ♗g5! dxe4 9 dxe4 ♗e7 10 e5! ♘d5 11 ♗xe7 ♘xe7 12 ♗b3 0-0 13 ♘d2 ±, and White's plan may be ♕e2, ♘e4 and ♖ad1) 6 d3 c6 7 ♗c4 (threatening 8 ♗xf7+ and 9 ♕h5+) 7...d6 8 ♕h5! ♕e7 9 ♘d2 ♘f6 10 ♕h4 and now on each of Black's alternatives White achieves a small plus:

e1)   10...0-0 11 ♘f3 h6 12 ♗f4 ±.
e2)   10...♗e6 11 c3! 0-0 12 ♗xe6
♕xe6 13 ♘b3 ±.
e3)   10...g5!? 11 ♕xg5! ♖g8 12
♕f4 ♗h3 13 g3 ♗xf1 14 ♔xf1 and
White has full compensation for
the exchange.
f) 3...d6. This is the Steinitz
Variation...the refined version of
which (3...a6 4 ♗a4 d6, the 'Improved Steinitz') we will see in
section II. 4 d4! ♗d7 (or 4...exd4 5
♕xd4!? ♗d7 6 ♗xc6 ♗xc6 7 ♘c3
♘f6 8 ♗g5, followed by 0-0-0 and
♖he1, when White stands more
freely) 5 ♘c3 ♘f6 6 0-0 ♗e7 7
♗xc6! ♗xc6 8 ♖e1 exd4 9 ♘xd4
♗d7 10 h3 0-0 11 ♕f3 ±, and with
12 ♗f4 and then ♖ad1 White keeps
the centre under fire.
These examples demonstrate
White's ideas well. Against even
slightly passive play by Black,
White plays for an immediate d2-
d4, often with the help of the preparatory move c2-c3. Then he
would gladly even give up the
bishop on b5 for the knight on c6
since the centre will be his!

A. 1 e4 e5 2 ♘f3 ♘c6 3 ♗b5 ♘f6 (Berlin Variation)

4 0-0
If White protects the pawn on
e4 with 4 d3 or 4 ♕e2 then Black
smoothly develops via 4...d6 followed by ...♗e7, ...0-0 and ...♗g4,
while 4 ♘c3 ♗b4 is the topic of the
Four Knights Game. 4 d4!? deserves attention, however: 4...exd4

5 e5 ♘e4 6 0-0 and now the lines
6...a6 7 ♗xc6 dxc6 8 ♖e1 ♘c5 9
♗g5! ♕d5 10 ♘xd4 ♘e6 11 ♘xe6
♗xe6 12 ♕h5!, with the threat of
13 ♘c3, or 6...d5 7 ♘xd4 ♗d7 8
♗xc6 bxc6 9 f3 ♘g5 10 f4, with
the nightmare of the rolling e-
and f-pawns, promise White an
advantage. The theoretical rec-
ommendation, 4 0-0, assures White
good chances as well.

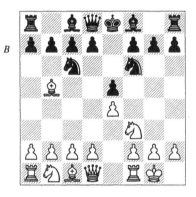

Here Black has to act actively
since after either 4...♗e7 5 d4
exd4 6 e5 ♘e4 7 ♖e1 ♘c5 8 ♘xd4
or 4...d6 5 d4 ♗d7 6 ♘c3 exd4 7
♘xd4 ♗e7 8 ♘f5!? ♗xf5 9 exf5 0-0
10 g4! he has problems. There are
two options:

A1.   4...♗c5 or
A2.   4...♘xe4.

A1. 1 e4 e5 2 ♘f3 ♘c6 3 ♗b5 ♘f6 4 0-0 ♗c5

5 c3!?
After 5 ♘xe5!? ♘xe4! (5...♘xe5
6 d4 c6 7 dxe5 ♘xe4 8 ♗d3 d5 9

exd6 ♘xd6? 10 ♖e1+ ♗e6 11
♖xe6+! with 12 ♕h5 and ♕xc5 +–)
6 ♕e2 ♘xe5 7 ♕xe4 ♕e7 8 d4 ♘c6!,
Black avoids dropping a piece in a
miraculous way. After 9 ♕xe7+
♗xe7 10 c3 Black is a little worse
but his position is solid, while on
9 ♕g4 Black achieves counterplay
on the kingside by 9...h5! 10 ♕xg7
♗xd4.

5...0-0 6 d4 ♗b6

6...exd4? 7 cxd4 ♗b6 8 e5 ♘d5 9
♗c4 ♘ce7 10 ♗g5! would be curtains for Black.

7 ♗g5!

This is the most unpleasant
move. After the inferior alternative 7 dxe5 ♘xe4 8 ♕d5 ♘c5 9
♗g5 ♘e7 10 ♕d1 ♘e4 11 ♗h4 d5!
12 ♘bd2 c6 Black gets nearly equal
chances.

7...h6!

A useful interpolation which
carries no risk as after 8 ♗xf6
♕xf6 9 ♗xc6 ♕xc6! 10 ♘xe5 ♕xe4
11 ♘d2 ♕f5 12 ♘df3 d6 White
has nothing.

8 ♗h4 d6

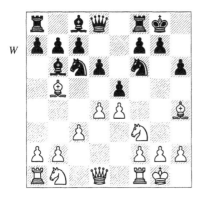

Plans and Counterplans:
White is evidently squeezing his
opponent but it is not easy to find
the correct sequence for the moves
♗xc6, dxe5, a2-a4, ♗xf6 and ♘bd2.
For example, **9 a4** a5 10 ♖e1 ♗g4
11 ♗xc6 bxc6 12 dxe5 dxe5 13
♕xd8?! (13 ♘bd2!?) 13...♖axd8 14
♘xe5 g5 15 ♗g3 ♘xe4 16 ♘xg4 f5
allows Black serious counter-
chances. An effective alternative
is **9 ♗xc6** bxc6 10 ♘bd2 ♖e8 (not
10...♗g4?! 11 dxe5 dxe5 12 ♕a4!
♗xf3 13 ♘xf3 ♕d6 14 ♖ad1 ♕e6
15 ♗g3 ♘d7 16 ♕b3! and Black
has a lost endgame on his hands)
11 ♖e1 exd4!? (11...g5 12 ♗g3
♘d7 13 ♕a4! ±) 12 ♘xd4 ♗d7 13
♕f3 g5!? 14 ♗g3 h5!? 15 h3! h4 16
♗h2 ±, and Black has many positional defects. For instance after
16...g4, 17 ♕f4! gxh3 18 ♘2f3 hxg2
19 e5! is strong, because Black's
weak king position is a decisive
handicap in such an open position.

**A2. 1 e4 e5 2 ♘f3 ♘c6 3 ♗b5 ♘f6
4 0-0 ♘xe4**

5 d4!

White should not drive the
knight away at once with 5 ♖e1 as
it may well have to retreat of its
own accord. After 5 ♖e1 ♘d6 6
♘xe5 ♗e7 7 ♗d3 0-0 8 ♘c3 ♘xe5 9
♖xe5 ♗f6 10 ♖e3 g6! Black is fine.

5...♘d6

The recommended continuation,
even though Black's tournament
results in this line are nothing to

boast about! On 5...a6, instead of 6 ♗xc6 dxc6 7 ♕e2 ♗f5 8 ♖d1 ♗e7 9 dxe5 ♕c8 10 ♘d4 0-0 =, White can transpose into the Open Variation of section II with 6 ♗a4. Also played is 5...♗e7, when 6 ♕e2 ♘d6 7 ♗xc6 bxc6 (or 7...dxc6 8 dxe5 ♘f5 9 ♖d1 ♗d7 10 ♘c3 0-0 11 ♘e4! ± followed by 12 ♗g5! and White seizes control of the dark squares) 8 dxe5 ♘b7 (on 8...♘f5, 9 ♕e4! g6 10 ♘c3 and ♖d1 gives Black problems) 9 ♘c3 (9 ♘d4 is worthy of attention: 9...0-0 10 ♘f5! d5 11 ♘xe7+ ♕xe7 12 b3! followed by ♗a3, when Black's queenside pawns and pieces are out of tune) 9...0-0 10 ♖e1 ♘c5 11 ♗e3 ♘e6 12 ♖ad1 ±, and Black has not even solved the problem of his d-pawn. On 5...♗e7 White can also react 6 ♖e1 ♘d6 7 ♗xc6 dxc6 8 dxe5 ♘f5 9 ♘bd2, when with the natural moves b2-b3, ♗b2, ♕e2 and ♘e4 he achieves a pleasant middlegame.

6 ♗xc6

White may also try the speculative 6 dxe5 ♘xb5 7 a4 d6 8 e6! fxe6 9 axb5 ♘e7 10 ♘c3 ♘g6 11 ♕d4!

6...dxc6

On 6...bxc6?! 7 dxe5 ♘b7 8 ♗g5! ♗e7 9 ♗xe7 ♕xe7 10 ♘c3 0-0 11 ♖e1 ±, Black is unable to construct a healthy setup.

7 dxe5

Now we can understand the real point of 5 d4! White regains the pawn and has achieved the following benefits:

a) The pawn on e5 restricts Black; it obstructs the development of his pieces.

b) By 'smuggling' his d-pawn to the e-file White has fundamentally improved his pawn structure. His three pawns on the queenside obstruct the Black quartet since the latter includes doubled c-pawns. Thus White has created a pawn majority on the kingside!

c) The previous two strategic gains are complemented by the momentary situation after 7 dxe5: the black pieces are unable to achieve harmony after the forthcoming queen trade. These three factors taken together guarantee White's advantage.

7...♘f5

On 7...♘e4 White should play not 8 ♕xd8+ ♔xd8 9 b3, as the way for the bishop on c8 is open, for example to g4, but 8 ♕e2 ♗f5 9 ♖d1 ♕c8 10 ♖d4!? ♘c5 11 ♗e3 ♗e7 12 ♘c3 0-0 13 ♘h4! ±.

8 ♕xd8+

It is worth swapping queens here as the black king cannot find a safe haven.

8...♔xd8 9 ♘c3 *(D)*

White should not give the check 9 ♖d1+ since Black's king stands better on e8 than on d8, but playable is 9 b3!? ♔e8 10 ♗b2 ♗e7 11 ♘bd2 a5 12 a4 ♗e6 13 ♘e4 ♖d8 14 ♖ad1 h6 15 h3 ±.

Plans and Counterplans:
Black would like to create some harmony in his game while White

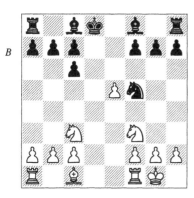

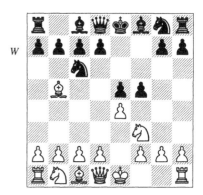

would like to lead the game into more and more simple endings by further developing his pieces. We can better understand Black's problems by examining three different continuations:

a) **9...♗e6** 10 ♘g5! ♔e8 11 ♘xe6 fxe6 12 ♘e4 ♖d8 13 c3!?, and after f2-f4 White is threatening both g2-g4 and the plan ♔f2-♔e2-♗d2-♖ad1, when he can still consider playing g2-g4 later.

b) **9...h6** 10 h3 ♗e6 11 g4 ♘e7 12 ♘d4 ♗d7 13 ♗f4 c5 14 ♘de2 ♔c8 15 ♖ad1 ±. Black's problems are not yet solved.

c) **9...♔e8** 10 h3 h6 (or 10...h5 11 ♖d1 ♗e6 12 ♘g5 ♗e7 13 ♘xe6 fxe6 14 ♘e4 c5 15 c3 ±) 11 ♗f4!? ♗e6 12 g4 ♘e7 13 ♗g3 ♘d5 14 ♘e4 c5 15 ♘h4! ♘b4 16 c3 ♗d5 17 ♘d2 ♘c6 18 ♘f5 ♖d8 19 ♖fd1 and ♘f5-e3 again drives Black back.

B. 1 e4 e5 2 ♘f3 ♘c6 3 ♗b5 f5!?
Jänisch (or Schliemann) Gambit

Let us first take a look at why Black did not interpose the moves

3...a6 4 ♗a4 before playing ...f7-f5. That is, in which lines is it important that the bishop stays on b5? After 4 d4 fxe4 5 ♘xe5 (not 5 ♗xc6 dxc6! 6 ♘xe5 ♕h4! 7 0-0 ♗d6 8 f3 exf3 9 ♘xf3 ♕h5 10 ♖e1+ ♘e7 and ...0-0, when Black is already better!) 5...♘xe5 6 dxe5 c6! At this point Black utilizes the position of the bishop on b5! Besides taking the bishop, Black is also threatening the pawn grab ...♕a5+ and ...♕xe5. For example 7 ♗e2 ♕a5+ 8 ♗d2 ♕xe5 9 ♗h5+ ♔d8 10 ♗c3 ♕g5 11 0-0 ♘f6 gives Black a clear pawn advantage. Later he will be almost winning with ...d7-d5. Therefore on 6...c6! White is forced to sacrifice a piece: 7 ♘c3! cxb5 8 ♘xe4 d5! 9 exd6 ♘f6 10 ♕d4! ♘xe4 11 ♕xe4+ ♔f7 12 ♗f4 ♕e8 13 ♗e5 ♗xd6! 14 ♕d5+ ♕e6 15 ♕xd6 ♕xd6 16 ♗xd6 ♖e8+ 17 ♔f1 ♗f5 and even though Black is a pawn behind, he seems to stand a little better! Before we move on to the main line with 4 ♘c3, let us take a look at a few rare lines for White:

a) 4 ♗xc6 dxc6 5 ♘xe5 ♛d4 6 ♘f3 ♛xe4+ 7 ♕e2 =.

b) 4 exf5 e4! 5 ♕e2 ♛e7 6 ♗xc6 dxc6 7 ♘d4 ♛e5! is a likely draw: 8 ♘f3 ♛e7 (8...♛xf5 9 d3!) 9 ♘d4 ♛e5, etc.

c) 4 ♕e2 fxe4 5 ♕xe4 ♘f6 6 ♕e2 ♗d6! 7 ♗xc6 dxc6 8 ♘xe5 0-0 9 d4 ♖e8 10 0-0 ♗xe5 11 dxe5 ♛d4 is equal.

d) 4 d3 fxe4 5 dxe4 ♘f6 6 0-0 ♗c5!? 7 ♘c3 (7 ♗xc6 bxc6 8 ♘xe5 0-0 9 ♘c3 d6 10 ♘d3 – if 10 ♘xc6 ♛e8! obtains excellent counter-play – 10...♗d4 11 ♘e2 ♗b6 12 ♘g3 ♘g4! gives Black a promising attack and he can continue with 13...♛h4) 7...d6 8 ♗g5!? 0-0 9 ♘d5 ♔h8 10 ♘h4 ♘d4 11 ♗c4 b5 12 ♗d3 c6 13 ♘xf6 gxf6 14 ♗e3 ♖g8 leads to a double-edged position.

So now let us see the antidote to the Jänisch Gambit!

4 ♘c3!

We need this knight on the battlefield.

4...fxe4

Weaker is 4...♘d4 5 exf5!? ♘xb5 6 ♘xb5 e4 7 ♘fd4 ♘f6 8 d3! ± or 4...♘f6 5 exf5!? e4 (5...♗c5 6 0-0 0-0 7 ♘xe5 ♘xe5 8 d4 ±) 6 ♘g5 d5 7 d3 ♗xf5 8 dxe4 dxe4 9 ♕e2 ♗b4 10 ♗d2 ♛e7 11 ♕c4! ±.

5 ♘xe4 d5

On 5...♘f6 the old answer 6 ♘xf6+ ♛xf6 7 ♕e2 ♗e7 8 ♗xc6 dxc6 9 ♘xe5 0-0 10 0-0 ♗d6 11 d4 is slightly better for White, but in this line 7 0-0!? could be an interesting improvement: 7...♘d4!? 8 ♖e1! ♘xf3+ 9 ♛xf3 and after

9...♛xf3 10 gxf3 White is threatening f3-f4.

6 ♘xe5! dxe4 7 ♘xc6

White could go astray with 7 ♛h5+? g6 8 ♘xg6 hxg6! 9 ♛xh8 ♛f6! 10 ♛xg8 ♗e6 11 ♗xc6+ bxc6 12 ♛h7 0-0-0 13 d4 ♖d7 and he drops his queen.

7...♛g5

Nobody plays 7...bxc6 8 ♗xc6+ ♗d7 9 ♛h5+ ♔e7 10 ♛e5+ ♗e6 any more, as after 11 f4 exf3 12 0-0 ♖b8 13 d4 White 'supposedly' has an attack, although he still has to prove this after 13...♛d6!? Instead of this risky piece sacrifice, 11 ♗xa8! ♛xa8 12 ♛xc7+ ♗d7 13 0-0 followed by 14 d3 is certainly superior for White. Another possibility for Black on the seventh move is 7...♛d5. Then on 8 c4! ♛d6 (not 8...♛g5 9 d4! ♛xg2 10 ♛h5+! g6 11 ♛e5+ and White is winning) 9 ♘xa7+ ♗d7 (or 9...c6 10 ♘xc8 ♖xc8 11 ♗a4 +–) 10 ♗xd7+ ♛xd7 11 ♛h5+! g6 (11...♔d8 12 ♘b5 ♘f6 13 ♛e2 ♗c5 14 0-0 ♖f8 15 d4! exd3 16 ♛e5 and Black is worse owing to his exposed king position) 12 ♛e5+ ♔f7 13 ♘b5 c6 14 ♛d4! and Black has insufficient counterplay for the two pawns.

8 ♛e2!

Not only protecting the bishop on b5 but also attacking the pawn on e4.

8...♘f6

The only move, because after 8...♛xg2? 9 ♛h5+! g6 10 ♛e5+ Black is losing straight away.

9 f4!
An excellent sacrifice, releasing the pawn on g2 from attack with gain of tempo.
9...♕xf4
On 9...♕h4+ an example taken from Timman is 10 g3 ♕h3 11 ♘e5+ c6 12 ♗c4 ♗c5 13 d3 ♘g4 (13...exd3 14 ♘xd3+ ♗e7 15 ♘e5 ±) 14 ♘f7! ♗f2+ 15 ♔d1 e3 16 ♕f3 ♘h6 17 ♕e4+ ♔f8 18 ♗xe3 ♗g4+ 19 ♔d2 ♖e8 20 ♘e5 1-0.
10 ♘e5+! c6 11 d4! ♕h4+ 12 g3 ♕h3 13 ♗c4 ♗e6
Or 13...♗d6 14 ♗f7+ ♔e7 15 ♗b3 ±
14 ♗f4
14 ♗g5 is similar: 14...0-0-0 15 0-0-0 ♗d6 16 ♗xe6+ ♕xe6 17 ♕c4 ♖he8 18 ♕xe6+ ♖xe6 19 ♘c4 ±, and the less pieces there are on the board, the weaker Black's e-pawn will become.
14...0-0-0
On 14...♖d8 15 0-0-0 ♗d6 the surprise move 16 ♗g5! puts White on top: 16...♕f5 17 ♗xf6 gxf6 18 ♖hf1! ♕g5+ 19 ♔b1 ♗xe5 20 ♗xe6 and the king is stuck in the middle, or 16...0-0 17 ♕f1!! ♔h8 18 ♕xh3 ♗xh3 19 ♘f7+ wins an exchange.
15 0-0-0 *(D)*

Plans and Counterplans:
White intends to play against the pawn on e4 either directly, or in a queenless endgame in which Black cannot create counterplay. Black needs to keep the pieces on the board, especially his nagging queen

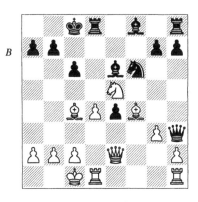

on h3. A short sample variation: 15...♗d6 16 ♔b1 ♖he8 17 ♗xe6+!? ♕xe6 18 h3! h6 19 g4 with slightly better prospects for White.

II. On the way to the Main Line: Systems with 3...a6

In this section we consider various alternatives after **1 e4 e5 2 ♘f3 ♘c6 3 ♗b5 a6**. The position after the moves **4 ♗a4 ♘f6 5 0-0 ♗e7 6 ♖e1 b5 7 ♗b3 d6 8 c3 0-0 9 h3** can be considered the starting position of the Spanish (Ruy Lopez) Main Line, but before we reach this important position, we need to become acquainted with the sidelines for both sides. At nearly every moment there are several ways to deviate from the main route, of which the following are definitely worth further examination:

A. Exchange Variation: 4 ♗xc6.

B. Improved Steinitz Variation: 4 ♗a4 d6.

C. Open Variation: 4 ♗a4 ♘f6
5 0-0 ♘xe4.

D. Marshall Attack: 4 ♗a4 ♘f6
5 0-0 ♗e7 6 ♖e1 b5 7 ♗b3 0-0 8 c3
d5!?

E. The Main Line of the variation.

Within each of the variations marked A-D, short passages named **'Sidelines'** will sum up other interesting possibilities for White and Black.

A. 1 e4 e5 2 ♘f3 ♘c6 3 ♗b5 a6 4 ♗xc6 (Exchange Variation)

4...dxc6
4...bxc6? is inferior in every respect: 5 d4 exd4 6 ♕xd4! ♕f6 7 e5 ♕g6 8 0-0 ♗b7 (White obtains a very strong attack after 8...♕xc2 9 ♘c3 followed by ♖e1 and ♘e4) 9 ♘bd2 (9 e6? fxe6 10 ♘e5 ♕xg2+!) 9...0-0-0 10 ♘b3 c5 11 ♕c3 f6 12 ♗f4 fxe5 13 ♗xe5 and ♗g3 is very good for White, but perhaps even stronger is 5 ♘c3!? d6 6 d4 exd4 7 ♕xd4 ♕f6 8 ♕c4! ♗d7 9 0-0 ±, and all White has to do is centralise his pieces (♗g5, ♖fe1, ♖ad1 and e4-e5). Let us see the position after 4...dxc6 (D).

White has voluntarily traded his bishop, rather than retreat it. Later by playing d2-d4 he will swap Black's e5-pawn for his own d-pawn to create a kingside pawn majority. On the queenside White

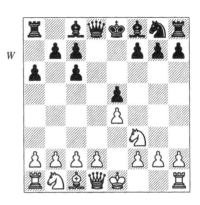

can block his opponent's four pawns with three of his own since Black has doubled c-pawns. The following king and pawn ending would certainly mean victory for White:

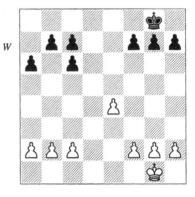

White can easily create a kingside passed pawn, while Black, for instance against the pawn constellation a3, b2, c3 could not do the same on the queenside. So if we took the pieces from our initial diagram, White would be winning! However, in the middlegame Black enjoys excellent chances as he has the bishop pair and his bishop on c8 can develop easily, enabling queenside castling. Although Black's prospects are by no means worse, he should always keep in mind that thoughtless exchanges can easily leave him in a difficult ending!

5 0-0

5 ♘xe5 does not come into consideration, as 5...♕d4 and ...♕xe4+ will only give White problems. Instead 5 ♘c3 ♕d6!? (5...f6 is also good) 6 d4 exd4 7 ♘xd4 (7 ♕xd4?! ♗g4 8 ♕xd6 ♗xd6 9 ♘d4 0-0-0 =) 7...♕g6 8 ♕f3 ♗g4 9 ♕g3 0-0-0 or 5 d4 exd4 6 ♕xd4 ♕xd4 7 ♘xd4 ♗d7 8 ♗e3 0-0-0 9 ♘c3 ♖e8!? 10 0-0-0 ♗b4 11 ♘de2 f5 12 exf5 ♗xf5 produces an equal game.

5...f6

Protecting the e5-pawn and preparing for a queen trade following White's d2-d4. A few other options are:

a) 5...♗d6 6 d4! exd4 7 ♕xd4 f6 8 e5!? fxe5 9 ♘xe5 ♕e7 10 ♖e1 ♗e6 11 ♘f3 0-0-0 12 ♗g5 ♘f6 13 ♗xf6 gxf6 14 ♕e3 ±.

b) 5...♘e7 6 ♘xe5 ♕d4 7 ♕h5!? g6 8 ♕g5 ♗g7 9 ♘d3 f5 10 e5 c5 11 b3!? h6 (11...♕xa1 12 ♘c3!) 12 ♕g3 f4 13 ♕f3 ♗f5 14 ♕xb7 ♗e4 15 ♕xc7 ♗xd3 16 cxd3 ♗xe5 17 ♕b7 ♖b8 18 ♕xa6 f3!? ∞. In this very unclear position it is probably White who is trying to hold on.

c) 5...♗g4 6 h3 h5!? 7 d3! (note that White must not capture the bishop for a long time as by opening the h-file he would get mated. However, with cautious play he

can pick the ideal moment) 7...♕f6! 8 ♘bd2 ♘e7 (8...0-0-0? 9 hxg4 hxg4 10 ♘h2 ♕h4 and 11 ♕xg4 is check!) 9 ♖e1 ♘g6 10 d4! ♗d6 (not 10...0-0-0 11 hxg4 hxg4 12 ♘h2 ♖xh2 13 ♕xg4+ ♔b8 14 ♔xh2 ♕xf2 15 ♖f1 ♕xd4 16 ♘b3 and Black's attack is over) 11 hxg4! hxg4 12 ♘h2 ♖xh2 (12...exd4 13 e5! ♘xe5 14 ♘e4 ♕h4 15 ♘xd6+ cxd6 16 ♗f4 +−) 13 ♕xg4 ♕h4 (13...♖h4 14 ♕f5! ♘e7 15 ♕xf6 gxf6 16 ♘f3 ♖h5 17 ♗e3 followed by g2-g3, ♔g2, ♖h1 and dxe5 with a huge plus for White in the endgame) 14 ♕xh4 ♖xh4 15 ♘f3 ♖h5 16 dxe5 ♘xe5 17 ♘xe5 ♗xe5 18 c3 ±, after g2-g3, ♔g2 and ♗e3 White can exchange rooks and then play f2-f4.

d) 5...♕d6!? A very popular move. 6 d3 (instead 6 ♘a3 ♗e6 7 ♘g5 ♗d7 8 d3 f6 9 ♘c4 ♕e7 10 ♘f3 ♕f7 ∞ or 6 d4!? exd4 7 ♘xd4 ♗d7 8 ♗e3 0-0-0 9 ♘d2 ♘h6! 10 h3 ♕g6 11 ♕f3 f5! 12 ♖ad1 fxe4 13 ♕xe4 ♘f5! with a very messy position) 6...f6 7 ♗e3 c5 8 ♘bd2 ♗e6 9 ♘c4 ♕c6 10 ♘fd2 ♘e7 11 a4 b6 12 f4 exf4 13 ♗xf4 ♘g6 14 ♗g3 ♗d6 15 ♘xd6+ cxd6 16 ♘c4 ♖d8 17 ♘e3 0-0 =. Black can later pick from the moves ...b6-b5, ...d6-d5 and ...♘e5.

6 d4

6 ♘c3 ♗g4 7 h3 ♗h5 is more comfortable for Black.

6...exd4

After 6...♗g4 7 dxe5! ♕xd1 8 ♖xd1 fxe5 9 ♖d3! ♗d6 10 ♘bd2 b5 11 b4! ♘f6 12 ♗b2 ♘d7 13 c4 ±

Black has some problems in view of his inferior pawn structure.

7 ♘xd4

7 ♕xd4 ♕xd4 8 ♘xd4 ♗d7 9 ♗e3 0-0-0 10 ♘c3 ♗b4 11 ♘de2 ♘e7 is just equal.

7...c5! 8 ♘b3 ♕xd1 9 ♖xd1 ♗g4!?

A slight finesse to weaken the diagonal a7-g1.

10 f3 ♗d7

The other, somewhat safer, plan is 10...♗e6, for example 11 ♗e3 b6 12 a4 ♘e7 13 ♗f4 c4! 14 ♘d4 0-0-0 15 ♘c3 ♖xd4 16 ♖xd4 ♘g6 17 ♗e3 ♗c5 18 ♔f2 ♗xd4 19 ♗xd4 with equality.

11 ♗f4 0-0-0 12 ♘c3 c4 13 ♘a5!?

13 ♘d4 ♘e7 14 ♖d2 ♘g6 15 ♗e3 ♗d6 gives Black sufficient counterplay.

13...♗c5+ 14 ♔f1 b5 15 ♘d5

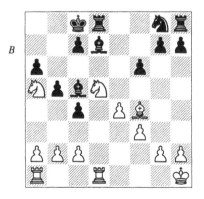

Plans and Counterplans:
With this attack on the pawn on c7 White has somewhat inflamed the opening after a lukewarm start. Karpov – true, in a blindfold game! – continued **15...c6** 16 b4! ♗a7 17 ♗e3 ♗xe3 18 ♘xe3 ♘e7 and it is hard to assess whether White's a5-knight is well-placed or not. A recognized pawn sacrifice is **15...♘e7!?**: 16 ♗xc7 ♘xd5 17 ♖xd5 ♔xc7 18 ♖xc5+ ♔b6 19 b4! (or 19 ♖d5 ♗e6! 20 ♖xd8 ♖xd8 21 b4 ♖d2 and White cannot move) 19...cxb3 20 ♘xb3 and now after 20...a5 21 ♖c3 b4 22 ♖e3 ♗b5+ or 20...♗e6 21 ♖c3 ♖c8! Black has adequate play for the pawn.

Sidelines

1 e4 e5 2 ♘f3 ♘c6 3 ♗b5 a6 4 ♗a4

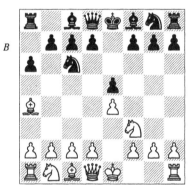

By inserting the moves 3...a6 and 4 ♗a4 Black has obtained a serious additional possibility. At any moment he can play ...b7-b5 gaining space on the queenside, creating a new way of development for the light-squared bishop on b7, and chasing away the white bishop from a4. Besides the main line **4...♘f6** and the Improved

Steinitz move **4...d6**, Black can choose from the following:

a) 4...♗c5 5 c3 b5 6 ♗b3 ♘f6 7 d4!? exd4 8 0-0 d5 9 exd5 ♘xd5 10 ♖e1+ ♗e6 11 ♘g5 0-0 12 ♕d3! g6 13 ♖xe6 fxe6 14 ♕h3, and Black's position is critical.

b) 4...b5 5 ♗b3 ♘a5 (on 5...♗c5 White obtains the initiative with 6 a4! ♖b8 7 axb5 axb5 8 0-0 d6 9 c3, and on 5...♗b7 6 d4! exd4 7 0-0 ♗c5 8 c3! gives him a superior position, as 8...dxc3? is impossible in view of 9 ♗xf7+ and 10 ♕d5+) 6 0-0 (the interesting piece sacrifice 6 ♗xf7+ ♔xf7 7 ♘xe5+ ♔e7 8 d4 is not advisable because White can reach a favourable position without taking any such risk) 6...d6 7 d4 ♘xb3 8 axb3 f6 9 ♘c3 ♗b7 10 ♘h4 ♕d7 11 ♘d5!? and White attacks Black's pawn chain via c2-c4 and f2-f4.

c) 4...f5?! 5 d4! (in section I on the Jänisch Gambit we saw why 4 d4 is bad in answer to 3...f5. But now this counter-thrust is almost winning!) 5...exd4 (5...fxe4 6 ♘xe5 ♕h4 7 0-0 ♘xe5 8 dxe5 e3 9 ♘c3 exf2+ 10 ♔h1, and by combining the moves ♕f3, ♗e3, ♘e4 and ♖xf2 White can start an attack along the open f-file) 6 e5 ♗c5 (on 6...♗b4+ 7 c3 dxc3 8 ♘xc3 ♘ge7 9 0-0 d5 10 exd6 ♕xd6 11 ♕e2 0-0 12 ♗g5 ♗xc3 13 bxc3 and ♖ad1 gives White good prospects) 7 0-0 ♘ge7 8 c3! dxc3 9 ♘xc3 d5 (or 9...0-0 10 ♗b3+ ♔h8 11 ♘g5 ♘xe5 12 ♘xh7 ♔xh7 13 ♕h5 mate!) 10 ♗g5!! and in this position Black

faces an insoluble problem, for example: 10...0-0 11 ♘xd5!, 10...b5 11 ♘xb5 axb5 12 ♗xb5 ♗b7 13 ♖c1 h6 14 ♗xe7 ♕xe7 15 ♕xd5, 10...♗e6 11 ♖c1 ♗a7 12 ♗xe7 ♔xe7 13 ♗xc6 bxc6 14 ♘a4, followed by ♘d4 and ♘c5, producing a total blockade, in the shelter of which White can march against the c-pawns and the enemy king or 10...♔f8 11 ♖c1 ♗a7 12 ♗xc6 bxc6 13 ♘e2 c5 14 ♘f4 c6 15 b4! and after 15...c4 16 ♖xc4 or 15...cxb4 16 ♖xc6 White smashes through the defences.

B. 1 e4 e5 2 ♘f3 ♘c6 3 ♗b5 a6 4 ♗a4 d6 (Improved Steinitz Variation)

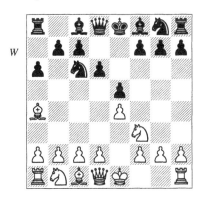

5 c3

How does the interpolation of 3...a6 and 4 ♗a4 'improve' the Steinitz Variation? Well, take a look at the following example: 5 d4?! b5! 6 ♗b3 ♘xd4 7 ♘xd4 exd4 8 ♕xd4? (8 c3 dxc3 9 ♕d5 ♗e6 10 ♕c6+ ♗d7 11 ♕d5 ♗e6 =) 8...c5 9 ♕d5 ♗e6 10 ♕c6+ ♗d7 11 ♕d5 c4 −+, and Black has netted the bishop on b3! So White cannot hope for an advantage with 5 d4?!, but besides 5 c3 he does have two other options:

a) 5 0-0!? ♗g4 (the variations 5...♘f6 6 ♗xc6+ bxc6 7 d4 ♘xe4 8 dxe5 ♗g4 9 exd6 ♗xd6 10 ♕e2 ♕e7 11 ♖e1 ♘c5 12 ♕xe7+ ♗xe7 13 ♘e5 and 5...♗d7 6 d4 b5 7 ♗b3 ♘xd4 8 ♘xd4 exd4 9 c3 dxc3 10 ♕h5 g6 11 ♕d5 ♗e6 12 ♕c6+ ♗d7 13 ♕xc3 are slightly better for White) 6 c3 ♕f6 7 ♗xc6+! bxc6 8 d4 ♘e7 9 ♘bd2 g5 10 ♖e1 ♘g6 11 ♕a4 ♗d7 12 dxe5 dxe5 13 ♘c4 g4 14 ♗g5! ♕e6 15 ♘fd2 h5 16 ♕b3 ♗c5 17 ♘a5!, and Black faces a tough endgame.

b) 5 ♗xc6+ bxc6 6 d4 f6! 7 ♘c3 ♘e7 8 ♗e3 ♘g6 9 ♕e2 ♗e7 10 0-0-0 ♗d7 11 h4 h5 12 ♘e1 ♕b8! 13 g3 ♕b4 14 f3 ♖b8 15 ♘d3 ♕c4 16 dxe5 ♘xe5 with a complex fight. It is worth remembering Black's manoeuvre ...♕d8-b8-b4, ...♖b8 as it is much stronger than ...♖b8, ...♕d8-c8-b7.

5...♗d7

On 5...f5!? White has to answer positionally: 6 exf5! ♗xf5 7 0-0 ♗d3 8 ♖e1 ♗e7 (8...e4 9 ♕b3!? ♖b8 − 9...b5 10 c4! − 10 ♘d4 ♘e7 11 c4 ±, threatening 12 ♘e6 as well as 12 ♘xc6 bxc6 13 ♗xc6+! ♘xc6 14 ♕xd3) 9 ♗c2 ♗xc2 10 ♕xc2 ♘f6 11 d4 0-0 (11...exd4 12 cxd4 0-0 13 ♘c3 d5 14 ♗g5 ±. White may play ♖ad1, ♘e5 and ♕b3) 12 d5! (12 dxe5 ♘xe5 13 ♘xe5 dxe5 14 ♖xe5? lets the spirit out of the bottle. After 14...♘g4 15 ♖e2 ♗c5 and ...♕h4 the genie is winning) 12...e4 (12...♘b8 13 ♘g5 ♕c8 14 c4 and White's knight invades on e6) 13 ♘g5 ♘e5 14 ♘e6 ♕d7 and now the correct way is not 15 ♘xf8?, as 15...♕g4! leaves Black with a strong attack, but 15 ♘d2! ♖fc8 16 ♘xe4 ♘xd5 17 ♘4g5 ♗xg5 18 ♘xg5 ±, according to analysis by the Indian grandmaster Viswanathan Anand.

6 d4 g6

A strange setup for Black arises after 6...♘ge7 7 ♗b3 h6 8 ♘bd2 ♘g6 9 ♘c4 ♗e7 10 ♘e3 ♗g5 11 ♘xg5 hxg5 12 g3 exd4 13 cxd4 ♔f8, when Lajos Portisch, in a game with Black, later complicated matters with ...♗h3, ...♕d7 and ...♖e8 and won. However, on 6...♘ge7 it is worth considering an approach typical of the middlegames of Closed Games: 7 d5! ♘b8 8 c4 ♘g6 9 h4!? ♗e7 10 h5 ♘h4 11 ♘xh4 ♗xh4 12 ♗xd7+ ♘xd7 13 ♕g4 ♗f6 14 ♘c3 ±. Besides his spatial plus White can also occupy the outpost f5 with the manoeuvre ♘c3-d1-e3-f5.

7 0-0 ♗g7 8 ♖e1!

Precise, White does not allow the knight on g8 to develop to f6! 8 dxe5 ♘xe5 9 ♘xe5 dxe5 10 f4 ♗xa4!? 11 ♕a4+ b5 12 ♕b3 exf4 13 ♗xf4 ♘f6 14 ♘d2 0-0 15 ♖ae1 ♘g4! gives mutual chances, while on 8 ♗e3 ♘f6! 9 ♗c2 0-0 10 h3 ♘h5! 11 ♘bd2 ♘f4, followed by ...♕f6 and ...♖ad8, Black is again fine.

8...♘ge7

8...♘f6? 9 ♗xc6 ♗xc6 10 dxe5 ♘xe4 (10...dxe5 11 ♕xd8+ ♖xd8 12 ♘xe5 ♗xe4 13 f3 ±) 11 exd6 ♕xd6 12 ♕xd6 cxd6 13 ♘g5 0-0 14 ♖xe4! ♗xe4 15 ♘xe4 ♖fe8 16 ♘bd2 d5 17 ♘g3 ♖e1+ 18 ♘gf1 followed by ♘b3 and ♗e3 ends Black's dreams of a back-rank pin. Let us return to the position after 8...♘ge7:

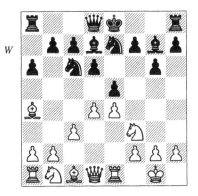

Plans and Counterplans:
White can follow two plans. He can open the centre, as José Capablanca once did: **9 ♗e3** 0-0 10 dxe5 ♘xe5 11 ♘xe5 ♗xe5 12 ♗b3 ♘c6 13 ♘d2 ♗g7 14 ♘f3 h6 15 ♘d4 and White definitely stands more freely but Black also cannot complain. Alternatively, those who prefer a closed centre will most probably prefer to follow Judit Polgar's play as White: **9 d5!?** ♘b8 10 ♗xd7+ ♘xd7 11 ♗e3! (it is important to accomplish the setup ♗e3 and ♘fd2 before Black can play ...h7-h6 and ...f7-f5, in order that the pawn on e4 can be

protected harmoniously by means of f2-f3) 11...h6 (11...f5? 12 ♘g5) 12 ♘fd2 0-0 13 c4 f5 14 f3. We have reached a middlegame typical of the King's Indian Defence in which White seeks play on the queenside with ♘c3, b2-b4, c4-c5 while Black can try to create a pawn storm on the kingside. Particularly in respect of the difference between the activity of the dark-squared bishops, White's position looks the more pleasing.

Sidelines

Returning to the 'Main Road', after **1 e4 e5 2 ♘f3 ♘c6 3 ♗b5 a6 4 ♗a4** we can make our next move, **4...♘f6**. Then White almost always plays **5 0-0**, but we should know about a few other options as well:

a) 5 d3 d6 (also possible is 5...b5 6 ♗b3 ♗e7 7 c3 d5 8 ♕e2 dxe4 9 dxe4 0-0 =, and later Black can opt for the piece setup ...♗d6, ...♘e7 and ...♗b7, while on 5...♗c5 interesting is 6 ♗e3!?) 6 c3 g6 7 0-0 ♗g7 8 ♖e1 0-0 =.

b) 5 ♘c3 b5 6 ♗b3 ♗e7 7 0-0 d6 8 ♘d5!? ♘a5 (8...♘xe4?! is dangerous in view of 9 d4!) 9 ♘xe7 ♕xe7 10 d4 ♗b7 11 ♗g5 0-0 12 dxe5 dxe5 with comfortable play for Black.

c) 5 ♕e2 b5 6 ♗b3 ♗c5 7 a4 ♖b8 8 axb5 axb5 9 ♘c3 0-0, and now instead of 10 ♘xb5? d5! 11 exd5 e4 12 ♘g5 ♘b4! White has to settle for a level game with 10 d3 d6 11 ♗g5 ♗b4 12 0-0 ♗xc3 13 bxc3 h6 14 ♗h4 ♕e7.

d) 5 ♗xc6 dxc6 6 d3 ♗d6 7 ♘bd2 ♗e6 8 ♕e2 ♘h5!? 9 ♘c4 ♗xc4 10 dxc4 ♕f6 and Black has no problems.

e) 5 d4!? ♘xe4?! (after the alternative 5...♘xd4?! 6 ♘xd4 exd4 7 e5 ♘e4 8 ♕xd4 ♘c5 9 ♘c3 ♗e7 10 ♕g4! 0-0 11 ♗h6 ♘e6 12 ♗b3! ♗g5 13 ♗xg5 ♕xg5 14 ♕xg5 ♘xg5 15 ♘d5, White obtains a significant advantage with the simple moves 0-0-0, ♖he1 and f2-f4) 6 ♕e2 b5 7 ♕xe4 d5 8 ♕e3 bxa4 9 ♘xe5 ♘xe5 10 0-0!? ♗e6 11 dxe5 ♕d7 12 ♘c3 ♗b4 13 ♕g3 0-0 14 ♗h6 f6 15 ♗f4 c5 16 ♖ad1 is slightly better for White. Instead of 5...♘xe4?! or 5...♘xd4?! Black does better to play 5...exd4 and now 6 e5 ♘e4 7 0-0 ♘c5! leads to an even position while 6 0-0 ♗e7! is again equal. This line is discussed under the move-order 5 0-0 ♗e7 6 d4 – see the next 'Sidelines'!

Now we can calmly play **5 0-0.**

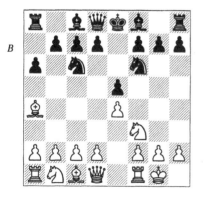

Besides **5...♘xe4** (the Open Variation) and **5...♗e7** (the Main Line), Black has the following alternatives:

a) 5...d6 transposes to the Improved Steinitz (see above).

b) 5...♗c5 6 ♘xe5!? (theory speaks kindly of the position after 6 c3 ♘xe4 7 d4 ♗b6 8 ♖e1 f5 9 ♘bd2 0-0 10 ♘xe4 fxe4 11 ♖xe4, although after 11...d6 12 dxe5 ♗f5 Black is not without chances) 6...♘xe5 7 d4 ♘xe4 8 ♖e1 ♗e7 9 ♖xe4 (after 9 dxe5 ♘c5 10 ♘c3 ♘xa4 11 ♘xa4 0-0 12 ♗f4 Black is still a little worse due to his backward d-pawn) 9...♘g6 10 c4 0-0 11 ♘c3 f5 (11...c6 12 d5!) 12 ♖e2 f4 13 f3 d6 14 ♗c2! ±. Black has some weaknesses: the pawn on f4 and the e6-square.

c) 5...b5!? 6 ♗b3 ♗b7. This is the very popular Archangelsk Variation. Let us see each of White's continuations in turn:

c1) 7 ♘g5? d5! 8 exd5 ♘d4 ∓.

c2) 7 d4 ♘xd4 8 ♗xf7+!? (8 ♘xd4 exd4 9 e5 ♘e4 10 c3 dxc3 11 ♕f3 d5 12 exd6 ♕f6 13 ♖e1 0-0-0 ∞) 8...♔xf7 9 ♘xe5+ ♔g8 10 ♕xd4 c5 11 ♕d1 ♕e8 12 ♘f3 ♕xe4 13 ♗g5!? ♕f5 14 ♗xf6 ♕xf6 15 ♘c3 ♖d8 with a complicated fight.

c3) 7 d3 ♗d6 (a strange looking move, but after ...0-0 and ...♖e8, the bishop will return to f8. Until then it strengthens the centre) 8 a4 0-0 9 ♘c3 b4 10 ♘e2 ♘a5 11 ♗a2 h6 12 ♘g3 ♖e8 13 h3 ♗f8 14 ♘h2 d5! 15 ♕f3 c5 16 ♘g4 ♖e6! 17 ♘e3 b3! 18 cxb3 ♖b6, and

Black has produced excellent play with his rook along the sixth rank.

c4) 7 ♘c3 ♗e7 8 d3 0-0 9 ♗d2!? (this move prevents a later ...♘c6-a5!) 9...d6 10 ♘d5!? ♘d7 11 a4 ♘c5! with mutual chances.

c5) 7 c3 ♘xe4 8 d4 ♗e7 (the move 8...♘a5 was strongly met in a game of Peter Leko's by 9 ♗c2 exd4 10 ♘xd4 c5 11 ♘f5 ♕f6 12 ♘d2! – a novelty of the young Hungarian grandmaster Zoltan Almasi! – 12...d5 13 ♘xe4 dxe4 14 ♘g3 ♗e7 15 ♘xe4 ♕c6 16 ♕h5!, and Black cannot play 16...0-0? owing to 17 ♘f6+ and 18 ♕xh7 mate) 9 ♖e1 (9 ♕e2 d5 10 dxe5 0-0 11 ♖d1 ♘a5 12 ♗c2 ♕c8! ∞) 9...d5 10 dxe5 ♘a5 11 ♗c2 0-0 12 ♘bd2 ♘c4!? with an adequate game.

c6) 7 ♖e1 ♗c5 8 c3 (not 8 ♘xe5? ♘xe5 9 d4 ♘fg4! 10 dxc5 ♕h4 –+) 8...d6 9 d4 ♗b6 10 ♗g5 (or 10 ♗e3 0-0 11 ♘bd2 h6 12 h3 ♖e8 13 d5 ♘a5 14 ♗xb6 cxb6 15 ♗c2 ♘c4 16 ♖b1 ∞) 10...h6 11 ♗h4 g5!? 12 ♗g3 0-0 and now 13 a4 exd4!? 14 cxd4 ♖e8 15 e5 dxe5 16 dxe5 ♕xd1 17 ♖xd1 ♘e4! or 13 ♕d3 ♘h5 14 ♘bd2 ♕f6 15 ♗d5 ♖ae8 16 a4 ♘xg3 17 hxg3 exd4 18 axb5 axb5 19 ♗xc6 ♗xc6 20 ♘xd4 ♗d7 is an interesting position with chances for both sides.

C. 1 e4 e5 2 ♘f3 ♘c6 3 ♗b5 a6 4 ♗a4 ♘f6 5 0-0 ♘xe4 (Open Variation)

The move 5...♘xe4 is the one that makes this variation 'open'.

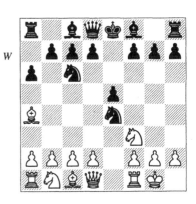

6 d4

The only way to fight for an edge. As we shall see, in this way White can regain the pawn via d4xe5, thus avoiding a symmetrical pawn formation. With the pawn on e5 White can play an active role both on the kingside and in the centre. After 6 ♖e1 ♘c5 7 ♘xe5 ♗e7 8 ♗xc6 dxc6 9 d4 ♘e6 10 ♗e3 0-0 11 f4 f6 12 ♘f3 ♗d6 Black has nothing to fear.

6...b5

Other choices are inferior:

a) 6...exd4 7 ♖e1 d5 8 ♘xd4 ♗d6!? 9 ♘xc6 ♗xh2+ 10 ♔h1 ♕h4 11 ♖xe4+! dxe4 12 ♕d8+! ♕xd8 13 ♘xd8+ ♔xd8 14 ♔xh2 ±. Material-wise Black is well off (a rook and two pawns in return for two pieces), but his king and his pawn on e4 will quickly become a target for the developing white pieces.

b) 6...♗e7 7 ♖e1 f5 8 dxe5 0-0 9 ♗b3+ ♔h8 10 ♗d5 (10 ♘c3!?) **10...♘c5 11 ♘c3 ±.** Black is undeveloped and has a 'hole' on d5.

7 ♗b3 d5

On 7...exd4 8 ♖e1 d5 9 ♘c3!
♗e6 (or 9...dxc3 10 ♗xd5 ♗b7 11
♗xe4! ♗e7 12 ♕e2 +-) 10 ♘xe4
dxe4 11 ♖xe4 ♗e7 12 ♗xe6 fxe6
13 ♘xd4 e5 14 ♕h5+ g6 15 ♘xc6
Black faces a lost endgame.

8 dxe5

Weaker are 8 a4 ♘xd4! 9 ♘xd4
exd4 10 axb5 ♗c5 and 8 ♘xe5
♘xe5 9 dxe5 c6 10 ♗e3 ♗e7 11
♘d2 ♘xd2 12 ♕xd2 0-0, when in
both cases Black has equalized.

8...♗e6 9 c3!?

A multi-purpose move, taking
up the fight for the d4-square
while vacating a square for the retreat of the bishop on b3. A few
other possibilities are:

a) 9 a4 b4! 10 a5 ♘c5 11 ♗g5
♕d7 (not 11...♗e7? 12 ♗xe7 ♘xe7
13 ♕d4 and Black's queenside is
in trouble) 12 ♘bd2 h6 13 ♗h4
♗e7 14 ♗xe7 ♘xe7 and 15...0-0 is
equal.

b) 9 ♗e3 ♗e7 (9...♗c5!?) 10
♘bd2 ♘c5 11 c3 ♗g4 12 ♗c2 ♘e6
13 ♕b1 ♗h5! and 14...♗g6 =.

c) 9 ♕e2 (the queen vacates its
place for the rook on f1) 9...♗e7
10 ♖d1 0-0 11 c4 bxc4 12 ♗xc4
♗c5 13 ♗e3 ♗xe3 14 ♕xe3 ♕b8!
15 ♗b3 ♘a5 16 ♘e1 ♘xb3 17
axb3 f5! ∞.

d) 9 ♘bd2!? ♘c5 10 c3 ♗g4!?
(10...♗e7 transposes into positions that arise after 9 c3 ♘c5 10
♗c2, while great confusion is
caused by 10...d4!? 11 ♘g5! ♕xg5
12 ♕f3 ♗d7 13 ♗xf7+ ♔e7 14
♗d5 ♘xe5 15 ♕e2 d3 16 ♕e1 c6 17
f4 ♕h6 18 ♗f3! ♔d8 19 fxe5,

when Black's king is unpleasantly
placed in the middle) 11 h3 ♗h5
12 ♗c2 ♘e6 and then ...♗e7, ...0-0
and ...♗g6 could be Black's next
few moves.

9...♗c5

Black has two nearly equiva-
lent options:

a) 9...♘c5 10 ♗c2 ♗g4 11 ♖e1
♗e7 (11...d4?! is premature, as after 12 h3! ♗h5 13 e6! fxe6 14 cxd4
♗xf3 15 ♕xf3 ♘xd4 16 ♕h5+
White has the upper hand) 12
♘bd2 ♕d7 (12...d4!? produces an
interesting position: 13 h3! ♗h5
14 ♘b3 d3 15 ♗b1 ♘xb3 16 axb3
♗g6 17 ♗e3 0-0 18 ♗d4!? ♘xd4
19 cxd4 ♗b4 followed by 20...d2,
and the weak pawn flees forward.
While White organizes the destruction of the pawn d2, Black
will have to assault the pawn on
d4) 13 ♘f1!? (13 ♘b3!? also comes
into consideration, with the idea
of taking possession of the d4-
square. For example, 13...♘e6 14
h3 ♗h5 15 ♗f5 ♘cd8 16 ♗e3 a5
17 ♗c5 a4 18 ♗xe7 ♕xe7 19
♘bd4! ♘xd4?! 20 cxd4 ♘e6 21 g4!
♗g6 22 ♖c1! ±. The dangers of
this line are materializing in
Black's position: he has a backward pawn on the open c-file, he
has lost control of the square c5
and even his kingside is con-
stricted. An improvement might
be 19...a3!? 20 b3 c6, instead of
19...♘xd4?!) 13...♖d8 14 ♘e3 ♗h5
15 b4 ♘e6 16 g4!? ♗g6 17 ♘f5 0-0
18 a4 d4!? ∞. This position is hard
to assess.

Black has produced excellent play with his rook along the sixth rank.

c4) 7 ♘c3 ♗e7 8 d3 0-0 9 ♗d2!? (this move prevents a later ...♘c6-a5!) 9...d6 10 ♘d5!? ♘d7 11 a4 ♘c5! with mutual chances.

c5) 7 c3 ♘xe4 8 d4 ♗e7 (the move 8...♘a5 was strongly met in a game of Peter Leko's by 9 ♗c2 exd4 10 ♘xd4 c5 11 ♘f5 ♕f6 12 ♘d2! – a novelty of the young Hungarian grandmaster Zoltan Almasi! – 12...d5 13 ♘xe4 dxe4 14 ♘g3 ♗e7 15 ♘xe4 ♕c6 16 ♕h5!, and Black cannot play 16...0-0? owing to 17 ♘f6+ and 18 ♕xh7 mate) 9 ♖e1 (9 ♕e2 d5 10 dxe5 0-0 11 ♖d1 ♘a5 12 ♗c2 ♕c8! ∞) 9...d5 10 dxe5 ♘a5 11 ♗c2 0-0 12 ♘bd2 ♘c4!? with an adequate game.

c6) 7 ♖e1 ♗c5 8 c3 (not 8 ♘xe5? ♘xe5 9 d4 ♘fg4! 10 dxc5 ♕h4 –+) 8...d6 9 d4 ♗b6 10 ♗g5 (or 10 ♗e3 0-0 11 ♘bd2 h6 12 h3 ♖e8 13 d5 ♘a5 14 ♗xb6 cxb6 15 ♗c2 ♘c4 16 ♖b1 ∞) 10...h6 11 ♗h4 g5!? 12 ♗g3 0-0 and now 13 a4 exd4!? 14 cxd4 ♖e8 15 e5 dxe5 16 dxe5 ♕xd1 17 ♖xd1 ♘e4! or 13 ♕d3 ♘h5 14 ♘bd2 ♕f6 15 ♗d5 ♖ae8 16 a4 ♘xg3 17 hxg3 exd4 18 axb5 axb5 19 ♗xc6 ♗xc6 20 ♘xd4 ♗d7 is an interesting position with chances for both sides.

C. 1 e4 e5 2 ♘f3 ♘c6 3 ♗b5 a6 4 ♗a4 ♘f6 5 0-0 ♘xe4 (Open Variation)

The move 5...♘xe4 is the one that makes this variation 'open'.

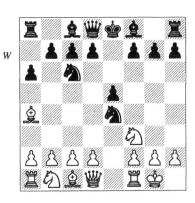

6 d4

The only way to fight for an edge. As we shall see, in this way White can regain the pawn via d4xe5, thus avoiding a symmetrical pawn formation. With the pawn on e5 White can play an active role both on the kingside and in the centre. After 6 ♖e1 ♘c5 7 ♘xe5 ♗e7 8 ♗xc6 dxc6 9 d4 ♘e6 10 ♗e3 0-0 11 f4 f6 12 ♘f3 ♗d6 Black has nothing to fear.

6...b5

Other choices are inferior:

a) 6...exd4 7 ♖e1 d5 8 ♘xd4 ♗d6!? 9 ♘xc6 ♗xh2+ 10 ♔h1 ♕h4 11 ♖xe4+! dxe4 12 ♕d8+! ♕xd8 13 ♘xd8+ ♔xd8 14 ♔xh2 ±. Material-wise Black is well off (a rook and two pawns in return for two pieces), but his king and his pawn on e4 will quickly become a target for the developing white pieces.

b) 6...♗e7 7 ♖e1 f5 8 dxe5 0-0 9 ♗b3+ ♔h8 10 ♗d5 (10 ♘c3!?) 10...♘c5 11 ♘c3 ±. Black is undeveloped and has a 'hole' on d5.

7 ♗b3 d5

On 7...exd4 8 Re1 d5 9 Nc3!
Be6 (or 9...dxc3 10 Bxd5 Bb7 11
Bxe4! Be7 12 Qe2 +−) 10 Nxe4
dxe4 11 Rxe4 Be7 12 Bxe6 fxe6
13 Nxd4 e5 14 Qh5+ g6 15 Nxc6
Black faces a lost endgame.

8 dxe5

Weaker are 8 a4 Nxd4! 9 Nxd4
exd4 10 axb5 Bc5 and 8 Nxe5
Nxe5 9 dxe5 c6 10 Be3 Be7 11
Nd2 Nxd2 12 Qxd2 0-0, when in
both cases Black has equalized.

8...Be6 9 c3!?

A multi-purpose move, taking
up the fight for the d4-square
while vacating a square for the retreat of the bishop on b3. A few
other possibilities are:

a) 9 a4 b4! 10 a5 Nc5 11 Bg5
Qd7 (not 11...Be7? 12 Bxe7 Nxe7
13 Qd4 and Black's queenside is
in trouble) 12 Nbd2 h6 13 Bh4
Be7 14 Bxe7 Nxe7 and 15...0-0 is
equal.

b) 9 Be3 Be7 (9...Bc5!?) 10
Nbd2 Nc5 11 c3 Bg4 12 Bc2 Ne6
13 Qb1 Bh5! and 14...Bg6 =.

c) 9 Qe2 (the queen vacates its
place for the rook on f1) 9...Be7
10 Rd1 0-0 11 c4 bxc4 12 Bxc4
Bc5 13 Be3 Bxe3 14 Qxe3 Qb8!
15 Bb3 Na5 16 Ne1 Nxb3 17
axb3 f5! ∞.

d) 9 Nbd2!? Nc5 10 c3 Bg4!?
(10...Be7 transposes into positions that arise after 9 c3 Nc5 10
Bc2, while great confusion is
caused by 10...d4!? 11 Ng5! Qxg5
12 Qf3 Bd7 13 Bxf7+ Ke7 14
Bd5 Nxe5 15 Qe2 d3 16 Qe1 c6 17
f4 Qh6 18 Bf3! Kd8 19 fxe5,
when Black's king is unpleasantly
placed in the middle) 11 h3 Bh5
12 Bc2 Ne6 and then ...Be7, ...0-0
and ...Bg6 could be Black's next
few moves.

9...Bc5

Black has two nearly equiva-
lent options:

a) 9...Nc5 10 Bc2 Bg4 11 Re1
Be7 (11...d4?! is premature, as after 12 h3! Bh5 13 e6! fxe6 14 cxd4
Bxf3 15 Qxf3 Nxd4 16 Qh5+
White has the upper hand) 12
Nbd2 Qd7 (12...d4!? produces an
interesting position: 13 h3! Bh5
14 Nb3 d3 15 Bb1 Nxb3 16 axb3
Bg6 17 Be3 0-0 18 Bd4!? Nxd4
19 cxd4 Bb4 followed by 20...d2,
and the weak pawn flees forward.
While White organizes the destruction of the pawn d2, Black
will have to assault the pawn on
d4) 13 Nf1!? (13 Nb3!? also comes
into consideration, with the idea
of taking possession of the d4-
square. For example, 13...Ne6 14
h3 Bh5 15 Bf5 Ncd8 16 Be3 a5
17 Bc5 a4 18 Bxe7 Qxe7 19
Nbd4! Nxd4?! 20 cxd4 Ne6 21 g4!
Bg6 22 Rc1! ±. The dangers of
this line are materializing in
Black's position: he has a backward pawn on the open c-file, he
has lost control of the square c5
and even his kingside is con-
stricted. An improvement might
be 19...a3!? 20 b3 c6, instead of
19...Nxd4?!) 13...Rd8 14 Ne3 Bh5
15 b4 Ne6 16 g4!? Bg6 17 Nf5 0-0
18 a4 d4!? ∞. This position is hard
to assess.

b) 9...♗e7 10 ♗e3 (after 10 ♕e2 0-0 11 ♖d1 ♘c5 12 ♗c2 ♗g4!? 13 b4 ♘a4 14 ♗f4 ♕d7!? 15 ♕d3 g6 16 ♕xd5 ♕xd5 17 ♖xd5 ♘b6 18 ♖d1 ♖ad8 Black has excellent play for the pawn, while after 10 ♘bd2 0-0 11 ♗c2 f5?! 12 ♘b3 ♕d7 13 ♘fd4 ♘xd4 14 ♘xd4 c5 15 ♘xe6 ♕xe6 16 f3 ♘g5 17 a4! White is threatening to rip open the loose black position on the queenside. In this line instead of 11...f5?!, Black should play 11...♗f5!? 12 ♘d4 ♘xd4 13 cxd4 f6!? 14 f4 fxe5 15 fxe5 ♕d7! with ample piece play) 10...♕d7!? 11 ♘bd2 ♖d8 12 ♖e1 0-0 13 ♗c2, and now 13...f5 14 exf6 ♘xf6 15 ♕b1 h6 or 13...♘xd2!? 14 ♕xd2 ♗f5 15 ♖ad1 ♖fe8 16 h3 ♕e6 produces a heavyweight clash.

10 ♘bd2

On 10 ♕e2 0-0 11 ♗e3 Black can obtain counterplay via 11...f6! 12 exf6 ♕xf6 13 ♘bd2 ♗d6.

10...0-0 11 ♗c2

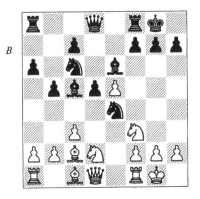

Plans and Counterplans:
White wants to get rid of the enemy knight on e4, and Black can

either protect it or swap it. For example:

a) 11...♘xd2?! 12 ♕xd2 (on 12 ♗xd2, 12...d4! is possible) 12...f6 13 exf6 ♖xf6 14 ♘g5 ♗f5 15 a4! ♘e7 16 ♗xf5 ♘xf5 17 ♕d3 ±. Black is in trouble because 17...h6 18 axb5 hxg5 19 ♗xg5 is overwhelming for White.

b) 11...♘xf2!? 12 ♖xf2 f6 13 exf6 ♗xf2+ 14 ♔xf2 ♕xf6 15 ♘f1 ♘e5 16 ♗e3 ♖ae8 17 ♗c5 ♘xf3 18 gxf3 ♖f7 19 ♔g2 and the two pieces against the rook and pawn secure White a slight advantage. With his larger share of the pieces, White can concentrate his forces in the middlegame, aiming for an attack rather than for an endgame.

c) 11...♗f5!? 12 ♘b3 ♗g6!? (or 12...♗g4 13 h3 ♗h5 14 g4! ♗g6 15 ♗xe4 dxe4 16 ♘xc5 exf3 17 ♗f4 ±) 13 ♘fd4 ♗xd4 14 ♘xd4 ♕d7 and now 15 a4 ♘xe5 16 f4 ♘c6 17 ♘xc6 ♕xc6 18 f5 ♕c5+ 19 ♕d4 ♗h5 20 ♗f4 ♕c6 (Judit Polgar's advice for Black) or 15 f4 ♘xd4 16 cxd4 f6! 17 ♗e3 ♖ad8 18 ♕e2 ♔h8 19 ♖ac1 c6 both give Black equal chances.

d) 11...f5 12 ♘b3 ♗b6 13 ♘fd4 ♘xd4 14 ♘xd4 ♗xd4 15 ♕xd4 (15 cxd4 f4! 16 f3 ♘g3! 17 hxg3 fxg3 18 ♕d3! ♗f5 19 ♕xf5 ♖xf5 20 ♗xf5 ♕h4 21 ♗h3 ♕xd4+ 22 ♔h1 ♕xe5 brings about a rare division of material: White has two pieces and a rook for Black's queen and three pawns. Analysts have come to the following useful conclusion:

'unclear') 15...c5 16 ♕d1 h6!? (or 16...f4 17 f3 ♘g3? 18 hxg3 fxg3 19 ♕d3 and now 19...♕h4 20 ♕xh7+ or 19...♗f5 20 ♕xf5 ♖xf5 21 ♗xf5 ♕h4 22 ♗h3 with a huge plus for White. Instead of 17...♘g3? worthy of attention is 17...♘g5 18 a4 b4 19 cxb4 c4! 20 b3! d4! 21 bxc4 ♗xc4 22 ♗b3 ♕d5 with some compensation for the pawn) 17 f3 ♘g5 18 ♗e3 ♖c8 19 ♕d2 and now Black can continue 19...a5 20 ♖ad1 ♕e7 or 19...d4!? 20 cxd4 cxd4 21 ♗f4 (21 ♗xd4? ♖xc2) 21...♕c7!? Hopefully these few pages have provided a broad feel for the Open Variation. With its lively middle-game and open-centered play, it is well worth studying more closely, although there is an immense amount of theory to know.

Sidelines

After **1 e4 e5 2 ♘f3 ♘c6 3 ♗b5 a6 4 ♗a4 ♘f6 5 0-0 ♗e7** we arrive at an important cross-roads. We can stay on the Main Road with **6 ♖e1**, while if we would like to deviate then the choices are the following:

a) 6 c3?! ♘xe4 7 ♖e1 ♘c5 8 ♘xe5 ♘xe5 9 ♖xe5 ♘xa4 10 ♕xa4 0-0 11 d4 ♗f6 and it is only Black, with his bishop-pair, who can be better.

b) 6 d3 b5 7 ♗b3 d6 8 a4 ♗d7!? (also playable are 8...♗b7 9 ♘c3 ♘a5 10 ♗a2 b4 11 ♘d5 ♗xd5 12 exd5 ♖b8! and 8...♗g4 9 c3 0-0. In both cases it is a battle of equal

forces) 9 c3 0-0 10 ♘bd2 ♘a5 11 ♗c2 c5 12 ♖e1 ♕c7 13 ♘f1 b4! 14 ♗g5 ♖ab8 15 ♘e3 ♗e6 =. Black's queenside play is beginning to take shape.

c) 6 ♗xc6 dxc6 (not 6...bxc6? 7 ♘xe5 ♘xe4 8 ♕g4 ♘d6 9 ♕xg7 ♗f6 10 ♖e1! ♗xg7 11 ♘g6+ ♕e7 12 ♘xe7 +−) 7 d3. This is the basic position of the Delayed Exchange Variation. White will play against the black e5-pawn, but if Black manages to regroup his pieces he can equalize. A good plan is 7...♘d7 8 ♘bd2 0-0 9 ♘c4 f6 10 ♘h4 ♘c5 11 ♕f3 ♘e6 12 ♗e3 g6 13 ♕g3 ♔h8 14 ♖ad1 ♘f4! 15 ♖fe1 ♗e6 16 b3 c5 followed by ...♕c8 and ...g6-g5, when Black can hope to assume the upper hand.

d) 6 d4 exd4 7 ♖e1 (or 7 e5 ♘e4 8 ♘xd4 0-0 9 ♘f5 d5 10 ♗xc6 bxc6 11 ♘xe7+ ♕xe7 12 ♖e1 ♖e8! 13 f3 ♘d6 14 b3 ♘f5 15 ♕d2 ♗e6 16 ♗a3 ♕h4 ∞) 7...b5 8 e5 (8 ♗b3 d6 9 ♗d5 ♗d7 =) 8...♘xe5 9 ♖xe5 (9 ♘xe5 bxa4 10 ♕xd4 0-0 11 ♕xa4 ♖b8) 9...d6 10 ♖e1 bxa4 11 ♘xd4 ♗d7 12 ♕f3 0-0 13 ♘c6 ♗xc6 14 ♕xc6 ♖b8!? 15 ♘c3 (after 15 ♕xa4 d5 and ...♘e4, Black has the attack ...♗c5/...♗d6, ...♕h4, ...♖b8-b6-g6 up his sleeve) 15...a3! 16 b3 ♖b6 17 ♕a4 d5 18 ♗xa3 ♗xa3 19 ♕xa3 ♖c6! gives Black the initiative. For example, after 20 ♕b2 ♘g4! he is threatening ...♕f6 and ...♕d6.

e) 6 ♕e2!? The Worrall Attack, the point of which is that the central action c2-c3 and d2-d4 will be supported by ♖d1, while the queen defends the e-pawn.

6...b5

This is the correct move, since now White cannot play his bishop to c2 without loss of time. For example, 6...d6 is met by 7 c3! 0-0 8 d4 ♗d7 9 ♗c2!, when White has a strong centre: after both 9...exd4 10 cxd4 ♘b4 11 ♘c3 ♘xc2 12 ♕xc2 ♗g4 13 ♘e1 c6 14 h3 ♗d7 15 ♗e3 and 9...♖e8 10 d5! ♘b8 11 h3 c6 12 dxc6 ♗xc6 13 c4 ♘bd7 14 ♘c3 he can maintain his advantage (±).

7 ♗b3 0-0 8 c3 d5!?

The most aggressive plan. Quieter play results from 8...d6:

a) 9 d4 exd4 10 cxd4 ♗g4 11 ♖d1 d5! 12 e5 ♘e4 13 ♘c3 ♘xc3 14 bxc3 ♕d7 15 h3 ♗f5 16 g4!? ♗g6 17 ♘e1 and White can increase his spatial advantage with f2-f4.

b) 9 h3 ♘a5 10 ♗c2 c5 11 d4 ♕c7 12 ♖d1 ♗d7!: Black intends 13...cxd4 14 cxd4 ♖ac8 with the queenside plan ...♘a5-c6-b4.

c) 9 ♖d1!? ♘a5 10 ♗c2 c5 11 d4 ♕c7 12 d5 c4 13 b4! cxb3 14 axb3 ♗g4 15 h3 ♗h5 16 ♗b2 ♖fc8 17 ♖c1! ±. After White has secured his queenside, his knight on b1 can get active via d2-f1-g3. Let us return now to 8...d5.

9 d3

White undertakes tremendous risks if he plays 9 exd5: 9...♗g4! 10 dxc6 (10 h3 ♗xf3 11 ♕xf3 e4 12 ♕e2 ♘a5! 13 ♗c2 ♕xd5 ∓. White is less developed and Black

can strengthen his position with ...♖ad8 and ...♖fe8) 10...e4 11 d4 exf3 12 gxf3 ♗h5!? 13 ♗f4 ♖e8 14 ♗e5 ♗d6 15 ♘d2 ♗xe5 16 dxe5 ♘d5 17 ♘e4 ♘f4 18 ♕e3 ♕h4 and Black has a dangerous attack.

9...♖e8

It is logical to bolster the centre due to the pressure on Black's d5- and e5-pawns. Other options are:

a) 9...♕d6 10 ♗g5! ♗e6 11 ♘bd2 ♖ad8 12 ♖fd1 ♘d7 13 ♗xe7 ♘xe7 14 d4! exd4 15 e5 ♕b6 16 ♘xd4!? ±. There is no coordination between the black pieces.

b) 9...d4 10 cxd4 ♘xd4 11 ♘xd4 ♕xd4 (on 11...exd4, 12 f4! would threaten the advance of the e- and f-pawns) 12 ♗e3 ♕d6 13 ♖c1!? ♗b7 14 ♘d2 and White controls the c-file and threatens ♘d2-f3-h4-f5.

10 ♘bd2

Black achieves lively play after 10 exd5 ♘xd5 11 ♘xe5 ♘xe5 12 ♕xe5 ♗b7.

10...♗f8 11 ♖e1 ♗b7

A balanced middlegame has arisen in which White can play ♘d2-f1-g3-f5 and ♗g5 while Black can group his forces with ...♘a5, ...♕d7 and ...♖ad8, awaiting the right moment to open the centre with d5xe4.

Having met White's sidelines, let us move forward to the main line!

1 e4 e5 2 ♘f3 ♘c6 3 ♗b5 a6 4 ♗a4 ♘f6 5 0-0 ♗e7 6 ♖e1 b5 White's threat was 7 ♗xc6 and 8 ♘xe5. **7 ♗b3.**

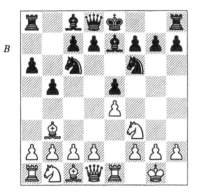

B

Here Black can opt for the hard strategic battle typical of the Spanish by playing either ...0-0 or ...d7-d6. However, if he wants to invite White to a tactical fight, then his only move is **7...0-0** after which he can play the **Marshall Attack**.

D. Marshall Attack

1 e4 e5 2 ♘f3 ♘c6 3 ♗b5 a6 4 ♗a4 ♘f6 5 0-0 ♗e7 6 ♖e1 b5 7 ♗b3 0-0 8 c3
This is the last moment at which White can avoid the Marshall Attack with one of the anti-Marshall systems:
  a) 8 ♘c3 ♗b7 9 d3 d6 10 a3 ♘d4! 11 ♘xd4 exd4 12 ♘d5 ♘xd5 13 exd5 ♗f6 14 ♕f3 ♖e8 15 ♗d2 ♕d7 =.
  b) 8 d4 ♘xd4 9 ♗xf7+ (9 ♘xd4 exd4 10 e5 ♘e8 11 ♕xd4 ♗b7 12 c3 d6 =) 9...♖xf7 10 ♘xe5 ♖f8 11 ♕xd4 c5 12 ♕d1 ♗b7 13 ♘c3 ♕e8! 14 h3 (14 ♘g4 ♕g6 15 ♘xf6+ ♗xf6 16 ♘d5 ♖ae8 17 ♘xf6+ ♖xf6 18 f3 d5! 19 e5 ♖f5 20 f4 d4 21 ♕e2

♖fxe5! 22 fxe5 ♖xe5, and Black gets a decisive attack) 14...d5! 15 exd5 ♖d8 16 ♘g4 ♘xd5 17 ♘xd5 ♗xd5 18 ♕e2 ♕c6 and now on 19 ♕xe7? ♖de8! wins.
  c) 8 a4!? A strategically justified concept, undermining the pawn on b5. In this way Black's attention and forces are distracted from the pawn sacrifice ...d7-d5. White has to be ready for two possible replies:
  c1) 8...b4 9 d3 (9 d4 d6 10 dxe5 ♘xe5 11 ♘xe5 dxe5 12 ♗g5 ♗c5! 13 ♕f3 h6 14 ♗xf6 ♕xf6 =) 9...d6 10 a5 (10 ♘bd2 ♘a5 11 ♗a2 ♗e6!? ∞) 10...♗e6 11 ♘bd2 ♕c8!? (11...♗xb3!? 12 ♘xb3 d5 13 ♕e2 ♖e8 14 ♗g5 h6 15 ♗h4 ♘h5! =) 12 ♗c4 ♖d8 13 ♘f1 h6! 14 ♘e3 ♗f8 with level chances.
  c2) 8...♗b7 9 d3 d6 (after 9...♖e8 10 c3!? h6 11 ♘bd2 ♗f8 12 ♗a2! Black has no good way of neutralizing the bishop sweeping down the a2-g8 diagonal. For example, the lines 12...d5 13 exd5 ♘xd5 14 d4 ♘f4 15 ♘e4 and 12...d6 13 ♘h4 ♕d7 14 ♘g6! demonstrate White's dominance) 10 ♘bd2 ♘d7 11 c3! ♘c5 (11...♗f6!?) 12 axb5 axb5 13 ♖xa8 ♗xa8 (or 13...♕xa8!? 14 ♗c2 b4 15 d4 bxc3 16 bxc3 ♘d7 ∞) 14 ♗c2 ♗f6 15 b4 ♘e6 16 ♘f1! d5! 17 exd5 ♕xd5 18 ♘e3 ♕d8 19 ♘g4 e4! leads to an unclear game.
  Note that 8...♖b8 is a poor response to 8 a4!?: 9 axb5 axb5 10 c3 d5 11 exd5 ♘xd5 12 ♘xe5 ♘xe5 13 ♖xe5 c6 14 d4 ♗d6 15 ♖e1 ±.

Black has stumbled into a poor Marshall in which he has lost control of the a-file.

8...d5!? 9 exd5

9 d3 is passive: 9...dxe4 10 dxe4 ♕xd1 11 ♗xd1 ♗b7 12 ♘bd2 ♘d7 13 ♘b3 a5 and Black is comfortably on top. 9 d4!? is more interesting, but Black has nothing to fear after 9...exd4 10 e5 ♘e4 11 cxd4 ♘a5!? 12 ♗c2 f5! 13 exf6 ♗xf6! ∞.

9...♘xd5

9...e4 is tricky but not good enough: 10 dxc6 exf3 11 d4 fxg2 12 ♗g5 ♗g4 13 ♕d3 followed by ♘d2, and Black's attack never gets going.

10 ♘xe5 ♘xe5 11 ♖xe5

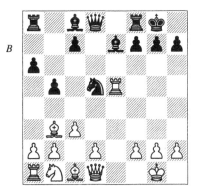

Black has sacrificed a pawn to get an attack on the kingside. His plan is justified by the cramped white queenside. White on the other hand pins his hopes on the move d2-d4 and the quick development of his light artillery. Let us see which side will win the debate!

11...c6

Black is planning ...♗d6 and ...♕h4, but first he has to do something about the knight on d5. Experience has shown that is best to protect it with a pawn, since after both 11...♘f6 12 d4 ♗d6 13 ♖e1 ♘g4 14 h3 ♕h4 15 ♕f3 ♘xf2!? 16 ♗d2! ♗b7! 17 ♕xb7 ♘d3 18 ♖e2 ♕g3 19 ♔f1 ♘f4 20 ♖f2! ♕h2 21 ♗xf4! ♗xf4 22 g3! and 11...♗b7 12 ♕f3 ♗d6 13 ♗xd5! c6 14 ♖e2 cxd5 15 d4 Black cannot find enough compensation for his material disadvantage. Even from these warm-up lines it becomes apparent that the ensuing positions are hard to assess in principle. After all, it is not enough for Black to have merely a potentially promising attack, he has to prove his point in concrete variations. In addition, White is often forced to defend his plus through a series of risky situations, or perhaps to bail out for a draw (if he can!) if things get too hot in the kitchen.

12 d4

Two other continuations are:

a) 12 ♗xd5 cxd5 13 d4 ♗d6 14 ♖e3 ♕h4 15 g3 (15 h3 ♕f4! 16 ♖e5! ♕f6 17 ♖e1 ♕g6 18 ♕f3 ♗e6 when Black is planning ...♖ae8 and ...♗g4) 15...♗g4 16 f3 ♗xg3 17 ♕e2 ♗f4 18 fxg4 f5! 19 gxf5 ♖xf5 20 ♖e8+ ♖xe8 21 ♕xe8+ ♖f8 22 ♕e6+ ♔h8 23 ♗xf4 ♕xf4 24 ♘a3 ♕f2+ and Black has a perpetual on f2 and f3.

b) 12 ♖e1!? ♗d6 13 g3 ♗b7! 14 d3 ♕d7 15 ♘d2 c5 16 ♘e4 ♗e7

17 ♗g5 f6 18 ♗d2 ♔h8 19 ♕h5 f5
20 ♘g5 ♗xg5 21 ♗xg5 ♕c6 22 f3
c4 23 ♗c2 b4 and the white king
is becoming a vulnerable target.

12...♗d6 13 ♖e1

13 ♖e2 is a less harmonious
move: 13...♕h4 14 g3 ♕h3 15 ♕f1
♕h5 16 f3 (16 ♘d2? ♘f4! 17 gxf4
♗h3 –+) 16...♗h3 17 ♕f2 f5 and
Black seizes the e-file. As a matter of fact, this position (after a
forty-move analysis!) is predicted
by theory to be a draw by perpetual.

13...♕h4 14 g3 ♕h3 15 ♗e3

On 15 ♖e4 the only reply is
15...g5!? followed by the plan of
...f7-f5 and ... ♖a7-g7. Of course
15...g5!? cannot be met by 16 ♗xg5
as 16...♕f5 picks up a piece.

15...♗g4 16 ♕d3

The queen can defend from f1.

16...♖ae8

All the forces are drawn into
the attack.

17 ♘d2 ♖e6

Also not entirely clear is 17...f5,
though the latest evidence goes
against it: 18 ♕f1 ♕h5 19 f4 ♔h8
20 ♗xd5 cxd5 21 ♕g2 ♖e4 22 h4!
(preventing ...g7-g5) 22...h6 23
♘xe4 fxe4 24 ♖f1 ♖f6 25 a4! and
White crawls out of Black's em-
brace.

18 a4!

Here it is not worth playing 18
♕f1 as after 18...♕h5 Black can
chase White's queen by 19...♗h3,
while 18 c4 ♗f4! 19 cxd5 ♖h6 20
♕e4 ♕xh2+ 21 ♔f1 ♗xe3 22 ♖xe3
♖f6! 23 f3 ♗f5 24 ♕e5 ♕xd2

brings about a success for Black.
Let us take a look at the position
after **18 a4!?**

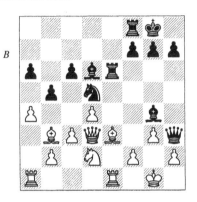

Plans and Counterplans:

Black must keep attacking but at
the same time he has to beware
that the a1-rook does not suddenly burst into the game and decide the battle. Here are a few
concrete lines as titbits:

a) 18...♖fe8? 19 ♗xd5 cxd5 20
♕f1 ♕h5 21 axb5 axb5 22 ♕xb5 ±.

b) 18...bxa4 19 ♖xa4 f5 20 ♕f1
♕h5 21 c4 f4 22 cxd5 ♖xe3 23 fxe3
fxg3 24 dxc6+ ♔h8 25 hxg3 ♖xf1+
26 ♖xf1 +–. White has too much
material for the queen and his c-
pawn is dangerously advanced.

c) 18...♕h5 19 axb5 axb5 20
♘e4!? (or 20 ♘f1 ♗f5 21 ♕d1 ♗g4
22 ♕d2 ♕h3 23 ♗d1 ♗xd1 24
♖axd1 f5! 25 f4 g5 26 fxg5 f4! 27
gxf4 ♗xf4 28 ♗xf4 ♘xf4 and Black
is threatening perpetual check by
29...♕g4+ 30 ♘g3 ♘h3+ 31 ♔g2
♘f4+) 20...♗c7 21 ♗d2 ♖fe8 22
♗d1! and Black faces a difficult
task. For example, 22...♗xd1 23

♖exd1 and now 23...♖xe4 would backfire due to 24 ♕xe4! ♕xd1+ 25 ♔g2 winning the black queen because of the mate threat on the back rank, while 23...f5 24 ♘g5 ♖e2 25 ♕f3! also thwarts Black's attack. We have the Indian grandmaster Viswanathan Anand to thank for this analysis of 22 ♗d1!

d) 18...f5!? 19 ♕f1 ♕h5 20 f4 bxa4 (White was hoping for the continuation 20...♖fe8 21 axb5 axb5 – 21...♖xe3 22 ♖xe3 ♖xe3 23 bxc6 ♖e2 24 ♗xd5+ ♔f8 25 h3! ♗xh3 26 ♗f3 +– – 22 ♗xd5 cxd5 23 ♕xb5 with a fatal invasion into the black position) 21 ♖xa4 ♖fe8 22 ♕f2 (not 22 ♖xa6 ♖xe3 23 ♖xe3 ♖xe3 24 ♖xc6 ♕e8 25 ♗xd5+ ♔f8 26 ♘e4 fxe4 27 ♖xd6 ♖d3 28 ♗b3 e3 –+) 22...g5 23 fxg5 f4 24 gxf4 ♗h3 and now 25 ♘f1? ♗xf1 26 ♔xf1 ♕h3+ or 25 ♗d1 ♖xe3! 26 ♗xh5 ♖xe1+ 27 ♘f1 ♖8e7 followed by 28...♗xf4 is to Black's advantage. White should therefore continue 25 ♔h1 ♕g4 26 ♖g1 and if the black queen moves, then he can hold with 27 ♖g3. Current theory suggests that this rather remote position presents chances to both sides.

Sidelines

After **1 e4 e5 2 ♘f3 ♘c6 3 ♗b5 a6 4 ♗a4 ♘f6 5 0-0 ♗e7 6 ♖e1 b5 7 ♗b3 d6** the main line runs **8 c3**. This move prepares d2-d4 and at the same time makes way for the bishop to retreat to c2. On 8

a4 Black should avoid 8...♘a5?! 9 axb5 ♘xb3 10 cxb3 ♗b7 11 bxa6 ♗xa6 12 d4 0-0 13 ♘c3 ♗b7 14 ♖a4 ±. The right direction is 8...♗g4 9 c3 0-0 10 h3 ♗h5 11 d3 ♘a5 12 ♗c2 c5 =.

8...0-0

Now, before we turn to the basic position of the Main Line with 9 h3, let us first take a look at White's alternatives on his ninth move:

a) **9 d3** ♘a5 10 ♗c2 c5 11 ♘bd2 ♖e8 (11...♘c6 12 ♘f1 ♖e8 13 h3 ♗b7 is discussed in the Main Line below) 12 ♘f1 ♗b7 13 a3!? h6!? 14 b4 cxb4 15 axb4 ♘c6 16 ♘e3 d5 is level.

b) **9 a4** ♗g4 (9...b4 is weaker: 10 h3 ♖b8 11 a5! ♗e6 12 ♗xe6 fxe6 13 d4 exd4 14 cxd4 ♖b5 15 ♘bd2 ♘xa5 16 ♘b3 ♘xb3 17 ♕xb3 ♕c8 18 ♘g5 ±) 10 h3 ♗h5!? (unless it is unavoidable, Black should avoid easing the tension with quick exchanges!) 11 d3 ♘a5 12 ♗c2 c5 13 ♘bd2 b4 14 g4 ♗g6 15 ♘f1 ♖b8 16 ♘e3 b3 17 ♗b1 ♖e8 ∞.

c) **9 d4!?** ♗g4 10 d5 (White can instead keep the position open with 10 ♗e3, but both 10...exd4 11 cxd4 ♘a5 12 ♗c2 c5!? – on 12...♘c4 13 ♗c1 and b2-b3 White regains the lost tempi – 13 dxc5 dxc5 14 ♘bd2 ♘c6 and 10...d5!? 11 exd5 exd4 12 ♗xd4 ♘xd4 13 cxd4 ♗b4 14 ♘c3 a5! 15 a3 ♗xc3 16 bxc3 a4 17 ♗a2 ♕d6 18 h3 ♗h5 ensure Black equality) 10...♘a5 11 ♗c2 ♕c8 12 h3 ♗d7 13 ♘bd2 c6!

(Black is obliged to fight against the white centre and open a queenside file for himself) 14 dxc6 ♛xc6 15 ♘f1 ♘c4!? 16 ♗d3 (or 16 ♘g3 ♖fc8!? 17 ♛e2 ♘b6 and Black's idea may be ...♘b6-a4-c5 followed by ...a6-a5) 16...♖ac8 17 ♛e2 ♖fe8 18 ♘g3 h6 =. Black can consolidate his kingside with 19...♗f8 and concentrate on ...d6-d5. The move ...♗c8-g4 is especially effective against an early seizure of the centre by White with d2-d4, as by attacking the knight on f3 Black weakens the pawn on d4. However, in connection with this one must know that a premature ...♗g4, for example after 8 c3, is a mistake, since 8...♗g4?! 9 d3! 0-0 10 ♘bd2 ♘a5 11 ♗c2 c5 12 h3 ♗h5 13 ♘f1 followed by g2-g4 and ♘g3 dooms the impatient bishop to total passivity.

E. Main Line: The basic position

1 e4 e5 2 ♘f3 ♘c6 3 ♗b5 a6 4 ♗a4 ♘f6 5 0-0 ♗e7 6 ♖e1 b5 7 ♗b3 d6 8 c3 0-0 9 h3 *(D)*

White has thwarted ...♗c8-g4 and is now ready to play d2-d4, after which, often with the help of the manoeuvre ♘b1-d2-f1-g3-f5, he wishes to gradually develope a kingside attack. Of course, Black's arena of play is on the queenside, but first he has to complete his development.

Among the many plans at his disposal, the following are worth close examination.

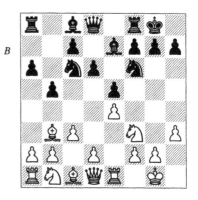

E1. Zaitsev Variation: 9...♗b7.
E2. Breyer Variation: 9...♘b8.
E3. Chigorin Variation: 9...♘a5.

Besides these options, the following lines are also frequently employed:

a) 9...a5 10 d4 a4 11 ♗c2 exd4 (11...♗d7 12 ♘bd2 ♖e8 13 ♘f1 ♗f8 14 ♘g3 h6 15 ♘h2! ♘a5 16 f4 c5 17 dxe5 dxe5 18 fxe5 ♖xe5 19 ♗f4 ±. With e4-e5 White will open up the diagonal of the bishop on c2 and commence a kingside attack) 12 cxd4 ♘b4 13 d5! (an excellent outpost has been created for a white knight on d4!) 13...♘d7 14 ♘a3 ♗f6 15 ♘xb5 a3 16 ♘bd4 axb2 17 ♗xb2 ♖xa2 18 ♖xa2 ♘xa2 19 ♘c6 and 20 ♛a1 rounds up the stray horse.

b) 9...♗e6 10 d4 (10 ♗xe6 fxe6 11 d4 ♛d7!? 12 dxe5 dxe5 13 ♛xd7 ♘xd7 14 ♗e3 ♘c5 is insufficient for an advantage. Black is active and his doubled isolated e-pawns control useful central squares) 10...♗xb3 11 axb3 (11 ♛xb3!? is worth considering, for example

11...♕d7!? 12 ♘bd2 ♖fb8 13 ♘f1 b4 14 ♕d1 bxc3 15 bxc3 ♖b5 16 ♘g3 ♖ab8 17 ♗g5 with mutual chances) 11...exd4 12 cxd4 ♘b4 (12...d5 is an interesting option, although after 13 e5 ♘e4 14 ♘c3 f5 15 exf6 Black must sacrifice a pawn with 15...♗xf6 as 15...♘xf6 is bad in view of 16 ♘g5) 13 d5! (just as we saw in the previous line, the f3-knight can again be directed to d4 while at the same White restrains the black c-pawn. 13 ♘c3 c5 14 ♗f4 ♖e8 and ...♕b6, ...♖ad8 leads to a balanced fight) 13...c5 14 dxc6 ♘xc6 15 ♘c3 and White is clearly better due to the weak d6-pawn.

c) **9...h6** (Black prevents the move ♘f3-g5 thus allowing the manoeuvre ...♖e8 and ...♗f8) 10 d4 ♖e8 11 ♘bd2 ♗f8 12 ♗c2!? (in the line 12 ♘f1 ♗d7 13 ♘g3 ♘a5 14 ♗c2 ♘c4 15 b3 ♘b6 16 ♗e3 c5!? Black obtains sufficient counterplay, while after 12 d5 ♘b8 13 ♘f1 ♘bd7 14 ♘g3 ♘c5 15 ♗c2 a5 Black's position is again satisfactory. 12 ♗c2!? prevents Black's queenside play from unfolding, for example, on 12...♘a5? 13 b4! Black is quite restrained) 12...♗d7 13 ♗d3!? ♕b8 14 b3 g6 15 ♗b2 ♗g7 16 d5 ♘d8 17 c4, and White stands more freely thanks to his spatial advantage.

d) **9...♘d7!?** (an idea of the Estonian grandmaster Paul Keres. The black knight is heading for the queenside while at the same time delegating his place to the

bishop, which will exert pressure on the d4-square from f6)

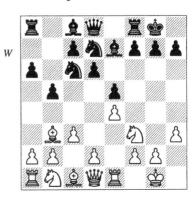

10 d4 ♗f6 (this is stronger than 10...♘b6 when after 11 ♘bd2 ♗f6 12 ♘f1 White can transport his b1-knight to the kingside) 11 a4!? (on 11 ♗e3 Black can reply 11...♘a5 12 ♗c2 ♘c4 13 ♗c1 ♗b7 14 b3 ♘cb6 15 ♗e3 ♖e8 16 d5 ♘c5, with the plan of ...c7-c6, while after 11 d5, playable is 11...♘a5 12 ♗c2 c5 13 ♘bd2 ♘b6 14 ♘f1 g6 15 g4!? ♗g7 16 ♘g3 ♗d7 17 b3 ♘b7 followed by ...a6-a5-a4) 11...♗b7 12 ♘a3!? (other moves are 12 d5!? ♘e7 13 axb5 axb5 14 ♖xa8 ♕xa8 15 ♘a3 ♗a6 16 ♘h2 g6 17 ♗c2!? ♕b7 18 b4 ♘b6, and Black can opt for ...c7-c6, or 12 axb5 axb5 13 ♖xa8 ♕xa8 14 d5 ♘a5!? 15 ♗c2 ♘c4 16 b3 ♘cb6 17 ♘a3 ♗a6 18 ♘h2 c6 with equality) 12...exd4 13 cxd4 ♖e8!? (13...♘b6 14 ♗f4 bxa4 15 ♗xa4 ♘xa4 16 ♕xa4 a5 17 ♗d2! ♖e8 18 d5 ♘b4 19 ♗xb4 axb4 20 ♕xb4 ♖b8 21 ♕c4 ♗xb2 22 ♖a2 ♗f6 23 ♘b5 ±) 14 ♕d2!? (White stops the move ...♘c6-a5

owing to 14 ♗f4 ♘a5! 15 ♗c2 b4 16 ♘b1 b3!? 17 ♗d3 c5!? ∞) 14...♖e7 15 ♖b1 bxa4 16 ♗xa4 ♘b6 17 ♗c2 a5 18 ♕c3 ♘b4 =. Here Black has good piece play due to the plan of ...exd4 and ...♖e8.

E1. 1 e4 e5 2 ♘f3 ♘c6 3 ♗b5 a6 4 ♗a4 ♘f6 5 0-0 ♗e7 6 ♖e1 b5 7 ♗b3 d6 8 c3 0-0 9 h3 ♗b7 (Zaitsev Variation)

10 d4

10 d3 is ineffective: 10...♘a5 11 ♗c2 c5 12 ♘bd2 ♘c6 13 ♘f1 ♖e8 14 ♘g3 g6!? 15 ♘h2 d5 =.

10...♖e8

Black is preparing for ...♗f8. The bishop on b7 and rook on e8 are both eyeing the white pawn on e4. 10...♘a5 is inferior: 11 ♗c2 ♘c4 12 b3 ♘b6 13 ♘bd2 ♖e8 14 ♗b2 ♗f8 15 c4! exd4 16 cxb5 axb5 17 ♘xd4, and the white pieces are ready to march against the black king with ♘f5 and ♕f3.

11 ♘bd2

Other possibilities are:

a) 11 a4 ♗f8 12 d5 ♘b8 13 axb5 axb5 14 ♖ax8 ♗xa8 15 ♘a3 c6 16 dxc6 ♗xc6 17 ♗g5 ♘bd7 and the black position looks a tough nut to crack.

b) 11 ♘g5 ♖f8 12 f4? exf4 13 ♗xf4 ♘a5 14 ♗c2 ♘d5! 15 exd5 ♗xg5 16 ♕h5 h6 17 ♗g3 g6! 18 ♕f3 ♘c4 and Black has seized the initiative. In this line, if White's ambitions are modest then instead of 12 f4? he can offer a draw by repetition with 12 ♘f3.

c) 11 dxe5 ♘xe5 (11...dxe5? loses to 12 ♗xf7+ ♔xf7 13 ♕b3+ and on 13...♔g6 14 ♘h4+ while on 13...♔f8 14 ♘g5 wins) 12 ♘xe5 dxe5 13 ♕f3 c5 14 ♘d2 c4 =.

11...♗f8 12 a4!?

12 ♘g5 is again ineffective: 12...♖e7 13 f4 h6 14 ♘df3 ♕e8!, and Black is better developed. White can also close the centre with 12 d5!? ♘b8 13 ♘f1 ♘bd7 14 ♘g3 g6!? (14...♘c5 15 ♗c2 a5!? 16 ♘h2 g6 17 ♕f3 h5 also comes into consideration) 15 ♗e3 ♘c5 16 ♗c2 c6 17 b4 ♘cd7 18 dxc6 ♗xc6 19 ♗b3 ♘b6 20 ♕d3 ♕c7, with a defensible game for Black, or by 12 ♗c2 g6!? 13 d5 ♘b8 14 b3 c6 15 c4 ♕c7 16 ♘f1 ♘bd7 17 ♗e3 ♘c5 18 ♘g3 a5 19 ♕d2 ♘fd7 20 dxc6 ♗xc6 21 cxb5 ♗xb5, with unclear consequences.

12...h6 13 ♗c2 exd4!?

A move that leads to some risky business! A safer choice is 13...g6!? and on 14 d5 ♘b8 15 b3 c6 16 c4 bxc4 17 bxc4 a5! 18 ♖b1 ♕c7 19 ♘b3 ♗a6 20 ♗d3 ♘bd7 21 ♗d2 cxd5 22 ♗xa5 ♕a7 23 cxd5 ♗xd3 24 ♕xd3 ♘c5! 25 ♘xc5 ♕xa5 the game becomes balanced.

14 cxd4

14 ♘xd4 ♘xd4 15 cxd4 c5 is unclear.

14...♘b4 15 ♗b1 c5

Here too a reliable option for Black is 15...g6!? 16 ♖a3 ♗g7 and the follow-up may be ...c7-c5.

16 d5 ♘d7 17 ♖a3 f5!?

A dramatic method of undermining the white centre, but with

the drawback that the black king position is significantly weakened.

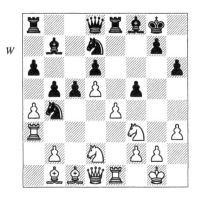

w

Plans and Counterplans:
Black aims at overthrowing the white centre while his opponent prepares a kingside attack for which he can transfer his rook along the third rank from a3 to g3. Here are a few examples taken from practice:

a) 18 e5?! ♗xd5 19 ♗xf5 ♗xf3! 20 ♕xf3 ♘xe5 21 ♕d1 c4 is clearly better for Black.

b) 18 exf5 ♘f6 19 ♘e4 ♗xd5 (19...♘bxd5 is also good) 20 ♘xf6+ ♕xf6 21 ♗d2 ♕xb2! 22 ♗xb4 ♗f7! and Black is on top.

c) 18 ♖ae3!? ♘f6 (18...f4 19 ♖3e2 ♘e5 20 ♘f1 ♘xf3+ 21 gxf3 ♕h4 ∞) 19 ♘h2 ♕d7! 20 exf5 ♖xe3 21 fxe3 ♗xd5 22 ♘g4 ♗e7 23 e4 ♗f7 and the fight is still completely open.

d) 18 ♘h2! (perhaps the best answer, opening the way for the rook on a3) 18...♔h8!? (also possible is 18...c4 19 exf5 ♘c5 20 ♖xe8 ♕xe8 21 ♖g3 ♘bd3 22 f6 g6 23 b3

♗xd5 24 bxc4 bxc4 25 ♗a3 or 18...♘f6 19 ♖f3 ♖e5 20 ♖xf5 ♖xf5 21 exf5 ♗xd5 with an immense fight) 19 ♖g3 ♘f6 20 ♘hf3! fxe4 21 ♘xe4 ♗xd5 22 ♘xf6 ♕xf6 23 ♗d2!? ♖xe1+!? 24 ♗xe1 ♗f7 ∞. The possibilities of attack and defence are not yet fully worked out in this variation, so one may be able to find stronger moves at some point ... for both parties!

Postscript: instead of 17...f5!? Black can also try 17...c4!? Then after both 18 ♘d4 ♕f6 19 ♘2f3 ♘c5 or 18 axb5 axb5 19 ♘d4 ♖xa3 20 bxa3 ♘d3 21 ♗xd3 cxd3 22 ♖e3 ♘c5 a complicated position arises with mutual chances.

E2. 1 e4 e5 2 ♘f3 ♘c6 3 ♗b5 a6 4 ♗a4 ♘f6 5 0-0 ♗e7 6 ♖e1 b5 7 ♗b3 d6 8 c3 0-0 9 h3 ♘b8 (Breyer Variation)

In the Breyer Variation, the knight withdraws to b8, ready to reappear on d7, while giving scope to the bishop when it comes to b7 and the c-pawn. Black obtains a flexible position with which to fight White's spatial plus.

10 d4
10 d3 is unreasonably modest: 10...♘bd7 11 ♘bd2 ♗b7 12 ♘f1 ♘c5 13 ♗c2 ♖e8 14 ♘g3 ♗f8 15 b4 ♘cd7 16 ♗b2 c5 17 a3 ♕c7 with equality.

10...♘bd7 11 ♘bd2
Black should meet 11 c4 with 11...c6. For example, 12 ♗g5 ♗b7 13 ♘bd2 c5 14 dxe5 ♘xe5 15 ♘xe5

dxe5, 12 c5 ♕c7 13 cxd6 ♗xd6 14 ♗g5 exd4 15 ♗xf6 gxf6 16 ♘xd4 (16 ♕xd4 ♘e5 17 ♘bd2 ♖d8 18 ♕e3 ♘d3) 16...♘c5! or 12 a3!? bxc4 13 ♗xc4 d5!? 14 exd5 cxd5 15 ♗a2 e4 16 ♘e5 ♗d6 17 ♘xd7 ♗xd7, with good play for Black in each case.

11...♗b7 12 ♗c2

White protects his pawn on e4 to allow the d2-knight to continue its migration towards the kingside.

12...♖e8

12...c5 can be met by 13 d5 g6 14 ♘f1 ♘h5 15 ♗h6 ♘g7 16 ♘e3 ♘f6 17 a4 ±.

13 ♘f1

Also possible are:

a) 13 a4 ♗f8 14 ♗d3 c6 15 ♘f1 g6!? 16 ♘g3 ♗g7 =.

b) 13 b4!? ♗f8 14 a4 ♘b6 15 a5 ♘bd7 16 ♗b2 ♖b8 17 ♖b1 ♗a8 18 ♗a1 g6 19 dxe5 ♘xe5 20 ♘xe5 dxe5 21 c4 bxc4 22 ♗c3 ♗c6 23 ♕e2 ♗b5 24 ♘xc4 c5 with unclear play.

13...♗f8

Black's dream of ...d6-d5 cannot be realized yet: 13...d5?! 14 ♘xe5 ♘xe5 (14...♘xe4 15 ♘xf7! ♔xf7 16 ♖xe4 dxe4 17 ♗b3+ ♔f8 18 ♕h5 g6 19 ♕xh7 +−) 15 dxe5 ♘xe4 16 f3 ♘g5 17 ♘g3 ♗c5+ 18 ♔h2 f6 19 ♗xg5 fxg5 20 ♕b1! h6 21 ♕d1! and the loose black king position is hard to defend.

14 ♘g3 g6

Black strengthens his king position against the forthcoming attack.

15 a4!?

This gives Black less chances of active counterplay than 15 b3, when two lines are perfectly playable:

a) 15...♗g7 16 d5 ♘b6 17 ♗e3 ♖c8 18 ♕e2 c6 19 c4 cxd5 20 cxd5 ♘bxd5! 21 exd5 ♘xd5 22 ♕d2 ♘c3 23 ♘e2 b4!, when Black's plan is ...d5-d4. His advancing central pawns provide excellent compensation for the piece.

b) 15...d5!? 16 ♗g5!? (16 exd5?! ♘xd5 17 dxe5 ♘xc3 18 ♕d3 ♘d5 19 ♗g5 ♕c8 20 ♕d4 ♗g7 ∓) 16...h6 17 ♗h4!? dxe4 (17...g5 18 ♘xg5 hxg5 19 ♗xg5 exd4 20 e5! ♖xe5 21 ♖xe5 ♘xe5 22 ♕xd4 and the threat of ♘f5 or ♘h5 creates a colossal attack against Black's king) 18 ♘xe4 g5 19 dxe5! ♘xe4 20 ♗xe4 ♗xe4 21 ♖xe4 gxh4 22 ♖d4 ♖e7 23 e6! ♖xe6! 24 ♖xd7 ♕e8 and in spite of appearances Black is no worse because he is threatening 25...♗d6 to entrap the white rook on d7.

15...c5

Now if 15...♗g7, then 16 d5! is strong, when White's target is the pawn on b5 and the entire black queenside.

16 d5

White cannot hope for an advantage after the feeble exchange 16 dxe5 dxe5. What is more it is even Black who threatens to assume the initiative with ...c5-c4 and ...♘c5.

16...c4 17 ♗g5 h6 18 ♗e3 ♘c5 19 ♕d2 h5 20 ♗g5 ♗e7

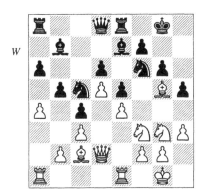

W

Plans and Counterplans:
White can double his rooks on the a-file and then open the way for an invasion with axb5. Black, in his turn, will try to neutralize the invading white rook. For example, 21 ♗h6 (White avoids any combinations that may become possible after a jump by the knight from f6, for instance, 21 ♖a2 h4 22 ♘xh4? ♘fxe4!) 21...♘h7 22 ♖a3 ♖b8 23 ♖ea1 ♗c8 24 axb5 axb5 25 ♗e3 ♗f6 26 ♘e2 ♗d7 27 ♖a7 ♕c8! and Black can pursue the rook on a7 with the manoeuvre ...♗f6-d8-b6.

E3. 1 e4 e5 2 ♘f3 ♘c6 3 ♗b5 a6 4 ♗a4 ♘f6 5 0-0 ♗e7 6 ♖e1 b5 7 ♗b3 d6 8 c3 0-0 9 h3 ♘a5 (Chigorin Variation)

10 ♗c2 c5
In this variation Black immediately mobilizes his c-pawn, creating instant tension in the centre and on the queenside. The drawbacks of this plan are that the knight on a5 has trouble finding

a good home and that the early ...c7-c5 removes the option of later nibbling at the white d5-pawn with ...c7-c6.

11 d4 ♕c7
Black protects his e5-pawn and at the same time already has the opening of the c-file in mind. There are of course several other moves:
a) 11...d5? 12 ♘xe5 dxe4 (after 12...♘xe4 13 ♘d2! ♘xd2 14 ♗xd2, White is threatening 15 b4 and 15 ♕h5) 13 ♗g5 cxd4 14 cxd4 ♗b7 15 ♘c3 ± and Black cannot hold his e-pawn.
b) 11...cxd4 12 cxd4 ♗b7 13 ♘c3 ♕c7 14 ♕e2 ♖ac8 15 ♗d3 ♖fe8 16 ♗g5 h6 17 ♗d2 ♗f8 18 d5 ± and then with ♖ec1 and at an apt moment a2-a4 or b2-b4 White takes over the initiative.
c) 11...♖e8? 12 dxe5 dxe5 13 ♘xe5 ♗d6 14 ♘xf7! ♔xf7 15 e5 ♕e7 16 ♗f4! ♗c7 (16...♗b8 17 ♘d2 ♘d5 18 ♕h5+ introduces an overwhelming attack) 17 ♖e3 ♕d7 18 e6+! ♖xe6 19 ♕xd7+ ♗xd7 20 ♗xc7 +−. Black has nothing for the pawn.
d) 11...♘c6 12 d5 ♘a5 13 ♘bd2 c4 14 ♘f1 ♘b7 15 g4! h5!? 16 gxh5 ♗xh3 17 ♘3h2 ♘h7 18 ♘e3 ♗g5 19 ♕f3 ♗d7 20 ♔h1, and White unfolds an attack on the kingside with the moves ♖g1 and ♘f5.
e) 11...♗b7 12 ♘bd2 cxd4 13 cxd4 exd4 14 ♘xd4 ♖e8 15 b4 ♘c6 (15...♘c4? 16 ♘xc4 bxc4 17 ♗a4! ♖f8 18 ♗g5 ±, and here White is threatening 19 ♘c6 or 19 ♘f5) 16 ♘xc6 ♗xc6 17 ♗b2 ♖c8 18 ♗b3!?

±, followed by 19 ♕f3, when the white bishops exert strong pressure on the black kingside.

f) 11...♘d7 12 ♘bd2 (12 dxc5 also comes strongly into consideration: 12...dxc5 13 ♘bd2 f6 14 ♘h4 ♘b6 15 ♘f5 ♖f7 16 ♘b3 ♘b7 17 ♗e3 ♕c7 18 ♘d2 ♗f8 19 a4!, and White assumes the initiative) 12...cxd4 13 cxd4 ♘c6 14 ♘b3 a5 15 ♗e3 a4 16 ♘bd2 exd4 (on any other move White follows the plan d4-d5, ♖c1, ♗b1, ♘f1 and ♕d2, when he can hope for activity on both the kingside and the c-file) 17 ♘xd4 ♘xd4 18 ♗xd4 ♘e5 19 a3!? ♘c6 20 ♗c3 ♗f6 21 ♕h5!? is much more pleasant for White. Not only is he threatening the pawn on b5, but also 22 e5 is in the air.

12 ♘bd2

It is not worth White closing the centre without a gain of tempo as his queenside is still undeveloped: 12 d5?! ♘c4 13 a4 ♗d7 14 b3 ♘a5 15 axb5 axb5 16 ♘bd2 g6! 17 ♘f1 ♘h5! 18 ♗h6 ♖fe8 19 ♘3h2 ♕d8 20 ♕d2 ♘f4 21 ♘f3 ♗f6, and if White should ever capture the knight on f4, the strength of the bishop on f6 multiplies.

12...cxd4

12...♘c6 is well met by 13 d5 ♘d8 14 a4 ♖b8 15 axb5 axb5 16 b4! c4 17 ♘f1 ♘e8 18 ♘3h2 f6 19 f4 ♘f7 20 ♘f3 g6 21 f5 ♘g7 22 g4, and White stands more freely, although of course it is still very hard to attack Black in such a closed position. Black's alternative is 12...♗d7 13 ♘f1 ♘c4 14 ♘e3

♘xe3 15 ♗xe3 ♖fc8 16 ♖c1 ♗c6 17 ♘d2 cxd4 18 cxd4 ♕b7 19 ♕f3 (19 d5 ♗e8 20 ♕e2 ♗d8!) 19...d5 20 dxe5 ♘xe4 21 ♗b3! ±. Black is unable to open the long diagonal with ...d5-d4 due to the weakness of the f7-pawn.

13 cxd4 ♘c6

Black is eyeing up the squares d4 and b4. Other possibilities are:

a) **13...♖d8** 14 b3 ♘c6 15 ♗b2 exd4 16 ♘xd4 ♘xd4 17 ♗xd4 ♗e6 18 ♖c1! ♕a5 19 ♗b1 d5 20 ♗c3 b4 21 ♗xf6 ♗xf6 22 e5 ♗g5 23 ♕e2 ♕b6 24 ♖cd1, and with the manoeuvre ♘d2-f3-d4 White takes control. On 24...♗xd2 25 ♖xd2, the plan ♖ed1, ♔h2 and f2-f4 also shows White's advantage.

b) **13...♗e6** 14 ♘f1 ♖fc8 15 ♗d3 ♘e8 16 ♘e3, and 17 ♗d2 gives White a clear advantage.

c) **13...♗d7** 14 ♘f1 ♖ac8 15 ♘e3 ♘c6 16 d5 ♘b4 17 ♗b1 a5 18 a3 ♘a6 19 b4!, and now 19...axb4 20 axb4 ♘xb4 is prohibited as 21 ♕b3 ♕c5 22 ♗d2 catches the black knight. White will now be able to seize the queenside initiative with 20 ♗d2 followed by ♗d3 and ♖c1.

d) **13...♗b7** 14 ♘f1 (14 d5!? is also not bad as it shuts down the bishop on b7) 14...♖ac8 15 ♖e2 ♘h5 (or 15...d5 16 dxe5 ♘xe4 17 ♘g3! ♘xg3 18 fxg3 and the black kingside is open to attack with 19 ♕d3) 16 a4!? bxa4 (on 16...b4, 17 b3 and 18 d5 cools the heels of the knight on a5, while 16...♘f4 17 ♗xf4 exf4 18 axb5 axb5 19 ♕d2! ♘c4 20 ♕xf4 ♘xb2 21 ♘g3 gives

White a tremendous attack) 17 ♗xa4 ♘f4 18 ♖c2! ±. Black is very disorganized: besides the knight on a5, the defence of the pawn on e5 is also causing trouble.

14 ♘b3

On 14 ♘f1, 14...exd4 is possible and on 14 d5 ♘b4 15 ♗b1 a5 16 a3 ♘a6, followed by ...♗d7 and ...♘c5 equalizes.

14...a5 15 ♗e3!

The bishop needs to be quickly developed in order to bring the knight back to d2.

15...a4 16 ♘bd2 ♘b4

16...♗d7 17 ♖c1 ♕b7 18 ♕e2 ♖fe8 19 a3!? g6 20 ♗b1! ♗f8 21 ♗a2! h6 22 dxe5 ♘xe5 (22...dxe5 23 ♗c5! and ♗xf8, ♕e3, ♖c5 brings about an advantage for White) 23 ♗d4 ♖ac8 24 ♗c3 ♗g7 25 ♘d4 ±.

17 ♗b1 ♗d7 18 a3 ♘c6 19 ♗d3

19 ♗a2!? is also possible.

19...♘a5 20 ♕e2 ♕b8 21 ♖ec1! *(D)*

Plans and Counterplans:

White is clearly better. He controls the play and with his excellent rook placement he has also prepared an unexpected plan: ♖ab1 and b2-b4! One possible continuation is 21...♖e8 22 ♖ab1! ♗d8 (or

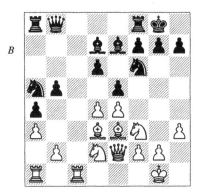

22...♗f8 23 ♗g5! ♘h5 24 b4!) 23 b4! axb3 24 ♘xb3 ♘xb3 25 ♖xb3 ♕b7 26 ♘d2 (the b5-pawn could not yet be taken due to the hanging pawn on e4) 26...h6 27 dxe5 dxe5 28 ♗xb5 ♗xb5 29 ♕xb5 ♕xb5 30 ♖xb5 ♖xa3 31 ♖c8 and White is unpleasantly squeezing Black on the eighth rank. In the Chigorin Variation Black has to live through some difficult moments so it is no wonder that the Zaitsev and the Breyer are more and more fashionable these days.

In the tough positional battle of the Main Line one can count on success only if one is familiar with all the typical plans and, according to the situation in the centre, is able to pick the one which grants active play at the right juncture.

Philidor's Defence

1 e4 e5 2 ♘f3 d6

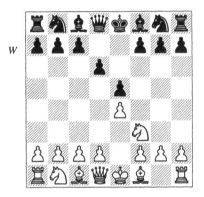

It is less active to protect the e5-pawn with 2...d6 than with 2...♘c6 because it is not a developing move and it shuts in the dark-squared bishop. However, the Philidor has the great advantage that it requires much less knowledge than 2...♘c6, although the initiative is clearly in White's hands.

3 d4

On 3 ♗c4 the correct answer is 3...♗e7, when after 4 d4 Black may transpose to the Hungarian Defence with 4...♘c6, or may play 4...exd4 5 ♘xd4 ♘f6 6 ♘c3 0-0. In both cases White stands slightly better. Note that it is inadvisable to meet 3 ♗c4 with 3...♗e6 as the weakening of the e6-square can cause serious problems: 4 ♗xe6 fxe6 5 d4 exd4 6 ♘xd4 e5 (6...♕f6 7 ♕h5+ g6 8 ♕b5+; 6...♕d7 7

♕h5+ g6 8 ♕h3) 7 ♘e6 ♕e7 8 ♕h5+ g6 9 ♕h3 and once he has castled White will be threatening f2-f4.

3...♘f6

Other moves favour White:

a) 3...♘c6 4 ♗b5 with a transposition into the Steinitz Variation of the Ruy Lopez.

b) 3...♗g4 4 dxe5 ♗xf3 5 ♕xf3 dxe5 6 ♗c4 with an initiative for White. Also good is 5 gxf3 dxe5 6 ♕xd8+ ♔xd8 7 f4 and White has good chances in the endgame due to his bishop pair.

c) 3...f5. This romantic move weakens Black's king position to a fatal degree. For example, 4 ♘c3 fxe4 5 ♘xe4 d5 6 ♘xe5! dxe4 7 ♕h5+ g6 8 ♘xg6 ♘f6 9 ♕e5+ ♔f7 10 ♗c4+! ♔g7 (10...♔xg6 11 ♕g5 mate) 11 ♗h6+! ♔xh6 12 ♘xh8 ♗b4+ 13 c3 and White continues the attack on the king and is also materially well off.

d) 3...♘d7 4 ♗c4 c6 ('natural' moves lose here: 4...♘f6? 5 dxe5 dxe5 6 ♘g5 or 5...♘xe5 6 ♘xe5 dxe5 7 ♗xf7+ ♔xf7 8 ♕xd8 ♗b4+ 9 ♕d2; 4...♗e7? 5 dxe5 dxe5 6 ♕d5 or 5...♘xe5 6 ♘xe5 dxe5 7 ♕h5 and 4...h6? 5 dxe5 dxe5 6 ♗xf7+ ♔xf7 7 ♘xe5+ 8 ♕d5) 5 0-0 ♗e7 6 dxe5 dxe5 7 ♘g5 ♗xg5 8 ♕h5 g6 9 ♕xg5 and, with the bishop pair and a more developed position, White is better.

e) **3...exd4** 4 ∆xd4 (also good is 4 ♕xd4, with the follow-up 4...∆c6 5 ♗b5, or 4...♗d7 5 ♗f4 ∆c6 6 ♕d2), and now Black should transpose to the Main Line with 4...∆f6.

After 3...∆f6 White has two possibilities:

I. 4 dxe5 or

II. 4 ∆c3.

I. 1 e4 e5 2 ∆f3 d6 3 d4 ∆f6 4 dxe5

4...∆xe4 5 ♕d5

The most forceful move. After 5 ∆bd2 ∆xd2 6 ♗xd2 ♗e7 7 ♗d3 (on 7 exd6 Black has to recapture with the queen while on 7 ♗f4 he plays 7...d5) 7...∆c6 8 ♕e2 ♗e6 9 0-0-0 dxe5 10 ∆xe5 ♕d5 Black is free of problems, while on 5 ♗d3 ∆c5 or on 5 ♗c4 c6 6 exd6 ∆xd6 7 ♗b3 ♗e7 8 0-0 0-0 9 ∆c3 ∆a6 is the most accurate continuation for Black.

5...∆c5 6 ♗g5

6 ∆g5 is ineffective after 6...♗e6 7 ∆xe6 fxe6 8 ♕f3 ∆bd7 9 exd6 ♗xd6 with an advantage to Black.

6...♕d7

Or 6...♗e7 7 exd6 ♕xd6 8 ∆c3 followed by queenside castling and White's initiative is extremely dangerous.

7 exd6 ♗xd6 8 ∆c3 0-0 9 0-0-0 ∆c6 (D)

Plans and Counterplans:

White's pieces are more naturally developed: He can try to make use

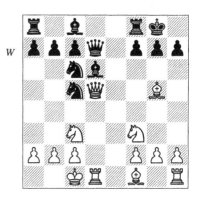

of the crowded state of Black's pieces and the pin on the d-file and may be able to mount an attack on the king. Black would like to free his queen and his light-squared bishop and then develop an attack against White's queen-side castling position. There might follow 10 ♗e3 ∆e7 11 ♕c4 b6 12 ♗xc5 bxc5 13 ♗d3 ∆g6 ±.

II. 1 e4 e5 2 ∆f3 d6 3 d4 ∆f6 4 ∆c3

4...exd4

Here it is more acceptable to play **4...∆bd7** than on the third move: **5 ♗c4 ♗e7** (Black should not play 5...c6 in view of 6 dxe5 dxe5 7 ∆g5) and now:

a) 6 ♗xf7+? (White, if he wants, can 'go wild', but he is not winning) 6...♔xf7 7 ∆g5+ ♔g8 8 ∆e6 ♕e8 9 ∆xc7 ♕g6 10 ∆xa8 ♕xg2 11 ♖f1 exd4 12 ♕xd4 ∆e5 13 f4 ∆fg4 and the white monarch runs into trouble.

b) The same idea in a revised form: **6 dxe5 dxe5** (also playable

is 6...♘xe5 7 ♗e2) 7 ♗xf7+ ♔xf7
8 ♘g5+ ♔g8 9 ♘e6 ♕e8 10 ♘xc7
♕g6 11 ♘xa8 ♕xg2 12 ♖f1 ♘c5,
and Black achieves enough counterplay with ...♗h3.

c) 6 ♘g5 0-0 7 ♗xf7+ ♖xf7 8
♘e6 ♕e8 9 ♘xc7 ♕d8 10 ♘xa8 b5!
11 dxe5! (not 11 ♘xb5? ♕a5+ 12
♘c3 ♘xe4 ∓) 11...♘xe5 12 ♗f4 b4
13 ♘d5 ♘xd5 14 ♕xd5 ♘g6 15
♗g3 ♗f8 16 0-0-0 ♗b7 and White
is somewhat better. These lines
are all very sharp and chaotic: in
a tournament game the better
versed player will be the one to
get on top!

d) 6 0-0. The natural continuation is 6...0-0 7 ♕e2 c6 8 a4 (of
course, ...b7-b5 must be stopped)
8...♕c7 9 h3 b6 10 ♖d1 ♗b7. White
has a spatial plus but Black's position is very solid. For players
with an active style this line can
be recommended as White. Black's
position is more suitable for 'snip-
ers' with a patient style of play.

5 ♘xd4

Here too the queen may recapture: 5 ♕xd4 ♘c6 6 ♗b5 ♗d7 7
♗xc6 with a spatial advantage and
a strong centralized queen for the
bishop pair.

5...g6

The bishop is better placed on
the long diagonal than on e7:
5...♗e7 6 ♗f4 (positions in which
White castles kingside are less
harmful for Black) 6...0-0 7 ♕d2
and after 0-0-0 White develops a
strong attack. Black has to try to
carry out ...d6-d5.

6 ♗g5

The most dangerous continuation. On 6 ♗f4 ♗g7 7 ♕d2 0-0 8
0-0-0 ♖e8 9 f3 ♘c6 10 ♘xc6 bxc6
11 e5 ♘d5 12 ♘xd5 cxd5 Black
obtains an attack on the open di-
agonals and files, while after 6
♗c4 ♗g7 7 0-0 0-0 8 ♗g5 h6 9
♗h4 ♘c6 10 ♘xc6 bxc6 11 f4 ♕e8
Black can have no complaints.

**6...♗g7 7 ♕d2 h6 8 ♗f4 g5 9
♗g3 ♘h5 10 ♗e2 ♘xg3 11 hxg3
♘c6**

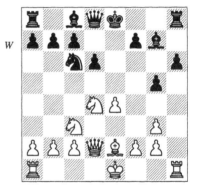

Plans and Counterplans:
White is more developed and has
the superior pawn structure. He
will castle queenside and try to
utilize the weakness of the squares
d5, f5 and h5. Black will have to
castle queenside as well and will
rely on the activity of his bishops.
There may follow 12 ♗b5 ♗d7 13
♘de2 ♕f6 with chances for both
sides.

Russian Game (Petroff's Defence)

1 e4 e5 2 ♘f3 ♘f6

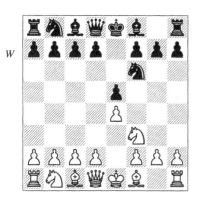

With 2...♘f6 Black does not bother to protect his pawn on e5. What is more, he wants to persuade White to spend time defending his own attacked pawn on e4. If White accedes to Black's will with 3 ♘c3 then after 3...♗b4!? 4 ♘xe5 0-0 5 ♗e2 (or 5 d3 d5! and the centre is opened in Black's favour) 5...♖e8 6 ♘d3 ♗xc3 7 dxc3 ♘xe4 8 0-0 d5 9 ♘f4 c6 10 ♗e3 ♘d6! 11 ♗d3 ♗f5 White cannot hope for any advantage. White therefore has to opt for more complex positions and an open centre(!) in which his extra tempo may be of importance. Even a slight inaccuracy will allow Black to equalize.

White's two possibilities are:

I. 3 ♘xe5 and
II. 3 d4.

I. 1 e4 e5 2 ♘f3 ♘f6 3 ♘xe5

3...d6

3...♘xe4? is catastrophic: 4 ♕e2 d5 (or 4...♕e7 5 ♕xe4 d6 6 d4 f6 7 ♘c3 dxe5 8 ♘d5 ♕d6 9 dxe5 fxe5 10 ♗f4 c6 11 0-0-0! cxd5 12 ♖xd5, with a winning attack for White) 5 d3 ♘f6?? (5...♕e7 6 dxe4 ♕xe5 7 exd5 ±) 6 ♘c6 winning the queen with a discovered check!

4 ♘f3

White's piece configuration is less natural after 4 ♘c4 ♘xe4 5 d4 d5 6 ♘e3, which Black can exploit with the following active plan: 6...♗e6 7 ♗d3 f5!? followed by ...♗d6, ...0-0, ...c7-c6 and ...♘bd7.

4...♘xe4 5 d4!

White does not chase the e4 knight so that later he will attack it with ♗d3. Other options do not promise any advantage:

a) 5 d3 ♘f6 6 d4 d5 (this is an Exchange French!) 7 ♗d3 ♗d6 8 0-0 0-0 9 ♗g5 ♗g4 10 ♘bd2 ♘bd7 11 c3 c6 =. White cannot interrupt Black's mirror-game.

b) 5 ♘c3 ♘xc3 (also playable is 5...♘f6 and ...♗e7, ...0-0 and ...♘c6) 6 dxc3 ♗e7 7 ♗f4 0-0 8 ♕d2 ♘d7!? 9 0-0-0 ♘c5 with equal chances.

c) 5 ♕e2 ♕e7 6 d3 ♘f6 7 ♗g5 ♕xe2+ 8 ♗xe2 ♗e7 9 ♘c3 c6! 10 0-0-0 ♘a6! 11 ♖he1 ♘c7, followed by 12...♘e6, neutralizing White's pressure along the open e-file.

d) 5 c4 ♗e7 (The best move. Black simply develops, preparing to castle shortly, while the pressure along the e-file has also vanished. A terrifying possibility is 5...♘c6 6 ♘c3 ♗f5?? 7 ♕e2 ♕e7 8 ♘d5 +−) 6 ♘c3 ♘xc3 7 dxc3 ♘c6 8 ♗d3 ♘e5! (not 8...♗g4 9 ♗e4! and Black can hardly find a plan while White, after 0-0, is ready to get going with b2-b4) 9 ♘xe5 dxe5 10 ♕c2 ♗g5! 11 0-0 ♗e6 12 ♖e1 ♗xc1 13 ♖axc1 ♕g5 14 ♖e3 0-0-0 with an equal position.

5...d5

It is necessary to act firmly in the centre. For example, on 5...♗e7 6 ♗d3 ♘f6 7 h3! 0-0 8 0-0 ♖e8 9 c4 White can complete his development with ♘c3, ♖e1 and ♗f4, when he has the choice between doubling on the e-file (♕d2, ♖e2 and ♖ae1) and a queenside expansion (with or without d4-d5): b2-b4-b5 and a2-a4. 5...♗g4 looks dangerous but after 6 h3 ♗h5 7 ♕e2 ♕e7 8 ♗e3 White inevitably comes out on top via 9 g4 and ♗g2, ♘c3 and 0-0-0.

6 ♗d3

White's aim is to undermine the position of the knight on e4 with 0-0, ♖e1 and c2-c4.

6...♗e7

Theory considers this to be the main line. The following moves are also sometimes seen in practice:

a) 6...♘c6?! 7 0-0 ♗g4 8 c4 ♘f6 (or 8...♗e7 9 ♘c3 ♘xc3 10 bxc3 0-0 11 h3 ♗h5 12 ♖b1 and White threatens 13 ♖b5 with fifth-rank pressure) 9 ♘c3 (9 cxd5 ♗xf3 10 ♕xf3 ♕xd5 11 ♕xd5! ♘xd5 12 ♘c3 0-0-0 13 ♗c4 gives White a small plus due to the bishop pair) 9...♗xf3 10 ♕xf3 ♘xd4 11 ♕h3 ♘e6 12 cxd5 ♘xd5 13 ♗g6!! ± and the knight on e6 becomes vulnerable. In such an open position White's development advantage means that the threats of ♕xe6+, ♖fe1 and ♖ad1 are all but decisive.

b) 6...♗d6!? 7 0-0 0-0 8 c4 (8 ♖e1 f5!? 9 c4 c6 10 ♕b3 ♔h8 11 ♘c3 ♘a6 ∞, since 12 cxd5 cxd5 13 ♘xd5?! ♗e6 14 ♕xb7 ♘ac5! 15 dxc5 ♗xd5 leads to a black initiative. The bishop on d5 is protected by the discovery ...♗xh2+) 8...c6 9 cxd5 (more critical than 9 ♘c3 ♘xc3 10 bxc3 dxc4 11 ♗xc4 ♗g4 12 ♕d3 ♘d7 =) 9...cxd5 10 ♘c3 ♘xc3 11 bxc3 ♗g4 12 ♖b1 b6 (12...♘d7!? 13 h3! − 13 ♖xb7? ♘b6 and ...♗c8 catches the white rook on b7 − 13...♗h5 14 ♖b5! ♘b6 15 c4!) 13 ♖b5 ♗c7 14 h3 a6 15 hxg4! axb5 16 ♕c2 g6 17 ♗xb5 with ample compensation for the exchange.

7 0-0 ♘c6

7...0-0 is weaker: 8 c4 ♘f6 (after 8...c6 9 cxd5 cxd5 10 ♘c3 Black is even a little more passive than if he had played 6...♗d6 instead of 6...♗e7) 9 ♘c3 ♗g4 10 cxd5 ♘xd5 11 ♗e4! and White is planning to increase his pressure on the light squares with ♕d1-d3.

8 ♖e1!?

Attacking e4 and vacating the f1-square for the bishop on d3 which would be needed after, for instance, 8 c4 ♘b4: 9 ♗e2 ♗e6 (not 9...dxc4 10 ♗xc4 0-0 11 ♘c3 with more active piece play for White) 10 ♘c3 0-0 11 ♗e3 f5!? 12 a3 ♘xc3 (after 12...♘c6? 13 cxd5 ♗xd5 14 ♘xd5 ♕xd5 15 ♖c1 Black's centre is exterminated) 13 bxc3 ♘c6 14 ♖b1 ♖b8 15 ♕a4 f4 16 ♗c1 ♔h8 17 ♖e1 dxc4 18 ♗xc4 ♗g4!? and Black can create good counter-chances.

8...♗g4

After 8...f5? 9 c4 ♗e6 10 cxd5 ♗xd5 11 ♘c3 ± Black has to abandon the knight outpost at e4.

9 c4

Nothing is gained by 9 ♗xe4 dxe4 10 ♖xe4 as after 10...♗xf3 11 ♕xf3 (11 gxf3? f5 12 ♖f4 0-0 13 d5 ♗g5 14 ♖a4 ♗xc1 15 ♕xc1 ♕xd5 ∓) 11...♘xd4 12 ♕d3 ♘e6 = White's most active pieces have been exchanged (♗d3, ♘f3).

9...♘f6 (D)

Black has to retreat the knight owing to 9...f5 10 ♘c3 ♗xf3 11 gxf3 ♘xc3 12 bxc3 0-0 13 cxd5 ♕xd5 14 ♕e2 ♔h8 15 ♖b1, threatening ♗c4 and then ♖xb7 or simply ♗f4, or 9...♗xf3 10 ♕xf3 ♘xd4 11 ♕e3 ♘f5 12 ♕f4 ♘fd6 13 cxd5 ±.

Plans and Counterplans:

White has forced the knight from e4 and now wants to take the d5-square away from his opponent to gain a free hand in the centre.

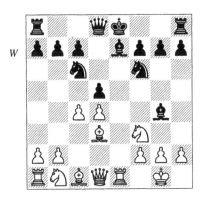

Black is counting on the irritating pin of his g4-bishop and an attack on the pawn at d4, but of course first he has to castle. Here are some examples:

a) **10 cxd5 ♘xd5 11 ♘c3 0-0** (11...♘xd4? 12 ♕a4+) 12 h3 (alternatively, 12 ♘xd5 ♕xd5 13 ♗e4 ♕d6 14 ♗xc6 bxc6 15 ♖e4!? ♗e6 16 ♗g5 ♗xg5 17 ♘xg5 ♗d5 18 ♖e3 h6 19 ♘e4 ♗xe4 20 ♖xe4 ♖ab8 leads to a drawish-looking heavy piece endgame or 12 ♗e4 ♗e6 13 a3 ♗f6 = with a difficult position in which Black has maintained the d5-square) 12...♗e6 (not 12...♗h5? 13 ♗xh7+ ♔xh7 14 ♘g5+ ♗xg5 15 ♕xh5+ ♗h6 16 ♗xh6 gxh6 17 ♕f5+ ♔g7 18 ♘xd5 +−) and now on 13 ♕c2 he can answer 13...♘f6, and 13 a3 ♖e8 14 ♗c2 ♘xc3 15 bxc3 ♗f6 16 ♕d3 g6 and ...♘a5 leads to mutual chances, while the interesting 13 ♘e4!? with the idea of harassing the bishop at e6 from the squares c5 or g5, still awaits practical testing.

b) **10 ♘c3!?** dxc4 (for 10...0-0 11 cxd5 ♘xd5 see 10 cxd5, while after 10...♘xd4 11 cxd5 ♘xf3+ 12 gxf3, followed by ♕e2, Black's king is stuck in the middle) 11 ♗xc4 0-0 12 d5 ♘a5 13 ♗d3 c6 14 h3 ♗h5 (not 14...♗xf3 15 ♕xf3 cxd5 16 ♗g5, threatening ♖xe7 and then ♘xd5) 15 ♖e5! and White holds the initiative. For example 15...cxd5 16 ♘xd5! ± or 15...♗g6 16 ♗xg6 hxg6 17 d6 ♗xd6 18 ♖xa5 ♕xa5 19 ♕xd6 ±. Best for Black is 15...♗d6!?, forcing White to sacrifice an exchange in return for an attack: 16 ♖xh5 ♘xh5 17 ♘g5 (17 ♗xh7+ ♔xh7 18 ♘g5+ ♔g6!) 17...♘f6 18 ♘ce4 with an unclear game in which positional factors (such as Black's knight on a5 and central disadvantage) take a back seat.

II. 1 e4 e5 2 ♘f3 ♘f6 3 d4

3...exd4

Other options are:

a) 3...d5 4 exd5 exd4 (or 4...e4 5 ♘e5 ♘xd5 6 ♗c4 ♗e6 7 0-0 ♗e7 8 f3! ± and Black's e4-outpost disappears while White gets ready to attack on the f-file) 5 ♕xd4 ♕xd5 6 ♘c3 ♕xd4 7 ♘xd4 c6! (it is important that the white knight does not attack the c7-pawn from either d5 or b5) 8 ♗g5 ± . White is more developed and can play 0-0-0, ♗d3 and ♘f5.

b) 3...♘xe4 4 ♗d3 (4 dxe5 d5 5 ♘bd2 ♘c5 =) and now after the traditional 4...d5 5 ♘xe5 Black has two ways to undermine the knight at e5:

b1) 5...♘d7!? 6 ♘xd7 (on 6 ♕e2 ♘xe5 7 ♗xe4 dxe4 8 ♕xe4 ♗e6 9 ♕xe5 ♕d7 10 ♗e3 ♗b4+ 11 c3 ♗d6 12 ♕a5 ♕c6, Black's bishop pair and activity on the light squares maintain the balance) 6...♗xd7 7 0-0 ♕h4 8 c4 0-0-0 (also playable is 8...♘f6 9 ♕e2+ ♗e7) 9 c5! (the dark-squared bishop must be sealed) 9...g5! 10 ♘c3 ♗g7 with mutual chances.

b2) 5...♗d6 6 0-0 0-0 7 c4 ♗xe5 (or 7...c6 8 ♘c3 ♘xc3 9 bxc3 ±) 8 dxe5 ♘c6 9 cxd5 ♕xd5 10 ♕c2 ♘b4 11 ♗xe4 ♘xc2 12 ♗xd5 ♗f5! 13 g4! ♗xg4 14 ♗e4 ♘xa1 15 ♗f4 and although the position is still up in the air, White is the one playing for an advantage.

After 4 ♗d3 a surprising novelty has brought new colour to this variation: 4...♘c6!? Now 5 d5 ♘c5 6 dxc6 e4 or 5 dxe5 d5 6 exd6 ♘xd6 7 ♘c3 ♗e7 8 ♘d5 ♗e6 9 ♘xe7 ♕xe7 and ...0-0-0 are perfectly playable for Black, so the critical line is 5 ♗xe4 d5 6 ♗g5 ♕d7 7 ♗d3 e4 8 0-0 f6! 9 ♖e1 ♗e7 10 ♗f4 exd3 11 ♕xd3 0-0, when Black is close to equality, for example 12 ♘c3 ♗b4 13 ♖e2 ♕f7 and the bishop on c8 is ready to venture out.

4 e5 ♘e4

Alternatives are worse: 4...♘d5 5 ♕xd4 ♘b6 6 ♘c3 ♘c6 7 ♕e4 ♗e7 8 ♗f4 with 0-0-0 and ♗d3 ± or 4...♕e7 5 ♗e2 ♘e4 6 ♕xd4 ♕b4+ 7 ♘bd2 ♘xd2 8 ♗xd2 ♕xd4 9 ♘xd4 ±.

5 ♕xd4 d5 6 exd6 ♘xd6 7 ♘c3

Nothing is gained by 7 ♗g5 ♘c6 8 ♕e3+ ♗e7 9 ♘c3 ♘f5 = or 7 ♗f4 ♘c6 8 ♕d2 ♕e7+ 9 ♗e2 ♘e4 10 ♕e3 ♘b4! 11 ♕c1 ♕c5 12 0-0 ♗e6! (12...♘xc2? 13 ♘c3! ♘xa1 14 ♘xe4 and the a1-knight will soon be lost) 13 c4 0-0-0 ∞. Since 7 ♗d3 ♘c6 8 ♕f4 g6 9 ♘c3 leads back to the line beginning with 7 ♘c3, let us now move on!

7...♘c6 8 ♕f4 g6

The apparent problems of developing the dark-squared bishop are thus solved. Other moves are problematic:8...♗e7 9 ♗d3 ♗e6 10 ♗d2 ♕d7 11 0-0-0 0-0-0 12 ♖he1 h6 13 ♗e3 and ♕a4 gives White the initiative; on 8...♗e6 9 ♗d3 g6 10 ♘d4! Black faces a difficult decision whether to capture d4 – but then kingside castling is impossible – or let White crash through on c6; while 8...♗f5 can be met by 9 ♗b5!, since after 9...♘xb5? 10 ♘xb5 Black must play 9...♕e7+ 10 ♗e3 ♘xb5 11 ♘xb5 ♕b4+ 12 ♕xb4 ♗xb4+ 13 c3 ♗d6, but then 14 ♘xd6+ cxd6 15 0-0-0 is clearly better for White.

9 ♗d3

9 ♗b5 is an interesting alternative, when 9...♘xb5 10 ♘xb5 ♗d6 11 ♘xd6+ ♕xd6 12 ♕xd6 cxd6 13 ♗f4 ± is inferior, but counterchances are offered by 9...♗g7 10 0-0 0-0-0 11 ♗xc6 bxc6 12 ♗e3 ♖b8 13 ♖ab1 a5 ∞. Another idea is 9 ♗e3 ♗g7 10 0-0-0 0-0 11 h4 and now Black has to play 11...h6 to meet 12 h5? with 12...g5.

9...♗g7 10 ♗e3 ♗e6

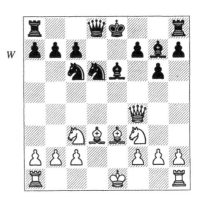

Plans and Counterplans:

White stands more freely. His standard moves after castling are ♘g5, ♘d4, ♗c5 and rooks to d1 and e1. Black has to generate some counterplay, but this is not easy. Let us see an example of each type of castling for White:

a) 11 0-0 0-0 12 ♘g5 ♖e8 13 ♖ad1 ♕f6 14 ♕xf6 ♗xf6 15 ♘xe6 and then ♘b5 ± with a pair of bishops and the initiative.

b) 11 0-0-0 ♕f6 (not 11...0-0 12 ♗c5! ♖e8 13 ♗b5! a6 14 ♗xc6 bxc6 15 ♘e4 ±) 12 ♘g5 ♕xf4 13 ♗xf4 ♗xc3 14 bxc3 0-0-0 15 ♘xe6 fxe6 16 ♖he1 ♖hf8 17 ♗g3 ♖de8 18 f3 and, with his bishop pair, White can look forward to a pleasant endgame (±).

In the Russian Game it is hard for Black to generate favourable complications. This opening is therefore recommended only on occasions when Black's aim is a simple position with equal play, hoping for a draw, for example, when the tournament situation or opponent's style justifies this.

King's Gambit

1 e4 e5 2 f4

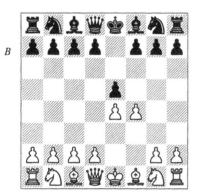

The King's Gambit is the 'king of the gambits', the pet variation of those who like romantic sacrifices. It is well worth experimenting with it, because there is no other opening in which tactical elements are combined with strategic aims in such diverse ways as in the King's Gambit. The kings often end up dancing a samba in the middle of the board; a few pawns, or perhaps even a piece less is not always decisive; and the most important motto for both sides is 'Activity, attack!'.

Before playing ♘g1-f3 White throws the strength of the f-pawn into the central fight and tries to undermine the e5-pawn. If Black accepts the gambit, he will try to obtain the initiative with quick piece development (♘f3, ♗c4 and 0-0) and an attack against the

f7-pawn along the open f-file. Alas, practice has also shown the weak points of the gambit, and Black has found ways to tame White's aggressive intentions. We shall take a look at the following responses in turn:

I. King's Gambit Declined
A. System with 2...♗c5
B. Falkbeer Counter-Gambit: 2...d5

II. King's Gambit Accepted
A. Classical Variation: 2...exf4 3 ♘f3 g5
B. The modern answer: 2...exf4 3 ♘f3 d5

I. King's Gambit Declined

A. System with 2...♗c5

1 e4 e5 2 f4 ♗c5
The pawn move f2-f4 weakens the dark squares in White's position. Black would like to immediately make use of this, and at the same time he also lays a trap: 3 fxe5?? ♕h4+ and Black captures the e4-pawn with check and wins. The following alternatives are feeble: 2...♘f6?! 3 fxe5 ♘xe4 4 ♘f3 ♘g5 5 d4 ♘xf3+ 6 ♕xf3 ♕h4+ 7 ♕f2 ♕xf2+ 8 ♔xf2 ♘c6 9 c3 d6 10 exd6 ♗xd6 11 ♘d2, followed by ♘c4 or ♘e4, when White has a

clear central plus (±), or 2...d6?! 3 ♘f3 ♘c6 4 ♗b5!? ♗d7 5 d3 exf4 6 ♗xf4, followed by 0-0, ♘c3 and d3-d4 with a perceptible White advantage. But 2...♕h4+ is playable: 3 g3 ♕e7 4 fxe5 (4 ♘c3 exf4 5 d4 fxg3 6 ♗f4 d5! ∞) 4...d6 5 exd6 ♕xe4+ 6 ♕e2 ♕xe2+ 7 ♘xe2 ♗xd6 8 ♗g2 ♘c6 9 c3 h5 ∞ and Black can focus on the g3-pawn with ...h5-h4.

3 ♘f3 d6

3...d5? 4 ♘xe5 dxe4 5 ♕h5 ♕e7 (5...♗e6 6 ♘xf7!) 6 ♗c4 g6 7 ♕e2 ♘h6 8 ♘c3 is favourable for White in view of the threats of 9 ♘d5 and 9 ♘xe4, while 3...♘c6 is extremely weak, as after 4 fxe5 d6 5 exd6 ♕xd6 6 c3! and d2-d4 White has an extra pawn and a powerful centre (±).

4 ♘c3

An equal game is reached by 4 c3 ♘f6 5 fxe5 (or 5 d4 exd4 6 cxd4 ♗b6 7 ♘c3 0-0 8 ♗e3 ♘c6 9 ♗d3 ♗g4 10 ♗c2 ♗xf3 11 gxf3 ♘h5 12 0-0 f5! with complicated play) 5...dxe5 6 d4 (6 ♘xe5 0-0 7 d4 ♗d6 8 ♘f3 ♘xe4 =) 6...exd4 7 cxd4 ♗b4+ 8 ♗d2 ♕e7 9 e5 (9 ♗d3 ♘xe4 10 ♗xe4 ♕xe4+ 11 ♔f2 ♗xd2 12 ♘bxd2 ♕d5 13 ♖e1+ ♗e6! 14 ♖e5 ♕d6 15 d5 ♘d7! and White is pushed back) 9...♘d5 10 ♘c3 ♗e6 =.

4...♘f6

4...♘c6 is a mistake, as after 5 ♗b5! ♗g4 6 d3 ♘f6 7 ♘a4! White eliminates the bishop on c5 and then castles.

5 ♗c4

Not 5 fxe5? dxe5 6 ♘xe5? ♕d4 7 ♘d3 ♗b6 and White is frozen in his tracks while Black can develop a victorious attack with ...0-0, ...♖e8 and ...♗g4.

5...♘c6 6 d3 ♗g4

On 6...0-0, 7 f5! shuts in the bishop on c8 and threatens the unpleasant 8 ♗g5. However, 6...♘a5!? comes into consideration, even though on 7 ♕e2!? ♘xc4 8 dxc4 there are still minor problems for Black, since after 8...exf4 9 ♗xf4, 10 ♗g5 and 10 e5 are simultaneously threatened, while on 8...♕e7 9 f5! followed by ♗d2 and 0-0-0 is again more attractive for White.

7 h3

An interesting alternative is 7 ♘a4!? ♗b6 8 ♘xb6 axb6 9 c3 (it is important that on 9...♘a5 10 ♗b5+ c6 11 ♗a4 b5 the bishop can flee via 12 ♗c2) 9...0-0 10 0-0.

7...♗xf3 8 ♕xf3

Plans and Counterplans:
White is threatening 9 ♘a4 or 9 ♗e3, while 9 g4 may be unpleasant as well, so Black cannot afford

to remain idle. On **8...♘d4** White, in the spirit of the gambit, can reply 9 ♕g3!, when both 9...♘xc2+ 10 ♔d1 ♘xa1 11 ♕xg7 ♖f8 12 fxe5 dxe5 13 ♗g5 ♗e7 14 ♖f1 ♘h5 15 ♗xf7+ ♔d7 16 ♕xe5, winning, and 9...0-0 10 fxe5 dxe5 11 ♗g5 ♕d6 (11...♘xc2+ 12 ♔d1 ♘xa1 13 ♘d5 ♗e7 14 ♘xe7+ ♕xe7 15 ♖f1 ♔h8 16 ♕h4 with ♖xf6 to follow +−) 12 0-0-0 ± give him the upper hand. More precise for Black is **8...exf4!?**: 9 ♗xf4 (not 9 ♕xf4? ♘e5! 10 ♖f1 0-0 11 ♗b3 ♘h5! 12 ♕g5 ♕xg5 13 ♗xg5 ♘g3 ∓) 9...♘d4 10 ♕d1 (not 10 ♕g3? ♘h5 11 ♕g4 ♘xf4 12 ♕xf4 ♘xc2+ 13 ♔d1 ♘e3+, followed by ...♘xc4, and Black is almost winning) 10...c6 and now 11 ♕d2?! d5 12 exd5 0-0 is excellent for Black (13 0-0-0 b5 14 ♗b3 ♘xb3+ 15 axb3 ♘xd5 ∓), but White can play 11 ♘a4! ♗b6 (White is also better after both 11...b5 12 ♘xc5 dxc5 − 12...bxc4 13 ♘b7 − 13 ♗b3 ± and 11...♕a5+ 12 c3 b5 13 ♘xc5 dxc5 14 b4! cxb4 15 ♗xf7+ ♔xf7 16 cxd4 ±) 12 c3 ♘e6 13 ♘xb6 axb6 14 ♗g3, when the bishop pair and open f-file offer White the better chances.

B. Falkbeer Counter-Gambit

1 e4 e5 2 f4 d5

Black grabs the chance to start an attack against the cornerstone of the white centre, the pawn on e4, while his own e-pawn is still taboo (3 fxe5? ♕h4+ followed by ...♕xe4+ and Black wins). Even though this idea is neat, White can still manage to secure an advantage. The fate of the Falkbeer Counter-Gambit proves the old adage: 'The best answer to a gambit is not a counter-gambit, but the acceptance of it and then giving back the sacrificed material at the appropriate moment.'

3 exd5 e4?!

This is what makes it a gambit. Note that Black could still have transposed into the Modern Variation via 3...exf4! 4 ♘f3 ♘f6, which is one of the most effective setups with Black. The other foxy continuation is 3...c6. If White is greedy, then he can get in trouble after 4 dxc6? ♘xc6 5 d3 ♗c5 6 ♘c3 ♘f6 7 ♘f3 0-0! 8 fxe5 ♘xe5 9 ♘xe5 ♖e8 10 ♗f4 ♘g4 11 ♕e2 ♗d4! But if he simply develops then he is better after 4 ♘c3! cxd5 5 fxe5 d4 6 ♘e4 ♕d5 7 ♗d3! ♘c6 8 ♕e2! ♘h6 (8...♘xe5 9 ♗b5+ ♗d7 10 ♗xd7+ ♕xd7 11 ♘f3 ♘xf3+ 12 ♕xf3 ±) 9 ♗c4 ♕a5 10 ♘f3 ♗g4 11 ♘d6+, and Black's king is stuck in the middle (±).

4 d3!

White immediately takes measures against the unpleasant e4-pawn. On 4 ♗b5+ c6! 5 dxc6 bxc6! 6 ♗c4 ♘f6 (6...♗c5!? 7 ♕h5 ♕e7 8 ♗xf7+ ♔f8! and 9...♘f6 is also far from simple!) 7 d4 ♗d6 8 ♘e2 0-0 9 0-0 c5 10 d5 ♘bd7, followed by ...♘b6, ...♗b7 and ...c5-c4, Black has sufficient chances. 4 ♘c3 ♘f6 5 ♕e2 ♗f5 6 d3? ♗b4! 7 ♗d2 0-0 8 dxe4 ♗xc3 9 ♗xc3 ♘xe4 ∓ also demonstrates that White has no alternative to 4 d3.

4...♘f6

After 4...exd3? 5 ♗xd3 ♘f6 (or 5...♕xd5 6 ♘c3 ♕e6+ – 6...♕xg2 7 ♗e4 – 7 ♘ge2 ♘h6 8 f5! ♘xf5 9 0-0 with a big attack for White, who can follow up with ♗g5 and ♘f4) 6 ♘c3 ♗e7 7 ♘f3 0-0 8 0-0 ♘bd7 9 ♗c4 ♘b6 10 ♗b3 ♗b4 11 ♘e5 ♗xc3 12 bxc3 ♘bxd5 13 ♗a3! ♖e8 14 ♕d4 c6 15 f5! ± Black is tied up, while 4...♕xd5 5 ♕e2 f5 6 ♘c3 ♗b4 7 ♗d2 ♗xc3 8 ♗xc3 ♘f6 9 dxe4! fxe4 10 ♕c4! ± is no improvement.

5 dxe4!

5 ♘d2 exd3 6 ♗xd3 ♘xd5 equalizes easily, while Black also stands well after 5 ♘c3 ♗b4 6 ♗d2 e3!? 7 ♗xe3 0-0 8 ♗d2 ♗xc3 9 bxc3 ♘xd5 10 ♕f3 ♖e8+ 11 ♘e2 ♘c6 ∞, and after 5 ♕e2 ♗g4 6 ♕e3 ♘xd5! 7 ♕xe4+ ♗e7, intending ...0-0, ...♘c6 and ...♖e8.

5...♘xe4 6 ♘f3

After 6 ♕e2 ♕xd5 7 ♘d2 f5 the white pieces are stuck.

6...♗c5

6...c6 is met by 7 ♘bd2 ♘xd2 8 ♗xd2 ♕xd5 9 ♗d3 ±, followed by 0-0 or ♕e2+, ♗c4 and 0-0-0, while on 6...♗f5, 7 ♗e3 c6 8 ♗c4 b5 9 ♗b3 c5 10 d6! c4 11 ♕d5 is winning for White.

7 ♕e2 ♗f5

The best chance since after 7...♕xd5 8 ♘fd2! f5 9 ♘c3 ♕e6 10 ♘dxe4 fxe4 11 ♕h5+! the bishop on c5 is lost; 7...♗f2+ 8 ♔d1 ♕xd5+ 9 ♘fd2! f5 10 ♘c3 ♕d4 11

♘xe4 fxe4 12 c3 ♕e3 13 ♕h5+ ♔f8 14 ♗c4 ♕xf4 15 ♕d5! allows White a mating attack (the threats are ♕d8 mate, ♘xe4 and ♖f1); 7...0-0 8 ♕xe4 ♖e8 9 ♘e5 f6 10 ♗b5! ♗d7 11 ♗e2 fxe5 12 fxe5 ± leaves Black helpless against the powerful e5- and d5-pawns; while 7...f5 8 ♗e3 ♕xd5 9 ♗xc5 ♕xc5 10 ♘c3 allows White a serious plus.

8 ♘c3 ♕e7

8...0-0 loses attractively to 9 ♘xe4 ♖e8 10 ♘e5 ♗xe4 11 ♕xe4 f6 12 d6! ♕xd6 (12...cxd6 13 ♗c4+ ♔f8 14 ♕d5) 13 ♗e3! (blocking the e-file) 13...♗xe3 14 ♕c4+ ♔h8 (14...♕e6 15 ♕xe6+ and ♗c4 +– or 14...♖e6 15 ♖d1 ♕e7 16 ♕xe6+! and ♖d8, mating) 15 ♘f7+ ♔g8 16 ♘h6+ + ♔h8 17 ♕g8+ ♖xg8 18 ♘f7 smothered mate!

9 ♗e3! ♗xe3

Not 9...♘xc3 10 ♗xc5! ♘xe2 11 ♗xe7 ♘xf4 12 ♗a3! ♘xd5 13 0-0-0 c6 14 ♘g5 ♘d7 15 ♗c4 ♗e6 16 ♖he1 and Black falls to pieces.

10 ♕xe3 ♘xc3 11 ♕xe7+ ♔xe7 12 bxc3

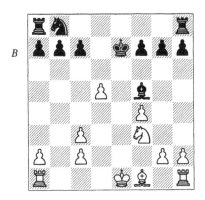

B

Plans and Counterplans:
White is threatening ♘d4, ♗d3 or
0-0-0. As for Black, he would like
to regain the pawn but he cannot
make up for his material and positional drawbacks at the same
time! For example:

a) 12...♗xc2 13 ♔d2 ♗g6 14
♖e1+ ♔d6 15 ♘d4! h6 16 ♘b5+
♔d7 17 g3! a6 18 ♗h3+ ♔d8 19
♘d4 ♘d7 20 c4 ♘c5 21 f5 ± and
the coordination of the black pieces
is non-existent (bishop on h7,
rook on a8).

b) 12...♗e4!? (a tricky move,
as after 13 c4? ♗xf3 14 gxf3 ♘d7
followed by ...♘c5 and ...♔d6 Black
is better despite being a pawn
down!) 13 ♘g5!! ♗xd5 14 0-0-0!
(development, attack!) 14...♗e6
(14...♗xa2 15 c4 or 14...c6 15 ♗d3
and ♖he1+ ±) 15 ♘xe6 fxe6 16
♗c4 ♘d7 17 ♖he1 ♘c5 18 ♗xe6!
♘xe6 19 f5 and White has good
winning prospects in the ending.

So the King's Gambit has to be
accepted!

II. King's Gambit Accepted

1 e4 e5 2 f4 exf4!

The advantage of accepting the
gambit is that Black permanently
weakens the enemy kingside; and
by releasing the central tension,
the counter-thrust ...d7-d5 also
becomes possible.

3 ♘f3

This is the King's Knight Gambit. In several other systems White
allows Black to play ...♕d8-h4+!

For instance:

a) 3 ♘c3 ♕h4+ 4 ♔e2 d5! 5
♘xd5 ♗g4+ 6 ♘f3 ♗d6 7 d4 ♘c6 8
e5 0-0-0 9 ♗xf4 (9 exd6? ♖xd6 10
c4 ♘f6 –+. The threat is ...♖he8+
and, after the disappearance of the
knight from d5, also ...♘xd4+)
9...♘ge7 10 c4 ♗b4! 11 ♗g3 ♕h5
12 ♘xe7+ ♗xe7 and White is losing as he cannot hold the pawns
on d4 and e5.

b) 3 d4 ♕h4+ 4 ♔e2 d5! 5 ♘f3
♗g4 6 exd5 ♘f6 7 ♕e1 (on 7 c4,
7...♗d6 followed by ...0-0 and
...♖e8+ or 7...c6!? come into consideration) 7...♕xe1+ 8 ♔xe1 ♗xf3
9 gxf3 ♘xd5 10 c4 ♘e3! 11 ♗xe3
fxe3, and after ...♘c6 and ...0-0-0
Black attacks d4 and invades the
undeveloped white position via
the dark squares (∓).

c) 3 ♗c4!? The King's Bishop
Gambit. Now 3...♕h4+ is again
possible, but after 4 ♔f1 White
can gain time with ♘f3, and his
king is not exposed on f1. The
best way to meet 3 ♗c4 is 3...♘f6!:
4 ♘c3 (4 e5 d5! 5 ♗b3 ♘e4 6 ♘f3
♗g4 7 0-0 ♘c6 8 d4 g5) 4...c6! 5
♗b3!? (5 d4?! d5 6 exd5 cxd5 7
♗b5+ ♘c6 8 ♗xf4 ♗d6 9 ♘ge2
0-0 10 0-0 ♗g4 ∞) 5...d5 6 exd5
cxd5 7 d4 ♗d6 8 ♘ge2 0-0 9 0-0
g5!? 10 ♘xd5 ♘c6 11 h4! h6 12
hxg5 hxg5 13 ♘ec3 with a double-edged position.

Let us get back to the most
popular line, the King's Knight
Gambit! *(D)*

In this position, **3...g5** (section
A) and **3...d5** (section B) are the

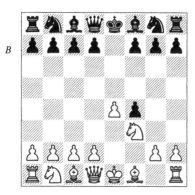

most effective weapons for Black, and we shall discuss these in detail. Besides these, a few other methods are worth mentioning:

a) 3...♗e7 4 ♗c4! (vacating the f1 square for the king. Now for example after 4...♗h4+ 5 ♔f1 and 6 d4 White has a spatial plus while Black is less developed and organized – what is the bishop doing on h4?) 4...♘f6 5 e5 ♘g4 6 0-0 (6 ♘c3 d6) 6...♘c6 7 d4 d5 8 exd6 ♗xd6 9 ♕e1+! ♘e7 10 h3 ♘h6 11 ♘e5 g5 12 h4 f6 13 hxg5 fxg5 14 ♘f3 ±. Black cannot go on protecting his g- and f-pawns (14...g4 15 ♘e5).

b) 3...d6 4 d4 (not 4 ♗c4 h6! 5 d4 g5 with resolute protection of the stolen pawn) 4...g5 5 h4 g4 6 ♘g1 ♗h6 (6...f5!? 7 ♘c3 ♘f6 8 ♗xf4 fxe4 ∞) 7 ♘e2 ♕f6 8 ♘bc3 c6 9 g3 f3 10 ♘f4 ♕e7 11 ♔f2, followed by ♗c4 and ♖e1, when White has good compensation for the pawn.

c) 3...♘f6 4 e5 ♘h5 5 d4 (5 ♗c4? d5!) 5...d6 (5...d5 6 c4! ♗e7 7 ♗e2 ♗h4+ 8 ♔f1) 6 ♕e2! d5 (the only move, because after 6...♗e7?

7 exd6 ♕xd6 8 ♕b5+! White wins a piece and the situation is similar after 6...dxe5 7 ♘xe5! ♕h4+ 8 g3! +–) 7 c4 ♗e6 8 cxd5 ♗xd5 9 ♘c3 ♘c6 10 ♗d2! ♗b4 11 ♘xd5 ♕xd5 12 0-0-0! ♕xa2 13 d5 ♗xd2+ 14 ♘xd2 and the black knight is hanging, though after 14...♕xd5 15 ♕xh5 ♕xe5 16 ♕xe5 ♘xe5 17 ♖e1 f6 18 ♘c4 0-0-0 he has three pawns for the piece. The ensuing position is assessed by theory as slightly better for White.

A. Classical Variation

1 e4 e5 2 f4 exf4 3 ♘f3 g5!?
The most ambitious continuation. Black protects his f4-pawn and at the same time is ready to chase the knight from f3 with ...g5-g4 in order to obtain the subsequent check ...♕d8-h4+.

4 h4
This is the last chance to force Black to play ...g5-g4 and thus to loosen up his kingside. If White puts off playing h2-h4 then Black can play ...♗g7 and on h2-h4, he can play ...h7-h6 as the h8-rook is protected.

Black need not fear 4 ♘c3: 4...♗g7 (White can produce extensive complications on 4...g4: 5 ♘e5 ♕h4+ 6 g3! fxg3 7 ♕xg4 ♕xg4 – 7...g2+? 8 ♕xh4 gxh1♕ 9 ♕h5! ♗d6 10 ♕xf7+ ♔d8 11 d4! and ♗g5 +– – 8 ♘xg4 d5 9 ♗h3! ∞, while 5 d4! gxf3 6 ♗xf4! is also possible with a considerable advantage in development and an attack along the f-file after queen-side castling) 5 d4 (on 5 h4 the right direction for Black is not 5...g4? 6 ♘g1 d6 7 d4 ♗h6 8 ♘ge2 as the pawn f4 has become feeble, but 5...h6! with a massive king-side) 5...d6 6 g3! ♘c6! 7 d5 ♘e5 8 gxf4 gxf4 9 ♗xf4 ♗g4 with active play for Black.

4 d4 is also harmless: 4...♗g7 5 h4 h6 6 g3!? d5! 7 exd5 g4 8 ♘e5 ♕xd5 9 ♖h2 ♗xe5 10 ♖e2 ♘c6 11 ♗xf4 ♕xd4 and Black has the ad-vantage.

An exciting fight is promised by 4 ♗c4:

a) **4...g4** 5 0-0!? (or 5 ♘e5 ♕h4+ 6 ♔f1 ♘c6 7 ♘xf7 ♗c5 8 ♕e1 g3 and now 9 ♘xh8? would be a mistake due to 9... ♗f2 10 ♕d1 ♘f6 11 d4 d5! 12 exd5 ♗g4 13 ♗e2 ♘xd4 14 ♗xg4 ♘xg4, and White cannot stop 15...♘xh2+, but after 9 d4! ♗xd4 10 ♘d2! Black has to struggle to hang on in view of the threat of 11 ♘f3!) 5...gxf3 6 ♕xf3 ♕f6 7 e5!? (also worth considering is 7 c3 and then d2-d4) 7...♕xe5 8 ♗xf7+!? ♔xf7 9 d4! ♕xd4+ 10 ♗e3 ♕f6 11 ♗xf4 ♘e7 12 ♘c3 ♘f5 13 ♘e4 ♕g6 14 g4 ♗e7, and now after 15 ♔h1 ♘h4 16 ♕b3+ ♔e8 17 ♖ae1 or 15 ♗g3!? White has an attack, although he is of course material down. Neither practice nor theory have demonstrated who is better in this extremely unclear position.

b) **4...♗g7!?** 5 0-0 (after 5 h4 h6 6 d4 d6 White has hardly any compensation for the pawn) 5...d6

6 d4 h6 (permitting the develop-ment of the knight from g8) 7 c3 (or 7 g3 ♗h3 8 ♖f2 ♘c6 9 c3 ♘f6 10 ♕c2 ♕d7, followed by ...0-0-0, and the weak white king position gives Black the advantage) 7...♘c6 8 g3!? ♗h3! (8...g4 9 ♘h4 f3 10 ♘d2 ♘f6 – 10...♗f6 11 ♕b3! – 11 ♘f5 ♗xf5 12 exf5 0-0 13 ♗d3 ∞) 9 gxf4! (9 ♖f2 ♕d7 ∓) 9...♕d7! and now White in the spirit of the po-sition, does not go in for the mis-erly 10 ♖f2? ♘f6 11 ♕e1 0-0-0, when after ...♖he8 he would face serious problems, but plays 10 f5! ♗xf1 11 ♕xf1 with chances for both sides.

4...g4 5 ♘e5

5 ♘g5 does not work owing to 5...h6 6 ♘xf7 ♔xf7 7 ♗c4+ (7 ♕xg4? ♘f6 8 ♕xf4 ♗d6 −+, while for 7 d4 f3!! 8 ♗c4+ d5!, see 7 ♗c4+) 7...d5! 8 ♗xd5+ ♔g7 9 d4 f3!! 10 gxf3 ♘f6! 11 ♘c3 ♗b4 12 ♗b3 ♘c6 13 ♗e3 ♘a5! and with watchful play Black has disarmed the white initiative while perse-vering the extra piece. The key move of the defence was 9...f3!! which sealed the f-file, destroyed White's king position and slowed down the development of the white pieces.

5...♘f6!

Defending the g4-pawn by at-tacking its counterpart on e4. A similar idea, but in a weaker form, is 5...h5 6 ♗c4 ♖h7 7 d4 d6 8 ♘d3 f3 9 gxf3 ♗e7 10 ♗e3 ♗xh4+ 11 ♔d2 gxf3 12 ♕xf3 ♘c6 13 c3, and Black has problems developing while White can obtain a strong initiative via ♔c2, ♘d2 and ♖af1.

6 d4

Necessary, in view of 6 ♘xg4 ♘xe4 7 ♕e2 ♕e7 8 ♘c3 ♘g3 9 ♕xe7+ ♗xe7 10 ♖h2 d5! −+ and 6 ♗c4 d5 7 exd5 ♗d6 8 d4 0-0!? 9 0-0 (9 ♗xf4? ♘h5 10 g3 f6 11 ♘d3 ♘xg3! −+) 9...♘h5 10 ♘xg4 ♕xh4 11 ♘h2 ♘g3 12 ♖e1 ♗f5, followed by ...♘d7 and ...♖ae8, when Black is on top.

6...d6 7 ♘d3 ♘xe4 8 ♗xf4 ♕e7!

Attacking along the e-file and preparing for queenside castling.

9 ♕e2 ♘c6!

Also possible is 9...♗g7 10 c3 h5 11 ♘d2 ♘xd2 12 ♔xd2 ♕xe2+ 13 ♗xe2 ♘c6 and ...♗e6 =.

10 c3 ♗f5 11 ♘d2 0-0-0 12 0-0-0 ♖e8

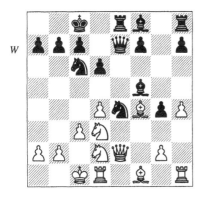

White has insufficient counterplay for the pawn. For instance:

a) **13 g3?** (this loses material) ♘xc3! 14 ♕xe7 ♘xa2+ 15 ♔b1 ♖xe7 16 ♔xa2 ♗xd3 17 ♗xd3 ♘b4+ and Black wins.

b) **13 d5** ♘xd2 14 ♕xd2 ♘e5 is clearly better for Black.

c) **13 ♖e1** ♕e6! 14 ♔b1 ♘xd2+ 15 ♗xd2 ♕xe2 16 ♗xe2 ♖xe2! and ...♗xd3+ wins a piece.,

d) **13 ♘c4** ♕d7 14 ♘e3 h5, with ...♗h6 to follow, is again good for Black.

So we can see that the main line of the King's Gambit is favourable for Black. But there are many, many opportunities for both sides to deviate from the main line and possibly to find new moves that will enrich this romantic variation.

B. The modern answer

1 e4 e5 2 f4 exf4 3 ♘f3 d5 4 exd5

On 4 e5? Black plays 4...g5! 5 d4 g4, when the piece sacrifice 6 ♗xf4 gxf3 7 ♕xf3 c6 8 ♗d3 ♗e6 is hopeless as White is unable to strengthen his attack with ♗f1-c4.

4...♘f6 *(D)*

Black's other options are:

a) **4...♕xd5** 5 ♘c3 ♕e6+ (after 5...♕h5 6 ♗e2 ♗g4 7 0-0 ± White's plan is to follow up with d2-d4 and h2-h3) 6 ♗e2 ♗d6 7 0-0 ♘e7 8 d4 0-0 9 ♘g5! ♕h6 10 ♘ce4! ±.

b) **4...c6** 5 d4 cxd5 6 ♗xf4 ♘f6 7 ♗d3 ±. White has an easy attack with 0-0, c2-c3, ♘bd2, ♘e5, ♘df3, ♕e1 and ♕g3 (♕h4).

c) **4...♗d6** 5 d4 ♘f6 6 c4 ♗g4 7 ♗d3 0-0 8 0-0 b6 9 ♕c2 c5 10 b4!

and the strength of the white centre pawns makes itself felt.

d) 4...g5 5 ♕e2+! and no matter how Black interposes on e7, the g5-pawn is *en prise*.

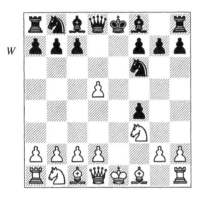

This is the basic position of 'the modern answer'. White has two more pawns on the queenside and in the centre while Black has the same advantage on the kingside and this naturally determines their objectives. White would like to advance his central pawns and restrict the black pieces, which could also lead to the capture of the f4-pawn. Black must protect f4 and try to gain counterplay through piece activity, helped by the weakness of the e3-square, caused by the lack of a pawn on f2. He can also play along the e-file with his rook and on the f5- and g4-squares with his bishop. Let us see these plans in practice:

a) 5 c4 c6!? (or 5...b5 6 ♘c3 bxc4 7 ♗xc4 ♗d6 8 d4 ♘bd7 9 0-0 0-0 10 ♘e5! ♘xe5 11 dxe5 ♗xe5 12 ♗xf4 ♗xf4 13 ♖xf4 ♕d6 14

♕d4 with a slight edge for White) 6 d4 (6 dxc6 ♘xc6 7 d4 ♗g4!? 8 d5 ♗xf3 9 ♕xf3 ♘e5 10 ♕xf4 ♗d6 with tremendous play for Black. The threat is 11...♘d3+, and if the white queen moves then a strong attack can be generated by the moves ...0-0, ...♖e8, ...♖c8 and ...♘eg4) 6...♗b4+ (on 6...cxd5 7 c5! is most inconvenient) 7 ♘c3 cxd5 8 ♗xf4 0-0 9 ♗e2 dxc4! 10 ♗xc4 (or 10 0-0 ♗xc3 11 bxc3 ♗e6!) 10...♘d5 11 ♗xd5 ♕xd5 12 0-0 ♗xc3 13 bxc3 ♗e6 is more comfortable for Black. His plan is ...♘c6, ...♖ac8 and ...♘a5, with an initiative on the vulnerable white queenside.

b) 5 ♗c4 ♘xd5 6 0-0 (6 ♗xd5 ♕xd5 7 ♘c3 ♕f5 8 ♕e2+ ♗e7 9 d4 c6 10 0-0 ♗e6 11 ♘e5 g5! 12 g3 ♘d7 and the white king position becomes vulnerable in the end) 6...♗e7 7 d4 ♗e6 (Black cannot go far wrong with 7...0-0 either) 8 ♕e2 0-0 9 ♘c3 ♘c6! (9...c6?! is weaker: 10 ♘xd5 ♗xd5 11 ♗xd5 cxd5 12 ♗xf4 ± and Black will always have to keep an eye on the d5-pawn) 10 ♘e4 ♖e8! 11 ♗b3 ♗f6! and it is White who must fight for equality.

c) 5 ♘c3 ♘xd5 6 ♘xd5 ♕xd5 7 d4 ♗e7 (7...♗g4!? 8 ♗xf4 ♘c6 9 ♗xc7!? ♖c8 10 ♗f4 ♕e4+! 11 ♕e2 ♗xf3 12 gxf3 ♕xe2+ 13 ♗xe2 ♘xd4 is more than attractive for Black. Instead of 10 ♗f4, White can seek to improve with 10 ♗g3 ♕e4+ 11 ♔f2!?) 8 c4 (8 ♗d3 ♗g4 9 ♗xf4 ♘c6 10 c3 0-0-0 =) 8...♕e4+

9 ♗e2 (9 ♔f2 ♗f5! 10 ♗e2 ♘c6 11 ♖e1 0-0-0 12 ♗f1 ♕c2 13 ♕xc2 ♗xc2 14 ♗xf4 ♖he8 ∞. The d4-pawn is attacked, and if White advances it then Black can play ...♗c5+ and ...♘b4) 9...♘c6 10 0-0 ♗f5 11 ♖e1 0-0-0 12 ♗f1 ♕c2 13 ♕xc2 ♗xc2 14 ♗xf4 ♖he8 with chances for both sides. Black can counterbalance White's spatial plus by exerting pressure on d4.

d) 5 ♗b5+!? (In this way White can exchange his d5 pawn for Black's c-pawn and try to exploit his central pawn majority. Black has to play more accurately than in the previous lines) 5...c6! (5...♗d7 6 ♕e2+ ♗e7 7 d6! cxd6 8 d4 0-0 9 ♘c3 ♖e8 10 ♗xd7 ♘bxd7 11 0-0 ♕b6 12 a4!? with the threat of a4-a5 followed by ♗xf4, regaining the pawn with a superior position) 6 dxc6 ♘xc6 (on 6...bxc6, White gets on top with 7 ♗c4 ♘d5 – 7...♗d6 8 ♕e2+! ♕e7 9 ♕xe7+ ♔xe7 10 0-0 ± – 8 0-0 ♗d6 9 ♘c3 ♗e6 10 ♘e4 ♗e7 – 10...♗c7 is strongly met by 11 b3, and then ♗a3!, or 11 ♘eg5 – 11 ♗b3 – the threat was ...♘e3 – 11...0-0 12 d4 ±. White's plan is ♕e2 and c2-c4, his target being the pawn on f4) 7 d4 ♗d6 (7...♕a5+ 8 ♘c3 ♗b4 runs into 9 0-0! ♗xc3 10 ♕e2+ and 11

bxc3 with a great advantage in development) 8 0-0 (Black can meet 8 ♕e2+ ♗e6 9 ♘g5 0-0 10 ♘xe6 with 10...fxe6 11 ♗xc6 bxc6 12 0-0 – not 12 ♕xe6+? ♔h8 13 0-0 f3! 14 ♖xf3 ♖e8! with a tremendous attack for Black. On any queen move the threat is ...♖e1+ and ...♘g4 – 12...♕c7! 13 ♘d2 – 13 ♕xe6+?! ♔h8 14 ♘d2 ♖ae8 15 ♕h3 c5! 16 ♘c4 ♖e2 and Black controls the game – 13...e5! =. However, even more interesting is 10...♕b6!?, e.g. 11 ♗xc6 bxc6 12 ♘xf8 ♖e8 13 ♕xe8 ♘xe8 14 c3 ♔xf8, when the black queen appears to be stronger than the two rooks due to White's underdevelopment and vulnerable kingside) 8...0-0 9 c4!? (or 9 ♘bd2 ♗c7! 10 c3 ♗f5 11 ♘c4 ♘d5 12 ♗xc6 bxc6 13 ♘fe5 g5! and, since the white centre has not been mobilized, the bishop on c1 is passive and the knight on e5 is vulnerable. For example, 14 ♘xc6 ♕e8 15 ♘6e5 f6! 16 ♘f3 ♕h5!? and Black has a dangerous offensive) 9...♗g4 10 ♘c3 ♖c8 11 ♘e2 a6! and now 12 ♗xc6 ♖xc6 13 b3 (13 c5? is a mistake owing to 13...♗xf3 14 ♖xf3 ♗xc5) 13...♘h5 or 12 ♗a4 ♘h5 produces a complicated battle with chances for both sides.

Vienna Game

1 e4 e5 2 ♘c3

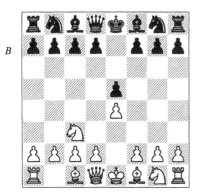

This move attempts to dissuade Black from playing ...d7-d5. Later he will aim for either ♗c4 or f2-f4 (or possibly both!) and will place his g1-knight, according to Black's setup, on e2 or f3.

2...♘f6

Other options are:

a) 2...♗c5?! 3 ♘f3! d6 (3...♘c6 4 ♘xe5! ♘xe5 – 4...♗xf2+ 5 ♔xf2 ♘xe5 6 d4 ± – 5 d4 ♗d6 6 dxe5 ♗xe5 7 f4 ±) 4 d4 exd4 5 ♘xd4 ♘c6 6 ♗e3 ±.

b) 2...♘c6 3 ♗c4 (3 f4?! exf4! 4 ♘f3 g5 5 d4 g4 6 ♗c4 gxf3 7 0-0 and now both 7...d5 8 exd5 ♗g4 9 ♕d2 ♘ce7 10 ♕xf4 ♘h6, and 7...♘xd4! 8 ♗xf4 – 8 ♕xd4? ♕g5!! –+ – 8...♗g7! offer Black chances of surviving with his extra piece intact) 3...♗c5?! (for 3...♘f6 see variation II) 4 ♕g4! g6 (4...♕f6? 5 ♘d5! ♕xf2+ 6 ♔d1 and besides

♘xc7 and ♕xg7, White also threatens 7 ♘h3 ♕d4 8 d3, followed by c2-c3 catching the black queen and excluding it from the assault ♘g5, ♖f1 and ♕h5) 5 ♕f3 ♘f6 6 ♘ge2 d6 7 h3!?, followed by d3 and Black is worse due to the enforced weakening ...g7-g6.

3 ♗c4

Other typical continuations are:

a) **3 g3** (White does not achieve an advantage by fianchettoing his f1-bishop in any line of the Open Games, because the bishop is less well placed on g2 than, for instance, c4. Furthermore, after the fianchetto the king's knight often has to go to the less active e2-square) 3...♗c5 (also playable is 3...d5 4 exd5 ♘xd5 5 ♗g2 ♘xc3 6 bxc3 ♗d6 and ...0-0, when Black is planning to neutralize the bishop on g2 by means of the manoeuvre ...♘d7, ...♖b8, ...b7-b6 and ...♗b7) 4 ♗g2 0-0 5 d3 ♖e8 6 ♘ge2 c6 7 0-0 d5 =.

b) **3 f4!?** d5! (the only reply, as on for example 3...d6? 4 ♘f3 ♘c6 5 ♗c4 ♗g4 6 d3 ♗e7 7 h3 ♗xf3 8 ♕xf3, White has an immense plus owing to the bishop pair and the chance of a kingside pawn-roller) 4 fxe5 (the moves 4 exd5 e4 or 4...exf4 lead to the King's Gambit) 4...♘xe4 5 ♘f3 (on 5 ♕f3, 5...f5! is pretty strong, as after 6 exf6 ♘xf6 Black can exploit the awkward position of the white queen with ...♗e7 and ...0-0. Since 5 d3 ♛h4+ 6 g3 ♘xg3 7 ♘f3 ♛h5 8 ♘xd5 is good for White, instead of 5...♛h4+ Black should play 5...♘xc3 6 bxc3 ♗e7 7 ♘f3 0-0 8 d4 f6! = and Black can undermine the outpost at e5) 5...♗e7 6 d4 (or 6 ♛e2 ♘xc3 7 dxc3 0-0 8 ♗f4 c5 9 0-0-0 ♛a5 followed by ...♗e6 and ...♘c6 =) 6...0-0 7 ♗d3 f5 8 exf6 ♗xf6! 9 0-0 ♘c6 10 ♘xe4 dxe4 11 ♗xe4 ♘xd4 =.

Let us get back to 3 ♗c4.

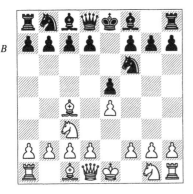

Black's two most important moves are:

I. 3...♘xe4 and
II. 3...♘c6.

Besides these moves Black can also consider the somewhat forgotten 3...♗c5, as after 4 d3 d6 5 f4 ♗e6! 6 ♗xe6 fxe6 7 fxe5 dxe5 and then ...♘c6 and ...0-0 Black is not badly placed since his doubled isolated e-pawns control all of the central squares.

I. 1 e4 e5 2 ♘c3 ♘f6 3 ♗c4 ♘xe4!?

In principle it is a good idea to reduce White's central control with exchanges. Both 4 ♘xe4 d5 and 4 ♗xf7+ ♔xf7 5 ♘xe4 d5! 6 ♛f3+ ♔g8 7 ♘g5 ♛d7! (not 7...♛xg5?? ♛xd5+ and mate!) 8 ♘e2 h6 are excellent for Black, so White steers the game straight into a tactical minefield!

4 ♛h5! ♘d6 5 ♗b3!?

The dull 5 ♛xe5+ ♛e7 6 ♛xe7+ ♗xe7 7 ♗b3 ♘f5 8 ♘d5 ♗d8 leads to complete equality.

5...♘c6

A quieter position is reached after 5...♗e7 6 ♘f3 (not 6 ♛xe5?! 0-0, followed by ...♘c6, when the white queen is on the run) 6...♘c6 7 ♘xe5 g6!? 8 ♛e2 and now 8...0-0 or 8...♘d4!? with chances for both sides.

6 ♘b5!

Direct play. White threatens to deliver mate on f7 by getting rid of the knight on d6. As the black queen is tied to the protection of the c7-pawn, the following moves are practically forced.

6...g6 7 ♛f3 f5

Black should avoid the line 7...f6? 8 ♘xc7+ ♛xc7 9 ♛xf6 and rook on h8 falls.

8 ♛d5

Now the queen must move from d8 to protect the f7-square.

8...♛e7 9 ♘xc7+ ♔d8 10 ♘xa8 b6!

White has won a rook but his knight a8 is doomed and Black is ready to counterattack with ...♗b7 and ...♘d4.

11 ♘xb6 axb6 12 ♕f3

Had Black played 8...♕f6?! instead of 8...♕e7 (so that his queen would now be standing on f6 instead of e7) then the road to simplification would be open with 12 d4! ♘xd4 13 ♘f3 ♗b7 14 ♕xd4! exd4 15 ♗g5.

12...♗b7 13 d3 ♘d4 14 ♕h3 *(D)*

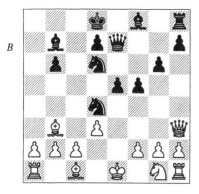

Plans and Counterplans:
White would like to secure his material plus (the exchange and a pawn) by castling queenside, while Black must exploit his development to launch an attack against the black king. He therefore needs to open up the centre, for example: 14...e4! 15 ♗e3 exd3 16 0-0-0 ♘xc2 17 ♗xb6+ ♔e8, and now with 18 ♕xd3 ♗h6+ 19 ♔b1 ♗e4 20 ♗xc2! ♗xd3 21 ♗xd3 White can sacrifice his queen and launch an offensive against the enemy king

in the middle. This line demonstrates how material can transform into initiative and attack on the chessboard.

II. 1 e4 e5 2 ♘c3 ♘f6 3 ♗c4 ♘c6

4 d3

On either 4 ♘f3 or 4 ♘ge2 Black would play 4...♘xe4 5 ♘xe4 d5. In fact, even after 4 f4, 4...♘xe4! is good: 5 ♗xf7+ ♔xf7 6 ♘xe4 d5 7 ♘g5+ ♔g8 8 d3 exf4 9 ♗xf4 h6 10 ♘5f3 g5! with ...♗g7 to follow and Black is better.

4...♗b4

Although Black can gain the bishop pair after 4...♘a5 5 ♘ge2 ♘xc4 6 dxc4 ♗c5 7 0-0 d6, it is White who is a little better due to his control of the centre: 8 ♕d3 c6 9 b3! ♗e6 10 ♘a4 ♘d7 11 ♘xc5 ♘xc5 12 ♕e3 and f2-f4 ±. The bishop on c1 can find targets (the pawns on d6 and e5) easier than its counterpart on e6. Worth considering is 4...♗c5!? 5 ♗g5 h6 6 ♗h4 d6 7 ♘a4 ♗b6 8 ♘xb6 axb6 9 f3 (preparing a bolt-hole for the dark-squared bishop) 9...♕e7 and ...♗e6, with an even position.

5 ♗g5

5 f4 and 5 ♘e2 are well met by 5...d5, but not 5 ♘f3: 5...d5?! 6 exd5 ♘xd5 7 0-0! ♗xc3 (7...♘xc3 8 bxc3 ♗xc3 9 ♘g5! 0-0 10 ♕h5 +−) 8 bxc3 0-0 9 ♘g5 h6 10 ♘e4 and White stands somewhat better. Black should therefore meet 5 ♘f3 with 5...d6 6 0-0 ♗xc3 (otherwise White jumps from c3 to d5

and the bishop on b4 turns out to be a spectator) 7 bxc3 ♘a5 8 ♗b3 ♘xb3 9 axb3 0-0 =.

5...h6!

The bishop must be forced to show its hand. If now 6 ♗h4 then after 6...d6 7 ♘e2 ♗e6 8 0-0 g5 9 ♗g3 h5! Black could exploit the position of the bishop at g3.

6 ♗xf6 ♗xc3+!

After 6...♕xf6 7 ♘ge2 and 0-0 White threatens ♘c3-d5.

7 bxc3 ♕xf6 8 ♘e2 d6 9 ♕d2 ♗e6 = *(D)*

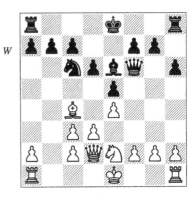

Plans and Counterplans:

The mass exchange of the minor pieces has led to an equal position. After both 10 ♗b3 ♗xb3 11 axb3 and 10 ♗b5 Black is justified in considering ...♕g5! The queen cannot be captured by White, as the black pawn on g5 and open h-file would strengthen Black's kingside influence. If the queen is not exchanged then it creates at least a sliver of tension in the otherwise dormant position.

Bishop's Opening

1 e4 e5 2 ♗c4

White immediately develops his bishop to a dangerous place from where it controls the d5-square and attacks f7. But as the bishop cannot act alone, Black can easily equalize or force White to transpose into complicated lines of other openings.

2...♘f6!

This is the natural reply, both developing and at the same time preparing the equalizing move ...d7-d5. 2...♕g5? is rebuffed by 3 ♘f3 ♕xg2 4 ♖g1 ♕h3 5 ♗xf7+ +−, and 2...♗e7? loses material in no time: 3 ♕h5! +−, while 2...f5? is best met by 3 d3! (3 exf5 ♘f6 followed by ...d7-d5 is favourable for Black) 3...♘f6 4 f4! d6 5 ♘f3 fxe4 6 dxe4, when the pawn on e4 is defended by the mate threat ♕d5, and the strength of the c4-bishop has been multiplied due to the advance of Black's pawn from f7. 2...c6?! is premature: 3 d4! d5 4 exd5 cxd5 5 ♗b5+ ♗d7 6 ♗xd7+ ♘xd7 7 dxe5 ♘xe5 8 ♘e2 followed by 0-0 and ♘bc3, and now Black must worry about his isolated d5-pawn (±). 2...♗c5!? is interesting, though, for example 3 c3 d5! 4 ♗xd5 (4 exd5 ♗xf2+! 5 ♔xf2 ♕h4+ and 6...♕xc4 is advantageous for Black) 4...♘f6 5 ♕f3 0-0, and now after 6 d4 exd4 7 ♗g5 dxc3 (7...♗e7!?) 8 ♗xf6 c2! 9 ♘c3 ♕xf6 10 ♕xf6 gxf6 followed by ...c7-c6 and ...f7-f5, or 6 ♗c4 ♗g4 7 ♕d3 ♕e7 Black obtains good play.

3 d3

3 ♘c3 leads to one of the basic positions of the Vienna Game. Two tricky continuations are:

a) 3 ♘f3?! ♘xe4 4 ♘xe5 (after 4 ♘c3 ♘xc3 5 dxc3 f6!? 6 0-0 d6 7 ♘h4 g6 8 f4 ♕e7 9 f5 ♕g7 10 ♕f3 ♗e7, followed by ...♘c6 and ...♗d7 White is struggling to prove the correctness of his sacrifice) 4...♕e7! 5 d4 d6 6 ♗xf7+ ♔d8 7 0-0 dxe5 8 dxe5+ ♗d7 and although White definitely has some compensation it is insufficient to justify such a large material disadvantage.

b) 3 d4 exd4 4 ♘f3 (4 e5 is met by the typical 4...d5!, solving all Black's problems since 5 exf6 dxc4 or 5 ♗b3 ♘e4 are both better for him) 4...♘xe4 5 ♕xd4 ♘f6 6 ♗g5 ♗e7 7 ♘c3 ♘c6 8 ♕h4 d6, followed by ...♗e6, and Black completes his development (∞).

3...c6!?

3...d5? would justify White's conception: 4 exd5 ♘xd5 5 ♘f3 ♘c6 6 0-0 ♗e7 7 ♖e1 f6 8 c3!, threatening 9 ♕b3 or 9 d4. (Black could only defend his e5-pawn by weakening the light squares) Alternatively, 3...♗e7!? 4 ♘c3 (4 f4? d5! 5 exd5 exf4 6 ♗xf4 ♘xd5 provides an overwhelming military success for Black: the white centre has been dissolved, the e3-square is weak and the first player is still undeveloped!) 4...c6! (not 4...0-0 5 f4! ± and Black cannot arrange ...d7-d5) 5 ♘f3 d6 6 a4! (to stop ...b7-b5) 6...0-0 and Black's plan may be either ...♗g4 or ...b6, ♗b7, ...a7-a6 and ...b6-b5. For 3...♗c5 4 ♘f3 ♘c6, see the Italian Game.

4 ♘f3

Neither 4 ♕e2 ♗e7 5 f4 d5! 6 exd5 exf4 7 ♗xf4 ♘xd5 nor 4 f4 exf4 5 ♗xf4 d5 6 exd5 ♘xd5 give any advantage to White. A general principle is that on f2-f4, Black plays ...d7-d5 and then on exd5 he achieves at least an equal game with ...exf4 and ...♘xd5.

4...d5 5 ♗b3

If White relieves the tension then Black is better due to his central control: 5 exd5 cxd5 6 ♗b5+ (6 ♗b3 ♗b4+! 7 c3 ♗d6 and now White cannot attack the pawn on d5 with ♘c3) 6...♗d7 7 ♗xd7+ ♘bxd7 and ...♗d6, ...0-0 ∓.

5...a5!?

Black would like to force a weakening of the enemy queenside. 5...dxe4? is a lemon due to 6 ♘g5! but the simple 5...♗d6 is playable: 6 ♘c3 dxe4 (after 6...d4? 7 ♘e2 followed by 0-0, ♘e1 White blows the centre to pieces with f2-f4) 7 dxe4 ♘a6, with a possible ...♕e7 and ...♗e6 to follow later.

6 ♘c3

Black would meet 6 a4 with 6...♗b4+! 7 c3 ♗d6 and ...♘a6-c5.

6...♗b4

Threatening 7...♗xc3+ followed by ...a5-a4, catching the bishop!

7 a3 ♗xc3+ 8 bxc3 ♘bd7 9 exd5!

Otherwise Black takes on e4 and the white pawn structure falls apart.

9...♘xd5!

After 9...cxd5 10 0-0 and ♖e1, ♗g5 Black will have problems with both of his pawns (e5, d5).

10 0-0 0-0

10...♘xc3? 11 ♕e1 ±.

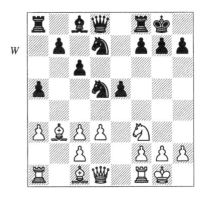

W

Plans and Counterplans:
Black would like to restrain the white bishops in order to allow his better pawn structure to prevail. White plans to open the position and obtain an attack for his minor pieces. For example 11 ♖e1 ♖e8 (11...♘xc3?! 12 ♕d2 ♘b5 13 ♗b2 and the e5-pawn is hanging, while White also threatens 14 ♘g5) 12 c4! (12 ♗d2 f6 stabilizes Black's position) 12...♘e7 13 ♘g5! h6! 14 ♘e4 a4 15 ♗a2 c5 with equality.

Scandinavian Defence

1 e4 d5

Only a few years ago chess theory considered this line to be very poor, as White gets the chance to attack the black queen with a tempo. This is true, but after exchanging the e4-pawn Black can quickly develop his pieces. In this clash of positional principles Black obtains a fully viable position, although he cannot fully counterbalance White's normal opening advantage.

2 exd5

2 e5? is mistaken in view of 2...♗f5 3 d4 e6 4 c3 c5 5 ♘f3 ♘c6 and Black will shortly attack the white centre with ...♕b6, ...♗g4, and ...♘h6-f5. This position is basically an Advance Caro-Kann with an extra tempo for Black (there he plays ...c7-c6-c5 instead of ...c7-c5) or an Advance French in which the black light-squared bishop is not clogged behind the black pawn chain. After 2 exd5 Black has two ways to regain the pawn:

I. 2...♕xd5 and
II. 2...♘f6.

I. 1 e4 d5 2 exd5 ♕xd5

---

3 ♘c3

Not 3 d4 e5!

3...♕a5!?

After 3...♕e5+ 4 ♗e2 White will win further tempi by attacking the enemy queen. On 3...♕d6 or 3...♕d8 White simply develops normally (d2-d4, ♗c4, ♘f3 or ♘ge2) and achieves an advantage in time and space.

4 d4 ♘f6 5 ♘f3 ♗g4

On 5...♘c6 the waiting move 6 h3! is very strong (after 6...♗f5 7 ♗b5! White can smash Black's pawn structure with ♗xc6). Or 5...c6 6 ♗c4 ♗g4 7 ♕d3!? ♘bd7 8 ♗d2 with a huge plus in view of the plan 0-0-0, ♖he1, h2-h3 and ♘c3-d5. Black loses immediately after 8...♗f5 9 ♕e2 ♗xc2 10 ♘b5! and ♘d6+, ♘xf7+.

6 h3 ♗h5

Or 6...♗xf3 7 ♕xf3 c6 8 ♗d2 ±.

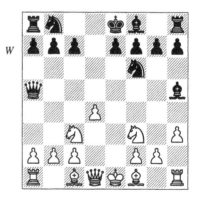

Plans and Counterplans:
White used to run down Black with **7 g4 ♗g6 8 ♘e5 e6** (not

8...♘bd7 9 ♘c4 ♕a6 10 ♗f4 threatening to win the queen with 10 ♘d6+!) 9 h4 ♗b4 10 ♖h3, but then Black came up with 10...♗xc3+ and now 11 bxc3 ♘bd7 =. And on 10 ♗d2 Black again has defensive resources: 10...♕b6 11 ♗g2 ♗xc3! 12 bxc3 ♗e4 13 ♗xe4 ♘xe4 14 ♖b1 ♕a6 15 ♕f3 ♘d6. White has to accept that he cannot advantageously undertake immediate action and settle for a more peaceful positional plan, such as **7 ♗d2!?** e6 (7...♘c6 8 ♗b5) 8 ♗c4 (threatening 9 ♘d5), when he stands better after 8...♗b4 9 a3 ♗xc3 10 ♗xc3 ♕b6 11 ♕e2. He can castle either side and besides d4-d5 he can consider g2-g4 followed by ♘e5.

II. 1 d4 d5 2 exd5 ♘f6

---

3 d4

White should not attempt to hold on to the pawn: 3 c4 c6!? 4 dxc6 (for 4 d4 cxd5 see the Panov Attack in the Caro-Kann Defence) 4...♘xc6 5 d3 e5 and Black has splendid compensation for the pawn (...♗c5, ...0-0, ...♗f5, ...♕d7, ...♖ad8, ...♖fe8 and ...e5-e4). Or on 3 ♗b5+ ♗d7 (3...♘bd7 4 c4 a6 5 ♗a4 b5!? 6 cxb5 ♘xd5 followed by ...♗b7 is unclear) 4 ♗c4 ♗g4 5 f3 ♗f5 (5...♗c8!? and ...♘b8-d7-b6) 6 ♘c3 and the sacrifice 6...c6!? or 6...♘bd7 intending ...♘b6-d5 are both interesting. Instead of 4...♗g4, 4...b5!? 5 ♗b3 a5! also deserves attention, e.g. 6 a4!? bxa4 7

♗a2 ♗g4 8 f3 ♗c8! 9 ♘c3 ♗b7 with ...♘xd5, ...e7-e6, ...♗e7, ...0-0 to follow, with an equal position.

3...♘xd5 4 c4 ♘b6

On 4...♘f6 5 ♘f3 and then ♘c3, ♗e2, 0-0, ♗e3, ♕d2, ♖ad1 with an edge for White.

5 ♘f3

5 ♘c3 e5!?

5...g6

The other way is 5...♗g4 6 ♗e2 (on 6 c5 not 6...♘d5? 7 ♕b3 but 6...♘6d7 followed by ...e7-e6 and ...♘c6) 6...e6 (6...♘c6 7 d5 ♗xf3 8 gxf3!? ♘e5 9 f4 ♘ed7 10 ♘c3 and ♗e3, ♕c2, 0-0-0) 7 0-0 ♘c6 8 ♘c3 ♗e7 (8...♗xf3 9 ♗xf3 ♘xc4 10 d5!) 9 d5! exd5 10 cxd5 ♘b4 11 ♕d4! ♗xf3 12 ♗xf3 0-0 (12...♘c2 13 ♕xg7 ♗f6 14 ♕h6 ♘xa1 15 ♖e1+ +−) 13 ♕e4! ±.

6 h3

This move protects the pawn on d4 by preventing ...♗g4.

6...♗g7 7 ♘c3 0-0

After 7...c5 8 ♗e3!? cxd4 9 ♗xd4 0-0 10 ♗xg7 ♔xg7 11 ♕d4+! both the endgame and the middlegame are better for White due to Black's misplaced knight on b6.

8 ♗e3 ♘c6

Or 8...c5 9 d5! followed by ♕d2 and ♖ad1.

9 ♕d2 e5

9...♖e8 10 0-0-0 e5 11 d5 ♘a5 12 b3! e4 13 ♘d4 c5 14 dxc6 ♘xc6 (14...bxc6 15 c5! ♘d5 16 ♘xd5 cxd5 17 ♗b5) 15 ♘xc6 ♕xd2+ 16 ♔xd2 bxc6 17 ♔c2 with a slight advantage for White.

10 d5

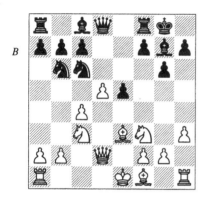

Plans and Counterplans:
Where should the knight go? On
10...♘e7 11 g4! f5 12 0-0-0! e4 (or
12...fxg4 13 ♘g5! threatening 14
c5 ♘d7 15 ♘e6 as well as 14 hxg4
♗xg4 15 ♗h3 with an immense
attack against squares h7 and e6,
and on 13...h6 14 ♘ge4 ±) 13 ♘g5
h6 14 ♘e6 ♗xe6 15 dxe6 and again
Black's misplaced knight on b6
tips the scales in White's favour.

10...♘a5 is more complicated:
11 b3 (11 ♗xb6 axb6 12 b4? ♘b3!
–+) 11...f5 and now 12 0-0-0?! e4
13 ♘e1 (on 13 ♘g5 either 13...f4!?
14 ♗xf4 ♕f6 or 13...h6 14 ♘e6

♗xe6 15 dxe6 ♕f6 are Black's
pleasant alternatives, while on 13
♘d4? f4! 14 ♗xf4 ♗xd4 15 ♕xd4
♖xf4 16 ♕c5 ♕f6 White is in grave
danger) 13...♕f6 14 ♗d4 ♕xd4 15
♕xd4 ♗xd4 16 ♖xd4 c5 17 ♖d1
♗d7 and then after the regrouping ...♘c8-d6 the game is level. After **10...♘a5** 11 b3 f5 the correct
move is 12 ♗g5!, as after 12...♗f6
13 ♗xf6 ♕xf6 14 ♘b5! e4 15 ♘fd4
c5 16 ♘c2! ♕b2 17 ♘ba3! the
placement of the knight on a5 is a
major drawback for Black.

If White wants to secure his advantage in a calm positional man-
ner he should vary his move-order
at the start. Thus on 1 e4 d5 2
exd5 ♘f6 3 d4 ♘xd5 first 4 ♘f3!?
If now 4...♗g4 then 5 c4 ♘b6 6
♗e2 transposes into the 4 c4 line.
But if 4...g6 then it is worth with-
holding c2-c4: 5 h3!? ♗g7 6 ♗e2
0-0 7 0-0 and now 7...c6 8 ♖e1
♘d7 9 ♗f1 ♖e8 10 c4 ♘c7 11 ♘c3
or 7...♘c6 8 c4 ♘b6 9 d5 ♘a5 10
♘a3! and Black faces a difficult
task after 11 ♕e1!

Caro-Kann Defence

1 e4 c6

The Caro-Kann is similar to the French Defence in principle. Black prepares to play ...d7-d5 and recapture with a pawn if White plays exd5, thereby avoiding the queen or knight recapture of the Scandinavian Defence. However, there are some important differences between the Caro-Kann and French. In the Caro-Kann the bishop on c8 is not locked behind its own pawns. On the other hand, in the middlegame Black would like to undermine White's d4-pawn with ...c7-c5 and this requires two moves in the Caro-Kann (...c7-c6-c5) compared to only one in the French (...c7-c5).

2 d4

White has a selection of several interesting independent lines:

a) 2 d3 e5!? 3 f4!? exf4! 4 ♗xf4 d5 5 e5 (5 ♘c3 dxe4 6 ♘xe4 ♗e7 and ...♘f6 =) 5...♘e7 and Black's setup is ...♘g6, ...♗e7, ...0-0, ...c6-c5 and ...♘c6.

b) 2 c4 d5 3 exd5 cxd5 4 cxd5 (4 d4 creates the basic position of the Panov Attack) 4...♘f6 5 ♗b5+ (5 ♕a4+ ♘bd7 6 ♘c3 g6 7 g3 ♗g7 8 ♗g2 0-0 9 ♘ge2 e6! and Black gets the pawn back as 10 dxe6? is wrong due to ...♘c5 and ...♘d3+) 5...♘bd7 (again it is the knight that Black should interpose as 5...♗d7? 6 ♗c4 guards the pawn!)

6 ♘c3 a6 7 ♕a4!? ♖b8 8 ♗xd7+ ♕xd7 and now on both 9 ♕xd7+ ♗xd7 and 9 ♕f4!? ♖a8 Black's bishop pair and the d5-pawn ensure a level position.

c) 2 ♘c3 d5 3 ♘f3 (3 ♕f3 dxe4 4 ♘xe4 ♘d7 – 4...d4?! 5 ♗c4! – 5 d4 ♘df6! 6 c3 ♘xe4 and ...♘gf6 =) 3...♗g4 (not 3...dxe4 4 ♘xe4 ♗f5?! 5 ♘g3 ♗g6 6 h4 h6 7 ♘e5! ♗h7 8 ♕h5 g6 9 ♗c4! e6 10 ♕e2 and the bishop on h7 is just an embarrassment) 4 h3 ♗xf3!? (dangerous is 4...♗h5?! 5 exd5 cxd5 6 ♗b5+! ♘c6 7 g4 ♗g6 8 ♘e5 and White has the initiative) 5 ♕xf3 e6!? (5...♘f6!?) and now 6 d4 ♘f6 7 ♗d3 dxe4 8 ♘xe4 ♘xe4 (8...♕xd4 9 c3 and 0-0, ♖d1 with a powerful attack) 9 ♕xe4 ♘d7 followed by ...♘f6, ...♗d6 and ...0-0 = or 6 g3 g6!? 7 ♗g2 ♗g7 8 0-0 ♘e7 9 d3 0-0 and ...♘d7 with equal chances.

2...d5

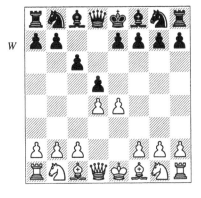

Now there are three main paths: for White:

I. Advance Variation: 3 e5.
II. Panov Attack: 3 exd5 cxd5.
III. Open Variation: 3 ♘c3 (or 3 ♘d2).

Among the less well-trodden tracks, 3 f3!? is interesting, with the idea of ♘c3, ♗e3, ♕d2 and 0-0-0. Now Black should avoid 3...dxe4?! 4 fxe4 e5 5 ♘f3 (5 dxe5? ♕h4+) 5...exd4 6 ♗c4!, whereupon White castles and exerts pressure on the f7-square along the f-file. The most exciting reply to 3 f3!? is 3...e5! 4 dxe5 ♗c5! 5 ♘c3 ♘e7 when Black achieves comfortable counterplay with his powerful dark-squared bishop and the future plan of ...♕b6, ...0-0, ...♖d8 and ...dxe4. 3...e6 4 ♘c3 ♘f6 5 e5 ♘fd7 6 f4 c5 transposes to the French Defence.

I. 1 e4 c6 2 d4 d5 3 e5 (Advance Variation)

3...♗f5
Black quickly develops his c8-bishop; after completing the plan ...e7-e6, ...c6-c5 and ...♘c6 this piece will play an active role in the attack against the white centre.
4 ♘c3
Not 4 g4? ♗e4! 5 f3 ♗g6 6 h4 h5 and White's kingside initiative fades away. What is more, after 7...e6 Black is threatening h5xg4,

when the h4-pawn is hanging. This cannot be hindered by playing g4-g5 as with ...♗f5, ...♘e7-g6, ...c6-c5 and ...♘c6 Black achieves his dream setup. On 4 h4 the answer is again 4...h5, and on 4 c3 e6 5 ♗e3 f6!? 6 ♘f3 ♘d7 7 ♘bd2 ♕c7! 8 exf6 ♘xf6 chances are even as well. However, the fashionable 4 ♘f3 e6 5 ♗e2 is anything but harmless. Black can play 5...♘d7 6 0-0 ♘e7 7 ♘h4 ♗g6 8 ♘d2 followed by 8...c5 9 c3 ♘c6 or 5...c5! straight away: 6 c3 ♘c6 7 0-0 ♗g4 with the idea of ...c5xd4, ...♘e7-f5, ...♗e7 and ...0-0 while White opts for gaining space on the queenside with ♘d2, a2-a3, b2-b4 and ♗b2.
4...e6 5 g4!?
With the knight on c3 White simply has to be aggressive; otherwise Black can start picking on the d4-pawn with ...c7-c5 which cannot be supported by c2-c3.
5...♗g6 6 ♘ge2
White's plan is h2-h4-h5, which, together with ♘f4, will be awkward for the bishop on g6.
6...c5!?
The best counter to a flank attack is an assault in the centre! A more restrained move is 6...f6, when after 7 ♘f4 fxe5 8 dxe5 the bishop on g6 is driven back to f7, but Black has a central pawn majority. The move 6...♘e7!? has also recently come into practice, threatening 7...h5 and protecting the bishop on g6 in advance against 8 ♘f4.

7 h4

After 7 ♗e3 ♘c6 8 dxc5 ♘xe5 White has two squares for his e2 knight:

a) 9 ♘f4 a6!? followed by ...♘f6, ...♗e7 and ... ♘c6 with the idea of mobilizing the centre pawns.

b) 9 ♘d4!? ♘d7! (defending against the threats f2-f4 and ♗f1-b5+) 10 ♗b5?! a6! 11 ♗a4 ♗xc5 12 ♘xe6 fxe6 13 ♗xd7+ ♕xd7 14 ♗xc5 ♘f6 15 ♕e2 ♖c8 16 ♗d4 0-0 17 0-0-0 b5 and Black has a strong attack on the c2-pawn. Instead of 10 ♗b5, 10 f4 or 10 ♘b3 come into consideration.

7...h5!?

The most resolute reply. After 7...cxd4 8 ♘xd4 h5 9 f4! hxg4 10 ♗b5+ ♘d7 11 f5! White has an attack. Also possible is an unexpected piece sacrifice: 7...♘c6 8 h5 ♗xc2!? 9 ♕xc2 cxd4 10 ♘b1 ♖c8 11 ♕a4 ♕d7 12 ♘a3 ♘xe5 13 ♕xd7+ ♔xd7 14 ♘xd4 ♘xg4 with an unclear game in which Black has gathered three pawns for the piece.

8 ♘f4 ♘c6!?

A move that violates all classical chess principles. The traditional path is 8...♗h7 9 ♘xh5 cxd4 10 ♕xd4 ♘c6 11 ♗b5 and now 11...♗xc2 or 11...♘e7 12 ♗h6!? ♖g8!? (12...gxh6?? 13 ♘f6 is mate! but 12...a6 is possible) 13 0-0-0 ♗g6 with double-edged play.

9 ♘xg6 fxg6 *(D)*

Plans and Counterplans:

Black's kingside looks bad but White has problems both with his

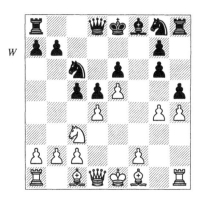

central pawns and with the g4-pawn. For example, **10 ♕d3** cxd4 11 ♘b5 hxg4! 12 ♕xg6+ ♔d7 13 ♕xg4 ♕b6 14 c3 dxc3 15 ♘xc3 ♘h6! is overwhelming for Black, as on 16 ♗xh6 ♕xb2 wins. Best for White is **10 ♘e2!** with the threat of ♘f4. Now 10...cxd4 11 ♘xd4 ♘xd4 12 ♕xd4 ♘e7 and 10...♘ge7 11 ♘f4 cxd4 12 ♗h3! (12 ♘xe6 ♕d7 and White has lost the initiative) 12...♘xe5 13 ♕e2 ♘7c6 14 ♘xe6 ♕a5+ 15 ♔f1 hxg4 16 ♗xg4 ♗d6 are very messy.

II. 1 e4 c6 2 d4 d5 3 exd5 cxd5 (Panov Attack)

4 c4

Or 4 ♗d3 ♘c6 5 c3 ♘f6 6 ♗f4 (6 ♘f3 ♗g4 and ...e7-e6, ...♗d6 and 0-0 =) 6...♗g4!? 7 ♕b3 ♕d7 8 ♘d2 e6 9 ♘gf3 ♗xf3 10 ♘xf3 ♗d6!? 11 ♗xd6 ♕xd6 12 ♕xb7 ♖b8 13 ♕a6 0-0 with sufficient counterplay for the pawn.

4...♘f6 5 ♘c3

Now Black has two completely independent variations:

A. 5...g6
B. 5...♘c6

A common alternative is 5...e6. Then play may continue 6 ♘f3 ♗e7 7 c5! (7 cxd5 ♘xd5 8 ♗d3 ♘c6 9 0-0 0-0 10 ♖e1 leads to the Semi-Tarrasch Defence of the Queen's Gambit) 7...0-0 8 ♗d3 b6 9 b4 a5 (or 9...♗b7!? followed by ...♘e4) 10 ♘a4! ♘fd7 11 h4 with a sharp game. White is threatening 12 ♘xb6 ♘xb6 13 ♗xh7+! ♔xh7 14 ♘g5+ ♔g8 15 ♕h5 ♗xg5 16 hxg5 f5 17 g6 and ♕h7 mate! To avoid White's infiltration with c4-c5, Black usually plays 6 ♘f3 ♗b4, reaching a position that is also known from the Nimzo-Indian: 7 ♗d3 dxc4 8 ♗xc4 0-0 9 0-0 b6 and then ...♗b7 and ...♘bd7 = or 7 cxd5 ♘xd5 8 ♗d2 0-0 9 ♗d3 ♘c6 10 0-0 ♗e7 11 a3 ♗f6 12 ♕e2 ♘xc3 13 bxc3 g6 14 ♗e4!? ♗d7 15 ♖ab1 b6 followed by ...♖c8 and ...♘a5, with counterplay for Black.

A. 1 e4 c6 2 d4 d5 3 exd5 cxd5 4 c4 ♘f6 5 ♘c3 g6

6 cxd5 ♗g7
Not 6...♘xd5 7 ♕b3 ♘xc3?! 8 ♗c4! e6 9 bxc3 ♗g7 10 ♗a3!
7 ♕b3
After 7 ♗b5+!? ♘bd7 8 d6! exd6 9 ♕e2+ ♕e7 10 ♗f4 ♕xe2+ 11 ♗xe2 ♔e7 12 ♗f3 Black is a little worse due to his weak pawn on d6 and his king position in the middle, although he should be able to make a draw with accurate play.

7...0-0 8 ♗e2 ♘bd7 9 ♗f3 ♘b6 10 ♗g5!?
White now has the option of capturing the knight on f6 to reduce the number of attackers on the d5-pawn.
10...a5!? 11 ♘ge2 a4 12 ♕b5 ♗d7 13 ♕b4 ♗f5 14 0-0

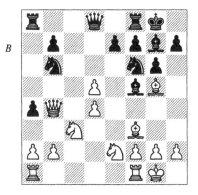

Plans and Counterplans:
Black would like to regain the pawn on d5 but right now he cannot capture it due to the hanging pawns on b7 and e7. **14...♗d3** 15 ♖fe1 ♕d6 16 ♕xd6 exd6 17 ♘f4 maintains the extra pawn (even if it is an ugly one), but the immediate **14...♕d6!?** 15 ♕xd6 exd6 deserves attention. Besides ...♗d3 Black can wheel and deal with ...♘c4, ...♖ac8 and ...h7-h6 while White attacks d6 via ♘g3-e4.

B. 1 e4 c6 2 d4 d5 3 exd5 cxd5 4 c4 ♘f6 5 ♘c3 ♘c6

6 ♘f3
The other line is 6 ♗g5!? Then on 6...dxc4? 7 ♗xc4 ♕xd4 8 ♕xd4

♘xd4 9 0-0-0 e5 10 f4! White has a forceful initiative, but 6...♗e6!? is interesting: 7 ♗xf6 exf6 8 c5 g6 9 ♗b5 h5 followed by ...♗h6 and ...0-0. Another frequently seen line is 6...♕a5!? 7 ♗xf6 exf6 8 cxd5 ♗b4 9 ♕d2 ♗xc3 10 bxc3 ♕xd5, although the pawn structure is in White's favour. Perhaps simplest is 6...e6 7 c5 ♗e7 8 ♗b5 (thwarting 8...b6) 8...0-0 9 ♗xc6 bxc6 10 ♘f3 ♘e4! and Black equalizes. This line resembles the 5...e6 variation in which Black tries to get loose from the c4-c5 bind with ...b7-b6 or ...♗e7 and ...♘e4.

6...♗g4 7 cxd5

After other moves Black is simply fine after ...e7-e6, ...♗e7, ...0-0 and ...dxc4 or ...♘e4.

7...♘xd5 8 ♕b3!

Simultaneously attacking d5 and b7.

8...♗xf3 9 gxf3 e6

9...♘xd4 loses to 10 ♗b5+! and on 9...♘b6 10 ♗e3 (10 d5 ♘d4! 11 ♕d1 e5) 10...e6 11 0-0-0 White is better in view of the threat of d4-d5.

10 ♕xb7 ♘xd4 11 ♗b5+ ♘xb5 12 ♕c6+!

12 ♕xb5+? ♕d7.

12...♔e7 13 ♕xb5 ♕d7! 14 ♘xd5+

14 ♕a5? ♘xc3 15 bxc3 f6! and ...♔f7 =.

14...♕xd5 15 ♕xd5 exd5 *(D)*

Plans and Counterplans:
We have gone straight into an endgame in which White has a

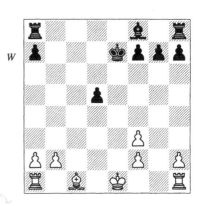

queenside pawn majority and possible threats against the black king, while Black relies on an attack on the weak white kingside pawns and the strength of the d5-pawn. The lines **16 0-0** ♔e6! 17 ♖e1+ ♔f5 18 ♗e3 ♗e7 and **16 ♗e3** ♔e6 17 0-0-0 ♗b4!? demonstrate that in this complicated ending chances are even.

III. 1 e4 c6 2 d4 d5 3 ♘c3 (Open Variation)

3...dxe4

On 3...g6 4 e5 ♗g7 5 f4 h5! followed by ...♘h6, ...♗g4 and ...♘f5 and Black has good play, so White should prefer 4 h3!? ♗g7 5 ♘f3 dxe4 6 ♘xe4 ♘d7 7 ♗c4 ♘gf6 8 ♘xf6+ ♘xf6 9 0-0 0-0 10 ♖e1 ±.

4 ♘xe4

Black's best moves are:

A. 4...♘d7 and
B. 4...♗f5.

The third option is considered worse: **4...♘f6?!** 5 ♘xf6+ and now on 5...exf6 6 c3 ♗d6 7 ♗d3 and ♘e2, ♕c2 White has the freer game and can hope for an endgame in view of Black's doubled f-pawns. The tactical answer is 5...gxf6!? but then, for example, 6 c3 ♗f5 7 ♗f4!? ♘d7 8 ♗d3 ♗g6 9 ♘e2 ♘b6 (or 9...e5 10 ♗e3!? and the black centre cannot make further progress without being seriously weakened while White can seize the f5-square via ♕c2 and ♘g3) 10 0-0 e6 11 ♗g3 ♗d6 12 b4!? ♕c7 13 a4 followed by c3-c4 and White is obviously on top. Black's strategic drawbacks – doubled pawns and a spatial disadvantage – are more significant than random tactical chances along the open g-file.

A. 1 e4 c6 2 d4 d5 3 ♘c3 dxe4 4 ♘xe4 ♘d7

5 ♗c4
Other lines are:
a) **5 ♘g5!?** ♘gf6 (5...h6?! 6 ♘e6! fxe6? 7 ♕h5+ and mate!) 6 ♗d3 e6 (6...h6? 7 ♘e6!) 7 ♘1f3 ♗d6 (7...h6?! 8 ♘xe6!? fxe6 9 ♗g6+ ♔e7 10 ♗f4 followed by 0-0, ♖e1 and c2-c4, when Black is tied up) 8 ♕e2 h6 9 ♘e4 ♘xe4 10 ♕xe4 ♘f6 (10...♕c7!? would prepare the plan ...b7-b6, ...♗b7, ...0-0-0 and ...c6-c5, but 11 ♕g4! is difficult to meet) 11 ♕e2 (on 11 ♕h4, 11...♔e7! is deadly, with the immediate threat 12...g5 and then ...g5-g4) 11...♕c7 12 ♗d2 b6 13 0-0-0 ♗b7 14 ♔b1 0-0-0! It is important for Black to castle, but not to the

kingside where he would be exposed to a white pawn rush. Now after 15 c4 c5 the position is level.
b) **5 ♘f3** ♘gf6 6 ♘g3 (6 ♘xf6+ ♘xf6 7 ♘e5 ♗e6!? 8 ♗e2 g6 and Black plays for ...♗g7, ...0-0, ...♕c7 and ...c6-c5 often combined with the regrouping ...♘f6-e8-d6 and ...♗f5 if White's bishop appears on d3) 6...e6 7 ♗d3 c5 8 c3 ♕c7 9 0-0 ♗e7 followed by ...0-0, ...b7-b6 and ...♗b7 =.
c) **5 ♕e2** ♘df6 (5...♘gf6?? 6 ♘d6 mate!) 6 c3 ♘xe4 7 ♕xe4 ♘f6 8 ♕c2 ♗g4 =.

5...♘gf6
This is the move that was prepared by 4...♘d7.

6 ♘g5
6 ♘xf6+ ♘xf6 7 ♘f3 (7 c3 ♕c7!? 8 ♘f3 ♗g4) 7...♗f5 (not 7...♗g4? 8 ♗xf7! +–) 8 ♕e2 e6 9 ♗g5 ♗e7 10 0-0-0 ♗g4 11 h3 ♗xf3 12 ♕xf3 ♘d5 13 ♗xe7 ♕xe7 and the white bishop is slightly superior to the black knight.

6...e6
6...♘d5 7 ♘1f3 h6 8 ♘e4 and later 0-0, ♗b3, c4 ±.

7 ♕e2
Not 7 ♘1f3? h6 and White is forced to withdraw to h3. 7 ♘e2 h6 8 ♘f3 ♗d6 is equal.

7...♘b6
The threat was ♘xf7 followed by ♕xe6+ leading to a quick mate. White now has to choose between the two lines:

A1. 8 ♗d3 and
A2. 8 ♗b3.

A1. 1 e4 c6 2 d4 d5 3 ♘c3 dxe4 4 ♘xe4 ♘d7 5 ♗c4 ♘gf6 6 ♘g5 e6 7 ♕e2 ♘b6 8 ♗d3

8...h6
The right moment to make this move since now the knight is forced to defend the d4-pawn from f3.
9 ♘5f3 c5 10 dxc5
After 10 ♗e3 ♘bd5 Black develops via ...a7-a6, ...♕c7, ...♗d6 and ...0-0.
10...♗xc5 11 ♘e5
White has to disentangle his knights. After 11 ♗d2 0-0 12 0-0-0 ♘a4! Black is threatening an attack with ...♕b6.
11...♘bd7
It is necessary to fight against the knight on e5. The bishop on c8 can only be developed with ...b7-b6 and ...♗b7.
12 ♘gf3 ♕c7 13 ♗f4!?
Not 13 ♗d2? ♘xe5 14 ♘xe5 ♗xf2+! 15 ♔xf2 ♕xe5 16 ♕xe5 ♘g4+ −+, while 13 0-0 0-0 14 ♗f4 ♗d6 15 ♖fe1 ♘xe5 16 ♘xe5 b6 and ...♗b7 is just equal.
13...♗b4+!? (D)
Not 13...♗d6 14 ♗g3! 0-0 15 0-0-0 ♘c5 16 ♔b1 ♖d8 17 ♗h4! ♗e7 18 g4! with a tremendous attack for White.

Plans and Counterplans:
White cannot play **14 c3** due to 14...♗xc3+. He therefore has an interesting choice between **14 ♘d2** ♗xd2+ 15 ♔xd2 0-0 (15...♘c5!?) 16 ♖hd1 and **14 ♔f1!?** ♗d6 15 ♖d1 ♘xe5 (15...♘h5 16 g3!?) 16

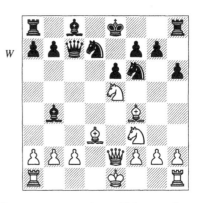

♘xe5 0-0 17 ♗g3 ♖d8 18 ♘c4 ♗xg3 19 hxg3 ♗d7.

A2. 1 e4 c6 2 d4 d5 3 ♘c3 dxe4 4 ♘xe4 ♘d7 5 ♗c4 ♘gf6 6 ♘g5 e6 7 ♕e2 ♘b6 8 ♗b3

8...h6
Just as on 8 ♗d3, 8...♕xd4? is met by 9 ♘f3 and 10 ♘e5 +−.
9 ♘5f3 a5
9...c5 at once is also playable: 10 ♗f4!? ♘bd5 11 ♗e5 ♕a5+ 12 ♘d2 cxd4 (12...b5!? 13 c4 bxc4 14 ♗xc4 ♘b6) 13 ♘f3 ♗e7 14 ♘xd4 0-0 15 0-0-0!? ♗d7 16 ♔b1 ♗a4!? with mutual chances.
10 a4!?
10 c3 a4 11 ♗c2 ♕d5!? or 10 a3 a4 11 ♗a2 c5 12 ♗e3 ♘bd5 makes life simpler for Black.
10...c5 (D)

Plans and Counterplans:
White wishes to castle queenside. He can play **11 ♗e3**, but this is met by 11...♕c7 (11...♘bd5? 12 0-0-0!) 12 ♘e5 ♗d6 13 ♘gf3 0-0 14 0-0 (14 0-0-0 ♗d7!?) 14...♘bd5.

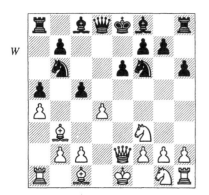

Sharp play results from **11 ♗f4!?** ♗d6 12 ♗g3!? 0-0 13 0-0-0?! c4! 14 ♗xc4 ♘xa4 with counterplay for Black, while **11 dxc5** ♘bd7! 12 ♘e5 ♘xe5 13 ♕xe5 ♘d7 14 ♕e2 ♗xc5 15 ♘f3 b6! (it is often better to let White castle first to avoid a kingside attack if he should castle queenside) 16 0-0 (16 ♗e3 ♗a6!) 16...0-0 is equal.

B. 1 e4 c6 2 d4 d5 3 ♘c3 dxe4 4 ♘xe4 ♗f5

5 ♘g3 ♗g6 6 h4!?

White undertakes a long-range strategic plan! The bishop on g6 cannot be tolerated but before White trades it with ♗d3 he clamps down on the black kingside. The price of this manoeuvre is that later he will have to keep an eye on the advanced h-pawn. Here are a few other possibilities:

a) 6 ♘1e2 ♘f6 7 ♘f4 e5!? 8 ♘xg6 (or 8 dxe5 ♕xd1+ 9 ♔xd1 ♘g4) 8...hxg6 9 dxe5 ♕a5+ 10 c3 ♕xe5+ 11 ♗e2 ♕c7 and Black can continue with ...♗d6 and ...0-0 =.

It is worth remembering this motif: the e5-pawn can be regained with ...♕a5+ and ...♕xe5!

b) 6 ♗c4 e6 7 ♘1e2 ♘f6 8 ♘f4 ♗d6 9 0-0 ♘d5! 10 ♘gh5 0-0 =.

c) 6 ♘f3 ♘d7! (White's 7 ♘e5 must be hindered as it would gain the bishop pair) 7 ♗e2 e6 8 0-0 ♗d6 9 b3!? (9 ♖e1 ♘gf6 10 ♗f1 ♕c7 11 c4 0-0 and Black controls the e5-square) 9...♘gf6 10 ♗b2 ♕c7 11 c4 0-0 12 ♘h4 ♖fe8 13 ♘xg6 hxg6 14 ♕c2 ♖ad8 =.

6...h6

6...h5? would destroy the option of kingside castling and create some horrible weaknesses: the pawn on h5 and the g5- square.

7 ♘f3 ♘d7

Black develops, prepares queenside castling and, not least, stops 8 ♘e5.

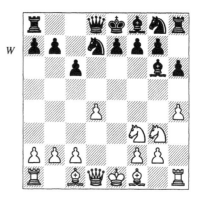

8 h5 ♗h7 9 ♗d3 ♗xd3

9...e6? 10 ♗xh7 ♖xh7 would be tragicomic.

10 ♕xd3 ♕c7

10...e6 11 ♗f4 ♕a5+ 12 ♗d2 ♕c7 may lead to the same thing,

although White may be able to profit from the difference with 12 c3 and 0-0, a2-a4 and b2-b4. 10...♕c7 avoids this by disallowing ♗f4.

11 ♗d2 e6 12 0-0-0 ♘gf6!
The perfect move-order. Following the principle 'make the essential moves first and then choose the best follow-up depending on the opponent's play' Black maintains the opportunity of castling on either side. 12...0-0-0?! is very strongly met by 13 ♕e2! ♘gf6 14 ♘e5 and after 14...♘xe5? 15 dxe5 ♘d5 16 f4 c5 17 c4 ♘b4 18 ♗xb4 ♖xd1+ 19 ♖xd1 cxb4 20 ♘e4 White is on top. In such positions Black should not capture on e5 as the pawn that recaptures will restrict his game. So instead of 14...♘xe5? it is better to continue 14...♘b6!?: 15 ♗a5 ♖d5 16 ♗xb6 (16 b4!?) 16...axb6 17 f4 or 15 c4!? ♖xd4 16 ♗e3! ♖xd1+ 17 ♖xd1, although Black's play is still somewhat problematic as 17...♕xe5? 18 ♖d8+ and 19 ♗xb6+ wins the queen and 17...♗d6 is met by 18 ♖xd6 followed by ♘xf7 +–. The only playable move seems to be 17...♖g8! 18 f4 c5 19 ♕d3 ♗e7!? 20 ♘xf7 ♘g4! but even here Black is not safe yet.

13 ♘e4!?
On 13 ♕e2 the difference becomes apparent: 13...c5! and, for example, 14 c4 cxd4 15 ♘xd4 ♖c8 16 ♔b1!? ♗c5 (16...♕xc4?? 17 ♖c1!

and White wins) followed by ...0-0 with equality.

13...0-0-0 14 g3! *(D)*
White prepares 15 ♗f4.

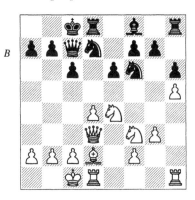

Plans and Counterplans:
Black has to play carefully in order to equalize. An example of the dangers is **14...♘xe4 15 ♕xe4 ♘f6?!** 16 ♕e2 c5? 17 dxc5 ♗xc5 18 ♖h4! and the rook from h1 will transfer to c4 with deadly strength. Instead of 15...♘f6?!, 15...♗d6!? 16 c4 ♘f6 17 ♕c2 c5 18 d5 exd5 19 cxd5 deserves attention as it prevents White occupying e5. Instead of 14...♘xe4, **14...♘c5!?** 15 ♘xc5 ♗xc5 comes into consideration, when White can achieve a slight plus with the plan c2-c4, ♗c3, ♕e2 and ♘e5.

Nowadays the Caro-Kann with ...♗f5 is not considered quite good enough to equalize, so Caro-Kann adherents tend to prefer the solid line 4...♘d7, and not without success!

French Defence

1 e4 e6

Black's intentions are honourable. He is planning ...d7-d5, and if White builds a pawn centre with e4-e5 then Black can undermine it with ...c7-c5 and ..f7-f6. The price of this strategy is the limited scope of the bishop on c8, which is obstructed by its own pawns (e6, d5).

The material is divided into four sections:

I. King's Indian Attack and other sidelines.
II. Advance Variation: 2 d4 d5 3 e5.
III. Tarrasch Variation: 3 ♘d2.
IV. Classical Main Line: 3 ♘c3.

I. King's Indian Attack and other sidelines

If he wants to sidestep the main lines (which require thorough preparation) White can choose between two independent lines:

A. King's Indian Attack: 2 d3
B. Exchange Variation: 2 d4 d5 3 exd5 exd5.

The following variations are less important:

a) **2 f4** d5 3 e5 c5 4 ♘f3 ♘c6 5 c3 d4!? 6 d3 ♘h6 to be followed by ...♘f5, ...♗e7 and ...0-0 =.

b) **2 c4** d5 3 exd5 exd5 4 cxd5 ♘f6 5 ♗b5+ ♘bd7 6 ♘c3 ♗e7 7 ♕f3 0-0 8 ♗xd7 ♕xd7!? 9 ♘ge2 ♖d8 10 ♘f4 ♗d6 and after returning the pawn White will stand worse due to his isolated d-pawn (∓).

c) **2 ♘c3** d5 3 ♘f3 d4!? (after 3...♘f6 4 e5 ♘fd7 5 d4 c5 play transposes to the 3 ♘c3 line) 4 ♘e2 c5 5 d3 ♘c6 and Black can build a very strong position with the plan ...e6-e5, ...f7-f6, ...♗e6, ...♕d7, ...♗d6 and ...♘ge7.

d) **2 ♕e2!?** (trying to dissuade Black from ...d7-d5 because White would capture and only the queen could recapture). 2...c5 (also good is 2...♗e7!? and then ...d7-d5) 3 f4 ♘c6 4 ♘f3 ♗e7 5 ♘c3 d5! 6 d3 (6 e5 ♘h6! followed by ...♘f5) 6...♘f6 7 e5 ♘d7 8 g3 b5 9 ♗g2 ♕b6 10 0-0 b4 11 ♘d1 c4+! 12 ♗e3 ♗c5 13 ♔h1 ♗a6! 14 ♗xc5 cxd3! 15 cxd3 ♘xc5 16 ♘f2 0-0 and Black is obviously better.

A. 1 e4 e6 2 d3 (King's Indian Attack)

White opts for a setup that resembles the King's Indian Defence. His idea is to play ♘d2, ♘gf3, g2-g3 and ♗g2. Then he will either open up the centre, counting on the strength of his bishop g2, or just the opposite, close it with e4-e5 to undertake a kingside attack with the manoeuvres h4-h5-h6, ♖e1 and ♘f1-h2-g4. The latter plan is more suitable when Black plays ...d7-d5, c7-c5, ...♘f6 and ...♗e7 than if Black develops with a kingside fianchetto, as it is harder to break down such a king position. Note that the positions in this section are often reached by a Sicilian move-order (1 e4 c5 2 ♘f3 e6 3 d3) instead of the French Defence.

2...d5 3 ♘d2

To avoid a queen swap after 3...dxe4 4 dxe4.

3...c5

After 3...♘f6 Black constantly needs to be on the alert against ...e4-e5.

4 ♘gf3 ♘c6 5 g3 ♗d6!?

5...♘f6 6 ♗g2 ♗e7 7 0-0 0-0 8 ♖e1!? and White is ready to play 9 e5 followed by the usual attacking plan of ♘f1, h2-h4-h5, ♘h2 and ♘g4.

6 ♗g2 ♘ge7! 7 0-0 0-0

The fight centres on the advance e4-e5.

8 ♖e1 ♕c7 9 ♕e2 f6! *(D)*

This is why the knight had to go to e7.

Plans and Counterplans:
White can hardly think of a kingside attack now since the black pieces are not separated from their king by a pawn on e5. Sooner or later White will have to play c2-c3 and then consider e4xd5. Black can complete his development with

...♗c8-d7 and then expand on the queenside with ...b7-b5, ...a7-a5 and ...b5-b4 or ...c5-c4. If White prematurely plays b2-b3 and ♗b2 Black can even consider ...d5-d4. Chances are even.

B. 1 e4 e6 2 d4 d5 3 exd5 exd5 (Exchange Variation)

The Exchange Variation is rather an unpretentious line in which – just as in other exchange variations (the Slav Defence, for example) – White cannot hope for an advantage.

4 ♗d3

4 c4 ♘f6 5 ♘c3 ♗e7 6 ♘f3 0-0 7 ♗e2 dxc4 8 ♗xc4 ♘bd7 followed by ...♘b6-♘d5 and ...c7-c6 is fine for Black.

4...♗d6

More exciting is 4...c5!? 5 ♘f3 ♘c6 6 dxc5 ♗xc5 7 0-0 ♘ge7 and ...0-0.

5 ♘f3 ♘f6 6 0-0 0-0 7 ♗g5 ♗g4 8 ♘bd2 ♘bd7 9 c3 c6

And now after the white moves ♖fe1, ♗h4 and ♗g3 Black will just copy with ...罝fe8, ...奠h5 and ...奠g6. Isn't this all just terribly boring?

II. 1 e4 e6 2 d4 d5 3 e5 (Advance Variation)

3...c5
Black attacks White's centre and prepares ♘c6. 'One should first develop the pawns and then the knights!'
4 c3
Otherwise after Black's 4...cxd4 the pawn-chain protecting the pawn on e5 is demolished.
4...♘c6 5 ♘f3
5 ♗e3 ♛b6 6 ♛d2 ♗d7 7 ♘f3 f6!? destroys the white pawn centre.
5...♛b6
Also possible is 5...♗d7 (5...f6? 6 ♗b5! and White controls e5) 6 ♗e2 (not 6 ♗b5?? ♘xe5) 6...f6 (6...♘ge7!? followed by ...♘f5 is also not bad) 7 0-0 fxe5 8 ♘xe5! ♘xe5 9 dxe5 and Black's position is a little loose, for example 9...♗c6 10 c4! ♘e7 11 ♗g5! threatening 12 ♗h5+.

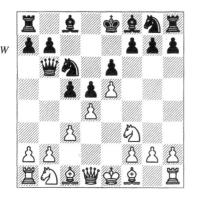

On 5...♛b6 White will usually answer:

A. 6 ♗e2
B. 6 a3!?

Also possible is 6 ♗d3, but this is only a trick based on 6...cxd4 7 cxd4 ♘xd4?? 8 ♘xd4 ♛xd4 9 ♗b5+ winning the queen. If instead of 7...♘xd4?? Black hinders the discovered check with 7...♗d7 then after 8 0-0!? ♘xd4 9 ♘xd4 ♛xd4 10 ♘c3 White has some compensation for the pawn. For example, 10...♛xe5 11 罝e1 ♛d6 (11...♛b8 12 ♘xd5) 12 ♘b5 or 10...a6!? 11 ♛e2 ♘e7 12 ♔h1 ♘c6 13 f4 ♘b4 14 ♗b1.

A. 1 e4 e6 2 d4 d5 3 e5 c5 4 c3 ♘c6 5 ♘f3 ♛b6 6 ♗e2

6...cxd4
Black would like to develop his king's knight to f5 but 6...♘ge7 7 dxc5 ♛c7 8 ♘d4!? ♘xe5? (8...♛xe5 9 0-0 and b2-b4) 9 ♘b5 ♛xc5 10 ♛d4! or 6...♘h6 7 ♗xh6 ♛xb2 8 ♗e3 ♛xa1 9 ♛c2 (the black queen is in trouble!) prevents this. However, after a swap on d4 this line is good for Black as his queen cannot be netted due to the hanging pawn on d4!
7 cxd4 ♘h6!
After 7...♘ge7 8 ♘a3 ♘f5 9 ♘c2 ♗b4+ 10 ♔f1 White 'castles' with g2-g3, ♔g2 and then unfolds with a2-a3 and b2-b4 or g2-g4.
8 ♘c3

Now 8 ♗xh6 is met by 8...♕xb2 9 ♗d2 ♕xa1 10 ♕b3 ♘xd4 11 ♗b5+ ♔d8 –+, but 8 b3!? is interesting: 8...♘f5 9 ♗b2 ♗b4+ 10 ♔f1 ♗e7! 11 ♘c3 f6!?

8...♘f5 9 ♘a4 ♗b4+ 10 ♗d2

On 10 ♔f1 Black plays 10...♕d8 and ...f7-f6.

10...♕a5 11 ♗c3 b5 12 a3! ♗xc3+ 13 ♘xc3 b4 14 axb4 ♕xb4 15 ♗b5 ♗d7 16 ♗xc6 ♗xc6 17 ♕d2 0-0 18 0-0 =

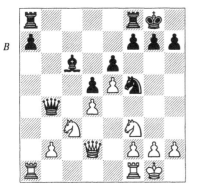

Plans and Counterplans:
The game is balanced. White attacks the pawn on a7 while Black does the same with the pawn on b2. But neither player can win the opposing pawn without abandoning their own.

B. 1 e4 e6 2 d4 d5 3 e5 c5 4 c3 ♘c6 5 ♘f3 ♕b6 6 a3!?

White's idea is 7 b4! cxb4 8 cxb4 with control of the queenside as 8...a5? 9 b5! ♘a7 10 a4 would completely disrupt Black's attempt to free himself.

6...c4!?

What happens if Black does not obstruct b2-b4? One line continues 6...♘h6 7 b4 cxd4 8 cxd4 ♘f5 9 ♗e3! (9 ♗b2 ♗e7 10 ♗d3 a5! 11 b5 ♘cxd4 is good for Black as after the exchanges there is no check on b5) 9...f6 10 ♗d3! ♘xe3 11 fxe3 fxe5 12 b5! e4 13 bxc6 and wherever Black captures his king runs into trouble. Black can also impede b2-b4 with 6...a5!?, e.g. 7 ♗d3 ♘h6! 8 0-0 cxd4 (8...♘f5 9 dxc5!) 9 cxd4 ♘f5 10 ♗xf5 exf5 and Black completes his development with ...♗e6, ...♗e7 and ...0-0 while White can aim for ♘c3-a4, ♗e3 and ♖c1.

7 g3

7 ♘bd2 would threaten 8 b3, which Black can meet by the preventive 8...♘a5 or the counterattack 8...f6. After 7 g3 White is ready for Black's ...f7-f6, as the white bishop will find a place on g2 or h3.

7...f6!? 8 exf6 ♘xf6 9 ♗g2

After 9 ♗h3 ♗d6 10 ♕e1 0-0 11 ♗xe6+ ♔h8 White has opened the position to his own detriment.

9...♗d6 10 0-0 0-0

Plans and Counterplans:
White plays against ...e6-e5 (11 ♘bd2? e5!). What is more, he would like to place a knight on e5 himself, but after 11 ♕e2!? (11 ♖e1 ♘e4! 12 ♘bd2 ♘xd2 13 ♘xd2? e5!) 11...♗d7!? 12 ♘e5 ♗e8! the bishop threatens to spring to life via 13...♗xe5 14 dxe5 ♗h5. After

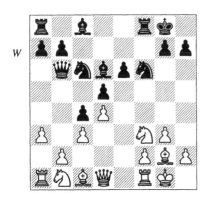

13 ♘xc6 ♕xc6 14 ♕xe6+ ♗f7 followed by ...♖e8, ...♗g6 and ...♗d3 Black again has good play for the pawn.

III. 1 e4 e6 2 d4 d5 3 ♘d2 (Tarrasch Variation)

If White does not push with 3 e5 he has to protect the pawn on e4. This can only be done with knight moves since after 3 f3? dxe4 4 ♘c3 (4 fxe4?? ♕h4+ −+) 4...♗b4!? White has nothing for the pawn and after 3 ♗d3 dxe4 4 ♗xe4 ♘f6 5 ♗f3 c5 6 ♘e2 ♘c6 7 c3 cxd4 8 cxd4 e5! Black seizes control. On 3 ♘d2 Black's main lines are:

A. Black captures on e4: 3...dxe4
B. Black accepts an isolated pawn: 3...c5
C. With a French centre: 3...♘f6.

3...♘c6?! is sometimes seen, but this is an anti-positional move as it impedes the pawn on c7 from

later advancing. White gains the advantage with simple moves: 4 ♘gf3 ♘f6 5 e5 ♘d7 6 ♗e2!? f6 7 exf6 ♘xf6 (7...♕xf6 8 ♘f1! ♗d6 9 ♘e3 followed by 0-0 and ♘g4 is also good for White) 8 0-0 ♗d6 9 c4! and White is threatening c4-c5. After 9...b6 10 cxd5 exd5 11 ♗b5 ♗d7 12 ♖e1 ♘e7 13 ♗xd7+ ♕xd7 14 ♘e5 White is markedly better (±).

A. 1 e4 e6 2 d4 d5 3 ♘d2 (or 3 ♘c3) 3...dxe4 (Black captures on e4)

4 ♘xe4
In this variation Black's position is slightly passive but in this Caro-Kann-like position White does not have a d4 and e5 pawn centre and cannot easily increase his opening advantage. This line, which is really only enough for a draw, is recommended for those who do not wish to plunge into the intricacies of 3 ♘d2 and 3 ♘c3. Of course 3...dxe4 can be played against both main lines, with little theoretical preparation.
4...♗d7!?
It is not without good reason that this line, activating the bishop on c8, is very fashionable. As other lines demonstrate, this bishop is Black's most troublesome piece:
a) 4...♘f6?! 5 ♘xf6+ ♕xf6 (or 5...gxf6 6 ♘f3 b6 7 ♗b5+! c6 8 ♗c4 and ♗f4, ♕e2, 0-0-0 ±) 6 ♘f3 h6 (to stop 7 ♗g5) 7 ♗d3 ♗d6 8 0-0 ♘c6 9 c3 0-0 10 ♘d2! e5 11 ♘e4 ♕d8 12 ♕h5! exd4 13 ♗xh6!

with a tremendous attack for White.

b) 4...♗e7 5 ♘f3 ♘f6 6 ♘xf6+ ♗xf6 7 c3!? b6 8 ♗d3 ♗b7 9 0-0 ♘d7 10 ♕e2 0-0 11 ♖d1 followed by ♗f4 and ♗e4 with a tiny but tangible advantage for White.

c) 4...♘d7!? 5 ♘f3 (5 g3!? ♘gf6 6 ♘xf6+ ♘xf6 7 ♗g2 c5 8 ♘e2 ±) 5...♘gf6 6 ♘xf6+ ♘xf6 7 ♗d3 b6 (7...c5 8 dxc5 ♗xc5 9 ♕e2 followed by 0-0, ♗g5 and ♖ad1 ±) 8 ♕e2 ♗b7 9 ♗g5 ♗e7 10 0-0 0-0 11 ♖ad1 and later White can continue with, for example, c2-c4, ♘e5, ♖fe1, ♗b1 and ♕c2 (±).

5 ♘f3 ♗c6 6 ♗d3 ♘d7 7 0-0 ♘gf6 8 ♘g3

Black's overcrowded state is eased after 8 ♘xf6+?! ♘xf6.

8...♗e7 9 b3!?

The c1-bishop would not be comfortable on f4 since if it is attacked it cannot retreat to g3.

9...0-0 10 ♗b2

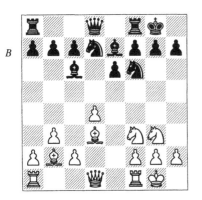

Plans and Counterplans:
White is now ready to increase his spatial advantage with natural moves: c2-c4, ♕e2 (♕c2), ♖fd1 and ♘e5. For example, **10...a5!?** 11 c4! a4 12 ♘e5 ♘xe5 13 dxe5 ♘d7 14 ♕c2 g6 15 ♖ad1 and Black has nothing to show for his inconvenience. Better is **10...♗xf3!** 11 ♕xf3 c6 12 c4 ± when White has a spatial plus and easy game (♖ad1, ♖fe1, h4-h5). However, Black's position is solid and he can also joust at White's queenside pawns (...♕a5 or ...a5-a4 comes into consideration in the long run).

B. 1 e4 e6 2 d4 d5 3 ♘d2 c5 (Black accepts an isolated pawn)

4 exd5

Practically compulsory as 4 dxc5?! ♗xc5 would help Black's development, while 4 c3?! cxd4 5 cxd4 dxe4 6 ♘xe4 ♘c6 7 ♘f3 ♗b4+ 8 ♘c3 ♘f6 and ...0-0 is comfortable for Black. On 4 ♘gf3 Black can answer 4...♘c6 5 ♗b5!? dxe4 6 ♘xe4 ♗d7 or even 4...cxd4, and now 5 exd5 is just a different move-order compared to 4 exd5, while 5 ♘xd4 ♘f6 6 e5 (6 exd5 ♘xd5 7 ♘2f3 ♗e7 8 ♗e2 a6 9 c4 ♘f6 10 0-0 ♕c7!? and besides ...e6-e5 Black can think about ...b7-b6, ...♗b7, ...♘bd7 and ...0-0) 6...♘fd7 7 ♘2f3 (7 f4? ♘xe5! 8 fxe5 ♕h4+ and the knight on d4 is hanging!) 7...♘c6 gives Black a pleasant game.

4...exd5!?

Even though 4...♕xd5 may seem tempting, the black pawn will be missed from the centre: 5 ♘gf3

cxd4 6 ♗c4 ♕d6 7 0-0 ♘c6 8 ♘b3
♘f6 (8...e5 9 ♘g5 and 10 f4 ±) 9
♘bxd4 ♘xd4 10 ♘xd4 a6 11 ♖e1
♗d7 (11...♗e7 12 c3 0-0 13 ♕e2
♕c7 14 ♗g5! ±) 12 c3 0-0-0 13 ♕e2
♕c7 14 h3 ♗d6 15 a4! e5 16 ♘c2!
and after 17 ♘e3 White can continue his attack with b2-b4-b5.

5 ♘gf3 ♘f6
5...c4?! is not very good: 6 b3
cxb3 7 ♗b5+ ♗d7 8 ♕e2+ ♕e7 9
♗xd7+ ♘bxd7 10 axb3 with a
better pawn structure and pressure along the a-file for White. On
the other hand 5...♘c6!? 6 ♗b5
♗d6 7 0-0 ♘ge7 8 dxc5 ♗xc5 9
♘b3 ♗d6 (9...♗b6 10 ♖e1 and 11
♗e3 ±) 10 ♘bd4 0-0 leads to an interesting middlegame which, with
colours reversed, can also arise
from a Nimzo-Indian. After an exchange of light artillery White
will start an attack on the d5-
pawn, but in the meantime he can
play h2-h3, ♗g5, ♖e1, c3, ♕d2 and
♖ad1. On the other hand, Black
must aim for complications. His
moves are ...♗g4, ...a7-a6, ...♕c7
and rooks to the middle.

6 ♗b5+ ♗d7
6...♘c6 is a mistake since the
knight is already on f6: 7 0-0 ♗e7
8 dxc5 ♗xc5 9 ♖e1+ ♗e7 (9...♗e6
10 ♘b3 with 11 ♘bd4 to follow ±)
10 ♕e2 and Black is uanble to castle.

7 ♕e2+
After 7 ♗xd7+ ♘bxd7 8 0-0 ♗e7
9 dxc5 ♘xc5 10 ♘b3 ♘ce4, followed by ...0-0 and ...♖e8, Black is
active.

7...♗e7
Interposing the queen is bad
since the exchange favours White.
Black's best plan is to capitalize
on the central strength of his isolated pawn in the middlegame.
**8 dxc5 0-0 9 ♘b3 ♖e8 10 ♗e3
a6**
Black can win the pawn back
immediately: 10...♗xc5!? 11 ♘xc5
♕a5+ 12 ♕d2 ♕xb5, but he wants
more than he would get after 13
0-0-0.
11 ♗d3
11 ♗xd7?! ♘bxd7 12 0-0 ♘xc5
makes life easier for Black.

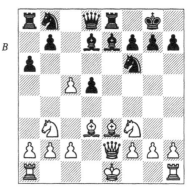

B

Plans and Counterplans:
Black cannot be careless with
11...♘g4 as after 12 0-0 a5, 13 c4!
is very strong. For example 13...a4
14 ♘bd4 dxc4 15 ♗xc4 ♗xc5 16
♗xf7+! and ♕c4+ wins. Therefore the pawn must be regained:
11...♗a4!? 12 ♘fd4 ♘bd7 13 0-0-0
♗xb3 14 ♘xb3 ♘xc5 15 ♕f3!?
♘xb3+! (15...♘xd3+ 16 ♖xd3 ±)
16 axb3 ♕a5 17 ♔b1 ♗c5 with
mutual chances.

C. 1 e4 e6 2 d4 d5 3 ♘d2 ♘f6 (With a French centre)

4 e5

4 ♗d3 c5 5 dxc5 dxe4 6 ♘xe4 ♘xe4 7 ♗xe4 ♕xd1+ 8 ♔xd1 ♗xc5 is dead equal.

4...♘fd7

After 4...♘e4 5 ♗d3 ♘xd2 6 ♗xd2 ± the black king position is deserted.

5 ♗d3

Here we have a typical 'French' centre. White's pawn centre (d4 and e5) pins down his opponent, who must fight the intruders with ...c7-c5 and ...f7-f6. White develops with ♗d3, ♘e2, ♘f3 and protects his pawn on d4 at the same time. His alternative idea is 5 f4!?, creating an even stronger pawn centre, the price of which is usually a king march instead of castling. For example: 5...c5 6 c3 ♘c6 7 ♘df3 (7 ♘gf3 ♕b6 8 ♘b3 cxd4 9 cxd4 a5!?) 7...♕b6 8 g3!? (preparing for the king journey e1-f2-g2. Another common line is 8 h4 cxd4 9 cxd4 f6 10 ♗d3 ♗b4+ 11 ♔e2 ♗e7 12 h5 0-0 13 ♕c2 f5 14 a3 a5 15 g4 ♕d8 16 gxf5 exf5 and now White should avoid 17 ♗xf5? ♖xf5! 18 ♕xf5 ♘dxe5) 8...cxd4 9 cxd4 ♗b4+ 10 ♔f2 g5!? 11 ♗e3!? (11 fxg5?! ♘dxe5 12 ♘xe5 ♘xe5 13 ♔g2 ♘c6 14 ♘f3 ♗f8 and ...♗g7) 11...f6!? 12 ♗h3? fxe5 13 fxe5 0-0 14 ♖c1 (14 ♗xe6+ ♔h8 threatening 15...♘dxe5) 14...♔h8 15 ♗g4 ♗e7 16 h4! gxh4 17 ♘h3! with a kingside initiative for White.

5...c5 6 c3 ♘c6 7 ♘e2

7 ♘df3 is met by 7...♕a5! with the threat of 8...cxd4, but 7 ♘gf3 is a viable gambit: 7...♕b6 8 0-0 cxd4 9 cxd4 ♘xd4 10 ♘xd4 ♕xd4 11 ♘f3 ♕b6 12 ♕c2 h6 (on 12...♕c5 White plays either 13 ♕e2 followed by ♗d2, ♖ac1 or 13 ♕b1!?) 13 ♗f4 ♗e7 14 ♖ac1 0-0 and now White can play 15 ♗e3 or 15 ♕e2 and ♗b1, ♕d3 with enough play for the pawn but probably no more.

7...cxd4 8 cxd4 f6!? 9 exf6

9 f4? is bad as after 9...fxe5 there is no good way to recapture: 10 dxe5 ♗c5! or 10 fxe5 ♘xd4! 11 ♘xd4 ♕h4+ and 12...♕xd4. The position suddenly becomes complicated after 9 ♘f4: 9...♘xd4 10 ♕h5+ ♔e7 11 exf6+ (11 ♘g6+ hxg6 12 ♕xh8 ♘xe5 -+) 11...♘xf6 12 ♘g6+ hxg6 13 ♕xh8 and White is an exchange up for a pawn, but Black can achieve equality with the active 13...♔f7 14 0-0 e5! followed by ...e5-e4.

9...♘xf6

In this position Black is ill-advised to try for a quick ...e6-e5, so 9...♕xf6?! is weak: 10 ♘f3 ♗b4+ 11 ♗d2 ♗xd2+ 12 ♕xd2 0-0 13 0-0 e5 14 dxe5 ♘dxe5 15 ♘xe5 ♘xe5 16 ♘d4! and Black's pawn d5 is insecure while White has ♖c1, ♗e2 and f2-f4 up his sleeve.

10 ♘f3 ♗d6

It is no use playing for exchanges with 10...♗b4+ 11 ♗d2 ♕a5 12 a3 ♗xd2+ 13 ♕xd2 ♕xd2+ 14 ♔xd2 as the e5 and d6 squares have been weakened and the difference in scope between the remaining bishops is even more apparent. The main line used to be 10...♕b6 but then people realized that after 11 0-0 ♗d6 12 ♘c3 0-0 13 a3! ♗d7 14 ♗e3 Black cannot take on b2 due to 15 ♘a4. Therefore the queen is misplaced on b6 because White's action b2-b4, ♖c1 and ♘a4-c5 will soon force it to withdraw.

11 0-0

11 ♗f4 ♕a5+ 12 ♔f1 ♕c7 is a very expensive trade for White.

11...0-0

Here Black can also try 11...♕c7 aiming to avoid the exchange of the dark-squared bishops. However, on one hand it is not clear that this exchange should be avoided, and on the other White can play 12 g3 0-0 13 ♗f4 e5 14 dxe5 ♘xe5 15 ♘xe5 ♗xe5 16 ♖c1 ♕d6 17 ♗xe5 ♕xe5 18 ♕b3 ♗h3 19 ♖fe1 ♖ae8 20 ♕c3! and Black's game is critical. His pawn on d5 will be fragile in the endgame while in the middlegame White is better due to his control over the d4-square.

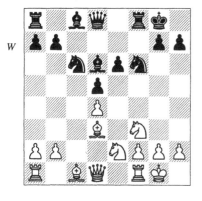

Plans and Counterplans:

White has an obvious target: the e6-pawn, or at least planting a knight on the square e5. Black plays a 'contra-game': he awaits a tactical opportunity to assault White's king position – often with an exchange sacrifice on f3 – or to attack the pawn on d4. Here are some examples:

a) 12 ♗f4 (the exchange of the bishops brings White closer to the seizure of the e5 square, but tactics crop up...) 12...♗xf4 13 ♘xf4 ♘e4! 14 ♘e2 (14 ♘h5 g6 15 ♘g3 ♘xg3 16 hxg3 ♕b6 17 ♕a4 a6! – Black cannot allow ♗b5 and ♗xc6 as this would immediately create a good knight vs. bad bishop game – 18 ♖ab1 ♗d7 19 ♗e2 ♘e5! = or 14 g3 ♕f6! 15 h4 h6 16 ♗xe4 – 16 h5? ♘g5! – 16...dxe4 17 ♘e5 ♖d8) 14...♖xf3! 15 gxf3 ♘g5 16 f4 (16 ♔h1 e5! 17 dxe5 ♘xf3 18 ♗xh7+ ♔h8 19 ♘g1 ♘cd4! 20 ♘xf3 ♗g4! and White has to sacrifice the queen: 21 ♘xd4! ♗xd1 22 ♖axd1 ♔xh7 =) 16...♘h3+ 17 ♔h1 ♕h4 and Black can start hunting the weak white pawns.

b) 12 ♗g5 ♕c7 13 ♗h4 ♘h5!? (to stop 14 ♗g3) 14 ♘c3 a6 15 ♖c1 g6 with complicated play. White can play the solid 16 ♗e2, planning ♘a4, when Black has 16...♕g7 and ...h7-h6 and ...g6-g5 (although this plan abandons the queenside, especially the b6-square) or can develop via 16...♗f4 17 ♖b1 ♗d7!? Black needs to be ready at any moment to counterbalance his positional weaknesses (the pawn on e6 and passive light-squared bishop) by tactical means.

IV. 1 e4 e6 2 d4 d5 3 ♘c3 (Classical Main Line)

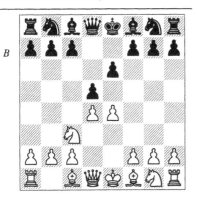

3 ♘c3 is the most aggressive move, and is therefore the favourite line of attacking players. Black cannot play an immediate 3...c5? in view of 4 exd5! exd5 5 dxc5 d4 6 ♗b5+! ♘c6 7 ♗xc6+ bxc6 8 ♘ce2 ♗xc5 9 ♘f3 ♗b4+ 10 ♗d2 ♗xd2+ 11 ♕xd2 c5 12 0-0-0 ♘f6 13 ♕g5! and the double attack (c5, g7) refutes Black's premature sortie. This leaves Black with:

A. 3...♘f6 and
B. 3...♗b4 (Winawer)

Both moves are designed to force White to play e4-e5 in order to make the central break ...c7-c5 possible. Besides these two main variations Black can also consider the interesting alternative move 3...♘c6, which is also known from the Nimzowitsch Defence (1 e4 ♘c6 2 d4 d5 3 ♘c3 e6). Play might continue: 4 ♘f3!? ♘f6 5 e5! (how much better this is now, compared to the previous move, pushing with a tempo!) 5...♘e4 6 ♗d3 ♗b4 7 ♗d2 ♘xd2 8 ♕xd2 f6 9 a3 ♗e7 10 exf6 ♗xf6 11 ♗b5! 0-0 12 ♗xc6 bxc6 13 ♘a4! ♕d6 14 0-0 e5 15 dxe5 ♗xe5 16 ♘xe5 ♕xe5 17 b3!? and besides his markedly better pawn formation White will also establish a knight on c5 (±). Instead of 5...♘e4, 5...♘fd7 6 ♗b5!? leaves Black with trouble finding counterplay, while the humble 3...♗e7 4 e5!? shuts in the knight on g8. Later White will have three plans to choose from: the sharp ♕g4, ♘f3 and h2-h4-h5; the strategic f2-f4 followed by ♘f3 or g2-g4 and f4-f5; and finally the most reliable ♘f3, ♗e2 (occasionally ♗b5+), 0-0.

A. 1 e4 e6 2 d4 d5 3 ♘c3 ♘f6

Here White achieves nothing after 4 ♗d3 c5 5 ♘f3 ♘c6!?, so his real alternatives are:

A1. 4 e5 and
A2. 4 ♗g5.

A1. 1 e4 e6 2 d4 d5 3 ♘c3 ♘f6 4 e5

4...♘fd7
On 4...♘e4, besides 5 ♘xe4 dxe4 6 ♗e3, 5 ♘ce2 (threatening 6 f3!) 5...f6 6 ♘f4 is strong, and if Black

hinders the threat of ♕h5+ and ♘g6 then the simple reply 7 ♗d3 secures White's advantage (±).

5 f4

After 5 ♘f3 c5 6 dxc5 ♘c6 7 ♗f4 ♗xc5 8 ♗d3 f6 Black is level, but his task becomes more difficult after 5 ♘ce2!? c5 6 c3 ♘c6 7 f4. The line 7...♕b6 8 ♘f3 f6!? has proved most successful, and after 9 a3 ♗e7 10 b4! cxd4 11 cxd4 0-0 12 ♖b1 (12 ♕d3 ♕c7! and the threat is 13...♘b6 while on 13 ♕c2 b5! is deadly!) 12...a5! 13 b5 a4! with equality.

5...c5 6 ♘f3 ♘c6

A brand new idea is 6...♕b6!? 7 ♗e3 a6 (now the pawn on b2 is hanging as after the capture White no longer has ♘c3-b5) 8 ♘a4 ♕c6 9 ♘xc5 ♘xc5 10 dxc5 ♗xc5 11 ♕d2 ♗d7 12 0-0-0 ♗xe3 13 ♕xe3 ♕a4! 14 ♔b1 ♘c6 15 ♗d3 0-0-0 16 c3 d4! 17 ♘xd4 (or 17 cxd4 ♘b4 18 a3 ♘xd3 and ...♗c6 with good counterplay) 17...♘xd4 18 ♕xd4 ♕xd4 19 cxd4 ♗c6 and Black has equalized. This plan of 6...♕b6!? and 7...a6 allows queenside castling by White only if he first captures on c5, and this concession reduces Black's problems.

7 ♗e3 ♕b6!?

On 7...cxd4 8 ♘xd4 ♗c5 9 ♕d2 ♘xd4 10 ♗xd4 ♗xd4 11 ♕xd4 ♕b6 12 ♘b5 (12 0-0-0!?) 12...♕xd4 13 ♘xd4 White has achieved his strategic goal. By blocking the d5-square he dooms the black army, and especially the bishop on c8, to passivity, while White can also

expand on the kingside and after 0-0-0, ♔b1, ♖c1 open up the queenside with c2-c4 at the right moment. The rook on h1 can be mobilized via the unusual solution h2-h4, ♖h3-c3 (d3).

8 ♘a4

8 a3 protects the pawn on b2 due to the trick ♘a4 but Black can equalize with 8...cxd4 9 ♘xd4 ♗c5 10 ♘a4 ♕a5+ 11 c3 ♗xd4 12 ♗xd4 ♘xd4 13 ♕xd4 ♘b8!! and ...♘c6.

8...♕a5+ 9 c3 c4!?

Black can sacrifice a piece with 9...cxd4 10 b4! (10 ♘xd4? ♘xd4 11 ♕xd4 b5 −+) 10...♘xb4!? 11 cxb4 ♗xb4+ 12 ♗d2 ♗xd2+ 13 ♘xd2 g5! 14 ♖b1! gxf4 15 ♗b5! ♔f8! 16 ♕e2 d3 17 ♕f2! ♘xe5 18 ♕xf4 ♘g6 19 ♕f6, but it seems that White's extra material will tell in the end. Positional players should take a close look at 9...c4!? or 9...b6!? (with the idea of continuing 10...♗a6) when the c5-square has been strengthened and Black can get rid of the bishop on c8.

10 b4

The threat was 10...b5.

10...♕c7 11 ♗e2 ♗e7 12 0-0 *(D)*

Plans and Counterplans:

White can opt for f4-f5 and ♘f3-g5 on the kingside or ♘a4-c5 and a2-a4-a5 on the queenside. However, Black can scupper White's kingside dreams with 12...f5!? After 13 exf6 ♘xf6 Black's plan is ...0-0 and ...♗d7-e8-g6, and on 13

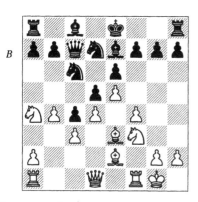

♞c5, 13...♞f8 followed by ...b7-b6 hounding the knight. Finally, on 13 ♞g5 ♞f8 14 g4 h6 15 ♞h3 b6!? Black awaits 16 gxf5?! exf5 so that he can play ...♣e6 and ...0-0-0, and daydream about ...g7-g5.

A2. 1 e4 e6 2 d4 d5 3 ♞c3 ♞f6 4 ♣g5

4...♣e7

4...dxe4 leads to almost equal chances: 5 ♞xe4 ♣e7 6 ♣xf6 ♣xf6 (6...gxf6 7 ♞f3 b6 8 ♣c4 ♣b7 9 ♕e2 and 0-0-0 is better for White) 7 ♞f3 0-0 8 c3 (8 ♕d2 ♣e7 9 0-0-0 b6 followed by ...♣b7, ...♞d7-f6 stops the attack ♣d3 and h2- h4) 8...♞d7 9 ♕c2 e5!. An exciting, although slightly inferior, alternative is 4...♣b4 5 e5 h6 6 ♣d2! (6 ♣h4 g5 7 ♣g3 ♞e4 8 ♞e2 c5 with lively play for Black or 6 exf6 hxg5 7 fxg7 ♜g8 8 h4 gxh4 9 ♕h5 ♕f6 =) 6...♣xc3 7 bxc3! ♞e4 8 ♕g4 g6 (8...♚f8 9 h4 and ♜h3, ♜g3 ±) 9 ♣d3 ♞xd2 10 ♚xd2 c5 11 h4! and now after 11...♕a5 12 ♞f3 ♞c6 13 ♕f4 b6 14 ♜hb1 ♣a6 15 a4 the

white king is unapproachable and White has a strong initiative, or on 11...♞c6 12 ♕f4! ♣d7 13 ♞f3 ♕e7 14 h5 g5 15 ♕f6! ♕xf6 16 exf6 c4 17 ♣f1 0-0-0 18 ♜e1 and 19 ♞e5 White is on top due to his spatial advantage in the endgame. It is surprising how the invincible king in the middle first helps out with the defence of the c3-pawn and is later well placed in the centre for the endgame!

5 e5

5 ♣xf6? ♣xf6 6 e5 ♣e7 followed by ...0-0, ...c7-c5 and ...♞c6 is better for Black.

5...♞fd7

After 5...♞e4?! 6 ♣xe7 ♕xe7 7 ♞xe4 dxe4 8 ♕e2 and 0-0-0 the pawn on e4 is in trouble.

6 ♣xe7

6 h4!? ♣xg5 7 hxg5 ♕xg5 is an amazing pawn sacrifice, but it works: 8 ♞h3! ♕e7 (8...♕h6? 9 g3 a6 10 f4! and ♕f3, 0-0-0 with a huge plus) 9 ♞f4 ♞c6 10 ♕g4 g6 11 0-0-0 h5!? (otherwise White has 12 ♜h6!) 12 ♕f3 ♞b6 13 g4 h4 14 ♞h3 and White regains the pawn with g4-g5, ♕f4 and ♞g1-f3.

6...♕xe7 7 f4 0-0 8 ♞f3 c5 9 ♕d2

Or 9 dxc5!? ♞c6 10 ♣d3 f6!? 11 exf6 ♕xf6 12 g3 ♞c5 13 0-0 ♣d7 14 ♕d2 ♞xd3 15 cxd3 e5!? ∞.

9...♞c6 10 dxc5

If White does not capture then after ...♞b6, and ...♣d7 Black can take on d4 and obtain counterplay with ...♜fc8.

10...♕xc5 11 0-0-0

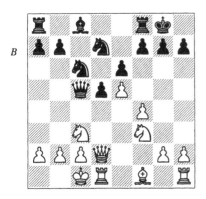

Plans and Counterplans:
Black has an attack on the queen-side with ...♖b8 and ...b7-b5 or ...♞b6, ...♗d7, ...♖fc8 and ...♞a5. White can try ♗d3, threatening a mating attack with ♗xh7, ♞g5, ♕d3-h3, or he can first weaken the black king position with h2-h4-h5-h6 and opt for an endgame with ♕d4 when time is ripe (for example after ...♞c6-a5).

B. 1 e4 e6 2 d4 d5 3 ♞c3 ♗b4

4 e5
Again a typical French pawn centre has taken shape. It is good general advice for White that he should not play ♕g4 as long as Black can answer it with the pawn sacrifice ...♞f6! For example, 4 ♕g4 ♞f6! 5 ♕xg7 ♖g8 6 ♕h6 ♖g6 7 ♕e3?! (7 ♕h4!?) 7...c5! and the white centre goes up in flames or 4 a3 ♗xc3+ 5 bxc3 dxe4 6 ♕g4 ♞f6! 7 ♕xg7 ♖g8 8 ♕h6 ♖g6 9 ♕e3 ♞c6!? 10 ♗b2 ♞e7 11 c4 b6 and ...♗b7, ...♞f5 and again Black is ahead in development (∓). But 4

♞ge2!? should not be underestimated: 4...dxe4 5 a3! ♗xc3 6 ♞xc3 f5?! 7 ♗f4!? (7 f3!?) 7...♞f6 8 ♕d2 0-0 9 0-0-0 followed by ♗c4 and f2-f3 and White is on top due to his control over the dark squares. Black should preserve his dark-squared bishop and instead of 5...♗xc3+ play 5...♗e7 6 ♞xe4 ♞f6 =. After, for example, 7 ♕d3!? ♞c6 8 ♗f4 0-0 9 0-0-0 e5! 10 dxe5 ♕xd3 followed by ...♞h5, or 10 ♗xe5 ♞xe5 11 dxe5 ♕xd3 and ...♞g4, he can obtain active counterplay.

4...c5
4...b6 is also seen occasionally: 5 a3 ♗xc3+ 6 bxc3 ♕d7!? 7 ♕g4 f5 8 ♕g3 ♗a6 9 ♗xa6 ♞xa6 10 ♞e2 ♔f7 11 a4 c5 12 ♕d3 ♕c8 13 ♗a3 and after 0-0 White is ready to shred Black's queenside with c3-c4!, ♖fb1 and a4-a5, and this cannot be hindered with ...c5-c4 as then the bishop on a3 would multiply in strength. 4...♞e7 5 a3 ♗xc3+ 6 bxc3 c5 is only a different move-order to 4...c5, leading to the same position.

5 a3!
To avoid trouble on d4 White 'induces' Black to swap minor pieces so that after he captures support will be provided by the pawn on c3. Other possibilities are:
a) 5 ♕g4 ♞e7 6 ♕xg7 ♖g8 7 ♕h6 cxd4 8 a3 ♗xc3+ (if on the seventh move White had played 7 ♕xh7? then now 8...♕a5! 9 axb4 ♕xa1 would be winning as the bishop on c1 is hanging. But with

the queen on h6 this line fails to 10 ♘b5!) 9 bxc3 ♕c7 10 ♘e2 dxc3 11 f4 ♗d7, followed by ...♘bc6 and ...0-0-0 with advantage to Black.

b) 5 ♗d2 ♘e7! (5...cxd4? 6 ♘b5! and the target is the d6-square) 6 ♘b5 ♗xd2+ 7 ♕xd2 0-0 8 dxc5 ♘d7 9 ♕c3 a6 10 ♘d6 ♕c7 and Black equalizes since the pawn on c5 cannot be maintained with 11 b4 due to 11...b6.

5...♗xc3+

Although the pawn on d4 will be more difficult to attack after this move, Black is able to destroy his opponent's queenside pawn formation. Other tries are: 5...cxd4 6 axb4 dxc3 7 ♘f3! ♕c7 (7...cxb2 8 ♗xb2 ♘e7 9 ♗d3 0-0 10 ♗xh7+! ♔xh7 11 ♘g5+ ♔g8 12 ♕h5 ♖e8 13 ♕xf7+ ♔h8 14 ♖a3! followed by ♖h3 mate. This slightly naive line nicely demonstrates White's possibilities) 8 ♕d4!? ♘e7 9 ♗d3 ♘d7 10 0-0 cxb2 11 ♗xb2 ♘b6 12 b5! ± and ♗a3 with a tremendous advantage. But 5...♗a5!? must be taken seriously: 6 dxc5? ♗xc3+ 7 bxc3 ♘e7 followed by ...♘d7, ...♕a5 is nearly losing for White, but 6 b4! cxd4 (6...cxb4? 7 ♘b5!) 7 ♕g4 (7 ♘b5 ♗c7 =) 7...♘e7 8 bxa5 dxc3 9 ♕xg7 ♖g8 10 ♕xh7 ♘bc6 11 ♘f3 ♕c7 12 ♗f4 ♗d7 followed by ...0-0-0 with a completely unclear position.

6 bxc3 ♘e7

6...♕a5 is premature due to 7 ♗d2, but 6...♕c7 is interesting with the idea of 7 ♕g4 f5, horizontally defending the pawn on g7. Still,

after 8 ♕g3! cxd4 9 cxd4 ♘e7 10 ♗d2 0-0 11 ♗d3 b6 12 ♘e2 ♗a6 13 ♘f4! ♕d7 14 ♗b4 White is on top.

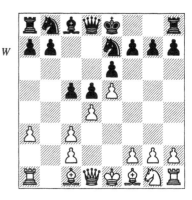

In this position White's main lines are:

B1. 7 ♕g4
B2. 7 ♘f3 and
B3. 7 a4.

It is a feature of all three lines that although White's pieces are more active, Black can counterbalance White's play with pressure on the centre. It is important that he does not open the position prematurely with ...c5xd4 as then the white bishops – especially the one on c1! – gain scope, but neither should Black close down the game too early with ...c5-c4, because this would make it difficult to obtain counterplay. So Black should maintain the central tension around the pawn on d4 and open or close the position according to White's plan.

B1. 1 e4 e6 2 d4 d5 3 ♘c3 ♗b4 4 e5 c5 5 a3 ♗xc3+ 6 bxc3 ♘e7 7 ♕g4

7...♕c7!?
This is sharper than 7...0-0 8 ♗d3!? ♘bc6!? (8...c4? 9 ♗h6 ♘g6 10 ♗xg6 fxg6 – or 10...hxg6 11 ♗g5 and h2-h4-h5 – 11 ♗e3 and h2-h4-h5, with a forceful attack on the black king, or 8...f5 9 exf6 ♖xf6 10 ♗g5 ♖f7 11 ♕h4 h6 12 ♗xe7 ♖xe7 13 ♕g3 ♕a5 14 ♘e2 c4 15 ♗g6 followed by f2-f4 and 0-0, also with an initiative for White) 9 ♕h5! ♘g6 (not 9...h6? 10 ♗xh6! gxh6 11 ♕xh6 ♘f5 12 ♗xf5 exf5 13 0-0-0! c4 14 ♘h3 and besides ♘g5 White is threatening to launch a mating attack by ♖h1-e1-e3-g3) 10 ♘f3 ♕c7 11 ♗e3!? (11 ♘g5 h6 12 ♘xf7 ♕xf7 13 ♕xg6 ♕xg6 = and the pawn will be regained on d4) 11...c4 12 ♗xg6 fxg6 13 ♕g4 ♕f7!? 14 h4 ♕f5 15 ♕xf5 ♖xf5 16 ♔e2, followed by g2-g4, ♖ag1, ♘e1 and f2-f4, when Black is struggling to keep his game alive.
8 ♕xg7
8 ♗d3 cxd4 (or 8...c4 9 ♗e2 0-0 and ...f7-f6 ∞) 9 ♘e2 dxc3 10 ♕xg7 ♖g8 11 ♕xh7 ♕xe5 12 ♗f4 ♕f6 is unclear.
8...♖g8 9 ♕xh7 cxd4 10 ♘e2 ♘bc6
Certainly not 10...♕xe5 11 cxd4 nor 10...dxc3 11 f4.
11 f4 ♗d7 12 ♕d3
12 cxd4?? ♘xd4 and 13 ♘xd4?? ♕xc3+ –+.
12...dxc3

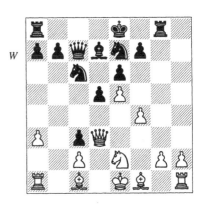

W

Plans and Counterplans:
What a crazy position! Black has given up his kingside in order to shatter White's centre. Black intends ...♘f5, ...0-0-0 and ...d5-d4 with a powerful centre. White should play 13 ♘xc3!? a6 (14 ♘b5 had to be stopped) and now 14 ♗d2 ♖c8 15 h4 ♘f5 16 ♖h3 or 14 ♖b1!? ♘f5 (14...0-0-0? 15 ♕xa6!! +–) 15 g4!? ♘xe5! (15...♖xg4 16 ♗h3 followed by ♗xf5 and ♘xd5 +–) 16 fxe5 ♕xe5+ 17 ♘e2 ♖xg4 with complete chaos.

B2. 1 e4 e6 2 d4 d5 3 ♘c3 ♗b4 4 e5 c5 5 a3 ♗xc3+ 6 bxc3 ♘e7 7 ♘f3

White chooses not to disturb the black kingside with 7 ♕g4. Instead he develops and strengthens his centre.
7...♗d7!?
Sooner or later this move will be necessary, so this is the right moment, leaving open the options for the queen (it can go to a5 or c7). Alternatively, 7...♕c7 8 a4!?

b6 9 ♗b5+ ♗d7 10 ♗d3 (the point of the preliminary check is that now Black will be unable to play ...♗a6) 10...♘bc6 11 0-0 h6 12 ♖e1 0-0 13 ♗a3 ± or 7...b6 8 a4!? ♗a6 9 ♗xa6 ♘xa6 10 0-0, and Black's a6 knight is misplaced while White is planning ♘g5, ♕h5.

8 dxc5

8 ♗d3 c4 9 ♗f1 (after g2-g3 the bishop will appear on h3) 9...♕a5 10 ♗d2 ♘bc6 followed by ...0-0-0 and ...f7-f5 =.

8...♕c7 9 ♗d3 ♗a4!

Vacating the d7-square for the knight.

10 ♖b1 ♘d7 11 0-0 ♘xc5

On 11...0-0?? again the typically French sacrifice decides the issue: 12 ♗xh7+ ♔xh7 13 ♘g5+ ♔g8 14 ♕h5.

12 ♖b4 ♘xd3 13 ♕xd3 ♗d7 =

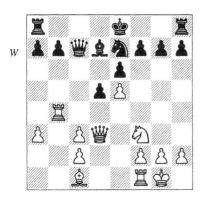

The position is level. For example 14 ♖e1 ♖c8 (not 14...0-0?? when 15 ♘g5! g6 16 ♕h3 h5 17 g4!? crushes the black kingside) 15 ♗d2 a6!? 16 a4 b5! 17 ♘d4 bxa4 18 ♕xa6 ♖b8 =.

B3. 1 e4 e6 2 d4 d5 3 ♘c3 ♗b4 4 e5 c5 5 a3 ♗xc3+ 6 bxc3 ♘e7 7 a4!?

This makes ♗a3 possible and controls the b5-square, where it will often protect the light-squared bishop. Sometimes this pawn will even make further progress to a5 and even a6.

7...♘bc6 8 ♘f3 ♕a5!? 9 ♗d2

This is the move that Black wanted to provoke. The bishop is now far away from the a3-f8 diagonal. 9 ♕d2 is no better owing to 9...♗d7 10 ♗a3 cxd4 11 cxd4 ♕xd2+ 12 ♔xd2 ♘f5 13 c3 ♘a5 14 ♖a2 f6 =.

9...♗d7

Trying to lure White into 10 c4?! as after 10...♕c7 11 cxd5 exd5 12 dxc5 0-0 13 ♗e2 ♘xe5 the white centre has vanished.

10 ♗b5!?

This is better than 10 ♗e2 as on 10...c4 11 0-0 f6 White now has 12 ♖e1 followed by the regrouping ♗d2-c1-a3!

10...♕c7

10...f6!? comes into consideration, in order to break up the white centre immediately, but not 10...0-0-0? 11 0-0 c4 12 ♗c1! ♕xc3 13 ♗d2 ♕b2 14 ♖b1 ♕a3 15 ♖e1 ♘f5 16 ♗xc6 ♗xc6 17 ♗b4 ♕xa4 18 ♕d2, when besides ♖a1, White is also threatening ♗c5 and then ♖a1 and ♖eb1.

11 0-0 0-0 12 ♗c1 b6 13 ♗a3 ♘a5 14 dxc5 ♗xb5! 15 cxb6 axb6 16 axb5

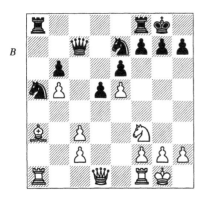

Plans and Counterplans:
Black has compensation for the sacrificed pawn in the form of an attack on the weak white pawns, but his first and most important task is to step out of the diagonal of the bishop on a3 with his pieces. So he should continue 16...♖fc8 17 ♗b4 (after 17 ♗d6 ♕d7 the c3-pawn is hanging and there is the threat of a double attack on d5 and b5 with 18...♘f5) 17...♘c4 18 ♖xa8 ♖xa8 19 ♖e1 ♘g6 20 ♗d6! (returning the pawn; after 20 ♕e2 ♕d7 the weak b5-pawn falls prey) 20...♘xd6 (or 20...♕d7!?) 21 exd6 ♕xd6 22 c4 and a roughly even endgame has arisen.

Sicilian Defence

1 e4 c5

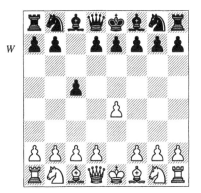

The Sicilian Defence is Black's most popular response to 1 e4, and one of the most important of all chess openings. The position becomes unbalanced right from the first move and often the players will castle on opposite wings. Both sides have their concrete plans and targets, but in 'Sicilian Wars' it is not the weapons that decide the battle but the ingenuity of the commanders-in-chief. The Sicilian is favoured on either side by those who prefer to play for victory from the very first moves.

White normally opens the position with 2 ♘f3 followed by 3 d4 (the Open Variation), in order to achieve a slight spatial plus and freer placement of his minor pieces. But let us first take a look at the alternatives.

White's two favourite ways of sidestepping the Open Variation are:

I. 2 c3 Variation
II. Closed Variation

In the Open Variation White has to be very well prepared to face several different lines, whereas in these two systems he can dispense with a large amount of study! Of course this choice will depend on individual preference. Here is a potpourri of other lines:

a) 2 ♗c4 e6 3 ♕e2 ♘c6 4 c3 ♗e7 and ....d7-d5 =.

b) 2 c4 ♘c6 3 ♘c3 g6 and Black opts for a setup which is frequently seen in the Closed Variation: ...♗g7, ...e7-e6, ...♘ge7 and ...d7-d6 or ...d7-d5 if possible.

c) 2 d3 ♘c6 3 ♘d2 and now either a King's Indian Attack setup (see the French Defence) with ...e7-e6, ...d7-d5, ...♗d6, ...♘ge7 or again a Closed Variation type of setup: ...g7-g6, ...♗g7, ...e7-e6(e5) and ....♘ge7.

d) 2 g3 d5!? 3 exd5 ♕xd5 4 ♘f3 ♗g4 5 ♗g2 ♕e6+! 6 ♔f1 ♘c6 7 h3 ♗h5 8 ♘c3 ♘f6 9 d3 ♕d7 followed by ...e7-e6, ...♗e7 (♗d6) with equality.

e) 2 b3 d6 3 ♗b2 ♘f6 4 ♗b5+ ♗d7 5 ♗xd7+ ♕xd7 6 ♗xf6 gxf6 7 ♕h5 (delaying ...f6-f5) 7...♘c6 8

♘c3 f5! 9 ♕xf5 ♕xf5 10 exf5 ♘d4 is level.

f) 2 f4 d5!? (again ...♘c6, ...g7-g6, ...♗g7, ...e7-e6 and ...♘ge7 is playable) 3 exd5 (3 e5? ♘c6 4 ♘f3 ♗g4 ∓) 3...♕xd5 4 ♘c3 ♕d8 5 ♘f3 ♘f6 6 ♘e5 e6 7 ♗b5+!? ♘fd7! (Black chooses this knight since it will later capture e5, when the other knight can come to c6), with ...a7-a6 to follow.

g) 2 b4!? (the Sicilian Wing Gambit) 2...cxb4 3 a3 (3 d4 d5 4 e5 ♘c6 and Black will develop via ...♕b6, ...♗f5 and ...e7-e6) 3...d5! 4 exd5 ♕xd5 (threatening 5...♕e5+ and a rook is attacked) 5 ♗b2 e5 6 axb4 ♗xb4 and ...♘c6, ...♘f6 and ...0-0, when Black is better.

h) 2 d4 cxd4 3 c3!? (the Smith-Morra Gambit) 3...dxc3 (3...♘f6 leads to the 2 c3 Sicilian) 4 ♘xc3 ♘c6 (also interesting is 4...e6 5 ♘f3 a6 6 ♗c4 d6 7 0-0 b5!? 8 ♗b3 ♖a7! and then ...♖d7 and ...♗b7, ...♘c6, neutralizing the d-file) 5 ♘f3 d6 6 ♗c4 e6 7 0-0 ♘f6 8 ♕e2 ♗e7 9 ♖d1! (the basic concept for White is the threat of e4-e5) 9...e5 10 h3 0-0 11 ♗e3. Black's moves are ...a7-a6, ...♗e6 while White usually opts for ♖c1 and b2-b4!? with roughly equal chances.

I. 1 e5 c5 2 c3

This move, which was once not rated very highly by chess theory, has become very fashionable, as White obtains an easily manageable middlegame.

2...d5

Black has to do something to counter d2-d4, otherwise he has no compensation for White's central plus: 2...d6?! 3 d4 ♘f6 4 ♗d3 cxd4 5 cxd4 g6 6 ♘c3 ♗g7 7 h3! 0-0 8 ♘f3 e5 9 dxe5 dxe5 10 0-0 ♘c6 11 ♗e3 ♗e6 12 ♗b5! and White's initial central advantage is transformed into a positional discrepancy between the dark-squared bishops. Black can instead counteract d2-d4 by attacking the e4-pawn with 2...♘f6!? 3 e5 ♘d5 4 d4 cxd4 5 ♘f3 ♘c6 and now White has a choice of the unclear lines: 6 cxd4 d6 7 ♗c4 ♘b6 8 ♗b5 dxe5 9 ♘xe5 ♗d7 10 ♗xc6 ♗xc6 11 ♘xc6 bxc6 12 0-0 g6! 13 ♖e1 ♗g7 14 ♗g5 ♘c8!? (14...♘d5? 15 ♘c3!) 15 ♕a4 0-0 16 ♕xc6 ♖b8 or 6 ♗c4!? ♘b6 7 ♗b3 d6 (7...dxc3? 8 ♘xc3 d6 9 exd6 ♕xd6 10 0-0! ♕xd1 11 ♖xd1 a6 12 ♗e3! and ♘d5 wins!) 8 exd6 ♕xd6 9 0-0 ♗e6!? 10 ♗xe6 ♕xe6 11 ♘xd4 ♘xd4 12 ♕xd4 ♖d8 13 ♕h4 ♕e2 (threatening 14...♖d1) 14 ♘d2. Black can also strongly consider 2...e6!? and after 3 d4 d5 4 exd5 (4 e5 transposes to the Advance Variation of the French) 4...exd5!? 5 ♘f3 ♘c6 6 ♗e2 ♗d6 7 dxc5 ♗xc5 8 0-0 ♘ge7 9 ♘bd2 0-0 10 ♘b3 ♗b6 11 ♘bd4 ♘f5!? Black destroys the knight's outpost on d4 and equalizes.

3 exd5 ♕xd5 4 d4 ♘f6 5 ♘f3 ♘c6!?

A practical move-order. After 5...e6 Black has to consider 6 ♗d3 as well as 6 ♘a3, but now 6 ♗d3

♗g4! and 6 ♘a3 ♗g4! 7 ♘b5 0-0-0! are better for Black.

6 ♗e2 cxd4

This is the first point at which c3-c4 has become a threat as the black queen has no check on e4.

7 cxd4 e6

Black must thwart the expansion ♘c3 and d4-d5.

8 ♘c3 ♕d6!?

Even more precise than 8...♕d8, because after ...♗e7 and ...0-0 the rook on f8 can use the d8 square.

9 0-0 ♗e7

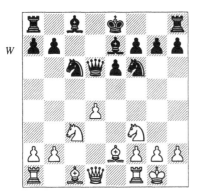

Plans and Counterplans:

On White's ♗e3, ♕d2, ♖d1, ♖ac1 Black answers ...0-0 and ...♖d8 and then places his bishop either on b7 (after ...b7-b6), or on d7-e8 to make room for his rook on c8. After 10 ♘b5 ♕d8 11 ♗f4 ♘d5 12 ♗g3 Black can choose between 12...0-0 13 ♗c4 a6 14 ♗xd5 axb5 15 ♗e4 ♖a5!? and 12...a6 13 ♘c3 0-0!? (13...♘xc3 14 bxc3 b5 15 a4! b4 16 c4 and d4-d5 is a powerful threat) and Black can construct a plan based on ...♘xc3, ...b7-b6 and

...♗b7 or ...♕b6, ...♖d8, ...♗d7-e8 and ...♖ac8. Meanwhile White can consider ♖c1, ♘a4, a2-a3 and b2-b4 or ♕d2, ♖fd1, ♘e4 and ♘e5.

II. 1 e4 c5 2 ♘c3 (Closed Variation)

2...♘c6

Black should not forget that White can still transpose to an Open Sicilian with 3 ♘f3 and 4 d4, so he should make a second move that would fit with his repertoire in an open game. For Paulsen players, 2...e6 is an alternative: 3 g3 d5 4 ♗g2 dxe4! 5 ♘xe4 ♗e7 followed by ...♘f6 and ...♘c6 with a pleasant game for Black.

3 g3

3 f4 g6 4 ♘f3 ♗g7 5 ♗c4 e6 6 f5!? ♘ge7! 7 fxe6 fxe6 8 d3 d5! 9, ♗b3 b5! leads to an exciting position in which the b5 pawn is protected by ...♕a5+ and ...d5-d4.

3...g6 4 ♗g2 ♗g7 5 d3 d6 6 f4

6 ♗e3 e5 7 ♕d2 ♘ge7 8 ♗h6!? 0-0! 9 h4? fails to 9...♗xh6 10 ♕xh6 f6!! and after 11 h5? g5 12 f4 ♔h8! 13 fxg5 ♘g8! the white queen falls! Instead of 6...e5 Black often plays 6...♖b8 followed by ...b5-b4.

6...e6

Also possible is first 6...♖b8 and then ...b7-b5-b4, ...e7-e6, and ...♘ge7 while White goes ♘f3, 0-0 with a kingside attack: h2-h3, g2-g4 and f4-f5 or ♘h4 and f4-f5. Since this kingside advance is exactly White's plan Black should not place his knight on f6 (so that it does not get attacked) and he can block the white pawns with ...f7-f5. Similar play results after 6...e5 followed by ...♘ge7, ...0-0 and ...♘d4.

7 ♘f3 ♘ge7 8 0-0 0-0

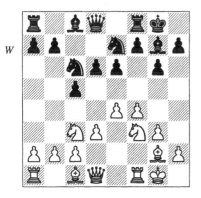

W

Plans and Counterplans:
On White's **9 g4** Black plays 9...f5 and 10 gxf5 exf5 =. More dynamic play results from **9 ♗e3**, threatening d3-d4 and, by attacking the pawn on c5, also enabling e4-e5. Black can answer 9...b6 when 10 d4 ♗a6! 11 ♖f2 ♘a5 leads to a double-edged game, but the most frequent reply to 9 ♗e3 is 9...♘d4! which again grants good chances. For example: 10 ♖b1 (alternatively: 10 ♘e2? ♘xe2+ and the pawn on b2 is hanging; 10 e5 ♘ef5 11 ♗f2 ♘xf3+ 12 ♕xf3 ♘d4 13 ♕d1 dxe5 14 fxe5 ♗xe5 15 ♘e4 f5 16 ♘xc5 ♕d6 =; or 10 ♗f2!? ♘xf3+ 11 ♗xf3 ♘c6 12 ♗g2 ♖b8 followed by ...b7-b6 and ...♗b7 =) 10...d5!? 11 ♘e2 ♘xf3+ 12 ♗xf3 d4 13 ♗f2 e5! 14 fxe5 ♘c6!, followed by ...♘xe5,

and the black pieces obtain active play.

Open Variation

1 e4 c5 2 ♘f3
White is now ready to open the centre with 3 d4. Black has the following options:

I. Paulsen Variation: 2...e6.
II. Scheveningen Variation: 2...d6 3 d4 cxd4 4 ♘xd4 ♘f6 5 ♘c3 e6.
III. Najdorf Variation: 2...d6 3 d4 cxd4 4 ♘xd4 ♘f6 5 ♘c3 a6.
IV. Four Knights Variation: 2...d6 3 d4 cxd4 4 ♘xd4 ♘f6 5 ♘c3 ♘c6.
V. Sveshnikov Variation: 2...♘c6 3 d4 cxd4 4 ♘xd4 ♘f6 5 ♘c3 e5.
VI. Dragon Variation and other systems involving ...g7-g6 and ...♗g7.

These lines encompass all the regular setups starting with 2...e6, 2...d6, 2...♘c6 and 2...g6. 2...d5? is bad in view of 3 exd5 ♕xd5 4 ♘c3 and d2-d4, but three minor lines are worth mentioning:
   a) 2...b6 3 d4 cxd4 4 ♘xd4 ♗b7 5 ♘c3 a6 6 ♗c4 e6 7 ♕e2 d6 8 ♗e3 followed by 0-0-0, f2-f3 and g2-g4 with a great attack for White,
   b) 2...a6!? 3 c3! (after 3 d4 cxd4 4 ♘xd4 ♘f6 5 ♘c3 Black's plan proves effective: 5...e5! and now White cannot jump to b5 to

threaten to go on to d6. 6 ♘f3 ♗b4! 7 ♘xe5? 0-0 8 ♗d3 d5! is better for Black!) 3...d5 4 exd5 ♕xd5 5 d4 e6 6 ♗e2 ♘f6 7 0-0 ♘c6 8 ♗e3! cxd4 9 cxd4 ♗e7 10 ♘c3 ♕d8 (10...♕d6!? is also possible) 11 ♘e5! ♘b4 (11...♘xe5 12 dxe5 ♘d7 13 f4 and ♘e4, ♖c1 ±) 12 ♗f3 0-0 13 ♕b3 ♘bd5 14 ♗g5 ±. Black cannot develop his queenside.

c) 2...♘f6!? 3 e5 ♘d5 4 ♘c3!? e6 (4...♘xc3 5 dxc3 followed by ♗f4, ♕d2, 0-0-0 ±) 5 ♘xd5 exd5 6 d4 ♘c6 7 c3!? (after 7 dxc5 ♗xc5 8 ♕xd5 d6! 9 exd6 ♕b6 Black has promising play: ...♗xf2+, ...♗e6 and ...0-0) 7...d6 8 ♗b5! ♗e7 9 exd6 ♕xd6 10 0-0 0-0 11 dxc5 ♕xc5 12 ♕a4! a6 13 ♗d3 ♕b6 14 ♖e1 ♗f6 15 ♘g5! and White has a strong attack, for example 15...h6? 16 ♘h7!, 15...♗xg5 16 ♗xg5 ♕xb2 17 ♕h4! or 15...g6 16 ♕h4 h5 17 ♕g3.

The various main lines can be reached with several different move-orders by Black. For example the basic position of section IV can arise through 2...d6 3 d4 cxd4 4 ♘d4 ♘f6 5 ♘c3 ♘c6 or 2...♘c6 3 d4 cxd4 4 ♘xd4 ♘f6 5 ♘c3 d6. Black has to decide which sidelines he will allow his opponent.

On the subject of sidelines, after 2 ♘f3 White can still change his mind and keep the position closed. For instance on 2...♘c6 or 2...d6 he has the option of playing 3 ♗b5(+). These sub-variations will be discussed in the main sections, the above-mentioned ones in sections II and V.

I. Paulsen Variation

1 e4 c5 2 ♘f3 e6 3 d4

An interesting position arises after 3 c3 d5 4 e5 (for 4 exd5 see the 2 c3 Sicilian) 4...d4!? (4...♘c6 5 d4 transposes to the Advance French) 5 cxd4 cxd4 6 ♗b5+ ♗d7! 7 ♘xd4 ♗xb5 8 ♘xb5 ♘c6 9 0-0 a6 10 ♘5c3 ♕d4!

3...cxd4

In the Sicilian Black always captures d4 as he would be tied up after d4-d5 (the knight on b8 and bishop on c8 respectively!). 3...d5?! is ineffective: 4 exd5 exd5 5 ♗b5+ ♘c6 6 0-0 and White is threatening ♘e5, ♖e1+ and ♘c3, but even if Black could survive this he would still be worse with his insecure isolated pawn on d5 after d4xc5.

4 ♘xd4

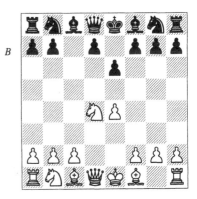

The flexibility of the Paulsen lies in the fact that the bishop on f8 can glide between its own pawns to reach b4, c5 or even d6!

And of course Black retains the option of a transposition into the Scheveningen Variation with ...d7-d6 and ...♗e7. He can choose the most appropriate deployment, depending upon White's moves. In the diagram position Black has two main continuations:

A. Original Paulsen: 4...a6
B. Modern Paulsen: 4...♘c6.

Beside the main lines, there are two independent sidelines:

a) 4...♘f6 5 ♘c3 (5 e5? ♕a5+! is worth remembering!) 5...♗b4?! 6 e5! ♘d5 (6...♘e4 7 ♕g4! ♘xc3 8 ♕xg7 ♖f8 9 a3 ♘b5+ – 9...♗a5 10 ♗h6 ♕e7 11 ♘b3 +– or 9...♕a5 10 ♘b3 ♕d5 11 ♗d3! +– – 10 axb4 ♘xd4 11 ♗g5! ♕b6 12 ♗h6 ♕xb4+ 13 c3 ♘f5 14 cxb4 ♘xg7 15 ♗xg7 ♖g8 16 ♗f6 ±. Black is tied up by the bishop on f6) 7 ♕g4!? (7 ♗d2!? ♘xc3 8 bxc3 ♗e7 9 ♕g4 ±) 7...0-0! (the best chance, since after 7...g6 8 ♗d2, 7...g5!? 8 ♘b5! and 7...♔f8 8 a3 ♗a5 9 ♗d2 ♘xc3 10 bxc3 ♕c7 11 ♕g3 Black has problems with his king) 8 ♗h6 g6 9 ♗xf8 ♕xf8 10 ♕g3 ♕c5 11 ♘e2 ♘c6 12 0-0-0! ♘xc3 13 ♘xc3 ♕xe5 14 ♕xe5 ♘xe5 15 ♘b5 ±. White's idea is to follow up with ♘d4 and f2-f4. Although Black has some activity due to his pawn majority and bishop pair, this does not fully counterbalance the loss of the exchange in this queenless position. The moral of this line is that if the bishop on f8 comes out too early

then White chases the knight from f6 with e4-e5 and sets about attacking the abandoned pawn on g7 with ♕g4.

b) 4...♕b6!? (eventually Black wishes to strike at the pawn on f2 via ...♕b6 and ...♗c5) 5 ♘b3!? (5 ♘c3 ♗c5 6 ♘a4 ♕a5+ 7 c3 ♗xd4 8 ♕xd4 ♘f6 =) 5...♘c6 6 ♘c3 ♘f6 7 ♗d3 ♗e7 8 0-0 0-0 9 ♗e3 ♕c7 10 f4 d6 and we reach a position resembling the Scheveningen Variation in which Black has lost a tempo with ...♕d8-b6-c7 and White has achieved ♘d4-b3. This means that Black cannot reach the c4-square with ...♘c6-a5-c4, although he can initiate play on the queenside (...a7-a6, ...b7-b5 and ...♗b7) while White plays on the opposite flank (g2-g4-g5!?).

A. 1.e4 c5 2 ♘f3 e6 3 d4 cxd4 4 ♘xd4 a6 (Original Paulsen)

The differences between this move compared to 4...♘c6 are that White cannot play ♘b5 and cannot simplify by exchanging on c6, but he can develop with ♗f1-d3. White's possible replies are:

A1. 5 c4
A2. 5 ♗d3 and
A3. 5 ♘c3.

A1. 1 e4 c5 2 ♘f3 e6 3 d4 cxd4 4 ♘xd4 a6 5 c4

This move, occupying the centre, is not correct at the moment as the bishop on f8 bursts from its home square.

5...♘f6 6 ♘c3

After 6 ♗d3 ♘c6 7 ♘xc6 dxc6 8 0-0 e5!, followed by ...♗c5, Black is better as his bishops can move more freely than White's (i.e. the bishop on d3!).

6...♗b4! 7 ♗d3

7 e5 ♘e4 8 ♕g4 ♘xc3 9 a3 (9 ♕xg7? ♘e4+ and ...♖f8 wins a piece!) 9...♗f8! 10 bxc3 ♕a5 11 ♕g3 d6! and if White takes twice on d6 then c3 is hanging. 7 ♗d2 0-0! (7...♗xc3? 8 ♗xc3 ♘xe4 9 ♕g4 ♘xc3 10 ♕xg7 ♖f8 11 bxc3 ±) 8 e5 ♗xc3 9 ♗xc3 ♘e4 and with ...d7-d5 (d6), ...♘xc3 and ...♘c6 Black is comfortable.

7...♘c6 8 ♘xc6 dxc6

Black has to capture this way to free his bishop on c8.

9 e5!

9 0-0?! e5! and the c8-bishop becomes active while its counterpart on d3 is passive.

9...♕a5!?

After 9...♘d7 10 f4 ♘c5 11 ♗c2 ♕xd1+ 12 ♔xd1 Black is worse due to his bishop on c8.

10 exf6 ♗xc3+ 11 bxc3 ♕xc3+ 12 ♗d2 ♕xd3 13 fxg7 ♖g8

Not 13...♕e4+ 14 ♔f1 ♖g8 15 ♗g5! ♕xc4+ 16 ♔g1 ♕d5 17 ♗f6 and despite Black's extra pawn White is winning: Black's pieces are out of play, the pawn on g7 is very strong and White can continue with ♕c2 and ♖d1 or h2-h4 and ♖h3-d3.

14 ♗h6

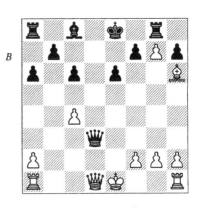

B

Plans and Counterplans:

Black plays against the pawn on g7 and will quickly castle queenside. White needs to secure his king and then swap as many heavy pieces as possible in order to make it easier for the g7-pawn to promote. So 14...♕c3+ 15 ♔f1 ♕f6 (15...♕xc4+ 16 ♔g1 ♕h4 17 ♕d2 and White is threatening ♗g5 and ♖d1) 16 ♕c1 e5, and now after 17 ♖b1? ♗e6! 18 ♖xb7 0-0-0! White falls into a trap as after, e.g. 19 ♖b1 ♖d4!? Black's game is very strong. Better is 17 c5 ♗e6 18 h4, preparing to offer the exchange of queens by ♕g5.

A2. 1 e4 c5 2 ♘f3 e6 3 d4 cxd4 4 ♘xd4 a6 5 ♗d3

Developing in the other direction is momentarily impossible: 5 g3?! d5! 6 exd5?! ♕xd5.

5...♘f6

A few other choices:

a) 5...♘c6 6 ♘xc6! dxc6 (after 6...bxc6 7 0-0 d5 8 c4! ♘f6 9 ♘c3 Black's centre collapses: 9...♗e7

10 cxd5 cxd5 11 exd5 exd5 – or 11...♘xd5 12 ♗e4 – 12 ♕a4+ ♕d7 13 ♖e1 ± or 9...d4!? 10 ♘e2 e5 11 h3!? and f2-f4 ±) 7 0-0 e5!? 8 ♘d2 ♗d6 (8...♗c5? 9 ♘c4 ♕c7 10 ♕h5! ±) 9 ♘c4 ♗c7 10 a4! ♘e7 11 a5 ♗e6 12 ♗e3 ± ♗xc4? 13 ♗xc4 ♗xa5 14 ♕g4! 0-0 15 ♖fd1 ♕c7 16 ♖d7 and White wins.

b) 5...b5 6 0-0 ♗b7 7 ♕e2 ♘e7 8 a4! b4 9 ♘d2 ♘bc6 10 ♘4b3 followed by f2-f4 ±.

c) 5...g6 6 c4!? ♗g7 7 ♘b3 ♘e7 (on 7...d6 White can attack d6 with ♘c3, ♗f4, ♕d2, ♗e2 and ♖d1) 8 0-0 0-0 9 ♘c3 ♘bc6 10 ♗g5! h6 (otherwise after ♕d2 the bishop can no longer be chased) 11 ♗h4 ±. White is planning ♕d2, ♖fd1, ♗e2, c5 and ♗g3 while it is hard to recommend anything for Black.

d) 5...♗c5!? 6 ♘b3 (6 c3 occupies the natural square of the knight on b1) 6...♗a7!? 7 ♘c3 ♘c6 8 ♕e2 d6 9 ♗e3 ♘f6 10 0-0-0 b5 11 f4 b4 12 ♘a4 e5 13 ♗xa7 ♖xa7 14 f5 0-0 15 g4 with a convincing attack for White.

6 0-0 d6 7 c4!?

Securing White's centre. The other setup ♔h1, f2-f4, ♘c3, ♕f3 and ♗e3 is also not bad.

7...♗e7

7...g6 8 ♘c3 ♗g7 9 ♗e3 0-0 10 ♗e2!? ♘bd7 (10...d5 11 cxd5 exd5 12 e5! ♘e4 13 ♘xe4 dxe4 14 ♕c2 ♗xe5 15 ♕xe4 followed by ♖fd1 and ♖ac1, when Black has opened the centre in vain as it is has only highlighted his lack of development. It is important to note that

in the given piece configuration the move ...d7-d5 – played against White's centre of e4 and c4 – is well met by cxd5 and then e5!) 11 ♕d2 ♘c5 12 f3 ♖b8 13 ♖fd1 ♕c7 14 ♘c2! ± and besides his spatial advantage. White has also found a specific target at d6.

8 ♘c3 0-0 9 ♗e3

Or 9 ♕e2 b6 10 f4 ♗b7 11 ♔h1 ♘bd7 with a tough fight in prospect.

9...♕c7 10 ♖c1 b6 11 f4 ♘bd7

11...♗b7? 12 f5! e5 13 ♘d5! is clearly better for White.

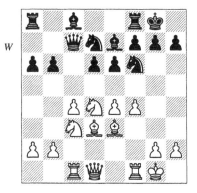

Plans and Counterplans:
Black has created a flexible 'hedgehog' setup but also this comes with a spatial disadvantage. White should not overextend with **12 g4?!** due to 12...♘c5 13 g5 ♘g4! 14 ♕xg4 ♘xd3 15 ♖c2 ♘b4 16 ♖c1 ♘d3, when he is forced to settle for a draw by repetition, unless he wants to lose the pawn on c4. So it is better to play **12 ♕e2!? ♗b7** 13 b4 ♖ac8 14 a3 ♖fe8 15 g4 g6, when the real struggle is yet to come.

A3. 1 e4 c5 2 ♘f3 e6 3 d4 cxd4 4 ♘xd4 a6 5 ♘c3

5...♕c7

After 5...b5 6 ♗d3 ♗b7 7 0-0 d6 8 ♖e1 ♘f6 9 a4! b4 10 ♘a2 ♗e7 11 c3! bxc3 12 ♘xc3 ± the queenside has opened up in White's favour. He is better developed and can continue ♖c1 and ♕b3.

6 ♗d3

On 6 g3 an important intermediate move is 6...♗b4!, when 7 ♗d2 (7 ♘e2 ♘f6 8 ♗g2 ♗e7 9 0-0 ♘c6 10 h3 0-0 11 f4 b5 is unclear) 7...♘f6 8 ♗g2 ♘c6! 9 ♘xc6 bxc6 and ...♗e7, ...d7-d6, ...0-0 equalizes. Instead 6 f4 b5 7 ♗d3 ♗b7 8 ♕f3 ♘f6 9 ♗e3 ♘c6 10 g4!? h5! 11 g5 ♘g4 12 ♗g1 ♘xd4 13 ♗xd4 e5! leads to sharp play.

6...♘c6

On 6...b5 White's scheme is quick castling and then ♖e1: 7 0-0 ♗b7 8 ♖e1 d6 9 ♗g5, threatening 10 ♘d5!, while 9...♗e7? 10 ♗xe7 ♘xe7 11 ♗xb5! axb5 12 ♘dxb5 and ♘xd6 wins for White.

7 ♘xc6!? dxc6!?

This move is still almost *terra incognita* in chess theory, but it looks better than 7...bxc6 8 0-0 ♘f6 9 ♕e2 ♗d6!? 10 f4 e5 11 f5! (11 fxe5? ♗xe5 and the invincible black bishop commands the board from the e5-square) 11...♗e7 12 ♔h1 h6 13 ♘a4! d5 14 c4 ♗b7 (after 14...d4 15 c5 ♘d7 16 b4 a5 17 a3 the play of Black's pieces is limited while the bishop on d3 is an excellent blockading piece,

controlling the diagonal a6-f1) 15 c5 and White has a firm grip on the e4-square while Black's bishop on b7 and his whole queenside is stymied. White is better (±).

8 0-0

On 8 a4!? the obligatory answer to the threat of a4-a5 is 8...a5.

8...♘f6 9 f4 e5!

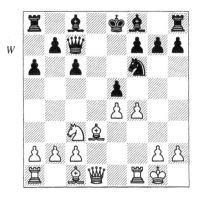

Plans and Counterplans:

9...e5! not only prevents 10 e5 but also prepares an attack using the g4-square, while putting the bishop on d3 on the shelf! For example, **10 fxe5?** ♗c5+ 11 ♔h1 ♘g4 12 ♕f3 0-0 followed by ♘xe5 when, with his control over the square e5, Black stands better. **10 f5** can also be met by 10...♗c5+: 11 ♔h1 h5 12 ♕f3 ♘g4 13 ♘d1 ♕b6! stops 14 ♗e3 and the black pieces cannot be driven away. White's best choice is **10 ♔h1!** and now 10...♗d6 would be a blunder as after 11 f5! Black is unable to thwart the simultaneous threats of 11 ♗e3 and 11 g4. So 10 ♔h1! ♗c5!? (10...h5?! 11 fxe5 ♘g4 12

♗c4!), with similar motives to the previous lines (...♘g4, or ...h7-h5 and then ...♘g4), keeping Black's counterplay alive.

B. 1 e4 c5 2 ♘f3 e6 3 d4 cxd4 4 ♘xd4 ♘c6 (Modern Paulsen)

Black intends ...♕c7, ...a7-a6 and ...♘f6, often combined with ...♘xd4 followed by ...♗c5. White's most important setups are:

B1. 5 ♘b5 and
B2. 5 ♘c3.

White cannot hope for an advantage with other continuations:
    a) 5 c4 ♘f6 6 ♘c3 ♗b4 7 ♘xc6 (7 f3 d5!) 7...bxc6 8 ♗d3 e5! =.
    b) 5 g3 d5! 6 ♗g2 ♕b6!? 7 ♘b3 dxe4 8 ♗xe4 ♘f6 =.
    c) 5 a3 ♘f6 6 ♘c3 and now with 6...d6 Black has a Scheveningen in which White's move a2-a3 is unnecessary.
    d) 5 ♘xc6 can be met by 5...bxc6 6 ♗d3 ♘f6 7 0-0 e5 with the idea of ...♗e7, ...0-0, ...d7-d6 and ...♗e6 or by 7...d5!? 8 e5 ♘d7 9 f4 ♘c5!? sweeping off the bishop on d3 so that White cannot play the typical attack ♗xh7+, ♕h5+, ♖f3-h3 against Black's kingside castling position.

B1. 1 e4 c5 2 ♘f3 e6 3 d4 cxd4 4 ♘xd4 ♘c6 5 ♘b5

5...d6
6 ♘d6+ should not be allowed.

6 c4!?
White opts to enforce the closure of the dark-squared bishop's diagonal followed by a blockade on the centre. But just as in the Sveshnikov Variation (section V) this can only be reached at the cost of several tempi, by galloping around with the knights while Black organizes his game. Instead of 6 c4 White can play 6 ♗f4 e5 7 ♗e3 a6 8 ♘5c3 ♘f6 9 ♗g5 ♗e7 10 ♗xf6 ♗xf6 11 ♘d5 0-0 12 ♘bc3 ♗e6 13 ♗c4 ♖c8 14 0-0 ♗g5! 15 ♗b3 ♘d4 with the idea of ...♔h8 and ...f7-f5.

6...♘f6
The most precise as now on 7 ♘5c3 Black need not answer 7...a6: 7...♗e7 8 ♗e2 0-0 9 0-0 b6 10 ♗f4 ♗b7 11 ♘d2 ♖c8 =.

7 ♘1c3 a6 8 ♘a3
After 8 ♘d4 ♗e7 9 ♗e2 0-0 10 0-0 ♗d7 11 ♗e3 ♘xd4 12 ♕xd4 ♗c6 13 f3 Black can prepare ...d6-d5 with 13...♕b8! For example, 14 a4 (...b7-b5 was also threatened!) 14...d5! 15 cxd5 exd5 16 exd5 (16 e5? ♘d7 17 f4 ♗c5 18 ♕d2 ♕a7! 19 ♗xc5 ♕xc5+ 20 ♔h1 d4! and after the isolated pawn gets moving Black stands better) 16...♖d8 17 ♗c4 b5 followed by ...b5-b4 and Black regains the pawn with an equal position.

8...♗e7
Black has the option of an interesting gambit: 8...d5!? 9 exd5 exd5 10 cxd5 ♘b4 11 ♗e2 and now 11...♗c5?! is bad in view of 12 ♗e3! ♗xe3 13 ♕a4+! ♘d7 14 ♕xb4 ♗c5

15 ♕e4+ ♔f8 16 0-0 ±, but the realistic 11...♘fxd5 12 0-0 ♗e6 is fine. Another move-order is 8...b6 9 ♗e2 ♗b7 10 0-0 ♘b8! 11 f3 ♗e7 12 ♗e3 ♘bd7 13 ♕d2 0-0 14 ♖fd1 ♕c7 15 ♖ac1 ♖ac8 and Black, as so often in the Paulsen, plays the hedgehog, that is, he employs the pawn configuration ...a7-a6, ...b7-b6, ...d7-d6 and ...e7-e6 with his pieces placed with ...♗b7, ...♘d7, ...♘f6, ...♗e7 and ...♕c7. The point of 10...♘b8! is not only to transfer the knight to d7, where it is really well placed, but also to attack the pawn on e4, thus provoking f2-f3 and at the same time preventing White from playing f2-f4 and ♗f3.

9 ♗e2 0-0 10 0-0 b6

The only route for the bishop.

11 ♗e3 ♗b7

The knight on c6 can still be shifted to d7 with 11...♘e5 12 f4 ♘ed7, but after 13 ♗f3 White definitely controls a larger territory. 11...♗b7 keeps ...d6-d5 in mind, for example 12 f4 d5! 13 cxd5 exd5 14 exd5 ♘b4 =.

W

Plans and Counterplans:

White would first like to obstruct Black's ...d6-d5 and then increase the pressure along the d-file to attack the pawn on d6. Black aims for ...d6-d5, but if this is out of reach then he will attack the pawns on c4 and e4 with, for example, ...♖c8 and ...♘e5. More specifically: **12 ♕b3** ♘d7 13 ♖fd1 ♘c5! 14 ♕c2 (14 ♗xc5? bxc5 15 ♕xb7?? ♘a5 nets the queen!) 14...♕c7 =. Black can continue ...♖ac8, ...♕b8, ...♖fd8 and sometimes ...♘b4 while White can opt for f2-f3, ♕d2 and ♘c2. On **12 ♖c1** Black can play 12...♖c8!? and 13 ♕d2 ♘e5 as now 14 f4? ♘eg4 15 ♗d4 e5! is already better for Black. Finally, one should note a trap that Black should avoid: **12 ♖c1** ♕c7? 13 ♘d5! exd5 14 cxd5 and White is strategically winning.

B2. 1 e4 c5 2 ♘f3 e6 3 d4 cxd4 4 ♘xd4 ♘c6 5 ♘c3

5...♕c7

5...♘f6 6 ♘db5 d6 7 ♗f4 e5 8 ♗g5 transposes to the Sveshnikov Variation, see the postscript in section V. 5...a6 6 ♗e2 ♘ge7 does not make much sense because after 7 ♗f4!? the d6-square is weak. After 5...♕c7 White's three possibilities are:

B2a. 6 g3
B2b. 6 ♗e2 and
B2c. 6 ♗e3.

After 6 ♘xc6 Black responds 6...bxc6 followed by ...d7-d5, while 6 ♘db5 can be met by 6...♕b8 7 a4 ♘f6 8 ♗d3 a6 9 ♘a3 d5!? and 6 f4!? by 6...a6 7 ♘f3 (7 ♘xc6 ♕xc6 8 ♗d3 b5 9 ♕e2 – 9 e5 f5! – 9...♗b7 10 ♗d2 ♗c5 and on e4-e5 – liberating the e4-square – it is worth remembering the typical reply ...f7-f5!) 7...♗c5 8 ♗d3 b5 9 ♕e2 ♘d4 10 ♘xd4 ♗xd4 11 ♗d2 ♗b7 12 e5! f5!! 13 exf6 ♘xf6 ∞.

B2a. 1 e4 c5 2 ♘f3 e6 3 d4 cxd4 4 ♘xd4 ♘c6 5 ♘c3 ♕c7 6 g3

6...a6

Now and hereafter Black can transpose to the Scheveningen Variation with ...d7-d6 (section II), but in the long run Black will need to play ...a7-a6 in any case to guard against the threat of ♘b5.

7 ♗g2 ♘f6

The kingside needs to be developed, otherwise after 0-0 and ♖e1 White will be threatening ♘d5.

8 0-0 ♗e7

After 8...♘xd4 9 ♕xd4 ♗c5 10 ♗f4! d6 (Black is undeveloped and draughty on the dark squares if the queens are exchanged) 11 ♕d2 h6 (11...0-0 12 ♘a4 e5 13 ♗g5 ±) 12 ♖ad1 e5 13 ♗e3 the king gets stuck in the middle as now 13...♔e7 is compulsory to defend the d6-square, e.g. 13...0-0? 14 ♗xc5 dxc5 15 ♕d6! with a winning endgame for White. After the exchange of queens there might follow ♖fd1 and ♘d5 or ♘a4-b6.

9 ♖e1 0-0

Now, with the rook on e1, playing 9...♘xd4 10 ♕xd4 ♗c5 makes more sense: 11 ♗f4 d6 12 ♕d2 ♘g4!, since the f2-pawn is hanging. Therefore instead of 11 ♗f4 it is better to continue 11 ♕d1!? (11...♘g4 is no go) with 12 ♗e3 to follow.

10 ♘xc6 dxc6

10...bxc6 11 e5 ♘d5 12 ♘a4! and c2-c4 ±.

11 e5

White has succeeded in carrying out e4-e5.

11...♖d8 12 ♕f3 ♘d5 13 h4!?

13 ♘e4 does not work as the pawn on e5 is hanging.

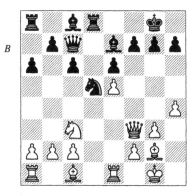

Plans and Counterplans:

White has the immensely strong threat of 14 ♗g5, exchanging the bishop on e7 which is protecting the vital square d6. For example, **13...b5?!** 14 ♗g5 ♗b7 15 ♘e4! c5 (15...♕xe5 16 ♘f6+ +−) 16 ♘d6! ±. Black should therefore play **13...♘xc3!** 14 ♕xc3 ♗d7 15 ♗g5 ♗e8 securing a defensible position.

For example, 16 ♖ad1 a5! (it is not good to mindlessly trade rooks and bishops as White is better in the queen endgame due to the difference between the light-squared bishops and the invasion of his queen on d6) 17 ♗xe7 ♕xe7 18 ♖xd8 ♕xd8 19 a3 ♕c7 20 ♖d1 ♖d8 21 ♖xd8 ♕xd8 22 ♕c5 and the queen swap should no longer be feared since after 22...h6! 23 ♕d6 ♕xd6 24 exd6 b6! 25 f4 c5! = Black has placed his queenside pawns on the opposite colour to his bishop, thus creating the possibility of centralizing with ...♗b5 and ...♔f8-e8-d7. Note also that 16 b4 ♗xg5 17 hxg5 a5! 18 b5 ♖ac8 leads to an even simpler ending. One certainly needs to be familiar with typical endgames in this variation!

B2b. 1 e4 c5 2 ♘f3 e6 3 d4 cxd4 4 ♘xd4 ♘c6 5 ♘c3 ♕c7 6 ♗e2

6...a6 7 0-0
After 7 f4 b5 8 ♘xc6 ♕xc6 9 ♗f3 ♗b7 10 e5 ♕c7 11 ♘e4 (11 0-0 ♘h6! 12 ♗xb7 ♕xb7 13 ♕d3 ♘f5 14 ♘e4 ♖d8 and ...d7-d6) 11...♖d8 12 ♕e2 d5 13 ♘g3 g6! 14 ♗e3 h5 Black is ready to seize the initiative on the kingside with ...♘e7, ...h5-h4 and ...♘f5.
7...♘f6
After 5...♕c7 Black's moves are nearly always ...a7-a6 and ...♘f6. Again 7...b5? is premature in view of 8 ♘xc6 dxc6 (or 8...♕xc6 9 ♗f3 ♗b7 10 ♗f4, followed by ♖e1, with

a significant advantage in development and threats of a2-a4 and ♘c3-d5) 9 ♗e3 ♗b7 10 a4! b4 11 ♘b1 c5 12 ♘d2 ± and White can opt for ♗d3, ♕e2, a4-a5 and ♘c4, when Black's weaknesses on a6 and b6 and the strength of the knight on c4 make themselves felt.
8 ♔h1
8 f4?? is, to say the least, premature due to 8...♘xd4 9 ♕xd4 ♗c5 and the queen is lost!
8...♘xd4
White is better after 8...♗b4 9 ♘xc6 bxc6 10 f4!, e.g. 10...♗xc3 11 bxc3 ♘xe4 12 ♕d4! ♘f6 13 ♗a3! and Black is beaten on the dark squares, or 10...d5 11 e5 ♘d7 (after 11...♗xc3 12 bxc3 ♘e4 13 ♗d3 c5 14 c4 ♗b7 15 ♕e1 White is threatening c4xd5 and c2-c4) 12 ♘a4! ♘b6 13 c4 ♗e7 14 ♗e3 ♘xa4 15 ♕xa4 then ♖ac1 ±, when Black's pawn on d5 is strong but his centre is still immobile. What is more, it is White who can choose the appropriate moment to play c4xd5, when he has already brought his rooks over to the queenside. Another possibility is 8...b5!? 9 ♘xc6 dxc6 10 f4 ♗b7 11 e5 ♖d8 12 ♕e1 ♘d5 13 ♘xd5 (13 ♘e4 c5) 13...cxd5 14 ♗d3 g6, and although White stands more freely it is difficult for him to get at his opponent.
9 ♕xd4 ♗c5 10 ♕d3
Not 10 ♗f4 ♗xd4 11 ♗xc7 ♗xc3 followed by ...♘xe4.
10...h5!?
Black cannot restrain f2-f4 and e4-e5 with 10...d6 due to 11 ♗g5

followed by ♖ad1 and ♘a4, so instead he immediately prepares counterplay by means of ...h7-h5 and ...♘g4. Weaker is 10...b5?! 11 f4 h5 (11...♗b7 12 ♗f3 – 12 e5 ♘d5 – 12...0-0 13 e5 ♘e8 14 ♗xb7 ♕xb7 15 ♘e4 ±) 12 e5 ♘g4 13 ♕h3! ♘h6 (13...♘f2+ 14 ♖xf2 ♗xf2 15 ♕f3 ♕a7 16 ♘e4 and because 16...♗c5 is wrong owing to 17 ♘xc5, the knight appears on d6 with deadly power!) 14 ♕xh5! ♗b7 15 ♗f3 0-0-0 16 ♗xb7+ ♕xb7 17 ♕f3 ♘f5! 18 h3! and Black is worse.

11 f4

An interesting alternative is 11 ♕h3, hindering ...♘g4.

11...♘g4 12 e5!?

Or 12 ♕g3 b5 13 e5 ♗b7 ∞.

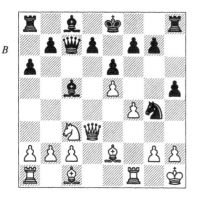

Plans and Counterplans:

Can Black win the exchange? Let us see: **12...♘f2+** 13 ♖xf2 ♗xf2 14 ♘e4 ♗c5 (preventing ♘d6) and now 15 ♕c3? b6 16 b4 ♗b7 17 ♗f3 d5! 18 exd6 ♗xd6 19 ♕xg7 (19 ♘xd6+ ♕xd6 20 ♗xb7? ♕d1+ and mate!) 19...0-0-0 and Black wins. But after 15 ♗e3! the bishop on c5

faces an uncomfortable decision. After 15...♗xe3 16 ♘d6+ and ♕xe3 the knight d6 is terribly powerful, much stronger than the black rooks, so it is White who is an 'exchange' up. He can assault the black monarch with ♖f1, ♗d3, f5. Neither can Black develop freely after 15...♗e7 16 ♘d6+! ♗xd6 17 exd6 ♕d8 18 ♗f3 ♖b8 19 ♗a7! ♖a8 20 ♗d4 0-0 21 c4! The threat is c4-c5 and the pawn on h5 is hanging (±). Therefore Black has to look for another way. **12...d6!?** 13 exd6 (after 13 ♘e4 d5! 14 ♘xc5 ♕xc5 15 ♗xg4 hxg4 16 ♗e3 ♕c7, followed by ...♗d7 and ...0-0-0 the rooks are ready to be doubled on the h-file) 13...♕xd6 14 ♕xd6 (14 ♕h3? ♘f2+ 15 ♖xf2 ♗xf2 16 ♘e4 ♕b4! and the threat is mate on e1!) 14...♗xd6 and it is unclear how White should fight off the black knight. For example, 15 ♘e4 ♗c7!? (15...♗e7 16 h3 ♘f6 is also not bad) 16 h3 ♗b6!? 17 ♗f3 f5 and after a knight move White is unable to escape from the repetition 18...♘f2+ 19 ♔h2 ♘g4+.

B2c. 1 e4 c5 2 ♘f3 e6 3 d4 cxd4 4 ♘xd4 ♘c6 5 ♘c3 ♕c7 6 ♗e3

6...a6 7 ♗e2

Also playable is 7 ♗d3 ♘f6 8 0-0 ♘e5!? 9 h3 (to stop 9...♘eg4) 9...♗c5 10 ♘a4 ♗a7 11 c4 d6 followed by ...0-0, ...♗d7, ...♖fd8 and ...♗e8. Instead of 8...♘e5!?, the alternative 8...♗d6!? is interesting: 9 ♘xc6 bxc6 (9...♗xh2+ is wrong due to 10 ♔h1 bxc6 11 g3 and the bishop goes) 10 f4 e5! 11 f5 ♗e7 and Black is ready for ...d7-d5. White can try to castle queenside with 7 ♕d2 ♘f6 8 f3 (in positions with ♗e3 and ♕d2 Black always threatens ...♘g4) 8...♘e5 9 0-0-0 ♗b4 10 ♘b3 b5 11 ♗d4 h6! with mutual chances. Black will play on the queenside while White aims to get his queen involved in a kingside attack.

7...♘f6

It is better to develop the kingside, although the curious 7...b5 8 ♘xc6 ♕xc6 9 f4?! ♗a3! stirs things up. Instead of 9 f4 White should play 9 0-0 ♗b7 10 ♗f3 followed by e4-e5, when White is somewhat better.

8 0-0

On 8 a3 it is best to transpose to the Scheveningen with 8...♗e7, ...d7-d6 and ...0-0 in which a2-a3 is hardly a move for White (section II).

8...♗b4

After 8...b5 9 ♘xc6 dxc6 10 f4 ♗b7 (10...b4 11 ♘a4 ♘xe4 12 ♗b6 and ♗f3 ±) 11 e5 ♖d8 12 ♕e1 ♘d5 13 ♘xd5 cxd5 14 c3! ♗c5 15 ♕f2 followed by a2-a4! White is nagging at the black queenside.

9 ♘a4!?

A strong move, aiming at the b6-square and at the same time liberating the c-pawn for a central fight!

9...0-0

After 9...♘xe4 10 ♘xc6 ♕xc6 11 ♘b6 ♖b8 12 ♕d4! ♗f8 13 ♗f3

f5 14 ♖ad1 Black cannot survive the pressure.

10 ♘xc6

Or 10 c4 ♗d6!?

10...bxc6

10...dxc6 11 c4 ♗d6 12 f4!? ♘xe4 13 c5! ♗e7 14 ♕c2 and ♘b6 completely ties Black up. 10...bxc6 is much more active due to the open b-file and the possibility ...d7-d5.

11 c4!?

Threatening to trap the bishop with 12 c5! The game would take on a tactical character after 11 ♘b6 ♖b8 12 ♘xc8 ♖fxc8 13 ♗xa6 ♖e8!? 14 ♗d3 ♗d6 15 f4 (15 ♔h1!?) 15...e5! 16 f5 ♖xb2, for example 17 g4 h6! 18 h4 ♗f8 19 g5 ♘d5! 20 exd5 e4! and if the bishop moves Black has a perpetual on g3. A reasonable alternative is 11 f4!?: 11...♖b8 (11...♘xe4 12 ♕d4) 12 ♗d3 ♗e7 13 c4 (13 e5 ♘d5 14 ♗d2 f5!?) 13...e5!! and now 14 fxe5 ♕xe5 15 ♖f5 ♕e6 16 ♕f3 d6 and 14 ♕f3 exf4 15 ♗xf4 ♗d6 are pleasant for Black. The game revolves around the e5-square. But back to 11 c4!?

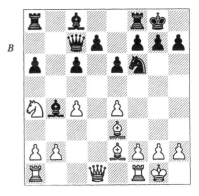

Plans and Counterplans:
Where should Black retreat the bishop? It was once believed that **11...♗e7** 12 ♕c2 c5! followed by ...d7-d6 and ...♗b7 was sufficient to equalize, but then came 11...♗e7 12 ♗f3!! d6 (12...c5?? 13 e5) 13 c5! d5 14 ♘b6 ♖b8 15 ♕a4! and Black is worse, e.g. 15...♗b7 16 e5! with a complete stranglehold (16...♕xe5 17 ♗f4). Therefore it is more advisable to play **11...♗d6!?**: 12 f4 ♘xe4 13 ♗d3 ♘f6 14 ♗b6!? (14 c5 ♗e7 15 ♗d4 ♖d8!? ∞) 14...♕b8 15 ♗d4 ♗e7 (not 15...e5? 16 ♗c3! and Black cannot ease the tension around the e5-pawn) 16 ♘b6 c5! 17 ♗xf6 ♗xf6 18 ♘xa8 ♕xa8 19 ♕c2 with a roughly equal game.

II. Scheveningen Variation

1 e4 c5 2 ♘f3 d6 3 d4
At this point White's ways of avoiding the Open Variation are:
a) 3 b3 ♘c6 4 ♗b2 e6 5 ♗b5 ♗d7 6 0-0 a6 7 ♗xc6 ♗xc6 8 ♖e1 ♖c8! (after 8...♘f6 9 e5! Black is in trouble) 9 d4 cxd4 10 ♘xd4 ♘f6 and ...♗e7, ...0-0 =.
b) 3 ♗c4 e6! 4 0-0 ♘f6 5 ♖e1 ♘c6 threatening 6...♘xe4 7 ♖xe4 d5, and if White sidesteps this then Black has the simple ...♗e7 and ...0-0 =.
c) 3 ♘c3 ♘f6 4 e5 dxe5 5 ♘xe5 a6! followed by ...e7-e6, ...♗e7, ...0-0 and ...♕c7 =.
d) 3 c3!? ♘f6 4 ♗e2 g6 (not 4...♘xe4?? 5 ♕a4+ +−, while after 4...♘c6 5 d4!? cxd4 6 cxd4

♘xe4 7 d5! ♕a5+! 8 ♘c3 ♘xc3 9 bxc3 ♘e5 10 ♘xe5 ♕xc3+ 11 ♗d2 ♕xe5 12 0-0 a6 13 ♖b1 White threatens 14 ♕a4+ ♗d7 15 ♗b5!) 5 0-0 ♗g7 6 ♖e1 0-0 7 ♗f1 ♘c6 8 h3 (8 d4? cxd4 9 cxd4 ♗g4!) 8...e5!? = 9 d4 cxd4 10 cxd4 exd4 11 ♘xd4 ♘xd4 12 ♕xd4 ♖e8 and the threat is ...♘xe4 attacking the queen.
e) 3 ♗b5+!? ♘c6 (3...♗d7 4 ♗xd7+ ♘xd7 5 0-0 ♘gf6 6 ♕e2 e6 and then ...♗e7 and ...0-0 =) 4 0-0 ♗d7 5 ♖e1 ♘f6 6 c3 a6 7 ♗f1 (7 ♗xc6 ♗xc6 8 d4!? ♗xe4 9 ♗g5 d5 ∞) 7...♗g4!? 8 h3 ♗xf3 9 ♕xf3 g6!? followed by ...♗g7 and ...0-0 with equality.

3...cxd4 4 ♘xd4
White develops unexpectedly quickly after 4 ♕xd4 ♘c6 5 ♗b5 ♗d7 6 ♗xc6 ♗xc6 7 ♘c3 ♘f6 8 ♗g5 e6 9 0-0-0 ♗e7 10 ♖he1, but Black can still achieve counterplay typical of positions with opposite-side castling: 10...0-0 11 ♕d2 (11 e5 dxe5 12 ♕h4 ♕e8 13 ♘xe5 h6 14 ♗xh6 gxh6 15 ♕xh6 ♘h7! 16 f4! ∞) 11...♕c7 12 ♘d4 (the regrouping of ♕d2 and ♘d4 has prepared f2-f4) 12...♖fd8 (although 12...b5 looks attractive as capturing would open files on the king, it is still not enough for equality: 13 ♗xf6 ♗xf6 14 ♘xc6 ♕xc6 15 ♕xd6 ♕xd6 16 ♖xd6 ♗xc3 17 bxc3 and the position is ±; not because of the extra pawn but because White's king is well located on the battlefield) 13 f4 ♖ac8 14 g4 b5! and now the pawn sacrifice is okay.

4...᎐f6 5 ᎐c3
5 f3?! makes a bad impression: 5...e5! 6 ᎐b3 (6 ᎐b5+ ᎐bd7 7 ᎐f5 d5!? 8 exd5 a6 9 ᎐xd7+ – 9 ᎐e2 ᎐b6 and ...᎐bxd5 – 9...᎐xd7! 10 ᎐e3 b5 11 c4 ᎐c5) 6...᎐e7 7 c4 0-0 8 ᎐c3 a5!? 9 ᎐e3 a4 10 ᎐d2 ᎐a5 11 a3 ᎐d7 and Black gets on top on the queenside with ...᎐a6-c5 and ...᎐fc8.
5...e6

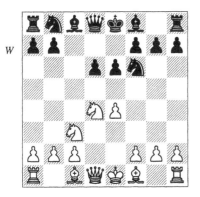

This position is the fundamental starting-point of the Scheveningen Variation. All the general characteristics of the Sicilian are present: White can try to exert pressure on d6 along the semi-open d-file, or he can try to carry through e4-e5 after the preparatory f4-f4, or he can try to use his central advantage to line up his pieces on the kingside, hoping for an attack. Black plans to invade along the c-file and on the queenside and is well-prepared to react dynamically to his opponent's play with his powerful pawn pair at e6 and d6.

White now has the following major choices:

A. Keres Attack: 6 g4
B. 6 f4 Variation
C. Sozin-like with 6 ᎐c4
D. Sicilian Killer: 6 ᎐e3
E. Positional Variation: 6 ᎐e2

Apart from the main lines, 6 g3 is also worth mentioning: 6...a6 7 ᎐g2 ᎐c7 8 0-0 ᎐e7 9 a4 (9 ᎐e1 ᎐c6 10 ᎐xc6 bxc6 11 e5! dxe5 12 ᎐xe5 0-0 13 ᎐f4 ᎐b7 14 ᎐a4 ±, but 9...0-0 10 g4 ᎐c6 11 g5 ᎐xd4 12 ᎐xd4 ᎐d7 gives Black good play) 9...᎐c6 10 ᎐b3 b6!? (hindering the advance of White's a-pawn) 11 f4 0-0 12 g4!? ᎐e8 13 g5 ᎐d7 14 ᎐e3 ᎐b7 ∞. After ᎐e2-f2 White can play for f4-f5, although after ...᎐f8 and ...᎐ac8 Black has play on the queenside with ...᎐b4 ...᎐c5 and can also consider the fearless ...g7-g6 and ...᎐g7. Note that if White does play f4-f5, this provides the black knight with the comfortable square on e5.

A. 1 e4 c5 2 ᎐f3 d6 3 d4 cxd4 4 ᎐xd4 ᎐f6 5 ᎐c3 e6 6 g4!? (Keres Attack)

White starts his kingside expansion at once, a plan that promises an instant 'military success' by chasing away the knight from f6.
6...h6!?
Black does not easily let his knight be hounded. Other moves are:

a) **6...e5** 7 &b5+! &d7 8 &xd7+
♕xd7 9 ♘f5! ± h5 10 gxh5 ♘xh5
11 &h6!! With this exceptional
move White attacks the knight on
h5. Black's various weaknesses
(the squares d5 and f5 and the
pawn on d6) are dominant.

b) **6...d5?!** (not a good idea) 7
exd5 ♘xd5 8 &b5+ &d7 9 ♘xd5
exd5 10 ♕e2+ ♕e7 (10...&e7 11
♘f5!) 11 &e3 g6 12 &xd7+ ♘xd7
13 ♘b5! ♘e5 14 0-0-0! and besides
♖xd5 White is also threatening
&c5! (±).

c) **6...a6** (as we have seen,
Black needs to be afraid of &b5+
if he is to play ...d6-d5 or ...e6-e5)
7 g5 (on 7 h3? Black really goes
for 7...d5! =) 7...♘fd7 8 &e3!? b5
9 a3 and White's plan is a kingside
pawn-storm with or without ♕d2
and 0-0-0. For example 9...♘b6 10
♖g1 ♘8d7 11 f4 &b7 12 f5! e5 13
♘e6! fxe6 14 ♕h5+ ♔e7 15 fxe6
with a tremendous attack: &h3,
g5-g6 and &g5.

d) **6...♘c6** 7 g5 ♘d7 8 &e3 a6
9 h4!? (again playable is the plan
of ♕d2, 0-0-0 and f2-f4) 9...&e7 10
♕h5!? (the pawn on e6 is hanging
and on g7-g6 the queen returns
and White will then harry the
black pawn structure with h4-h5)
10...0-0 11 0-0-0 ♖e8 12 f4 &f8 13
&d3! ♘xd4?! 14 &xd4 e5 15 &c4!
g6 16 &xf7+! ♔xf7 17 ♕xh7+ &g7
18 fxe5 +–. White threatens 19
♖hf1+ as well as 19 e6+.

e) **6...&e7!?** 7 g5 ♘d7 8 &e3
♘c6 9 h4 0-0 10 ♕d2 ♘de5!? 11
&e2 (not 11 f4?? ♘xd4! with a

'family check' on f3 or 11 0-0-0
♘g4!) 11...♘a5!? 12 b3 ♘ac6 13
0-0-0 ♘xd4 14 &xd4 ♘c6 15 &e3,
and now after 15...♕a5 or 15...a6!?
followed by ...b7-b5 Black has
some counter-chances.

7 ♖g1

An interesting alternative is 7
g5!? hxg5 8 &xg5 ♘c6 9 h4 a6 10
♕d2 ♕b6 11 ♘b3 &d7 12 0-0-0
0-0-0, where after f2-f4, &e2, h4-
h5 and &f3 White often plays h5-
h6 with an invasion on the open
kingside files, while Black creates
a flexible position with ...♔b8,
...&c8, ...&e7 and ...♕c7, awaiting
the right moment for ...d6-d5.

7...♘c6 8 h4 d5!

This central blow is the logical
answer to White's kingside ag-
gressions. After 8...h5 9 gxh5 ♘xh5
10 &g5 ♘f6 11 ♕d2 and 0-0-0
White is on top.

9 &b5!?

9 exd5 ♘xd5 10 ♘xd5 ♕xd5 11
&g2 ♕e5+ 12 &e3 ♘b4! 13 c4 (to
prevent 13...♘d5) 13...&c5! and
Black plans to take twice(!) on d4
and eventually win a piece with
...♘c2+.

**9...&d7 10 exd5 ♘xd5 11
♘xd5 exd5 12 &e3** (D)

Many players would refuse to
play the position after 12 ♕e2+
&e7 13 ♘f5 &xf5 14 exf5 ♔f8 followed by ...&f6! with either colour
(∞).

Plans and Counterplans:

By escaping the g4-g5 attack with
his knight at the last minute,

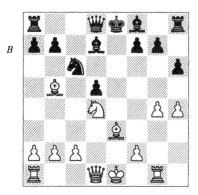

Black has slowed down White's assault and made a target out of the white pieces. But White still has a spatial advantage and superior development. After 12...♕xh4 13 ♕f3 (13 ♕e2 ♘xd4 14 ♗xd4+ ♕e7 15 ♗xd7+ ♔xd7 16 ♗e3 ♖d8! 17 0-0-0 ♔c8 ∞) 13...a6 14 ♗xc6 bxc6 15 0-0-0 ♗d6 16 ♘f5 ♗xf5 17 gxf5 ♗e5! Black manages to defend his position.

B. 1 e4 c5 2 ♘f3 d6 3 d4 cxd4 4 ♘xd4 ♘f6 5 ♘c3 e6 6 f4

The principle of 6 f4 is similar to that of the Keres Attack. The difference is that the intensity of the attack is not so strong, but here White can more easily develop his pieces (♗e3, ♕f3).

6...a6
Black needs to be careful, for example 6...♗e7? 7 ♗b5+ ♘fd7 (or 7...♗d7 8 e5! ±) 8 f5! e5? 9 ♘e6! fxe6 10 ♕h5+ ♔f8 11 fxe6 ♕e8 12 0-0+ ♗f6 13 exd7 ♘xd7 14 ♖xf6+! and 14...♘xf6 15 ♗xe8 ♘xh5 16 ♗xh5 +– or 14...gxf6 15 ♕h6+

♔e7 16 ♘d5+ ♔d8 17 ♗xd7 +–. But 6...♘c6!? is a sensible alternative: 7 ♗e3 ♗e7 8 ♕f3 ♕c7 9 0-0-0 0-0 10 g4 ♘xd4 11 ♗xd4 e5! 12 fxe5 dxe5 13 ♕g3! ♘xg4 14 ♘d5 ♕d6 with a difficult position for both sides.

7 ♕f3
On 7 ♗d3 b5 8 0-0 ♗b7 9 a3 ♘bd7 10 ♔h1 ♗e7 and ...0-0 =, while on 7 ♗e3 b5 8 ♕f3 ♗b7 9 ♗d3 b4 10 ♘ce2 ♘bd7 11 g4 e5! 12 ♘b3 exf4 13 ♗xf4 ♕e7 14 0-0-0 ♘e5! (14...♗xe4 15 ♗xe4 ♕xe4 16 ♕g3 and after ♖he1 the e-file opens on Black) 15 ♕g3 ♖c8 16 ♘ed4 ♕c7 17 ♔b1 g6 and after ...♗g7, ...0-0 Black reaches the haven of an equal game. Black should only consider ...e6-e5 if White cannot take his d4 knight to b5 or Black can kick it away with ...g7-g6 if it goes to f5.

7...♕b6!?
Black opts for his usual plan of counterplay by ...b7-b5, ...♗b7 and ...♘bd7. But it is wrong to play the immediate 7...b5, as after 8 e5 dxe5 9 ♕xa8 the knight on b8 is also hanging. Therefore apart from this move, pushing the knight from d4, 7...♕c7 also comes into consideration.

8 a3!
The knight on d4 is now protected by the queen trap 8...♕xd4?? 9 ♗e3. On 8 ♘b3 ♕c7 9 g4 b5 10 ♗d3 ♗b7 11 g5 ♘fd7 12 ♗e3 ♘c6 13 ♕h3 b4 14 ♘e2 g6 15 0-0-0 ♗g7 16 ♔b1 0-0 17 f5 exf5 18 exf5 ♖fe8! 19 ♖hf1 ♘ce5! 20 ♘f4 ♘c5

the black central knights fortify the position.

8...♘c6!

Black cannot go back to the scheme ...♕c7, ...b7-b5, ...♗b7 and ...♘bd7 since then White's extra move a2-a3 would turn out to be very useful.

9 ♘xc6

On 9 ♘b3, 9...g6 10 ♗e3 ♕c7 11 0-0-0 ♗g7 followed by ...0-0 and ...b7-b5 deserves attention.

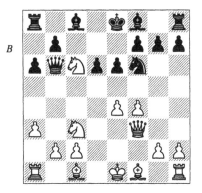

B

Plans and Counterplans:

Black can either continue simply with **9...♕xc6** 10 ♗d3 b5 11 0-0 ♗b7 or complicate matters with **9...bxc6** 10 b3 ♗b7 11 ♗b2 c5 12 0-0-0 0-0-0! 13 ♗c4 ♕c6 with the idea of ...d6-d5.

C. 1 e4 c5 2 ♘f3 d6 3 d4 cxd4 4 ♘xd4 ♘f6 5 ♘c3 e6 6 ♗c4 (Sozinlike)

6...a6

6...♘c6 is the real Sozin, see section IV.

7 ♗b3

The threat was ...b7-b5-b4 endangering the pawn on e4. Holding this advance up with 7 a4 cannot be recommended due to 7...♗e7 8 0-0 0-0 9 ♗e3 ♘c6 10 ♔h1 ♕c7 and Black can easily achieve queenside play with ...♗d7, ...♖ac8 and ...♘a5-c4.

7...b5

A similar concept in a different guise is 7...♘bd7!? 8 f4 ♘c5 9 f5!? ♗e7 10 ♕f3 0-0 11 ♗e3 e5! 12 ♘de2 b5! and now 13 ♘d5 ♘xb3 14 ♘xf6+ ♗xf6 15 cxb3 d5! would represent a total opening success for Black because after 16 exd5 e4! he has activated all his pieces and the white king is still sitting in the middle! After 13 g4 ♗b7 14 ♗xc5 dxc5 15 g5 c4 White's activity again seems to have vanished.

8 0-0 ♗e7

Here it is a mistake to play 8...b4?! 9 ♘a4 ♘xe4?, as after 10 ♖e1 White's development advantage is just too much. For example, 10...♘f6 11 ♗g5 ♗e7 12 ♘f5! exf5 (or 12...0-0 13 ♘xe7+ ♕xe7 14 ♘b6 ♖a7 15 ♘d5 ♕d8 16 ♘xf6+ gxf6 17 ♗h6 threatening ♕g4 and mate) 13 ♗xf6 gxf6 14 ♕d5 wins for White, or 10...d5 11 ♗f4 ♗d6 12 ♗xd6 ♕xd6 13 ♘f5 exf5 14 ♕xd5 ♕xd5 15 ♗xd5 ♖a7 16 f3 and White commands the forthcoming endgame.

9 ♕f3

The queen rushes to g3 to attack the black king position. Black can crawl out of the grip after 9 f4 ♗b7 10 e5 dxe5 11 fxe5 ♗c5 12

♗e3 ♗xd4 13 ♗xd4 ♘c6 14 ♖f4 ♕c7! 15 ♕e2 0-0-0!

9...♕c7

Now 10 e5 would be answered by 10...♗b7.

10 ♕g3!? 0-0 11 ♗h6!? ♘e8

White has thrown his opponent into retreat with his threats.

12 ♖ad1 ♗d7

Always be vigilant! 12...♗b7? 13 ♗xe6 fxe6 14 ♘xe6 wins.

13 a3 ♘c6 14 ♘xc6 ♗xc6

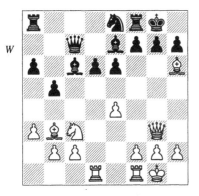

Plans and Counterplans:

After the exchange of knights the tension has eased. White will target the d6-pawn, while Black will launch a minority attack with his a- and b-pawns. One example is: 15 ♗f4 ♕b7 16 ♖fe1 a5 17 e5 dxe5 18 ♗xe5 ♗f6 19 ♖d4 ♖d8 20 ♖xd8 ♗xd8 21 ♘e2 a4 22 ♗a2 b4 =.

D. 1 e4 c5 2 ♘f3 d6 3 d4 cxd4 4 ♘xd4 ♘f6 5 ♘c3 e6 6 ♗e3 (Sicilian Killer)

White has been immensely successful with this move in the past

few years, in conjunction with the very direct plan ♕d2, f2-f3, 0-0-0 and g2-g4. Of course, this is partly attributable to the fact that this is the pet line of several young superstars. In their hands even a toy gun can turn into a Winchester!

6...a6

6...♘c6!? leads to immediate complications: 7 ♕d2 ♗e7 (now 8...♘g4 is already threatened) 8 f3 0-0 9 0-0-0 (9 g4 d5 10 g5 ♘d7 11 exd5 ♘xd4 12 ♕xd4 ♗xg5 13 0-0-0 – 13 dxe6 ♗xe3 14 ♕xe3 ♕h4+ 15 ♕f2 ♕xf2+ 16 ♔xf2 fxe6 = – 13...exd5 14 ♘xd5 ♘b6 =) 9...d5! 10 exd5 ♘xd5 11 ♘xd5 ♕xd5 12 ♘b3 ♕xd2+ 13 ♖xd2 ♖d8 14 ♖xd8+ ♘xd8 =. Just as in the Keres Attack, it is a good plan for Black to open the centre with ...d6-d5. 'A central blow against a flank attack...' as our chess ancestors used to say.

7 ♕d2

7 g4!? brings about mind-boggling complications: 7...h6 8 ♕f3 ♘bd7 9 ♕h3! e5 (safer is 9...♘c5!? 10 f3 e5 11 ♘b3 ♗e6 ∞) 10 ♘f5 g6 11 g5! gxf5 12 exf5 d5! 13 gxf6 d4 14 ♗c4 ♘xf6 15 0-0-0 ♕c7!? ∞ or 7...e5 8 ♘f5 g6 9 g5 gxf5 10 exf5 d5 11 gxf6 d4 12 ♗c4 ♕c7 13 ♕d3 dxc3 14 0-0-0 ♘c6 15 ♖he1 ∞. Black has become more and more successful in these complications, but this might be because Bela Perenyi, the excellent Hungarian IM who used to handle the white side with sparkling fantasy, is

long gone from the other side of the board.

7...b5

7...♘g4 would be met by 8 ♗g5.

8 f3 ♘bd7 9 g4 h6 10 0-0-0

On 10 h4? b4 11 ♘ce2 d5!, Black seizes the initiative.

10...♗b7 11 h4 b4 12 ♘ce2 d5!

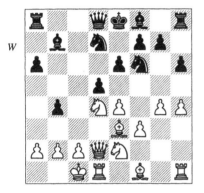

W

Plans and Counterplans:
Black has achieved the desired central counter-thrust, but he has not castled yet. In fact his activity counterbalances his lack of development. For example: **13 exd5** ♘xd5 14 ♘f4 ♘xf4! (the pressure on e6 must be reduced, though 14...♘e5!? is interesting) 15 ♗xf4 ♗e7 16 ♗c4 ♘b6 17 ♕e2 ♗d5 and with careful play Black can avoid White's threatened combinations on e6; **13 ♘g3** ♕a5 (13...♗d6 14 ♖g1 ♕c7 15 g5 hxg5 16 hxg5 ♗xg3 17 gxf6 ♘xf6 18 ♕b4 ♗d6 19 ♕a4 ±) 14 ♔b1 dxe4 15 g5 hxg5 16 hxg5 ♖xh1 17 ♘xh1 ♘d5 18 g6! 0-0-0!? ∞; or **13 ♗h3!?** dxe4 14 g5 hxg5 15 hxg5 exf3 16 ♘f4 (16 ♘g3 ♘e4 17 ♘xe4 ♗xe4 18 ♘xe6 fxe6

19 ♗xe6 ♘c5! with a material advantage for Black) 16...♘e4 17 ♕e1 ♗xh3!! and now after 18 ♘xh3 e5 White's activity has vanished. Both 19 ♘xf3? ♕a5 20 ♔b1 ♘c3+! –+ and 19 ♘b3 a5 20 ♘d2 ♕c7 demonstrate the correctness of Black's exchange sacrifice.

Those who wish to dabble in 6 ♗e3 should be aware that general chess principles are irrelevant in this line: concrete calculation will decide the game.

E. 1 e4 c5 2 ♘f3 d6 3 d4 cxd4 4 ♘xd4 ♘f6 5 ♘c3 e6 6 ♗e2 (Positional Variation)

After a swift 0-0, White is planning ♗e3, f2-f4 and ♕e1-g3 with pressure on the black kingside.

6...a6

Black may also play without ...a7-a6: 6...♘c6 7 0-0 ♗e7 8 ♗e3 0-0 9 f4 ♗d7!? and now 10 ♘b3 ♕c7 11 ♗f3 ♖fd8 12 ♕e1 ♗e8, and then either ...a7-a6 and ...b7-b5 or ...♘d7-c5, or 10 ♘xd4 11 ♗xd4 ♗c6 12 ♕g3 g6! 13 ♗f3 (13 ♗d3 ♘h5 14 ♕f2 ♘xf4! 15 ♕xf4 e5 or 13 f5 e5 14 ♗e3 ♘xe4 15 ♘xe4 ♗xe4 16 ♗h6 ♖e8 offers Black good play) 13...b5! 14 a3 a5!, followed by ...b5-b4, when Black has saved the move ...a7-a6.

7 0-0

7 ♗e3!? is a cunning move as, for example, on 7...♘bd7?! White can go wild with 8 g4 h6 9 f4 b5 10 g5, when it is hard to rescue the knight on f6. So it is better to

leave the d7-square open and continue with either 7...♘c6 or 7...♕c7 followed by ...b7-b5 and ...♗b7.

7...♗e7

7...b5? is an educational mistake in view of 8 ♗f3! ♗b7?? 9 e5! ♗xf3 10 ♕xf3 dxe5 11 ♕xa8 and White is winning. When Black plays ...b7-b5 he has to be ready for White's e4-e5 and for tactical tricks on the open h1-a8 diagonal. Instead of 8...♗b7??, 8...♖a7 9 ♗e3 ♖d7!? is just about playable but the rook still looks bad in front of the minor pieces and the queen.

8 f4 ♘c6 9 ♗e3 0-0 10 ♕e1

It is vital to know that after 10 a4!? ♕c7 11 ♘b3 Black must prevent a4-a5 with 11...b6! followed by ...♗b7. On 10 ♔h1 Black should consider playing 10...♗d7 followed by ...♘xd4 and ...♗c6.

10...♕c7

Or 10...♘xd4 11 ♗xd4 b5 12 ♖d1 ♗b7 13 ♗f3 ♕c7 14 e5 dxe5 15 fxe5 ♘d7 16 ♗xb7 ♕xb7 17 ♘e4 ♕c7!, when Black's idea is ...♖ad8, while ♕g3 can be met by ...♔h8 or ...f7-f5!?

11 ♕g3 ♘xd4 12 ♗xd4 b5 13 a3

13 e5 dxe5 14 ♗xe5 ♕c5+ 15 ♔h1 ♗b7 16 ♗d3 should be met by 16...g6!?

13...♗b7 14 ♖ae1! ♗c6 (D)

Preparing the action ...♕b7, ...a6-a5 and ...b5-b4.

Plans and Counterplans:
If White hesitates he cannot hope for an advantage: **15 ♔h1** (the

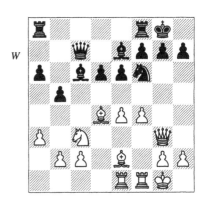

point of this move is to avoid a check in the concrete lines that follow) 15...♕b7! 16 ♗d3 b4! 17 axb4 (17 ♘d1 is interesting, intending ♘f2-g4) 17...♕xb4 18 ♘e2 ♕b7 19 e5 ♘h5! 20 ♕h3 g6! and Black is fine. But **15 ♗d3!?** is a lot more dangerous: 15...e5?! 16 fxe5 ♘h5 17 exd6! ♘xg3 18 dxc7 ♘xf1 19 ♘d5! and White is well on top with his c7-pawn. It is better to play 15...♕b7, but after 16 e5! dxe5 17 ♗xe5 White is threatening an attack with ♕h3 or f4-f5. So Black should keep the queen on c7 as long as e4-e5 is a threat: 15...♖ad8 16 e5 ♘e8! with 17...dxe5 18 ♗xe5 ♗d6 in mind.

III. Najdorf Variation

1 e4 c5 2 ♘f3 d6 3 d4 cxd4 4 ♘xd4 ♘f6 5 ♘c3 a6 (D)

In this variation Black leaves all his development options open and first makes a useful waiting move, taking the b5-square away from the white pieces and preparing for queenside counterplay by

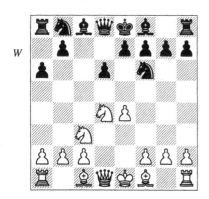

means of ...b7-b5. The value of this tiny move is perfectly demonstrated by the line 5...e5? 6 ♗b5+! ♗d7 (6...♘bd7 7 ♘f5 a6 8 ♗xd7+ ♕xd7 9 ♗g5! ±) 7 ♗xd7+ ♕xd7 8 ♘de2 ♕c6 9 ♘g3 ±. White meets a premature ...e7-e5 with ♗b5+ and – after the exchange of light-squared bishops – seizes control of the squares d5 and f5.

Two of Black's typical setups in the Najdorf are ...e7-e6 and then ...♗e7, ...♕c7, ...b7-b5, ...♗b7 and ...♘bd7 or ...e7-e5 and then ...♗e6, ...♗e7, ...♕c7 and ...♘bd7. We have divided the material into two main sections:

A. Main Line with 6 ♗g5
B. Kaleidoscope: everything but 6 ♗g5

A. 1 e4 c5 2 ♘f3 d6 3 d4 cxd4 4 ♘xd4 ♘f6 5 ♘c3 a6 6 ♗g5 (Main Line)

White's most aggressive setup in the Sicilian is to castle queenside. The move 6 ♗g5 plans f2-f4 and

♕f3, clearing the way for a quick 0-0-0.
6...e6
6...♘bd7 is well met by 7 f4 ♕b6 8 ♕d2 (8 ♘b3?! h6! 9 ♗h4 ♕e3+ and 10...♕xf4 costs White a pawn) 8...♕xb2 9 ♖b1 ♕a3 10 ♗xf6! gxf6 (10...♘xf6 11 e5) 11 ♘d5 ♕c5 12 ♖b3!, followed by ♖c3 and ♘c7, with a clear edge for White.
7 f4
This pawn not only protects the bishop on g5 against various tactical motifs, but may also preface an advance with e4-e5 or f4-f5. After 7 ♕e2 h6 8 ♗h4 ♗e7 Black is already threatening to win a pawn with 9...♘xe4 10 ♗xe7 ♘xc3 11 ♗xd8 ♘xe2 and 7 ♕d3 ♘bd7 8 0-0-0 b5 followed by ...♗b7 is also comfortable for Black. Black's queenside play can be hindered by 7 ♕f3, but then 7...h6! 8 ♗h4 (8 ♗xf6 ♕xf6! 9 ♕xf6 gxf6 is fine for Black in view of a later ...h6-h5 and ...♗h6 with a healthy bishop pair) 8...♘bd7 9 0-0-0 ♘e5 10 ♕e2 g5 11 ♗g3 ♗d7 12 h4 ♖g8 planning ...♕c7, ...b7-b5 is more than adequate.

Black has two major replies to 7 f4:

A1. 7...♕b6!? and
A2. 7...♗e7.

The following rather rare variations serve to demonstrate some of the typical tactical themes in this line:

a) **7...♕c7?!** 8 ♕f3 b5 9 0-0-0 b4 10 e5! ♗b7 11 ♘cb5! ♕b6 (or 11...axb5 12 ♗xb5+ ♘bd7 13 ♕h3! and if the knight on f6 moves then 14 ♘xe6! wins) 12 ♕h3! and now a 'help-mate': 12...♘d5 13 ♘xe6! axb5 14 ♖xd5 ♗xd5 15 ♘xg7+ and ♕c8 check and mate!

b) **7...♘bd7** 8 ♕f3 (White's attack does not penetrate after 8 ♗c4 b5 9 ♗xe6 fxe6 10 ♘xe6 ♕a5 11 0-0 ♗b7!) 8...♕c7 9 0-0-0 b5 10 ♗xb5! axb5 11 ♘dxb5 ♕b8 12 e5 ♖a5 (the threat was 13 ♕xa8 and ♘c7 with a family check; and on 12...♗b7, 13 ♕e2 followed by ♕c4 and ♘c7+) 13 exf6 gxf6 14 ♗h6! ♗xh6 15 ♘xd6+ ♔e7 16 ♔b1! ♘b6 17 ♘ce4 ♘a4 18 ♘xc8+ ♖xc8 19 ♕a3+ ♘c5 20 ♕xa5 ♘xe4 21 ♕a3+! ♘c5 22 g3 and White is better, especially if he can manage to liquidate to an endgame.

c) **7...h6?** 8 ♗h4 ♕b6 9 a3! and now 9...♕xb2 is wrong in view of 10 ♘a4 trapping the queen, whilst otherwise 10 ♗f2 drives the queen back.

d) **7...b5!** 8 e5 dxe5 9 fxe5 ♕c7! 10 exf6 ♕e5+ 11 ♗e2 ♕xg5 12 ♕d3 ♕xf6 13 ♖f1 ♕e5 14 ♖d1 (White wants to move his knight from d4 but he does not want to allow Black to check him with 14...♕g5 after 14 0-0-0) 14...♖a7! 15 ♘dxb5! ♖d7 16 ♕c4 and in this complicated position Black has a vast number of moves to choose from (...♗c5, ...♕c5, ...♗b7, ...♖xd1+). White's typical sacrifices in the Najdorf are ♗xb5 with ♘xb5 to

follow or ♗xe6 after ...♘bd7, while if White's queen is on f3 then e4-e5 to open the h1-a8 diagonal is also a fine motif. Black has to trust in his protective forces and get going with his queenside play as soon as possible (...b7-b5, ...♕c7, ...♘bd7 and ...♗b7).

A1. 1 e4 c5 2 ♘f3 d6 3 d4 cxd4 4 ♘xd4 ♘f6 5 ♘c3 a6 6 ♗g5 e6 7 f4 ♕b6!?

By attacking the b2-pawn Black aims to delay White's 0-0-0.

8 ♕d2!?

8 b3? and 8 ♖b1? are both out of the question as they mess up the white queenside. Also artificial is 8 a3?!: 8...♘c6 (8...♕xb2?? 9 ♘a4 +−) 9 ♘b3 ♗e7 10 ♕f3 h6 11 ♗h4 g5! 12 fxg5 ♘e5 13 ♕e2 ♘fg4! 14 h3 hxg5 and Black has the initiative. However, 8 ♘b3!? deserves attention, after which 8...♕e3+ 9 ♕e2 ♕xe2+ 10 ♗xe2 ♘c6 11 ♗f3 ♗d7 12 0-0-0 ♗e7 13 ♘a4! leaves White a whole lot better (±). In this example the queen exchange has only highlighted White's spatial advantage, the semi-open d-file and the weak square on b6. So after 8 ♘b3!? Black – glad that the knight on d4 has been withdrawn – should play 8...♘bd7 and then ...♗e7, ...♕c7, ...b7-b5 along the lines of 7...♗e7 (see the next section).

8...♕xb2 9 ♘b3

This is more restrained than 9 ♖b1 ♕a3 and now:

a) 10 ♗xf6 gxf6 11 ♗e2 ♘c6 12 ♘xc6 bxc6 13 0-0 ♕a5!? 14 ♔h1 ♗e7 15 f5 h5!? ∞.

b) 10 e5 dxe5 11 fxe5 ♘fd7 12 ♗c4 ♕a5! (Black needs the queen for the defence as White is threatening both ♗xe6 and 12...♘xe5 13 ♘xe6!) 13 0-0 ♘xe5 14 ♖be1 ♘xc4 15 ♕f4 ♘d6 16 ♘e4 ♕c7 17 c4! (the immediate 17 ♘f5? is bad due to 17...♕b6+) 17...♘b5! (not 17...h6? 18 ♘f5! ♕b6+ 19 c5! and wins) 18 cxb5 ♕xf4 19 ♗xf4 and although White's advantage in development is enormous, he needs something more concrete for the two pawns (∓),

c) 10 f5!? ♘c6! 11 fxe6 fxe6 12 ♘xc6 bxc6 13 e5 dxe5 14 ♗xf6 gxf6 15 ♘e4 ♗e7 16 ♗e2 h5! 17 ♖b3! ♕a4, reaching the starting point of some extensive theoretical analysis! For example 18 ♘xf6+!? (or 18 c4 f5 19 0-0 fxe4 20 ♕c3 ♕xa2! 21 ♗d1 ♖f8! 22 ♗xh5+ ♔d8 23 ♖d1+ ♗d7 24 ♕e3! ♕a5 25 ♖b7 ♗c5 26 ♖dxd7+ with a perpetual along the seventh rank) 18...♗xf6 19 c4 ♗h4+ 20 g3 ♗e7 21 0-0 ♖a7! 22 ♖b8 ♖c7, when the black king may go wandering via e8-e7-d6 after ...♗c5+ and ...♗d4. White's attack is more or less balanced by his material sacrifices. The moral of the Najdorf is that an attack on the king may look promising, but Black has a flexible position and may just establish a material advantage ... often White runs into trouble after his attack loses steam.

9...♕a3

The main alternative is 9...♘c6, thwarting the queen trap 10 a3 and ♖a2 with 10...♘a5. So on 9...♘c6 White plays 10 ♗xf6 gxf6 11 ♘a4 ♕a3 12 ♘b6 ♖b8 13 ♘c4 ♕a4 14 a3 b5 15 ♘xd6+ ♗xd6 16 ♕xd6 ♕xe4+ 17 ♗e2 ♕d5 18 ♕xd5 exd5 19 0-0-0, and after 19...♘e7 20 ♗f3 ♗e6 21 ♖he1 0-0 22 g4 f5! an equal endgame is reached.

10 ♗xf6

After 10 ♗d3 ♗e7 11 0-0 h6!, it is bad to play 12 ♗h4? in view of 12...♘xe4, while after 12 ♗xf6 ♗xf6 13 e5 dxe5 14 ♘e4 ♘d7 15 f5! exf5 16 ♖xf5 ♗e7 17 ♗c4 ♘f6 18 ♖xe5 0-0 White still has to prove the correctness of his sacrifice.

10...gxf6 11 ♗e2 ♘c6 12 0-0 ♗d7 13 ♔h1 h5!

Simultaneously attacking, making ...♗f8-h6 possible and, above all, hindering ♗e2-h5.

14 ♘d1

The knight is en route to c4 to attack the d6-pawn.

14...♖c8 15 ♘e3 ♕b4

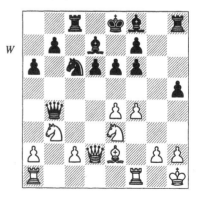

Plans and Counterplans:
White will sidestep the exchange of queens and aims to strike at the weak squares on b6 and d6. As for Black, we should ask the best 'Najdorfer' in the world, namely Garry Kasparov: 16 c3 ♕xe4 (not 16...♕b6? when 17 ♘c4 and ♖ad1 wins the d6-pawn) 17 ♗d3 ♕a4 18 ♘c4 ♖c7 19 ♘b6 ♕a3 20 ♖ae1 ♘e7! 21 ♘c4 ♖xc4! 22 ♗xc4 h4! followed by ...f7-f5 and ...♗g7 when Black takes over. White should therefore settle for a draw with a 'perpetual check on the queen' after 20 ♘c4.

A2. 1 e4 c5 2 ♘f3 d6 3 d4 cxd4 4 ♘xd4 ♘f6 5 ♘c3 a6 6 ♗g5 e6 7 f4 ♗e7

8 ♕f3 ♕c7
The tempting 8...h6 9 ♗h4 g5 10 fxg5 ♘fd7 fails to 11 ♕h5!: 11...♘e5 (11...♗xg5?? 12 ♘xe6!) 12 ♗g3 ♗xg5 13 ♗e2 ♕b6 14 ♖d1 ♕xb2 15 0-0 ♖f8 16 ♘db5! axb5 17 ♘xb5 ♔e7 18 ♘xd6 and Black must throw in the towel.

9 0-0-0 ♘bd7
In this position Black should place castling behind development moves. For example, 9...0-0? 10 ♗d3! ♘c6 11 ♘xc6 bxc6 12 e5! dxe5 13 ♕h3! h6 (13...g6 14 ♕h4 +−) 14 ♗xh6!! gxh6 15 ♕xh6 e4 16 ♘xe4 ♘xe4 17 ♗xe4 f5 18 ♕g6+ ♔h8 19 ♗xc6! ♕xc6 20 ♗d3 and, with the help of reinforcements, White's attack prevails.

10 g4!

White cannot make progress without this pawn:
a) **10 f5?!** e5 11 ♘b3 b5 12 a3 ♗b7 13 h4 ♖c8 (this threatens 14...♘xe4!) 14 ♗d3 h5! and White runs out of breath. Black can trek his knights to c4 or g4.
b) **10 ♗e2.** The point of this move is that on 10...h6 11 ♗h4 g5 12 fxg5 ♘e5 13 ♕e3! the bishop keeps the black knights out of the g4-square since after 13...♘fg4 14 ♗xg4! ♘xg4 15 ♕d2 ♖g8 16 ♘f3 ♕d8 17 ♗g3! the d6-pawn falls. Black needs both knights in the fight for the dark squares. So on 10 ♗e2 Black should play 10...b5! 11 ♗xf6 ♘xf6 12 e5 ♗b7, when Black is fine even after the interesting queen sacrifice 13 exf6! ♗xf3 14 ♗xf3 ♗xf6 15 ♗xa8 d5 16 ♗xd5! ♗xd4! 17 ♖xd4 exd5 18 ♘xd5 ♕c5 19 ♖e1+ ♔f8 20 c3 h5!, when the rook on h8 can join the game from h6.
c) **10 ♗d3!?** (preparing ♖he1 and then often ♘d5!) 10...b5 (or 10...h6 11 ♗h4 g5 12 fxg5 ♘e5 13 ♕e2 ♘fg4 14 ♘f3! hxg5 15 ♗g3! − it is worth much more than a pawn to loosen Black's grip − 15...♘xf3 16 gxf3 ♘e5 17 f4 gxf4 18 ♗xf4 ♗d7 19 ♖df1!! and Black can hardly castle queenside owing to ♗xe5 and ♖xf7, while otherwise the h-pawn is on the march!) 11 ♖he1 ♗b7 12 ♕g3!? b4! (but not 12...0-0-0? 13 ♗xb5! axb5 14 ♘dxb5 ♕b6 15 e5 dxe5 16 fxe5 ♘d5 17 ♗xe7, to be followed by 18 ♘d6+ and ♘xf7 +−) 13 ♘d5!

exd5 14 exd5 ♔d8 15 ♕e3 ♘b6 16 ♘f5 ♘bxd5 17 ♕d4 ♗f8 18 ♗e4 ♔c8 19 ♘xg7! with great complications.

10...b5 11 ♗xf6 ♘xf6

After 11...gxf6 12 f5 ♘e5 13 ♕h3 0-0 14 ♖g1 ♔h8 15 ♘ce2! ♕b7 16 ♘f4 the e6-pawn is hanging, while on 16...♕xe4, 17 ♘h5 threatens ♗g2 and ♕h4. Instead, 11...♗xf6 12 g5 (12 ♗xb5?! ♖b8! 13 ♗xd7+ – 13 ♗e2? ♗xd4 14 ♖xd4 ♖xb2! – 13...♗xd7 and ...0-0, ...♖fc8, ...a6-a5 with attack) 12...♗e7 leads to the same position as 11...♘xf6.

12 g5 ♘d7 13 f5!?

A brave move, but there is no time to fool around since Black is threatening to assail the e4-pawn with ...b5-b4 and then ...♗b7 and ...♘c5. If White tries to prevent this advance with 13 a3 then 13...♖b8! 14 h4 b4 15 axb4 ♖xb4 16 ♗h3! ♕c5! (not 16...♕b6 17 ♘f5! exf5 18 ♘d5 ♕c5 19 exf5! and the threat is 20 ♖he1) 17 ♘b3 ♕b6 18 h5 ♘c5 19 ♘xc5 dxc5 20 g6 fxg6 21 hxg6 h6 with a double-edged fight.

13...♘c5!

13...♘e5 is wrong due to 14 ♕g3 b4 15 ♘ce2, threatening 16 ♘f4 when the pawn on e6 is defenceless as ...e6xf5 would hand the d5-square to White on a silver platter. It is also risky to snatch the pawn on g5: 13...♗xg5+ 14 ♔b1 ♘e5 15 ♕h5! and both the bishop on g5 and the pawn on e6 are hanging.

14 f6

After 14 h4 b4 15 ♘ce2 (or 15 fxe6 fxe6! 16 ♘ce2 g6 17 ♔b1 ♗b7 18 ♘g3 ♖f8 19 ♕e3 e5 20 ♘b3 ♘e6 and Black seizes the initiative) 15...e5 16 ♘b3 ♘xe4! 17 ♕xe4 ♗b7 18 ♖d5 ♖c8 19 c3 ♕c4! 20 ♕xc4 ♖xc4 21 ♗g2 ♗xd5 22 ♗xd5 ♖xh4, a rook and two pawns plus an active position, for two pieces, is not a bad trade.

14...gxf6

Not 14...♗f8? 15 ♗xb5+!! axb5 16 ♘dxb5 and the queen has serious problems escaping in view of 17 fxg7 and then ♘xd6.

15 gxf6 ♗f8

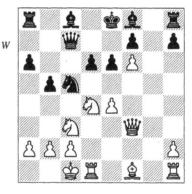

Plans and Counterplans:

Black is again planning ...b5-b4 and ...♗b7. If White prevents this with **16 a3** then Black can follow up with 16...♖b8!? with the idea of ...b5-b4, since 17 b4! ♘d7 and 18...♘e5 is more pleasant for Black. White should therefore play for an attack, but how? **16 ♗h3** b4 17 ♘d5!? exd5 18 exd5 ♗xh3 19 ♖he1+ ♔d8 20 ♘c6+ ♔c8 21 ♕xh3+ ♕d7! and 22 ♖e8+ ♔c7 23

♕xd7+ ♔xd7 24 ♖xa8 does not win the rook in view of 24...♗h6+ and 25...♖xa8, and a piece is a piece. Therefore it seems logical to play **16 ♕h5** so that after a piece sacrifice on d5 and ♖he1+ White can win the pawn on f7 by chasing the black king to d8. Black cannot play 16...b4? 17 ♘d5 exd5 18 exd5 ♗d7 19 ♖e1+ ♔d8 20 ♔b1! ♔c8 21 ♕xf7 ♔b7 22 ♘e6 (±), but he does have 16...♗d7 17 ♗h3 b4 and 18 ♘d5 exd5 19 exd5 0-0-0, even though White still has an initiative for the piece. The latest invention is **16 ♖g1!?**, intending ♖g1-g7, with a number of threats. For example, 16...♗d7 17 ♖g7! ♗xg7 18 fxg7 ♖g8 19 e5! 0-0-0 20 exd6 ♕b7 21 ♕xf7 b4 22 ♘ce2 ♕d5 23 ♕f2! ♕xa2 24 ♘b3 ♘xb3+ 25 cxb3 and the black king falls prey to the white queen or 16...b4 17 ♘d5 ♕b7 18 ♖g7! exd5 19 exd5 ♗d7 20 ♘c6 ♗xc6 21 dxc6 ♕c7 22 ♕e3+ and it is curtains for Black. The only move that has withstood practical tests is 16 ♖g1!? h5!?, although even now White has a strong attack. Play may continue: 17 a3 ♗d7 18 ♗h3!? (after 18 ♖g7 ♖c8 19 ♗h3 ♕d8! 20 ♖dg1 ♖h6! 21 b4 ♕xf6! 22 ♕xf6 ♖xf6 23 bxc5 ♗xg7, followed by ...♖xc5, Black is winning) 18...♘a4 19 ♘xa4 bxa4 20 e5 and now after 20...♖c8? 21 exd6 ♗xd6 22 ♔b1 ♗e5 23 c3 (±) Black has not a shred of counterplay so he should play 20...♖b8!?, which still awaits practical testing. The other option on 16 ♖g1!?

h5!? is the immediate 17 ♖g7: 17...b4 18 ♘d5 exd5 19 exd5 ♗g4! 20 ♖e1+ ♔d8 and now White can sustain his attack with either 21 ♕e3 ♔c8 22 ♘e6!? or 21 ♕f4 ♔c8 22 ♘c6. In tournament practice a delicate balance between attack and defence is starting to take shape, but this balance may be disrupted by new moves for either side.

B. Kaleidoscope

1 e4 c5 2 ♘f3 d6 3 d4 cxd4 4 ♘xd4 ♘f6 5 ♘c3 a6

In this section we deal with White's alternatives to 6 ♗g5 in the Najdorf consists of the following tracks:

B1. 6 h3
B2. 6 a4
B3. 6 g3
B4. 6 f4
B5. 6 ♗e2
B6. 6 ♗c4 and
B7. 6 ♗e3.

B1. 1 e4 c5 2 ♘f3 d6 3 d4 cxd4 4 ♘xd4 ♘f6 5 ♘c3 a6 6 h3?!

This unnecessary move gives Black the opportunity to transpose to other variations – with an extra tempo!
   6...e6!
   6...e5? plays into White's hands as after 7 ♘de2 and 8 g4 the knight goes to g3 and threatens ♘f5 or g4-g5. But 6...g6!? 7 g4 ♗g7

8 g5 ♘h5 9 ♗e2 e5 10 ♘b3 ♘f4!? comes into consideration, since if White captures the knight on f4 then Black rules the dark squares.

7 g4

Now we have reached the Keres Attack of the Scheveningen Variation, only here White has spent time on the tempo-losing h2-h3.

7...d5! 8 exd5 ♘xd5 9 ♘de2! ♗b4! 10 ♗g2 0-0 11 ♗d2 ♘b6 ∞.

B2. 1 e4 c5 2 ♘f3 d6 3 d4 cxd4 4 ♘xd4 ♘f6 5 ♘c3 a6 6 a4?!

By including the moves ...a7-a6 and a2-a4 Black's position is more favourable in nearly every variation. For example, in the Dragon after 6...g6 7 ♗e2 ♗g7 8 0-0 0-0 9 ♗e3 ♘c6 or in the Four Knights Variation with 6...♘c6!? 7 ♗e2 e5 8 ♘f3 (or 8 ♘xc6 bxc6 and now 9 f4 a5! or 9 a5 d5! is already better for Black) 8...h6 followed by ...♗e6, ...♗e7, ...0-0 and ...♖c8, giving Black good play.

B3. 1 e4 c5 2 ♘f3 d6 3 d4 cxd4 4 ♘xd4 ♘f6 5 ♘c3 a6 6 g3

6...e5!? 7 ♘de2

Or 7 ♘b3 ♘bd7 8 a4 b6 9 ♗g2 ♗b7 10 ♘d2 ♖c8 11 0-0 ♗e7 12 ♖e1 ♖c5! hindering ♘c3-d5 whilst preparing for an attack on the e4-pawn: 13 ♘f1 ♕a8! with an active position for Black.

7...b5!? 8 ♗g2

After the faulty 8 a4 b4? 9 ♘d5 ♘xd5 10 ♕xd5! White is on top,

but instead of 8...b4, 8...♗b7! 9 ♗g2 ♘bd7!? 10 axb5 axb5 11 ♖xa8 ♕xa8 12 ♘xb5 ♕a5+ and ...♘xe4 is better for Black.

8...♗b7 9 0-0 ♗e7 10 h3

White opts for the typical plan of a slow expansion with h2-h3, g3-g4 and ♘g3.

10...0-0 11 g4 ♘bd7 12 ♘g3 b4! 13 ♘d5 ♘xd5 14 exd5 g6!? 15 ♗h6 ♖e8 16 ♕d2! a5 17 f4 ♗a6 18 ♖f3

Or 18 ♖f2 ♗h4 19 ♔h2 e4! ∞.

18...exf4!

19 ♕xf4 ♘e5 or 19 ♗xf4 ♗f6! gives Black sufficient counterplay.

B4. 1 e4 c5 2 ♘f3 d6 3 d4 cxd4 4 ♘xd4 ♘f6 5 ♘c3 a6 6 f4

6...e5 7 ♘f3 ♘bd7 8 a4

Otherwise Black obtains easy play with ...b7-b5, ...♗e7, ...♗b7, ...0-0 and ...♕c7.

8...♗e7 9 ♗d3 0-0 10 0-0 exf4!?

A good decision since on 11 ♗xf4 ♕b6+ 12 ♔h1 ♕xb2 13 ♕e1 ♕b6 14 ♘d5 ♘xd5 15 exd5 ♕d8! Black steals a pawn for nothing, and although 11 ♔h1 ♘e5 12 ♗xf4 ♕c7 13 ♕d2 ♗e6 14 ♘d4 ♖fe8 15 ♗xe5 dxe5 16 ♘xe6 fxe6 looks ugly for Black owing to his doubled isolated e-pawn, these pawns exert excellent control over all of the central squares and Black is strong on the dark squares (=). On 11 ♔h1, 11...♘h5!? is interesting:12 ♘d4 g6 13 ♗e2 ♘df6 14 ♘f5 ♗e6 =.

B5. 1 e4 c5 2 ♘f3 d6 3 d4 cxd4 4 ♘xd4 ♘f6 5 ♘c3 a6 6 ♗e2

6...e5 7 ♘b3

7 ♘f3 bottles up the strength of the f2-pawn: 7...h6! (preventing ♗g5xf6 which would consolidate White's grip on the d5-square) 8 0-0 ♗e6 9 ♖e1 ♘bd7 10 ♗f1 ♗e7 11 a4 b6! (hindering a4-a5 which would clamp down on Black) 12 b3 0-0 13 ♗b2 ♕c7 14 h3 ♖fc8 15 ♕d2 ♕b7! and Black aims for ...b6-b5. 7 ♘f5 looks strange but it should not be taken lightly: 7...♗xf5 8 exf5 h6 (8...d5 9 ♗g5) 9 ♗f3! and Black does not achieve ...d6-d5. Correct is 7...d5!? 8 ♗g5! d4! 9 ♗xf6 ♕xf6 10 ♘d5 ♕d8 11 c4 g6 12 ♘g3 h5! 13 ♗f3 ♗e6 14 ♘e2 ♗g7 and ...0-0 with equal chances.

7...♗e7

On 7...♗e6?! White has the excellent 8 f4! ♕c7 9 g4! exf4 10 g5! ♘fd7 11 ♗xf4, followed by ♕d2 and 0-0-0 ±.

8 0-0

8 f4 0-0 9 g4 d5! 10 exd5 ♗b4! is heavenly for Black as besides ...♘xd5 and ...♘e4 he also threatens ...♘xg4 followed by ...♕h4+.

8...0-0 9 f4 ♕c7 10 a4 ♗e6 11 f5 ♗c4 12 a5 ♘bd7 13 ♗e3 b5! 14 axb6 ♘xb6 15 ♔h1 ♖fc8 16 ♗xb6 ♕xb6 17 ♗xc4 ♖xc4 18 ♕e2 ♖ac8 19 ♖a2 ♗d8! 20 ♖fa1 ♕b7!

Now the pawn on e4 is hanging and on 21 ♖a4, 21...♖xa4 22 ♖xa4 a5! secures the a-pawn.

B6. 1 e4 c5 2 ♘f3 d6 3 d4 cxd4 4 ♘xd4 ♘f6 5 ♘c3 a6 6 ♗c4

6...e6

Not 6...e5? 7 ♘f5 ♗xf5 8 exf5 and Black has a permanent hole on d5. After 6...e6 play transposes into the Scheveningen Variation (section II).

B7. 1 e4 c5 2 ♘f3 d6 3 d4 cxd4 4 ♘xd4 ♘f6 5 ♘c3 a6 6 ♗e3!?

This dangerous move needs to be examined more carefully. White is planning to storm the black kingside with f2-f3, ♕d2, 0-0-0 and then g2-g4-g5, when by chasing away the knight from f6 White increases his control over d5.

6...♘g4!?

Black may as well make use of his control over the g4-square. 6...e5 results in nerve-racking complications: 7 ♘b3 (7 ♘f3 ♗e7 8 ♗c4 0-0 9 0-0 ♘c6 10 ♕e2 ♘a5 11 ♗b3 h6 12 ♖fd1 ♘xb3 13 axb3 ♕e8! 14 ♘d2!? b5!, followed by ...♗e6 and ...♕c6, with an equal position and a peaceful old age) 7...♗e6 8 f3!? (or 8 f4 exf4 9 ♗xf4 ♘c6 10 ♕e2 ♖c8 11 h3 g6!? 12 g4 – 12 0-0-0 ♘h5! 13 ♗h2 ♘g3!! 14 ♗xg3 ♕g5+ and ♕xg3 ∓ – 12...h5 13 g5 ♘d7 14 0-0-0 ♗e7 15 ♖g1 ♘ce5 ∞) 8...♗e7 (not 8...d5?! 9 exd5 ♘xd5 10 ♘xd5 ♕xd5 11 ♕xd5 ♗xd5 12 0-0-0 and White is much better developed) 9 ♕d2 ♘bd7 (9...0-0!? comes into consideration). Now 10 g4! d5 is fine for Black, while 10 0-0-0 a5!? 11 ♗b5! ♘c6 12 g4 ♘e8, followed by ...♘c7 and ...♕b8 and ...a5-a4 is also playable. Of course in the meantime White is also rushing forward on the other flank with g4-g5, h2-h4, ♕g4, and g5-g6!) 10 g4 h6! (after 10...b5 11 a4! b4 12 ♘d5 ♗xd5 13 exd5 White is threatening 0-0-0 and ♕xb4 or g4-g5, h2-h4, ♖g1 and has control over the light squares with his bishop on f1) 11 h4 b5 12 ♖g1 b4 13 ♘a4 d5 14 g5! (White has to put aside 0-0-0 for the moment to deal with Black's counter in the centre) 14...d4 15 ♗xd4 ♗xb3 16 gxf6 ♗xf6 17 axb3 exd4 18 0-0-0 ♘e5 19 f4! ♘f3 20 ♕g2 ♘xg1 21 e5!! 0-0 22 ♗d3 ♗xe5 23 fxe5 ♕xh4 24 ♖xg1 and White has an attack. The most successful exponent of 6 ♗e3, the Indian grandmaster Viswanathan Anand, has been our tutor in this line.

7 ♗g5 h6 8 ♗h4 g5 9 ♗g3
After 9 ♘f5 Black can win the pawn with 9...♘f6! 10 ♗g3 ♘xe4 11 ♘xe4 ♗xf5, while Black also obtains excellent play after 9 ♗e2?! ♗g7 10 ♗g3 h5! 11 h4 ♘c6 12 ♘b3 gxh4, as after both 13 ♗xh4 ♗e6 14 ♕d2 ♕b6! and 13 ♖xh4 ♗e6 14 ♕d2 ♕b6! White has problems with his pawn on f2 and Black is also threatening ...♗h6.

9...♗g7 10 ♕d2 ♘c6 11 ♘b3 (D)

Plans and Counterplans:
White is preparing for queenside castling and will hamper Black's

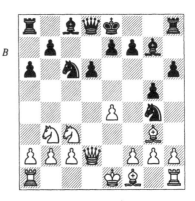

B

kingside initiative with h2-h4 or f2-f3. Black can continue **11...♗e6** 12 f3 ♘ge5 13 ♘d5 b5 (13...♘g6!? intending ...h5-h4) or **11...f5!?** 12 exf5 ♗xf5 13 ♗d3 ♕d7 14 0-0 0-0 15 ♘d5 ♗xd3 16 ♕xd3 ♕f5 with equal chances.

The standard 'Najdorf reply' ...e7-e5 is a good response in most of these sidelines, but Black always has the option of the flexible ...e7-e6 if he prefers, transposing to the Scheveningen Variation (see section II).

IV. Four Knights Variation

---

1 e4 c5 2 ♘f3 d6 3 d4 cxd4 4 ♘xd4 ♘f6 5 ♘c3 ♘c6 (D)
The Four Knights Variation is very closely related to the Scheveningen (where instead of 5...♘c6 Black plays 5...e6) and the Najdorf (where the fifth move is 5...a6). Often the same position can arise from all three move-orders. The most typical feature of the Four Knights Variation is that Black controls the square g4. So

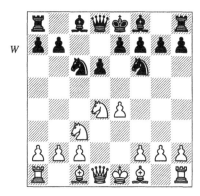

W

here White cannot copy the Keres Attack of the Scheveningen (5...e6 6 g4!?). And what is more, 6 ♗e3, which is playable against both the Najdorf and Scheveningen, is now harmless in view of 6...♘g4! 7 ♗b5 ♘xe3 8 fxe3 ♗d7 9 0-0 (9 ♗xc6?! bxc6 10 0-0 e5! 11 ♕f3 f6 and White's initiative is beaten back) 9...e6 10 ♗xc6 bxc6 and now after either 11 ♕f3 ♕f6 12 ♕e2 ♕g5 or 11 e5 ♗e7 12 ♕h5 0-0 Black's king finds safety and sooner or later the weaknesses of White's pawn structure and the difference between the knight pair and bishop pair will make themselves felt.

In this section we consider three possibilities for White:

A. Boleslavsky Variation: 6 ♗e2 e5.
B. Sozin Variation: 6 ♗c4.
C. Rauzer Variation: 6 ♗g5.

On moves of lesser importance Black usually equalizes quite easily:

6 g3?! ♗g4! Forcing a weakening. 7 f3 ♗d7 8 ♗g2 a6 9 ♘b3 e6 10 ♗e3 b5 followed by ...♖c8, ...♗e7, ...0-0 and ...♕c7 or **6 f4** e5!? 7 ♘f3 (7 ♘xc6 bxc6 8 fxe5 ♘g4!? 9 exd6? ♗xd6 with a huge initiative for the pawn) 7...♗e7 8 ♗c4 0-0 9 0-0 exf4! 10 ♗b3 (10 ♗xf4 ♕b6+ and ...♕xb2) 10...♘g4 threatening 11...♘e3 and 11...♕b6+ followed by ♘f2+.

A. 1 e4 c5 2 ♘f3 d6 3 d4 cxd4 4 ♘xd4 ♘f6 5 ♘c3 ♘c6 6 ♗e2 e5 (Boleslavsky Variation)

6...♘xd4?? would be a mistake, since although Black has 'forced' the queen to the centre with 7 ♕xd4 but there is nothing to attack and chase it with. The situation is completely different for example in the Scandinavian Defence where after 1 e4 d5 White captures d5 in order to win a tempo and chase the well-placed queen after 2 exd5 ♕xd5 3 ♘c3! For 6...e6 see section II, and for 6...g6 section VI.

7 ♘f3

7 ♘xc6 is unpretentious: 7...bxc6 8 0-0 ♗e7 9 ♕d3 ♘d7! 10 ♕g3 0-0 11 f4 exf4! 12 ♗xf4 ♘e5! 13 ♗xe5 dxe5 14 ♕xe5 ♗d6 15 ♕h5 ♕b6+ with ...♕xb2 to follow and Black is better. An important manoeuvre on f2-f4 is e5xf4 and then the knight – brought to d7 well in advance – jumps to e5. 7 ♘f5? ♗xf5 8 exf5 d5 9 ♗g5 ♗b4, and 7 ♘db5? a6 8 ♘a3 b5!? (8...♗e6!?)

are both ill-advised lines. But White should consider 7 ②b3 ♗e7 8 0-0 0-0 9 f4!? a5! 10 a4 ②b4 11 ♔h1 b6 (also possible is 11...♗e6 12 f5 ♗d7 and ♗c6) 12 ♗f3 ♗b7 with an unclear game in which White has to know that he cannot ease central pressure with f4-f5, due to d6-d5, or with f4xe5, owing to the weakening of the e4-pawn.

7...h6!?

Hindering White's plan of ♗g5-♗xf6-②d5.

8 0-0 ♗e7 9 ♖e1

Or 9 ♗e3 0-0 10 ♕d2 ♗e6 11 ♖fd1 ♕d7 and ...♖fd8 =.

9...0-0 10 h3

White is aiming for 11 ♗f1 as the immediate 10 ♗f1 is met by 10...♗g4 11 h3 ♗xf3 12 ♕xf3 ②d4.

10...♗e6 11 ♗f1

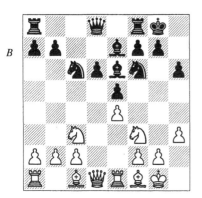

Plans and Counterplans:
White has cautiously protected the pawn on e4 and now he is planning ②c3-d5. This cannot be thwarted with **11...d5?** as after the exchanges on d5 Black loses

the pawn on e5, and **11...♕a5** 12 ♗d2 ♕d8 (12...♕b6 13 ②a4 and c2-c4 ±) 13 ②a4!? d5 14 exd5 ♕xd5 15 c4! ♕d6 16 ♗c3 is also better for White owing to the pawn on e5 and the mobile white queenside. Black therefore has to get ready for 12 ②d5: **11...♖c8?!** 12 ②d5 ♗xd5 13 exd5 ②b8 14 c4! ②bd7 15 b4 a5 16 a3 and White's bishop pair and queenside initiative speak for themselves (±). More precise is **11...②b8!** 12 ②d5 ②xd5 (12...♗xd5 13 exd5 ②bd7 14 c4 a5! and White can hardly get in b2-b4 and the mobilization of his queenside!) 13 exd5 ♗f5 14 c4 ②d7 and now 15 ♗e3 e4!? 16 ②d4 ♗g6, followed by the manoeuvre ...②d7-e5-d3, or 15 a3 ♗f6! with the constant threat of playing ...e5-e4, offers Black level chances.

B. 1 e4 c5 2 ②f3 d6 3 d4 cxd4 4 ②xd4 ②f6 5 ②c3 ②c6 6 ♗c4 (Sozin Variation)

White chooses an aggressive attacking setup. At times like this Black is easily punished for any naiveté: 6...g6?! 7 ②xc6 bxc6 8 e5! dxe5?? (8...②g4 9 ♗f4 ±) 9 ♗xf7+! ♔xf7 10 ♕xd8 +−.

6...e6

A natural move, which also defends the weak f7-square from possible combinations by the bishop on c4. Obviously bad is 6...e5?! 7 ②de2 followed by ♗e3, f3, ♕d2, 0-0-0 and White is in control. But an interesting intermediate move is 6...♕b6!?, forcing the knight on d4 to a more passive square. Black need not fear 7 ♗e3 ♕xb2 8 ♘db5 on account of 8...♕b4! 9 ♗d3 ♕a5. Better is 7 ♘de2 e6 8 0-0 a6 (also playable is the simple ...♗e7, ...0-0) 9 ♗b3 ♗e7 10 ♗g5 ♕c7 and then ...b7-b5 and Black can consider exchanging the bishop on b3 with ...♘a5. Finally, on 6...♕b6 perhaps best is 7 ♘b3!?: 7...e6 8 0-0 ♗e7 9 ♗g5 0-0!? 10 ♗xf6 ♗xf6 11 ♕xd6 ♖d8 (11...♗xc3!?) 12 ♕g3 ♗e5!? 13 ♕h3 a5 with excellent compensation for the pawn.

7 ♗e3 ♗e7

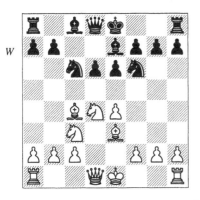

White's two continuations of different temperament are:

B1. 8 0-0
B2. 8 ♕e2 and **0-0-0**.

B1. 8 0-0

8...0-0 9 ♗b3
White has f2-f4 in mind but right now this is premature in view of 9 f4? d5!

9...a6!?
Black prepares queenside play, namely ...b7-b5. He has to live with the bishop on b3 as after 9...♘a5 10 f4 b6 11 e5! the absence of the knight from the centre is really felt. Here is a sample line: 11...dxe5 12 fxe5 ♘d7 (12...♘d5 13 ♘xd5 exd5 14 ♕f3! ±/±) 13 ♖xf7! and Black is in trouble owing to the e6-square (+−). Thus if White is threatening f2-f4 and e4-e5, Black ought to keep the knight on c6!

This position can be reached via the Najdorf as well: 1 e4 c5 2 ♘f3 d6 3 d4 cxd4 4 ♘xd4 ♘f6 5 ♘c3 a6 6 ♗c4 e6 7 ♗b3 (the threat was 7...b5 8 ♗b3 b4 and the pawn on e4 is lost) 7...♗e7 8 0-0 0-0 9 ♗e3 ♘c6.

10 f4 ♘xd4!? 11 ♗xd4 b5 12 e5!
Otherwise White is doomed to passivity: 12 a3 (to stop 12...b4 which would win the e4-pawn) 12...♗b7 13 ♕e1 a5! and Black has the initiative.

12...dxe5 13 fxe5 ♘d7 14 ♘e4
Not 14 ♕f3?! ♘c5! 15 ♕xa8? ♕xd4+ 16 ♔h1 ♗b7 17 ♕a7 ♕xe5 and apart from ♗d6, White is also threatening ♕c7, trapping the queen.

14...♗b7 15 ♘d6 ♗xd6 16 exd6 ♕g5 ∞.

Plans and Counterplans:
White can pin his hopes on the d6-pawn and hope that Black will neglect his kingside when White can have a go at it with the bishop

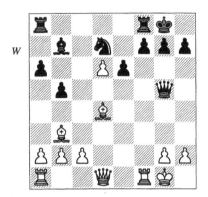

pair. Black can trust his active bishop b7, the open c-file and perhaps the expansion ...e6-e5 and ...f7-f5. For example, 17 ♖f2 a5 (17...e5?! 18 ♗c3 and ♕f1 ties Black down to f7) 18 a4 e5 19 ♗c3 b4 20 ♗d2 ♕g6 or 17 ♕e2 e5 18 ♗c3 ♕g6 19 ♖ad1 ♔h8 20 ♗d5! ♗xd5 21 ♖xd5 ♕e6 22 ♖fd1 ♖fc8!? produces a dynamic fight.

B2. 1 e4 c5 2 ♘f3 d6 3 d4 cxd4 4 ♘xd4 ♘f6 4 ♘c3 ♘c6 6 ♗c4 e6 7 ♗e3 ♗e7 8 ♕e2

8...a6
Nowadays Black typically delays castling in order to create a rapid queenside attack, although he has chances with 8...0-0 9 0-0-0 ♕c7 10 ♗b3 a6 11 ♖hg1 (11 g4 ♘xd4 12 ♗xd4? e5! and the pawn on g4 is hanging; 12 ♖xd4! ∞) 11...♘d7 12 g4 ♘c5 13 g5 ♗d7 14 ♕h5 ♖fc8! 15 ♖g3 g6 16 ♕h6 ♗f8 17 ♕h4 ♘xd4 18 ♖xd4 b5! 19 ♖h3 h5 20 gxh6 ♔h7! and Black holds up the white pawn h6 as a shield (∓). In this line instead of 13 g5

White has the typical Sozin sacrifice 13 ♘f5!? which it is more than risky to accept: 13...exf5? 14 gxf5 ♗d7 15 ♘d5 ♕d8 16 ♕h5 ♔h8 17 ♖xg7! ♔xg7 18 f6+! and a quick mate. Black has to try the cold-blooded line 13...b5 14 ♗d5! (it is worth a piece to get a knight in to d5!) 14...♗b7 15 g5 ♖fc8, even though White's pieces have advanced in frightening fashion.

9 0-0-0 ♕c7 10 ♗b3
10 ♖hg1 ♘a5 11 ♗d3 b5 12 g4 b4 13 ♘b1 and now Black can play either ...♘f6-d7-c5 or 13...♗b7 14 ♘d2 d5!?

10...♘a5
10...b5? 11 ♘xc6! ♕xc6 12 ♗d4 and Black's queenside play has diminished.

11 g4 b5 12 g5 ♘xb3+
12...♘d7? 13 ♗xe6!
13 axb3 ♘d7 ∞

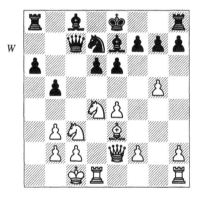

Plans and Counterplans:
White has two 'speed gears' at his disposal. The slower line is **14 h4** b4 15 ♘a4 ♘c5 16 h5 ♗d7 17 g6 ♘xb3+ 18 ♘xb3 ♗xa4 19 h6! fxg6

20 hxg7 罝g8 21 ♘d4 e5 22 ♘e6 豐c6 23 罝xh7 ♗b3! 24 罝d5! with complete disorder. The faster one goes **14 ♘f5!?** exf5 15 ♘d5 豐d8 (15...豐a5 loses beautifully: 16 exf5 ♗b7 17 ♘xe7 豐a1+ 18 ♔d2 豐xb2 19 ♘c6!! 0-0 20 ♗d4 豐a3 21 罝a1 +−) 16 exf5 ♗b7 (16...0-0? 17 f6 gxf6 18 ♗d4 ♘e5 19 gxf6 ♗xf6 20 罝g1 ♗g7 21 ♗xe5 +−) 17 f6 gxf6 18 罝he1 ♗xd5 19 罝xd5 罝g8 20 gxf6 ♘xf6 21 罝f5 罝b8 (to stop the threat of 22 ♗b6) 22 h4!? ♘g4 23 ♗g5 f6 24 豐xg4 fxg5 25 豐h5+ ♔d7 26 罝xe7+ 豐xe7 27 罝f7 gxh4 28 罝xe7+ ♔xe7 29 豐xh7+ with an even endgame. This practical example again shows that even a wild 'shoot-out' can have a peaceful outcome.

C. 1 e4 c5 2 ♘f3 d6 3 d4 cxd4 4 ♘xd4 ♘f6 5 ♘c3 ♘c6 6 ♗g5!? (Rauzer Variation)

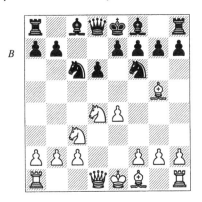

White prepares 豐d2 and 0-0-0, after which he often tries to convert his activity into a more tangible advantage by means of the breakthrough f2-f4 and e4-e5. Black can try to respond on the queenside or seek counterplay in the centre. The main lines are:

C1. 6...♗d7 and
C2. 6...e6.

Others are less significant:

a) 6...g6? 7 ♗xf6 exf6 8 ♗c4 ♗g7 9 ♘db5 0-0 10 豐xd6 ±.

b) 6...e5? 7 ♗xf6! gxf6 (7...豐xf6 8 ♘d5 followed by ♘b5 +−) 8 ♘f5! and, with White controlling the d5- and f5-squares, Black's game is in distress (±).

c) 6...豐a5 7 ♗xf6 gxf6 8 ♗b5 ♗d7 9 ♘b3 豐c7 10 ♘d5 豐d8 11 豐h5! (a multi-purpose move: while preparing queenside castling for White, the queen makes the same castling difficult for Black by a permanent attack on the f7-pawn. This move also prevents Black's active ...h7-h5, ...♗h6 plan) 11...e6 12 ♘e3 and 0-0-0 ±.

d) 6...豐b6 7 ♘b3 e6?! 8 ♗xf6 gxf6 9 ♗e2 a6 10 ♗h5! ♗d7 11 0-0 罝g8 12 ♔h1 罝g7 13 f4 0-0-0 14 a4! and White has an attack.

e) 6...a6 7 ♗xf6 gxf6 8 ♗e2 e6 (8...f5!?) 9 ♘b3 b5 10 0-0 ♗b7 11 f4 ♗g7 and 0-0 ∞. 7 豐d2 e6 instead of 7 ♗xf6 transposes into the 6...e6 main line.

C1. 1 e4 c5 2 ♘f3 d6 3 d4 cxd4 4 ♘xd4 ♘f6 5 ♘c3 ♘c6 6 ♗g5 ♗d7

Black starts his manoeuvres on the queenside at once. Typically

he will eventually sacrifice the exchange on c3!

7 ♕d2

Worse is 7 ♗xf6 gxf6 8 ♗e2 ♕b6!
9 ♘b3 f5! and Black has got rid of
his doubled pawns.

7...♖c8 8 f4!

Black has several opportunities
to sacrifice on c3. For example, 8
0-0-0 ♘xd4 9 ♕xd4 ♕a5 10 f4
♖xc3!? 11 bxc3 e5 12 ♕b4 ♕xb4 13
cxb4 ♘xe4 14 ♗h4 g5! (14...♘xc3
15 ♖d3 ♘xa2+ 16 ♔b2 ♘b4 17
♖b3 and White's rook invades the
black position) 15 fxg5 ♗e7 with a
perfectly playable game for Black.

8...♘xd4

After 8...h6 9 ♗xf6 (9 ♗h4?! g5!
10 fxg5 hxg5 11 ♗xg5 ♘g4! followed by ...♗g7 and Black has the
e5 square with control over d4)
9...gxf6 10 ♘f5! ♕a5 11 ♗d3 ♘b4
12 0-0 ♘xd3 13 ♕xd3 ♕c5+ 14
♔h1 e6 15 ♘e3 with ♖ad1 and especially f4-f5! to follow. Black's
pawns in the centre are immobile
and he has a hard time finding a
safe place for his king.

9 ♕xd4 ♕a5 10 e5!

This is how White can avoid 10
0-0-0 ♖xc3.

10...dxe5

Not 10...♖xc3 11 bxc3 ♘e4 12
♕xe4! ♕xc3+ 13 ♔f2 ♕xa1 14
♗b5!! ♕c3 (14...♕xh1 15 ♕xb7
♗xb5 16 ♕c8 mate!) 15 ♗xd7+ and
16 ♕xb7+ and White overwhelms
the undeveloped black position.

11 fxe5 e6 12 0-0-0

White cannot take on f6 because of the 'hanging' g5-bishop.

12...♗c6

Again bad is 12...♖xc3? 13 ♗d2!
♗c5 14 ♗xc3 ♗xd4 15 ♗xa5 ♗xe5
16 ♗b5! b6 17 ♗xd7+ ♘xd7 18
♗b4! ± and the black queenside is
cramped.

13 ♘b5! ♗xb5 14 exf6

This is why it was necessary to
close the fifth rank with a piece
sacrifice.

14...♗a4

14...♗c6 15 h4! ±.

15 ♗d2

15 h4? gxf6 16 ♗xf6 ♗h6+! 17
♗g5 ♗xg5+ 18 hxg5 ♕xg5+ ∓.

15...♖xc2+ 16 ♔b1 ♖xd2

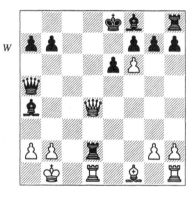

For a long time theoretical books
gave **17 ♖xd2** gxf6 'unclear' as
the end of this line, until it turned
out that after **17 ♕xd2!** White is
better! For example: 17...♗b4 18
♕c1! (18 fxg7 ♖g8 19 ♕c1 ♗xd1
20 ♕c8+ ♔e7 21 ♕xg8 ♕f5+ 22
♔a1 ♕c2! ∞) 18...0-0 (certainly not
18...♗xd1?? 19 ♕c8+ ♕d8 20
♗b5+ with mate) 19 fxg7 ♔xg7
20 ♖d4 ♖d8 21 ♖xd8 ♕xd8 22 ♗e2
and Black is an exchange down

without compensation. Alternatively, 17...♛xd2 18 ♖xd2 gxf6 19 ♗e2 ♘c6 20 ♗f3! ♗xf3 21 gxf3 followed by ♖c1 and the white rooks invade on the c- and d-files and win. It is worth noting that only a late novelty (17 ♛xd2! instead of 17 ♖xd2) made this whole line attractive for White if he plays the correct move-order (8 f4! instead of 8 0-0-0) right to the end. This line gives a little insight into the world of the 'pros' in which opening novelty after opening novelty help to form the repertoire of the great chess stars.

C2. 1 e4 c5 2 ♘f3 d6 3 d4 cxd4 4 ♘xd4 ♘f6 5 ♘c3 ♘c6 6 ♗g5 e6

7 ♛d2
Another line is 7 ♛d3. Black has to watch out since the white queen is heading towards g3 with a kingside attack! So 7...♗e7 8 0-0-0 0-0 9 f4 and now not 9...♗d7?! 10 ♘b3 ♛b6 11 a3 ♖fd8 12 ♛g3!, but 9...♘xd4 invalidating the difference between 7 ♛d3 and 7 ♛d2. Finally there are two bishop moves: 7 ♗e2 ♗e7 8 0-0 0-0 9 ♛d2 ♘xe4! 10 ♘xe4 ♗xg5 11 ♘xg5 ♘xd4 12 ♛xd4 ♛xg5 13 ♛xd6 ♛d8! (13...♖d8 14 ♛c7 ±) =; and 7 ♗b5!? ♗d7 8 ♗xc6! bxc6 (8...♗xc6 9 ♘xc6 bxc6 10 e5! dxe5 11 ♛f3 with strong initiative for White) 9 ♛f3 h6 10 ♗h4 e5!? 11 ♘f5 ♗xf5 12 ♛xf5 ♛d7 13 ♛f3 ♗e7 ∞. On 7 ♛d2 Black has two viable possibilities:

C2a. 7...♗e7 or
C2b. 7...a6.

Other moves are practically out of the question as White is threatening to bear down on the d6-pawn with 0-0-0, ♘db5.

C2a. 7...♗e7

8 0-0-0
8 ♗xf6?! ♗xf6 9 ♘db5 0-0! 10 ♘xd6 ♛a5 11 ♘c4 ♛c5 ∞.
8...0-0 9 f4
When Black is already castled it is no longer worth winning a pawn with 9 ♘db5 ♛a5 10 ♗xf6 ♗xf6 11 ♘xd6 because 11...♖d8 12 f4 e5! causes trouble. Also possible is 9 ♘b3 ♛b6 10 f3 ♖d8 11 ♗e3 ♛c7 12 ♛f2 d5 with an unclear position.
9...♘xd4
Black is ill-advised to play 9...e5? 10 ♘f5! ♗xf5 11 exf5, when the d5-square belongs to White. Later he will opt for ♗c4, ♗xf6 and ♘d5. 9...d5? is also wrong on account of 10 e5! ♘d7 11 h4 ♘b6 12 Bx7 ♛xe7 13 h5 and White is on top. Also bad is 9...♛a5 10 ♘b3! and the black queen is shoved off the fifth rank from where it could have kept an eye on the e5-square and might also attack the bishop on g5.
10 ♛xd4 ♛a5
On 10...h6 11 ♗h4 ♛a5 the difference favours White as his dark-squared bishop is not attacked by the enemy queen.

11 ♗c4

Premature is 11 e5? dxe5 12 fxe5 ♖d8! 13 ♕f4 ♖xd1+ followed by ...♘d5 and Black has seized control (∓). But after 11 ♗c4, e4-e5 turns into a forceful threat!

11...♗d7!

Black has to grab the chance to develop the bishop! Not 11...h6? 12 h4! hxg5? 13 hxg5 ♘g4 14 ♖d3 and ♖dh3 with an imminent mating attack, while on 11...♖d8? 12 ♖hf1 ♗d7 13 f5! exf5 14 exf5 ♗xf5? 15 ♘d5! ♘xd5 16 ♖xf5 White wins a piece. Black has to keep his balance on a narrow ledge, just one bad move and ...

12 e5

White has no time to wait as after ...♗c6 and ...♖fd8 Black consolidates and starts to think about a queenside attack. But White has yet another active option: 12 ♗xf6 ♗xf6 13 e5! (not 13 ♕xd6? ♗xc3 14 ♕xd7 ♖ad8! 15 ♕b5 ♗d2+ with ...♕xb5 and ...♗xf4 to follow) 13...♗e7 14 exd6 ♗f6 15 ♕d3 ♗xc3 16 ♕xc3 ♕xc3 17 bxc3 ♖ac8 18 ♗b3 ♖xc3 and Black holds in the endgame. A brand new idea is 12 ♖d3!?: 12...♖ad8 13 ♖g3! ♔h8! (sidestepping the threat of 14 ♗h6) 14 e5 dxe5 15 fxe5 ♗c6 16 ♕e3 ♘g8! 17 h4! ♕b6! with a sharp game.

12...dxe5 13 fxe5 ♗c6!

The knight on f6 is naturally taboo since the bishop on g5 would be hanging!

14 ♗d2! ♘d7 15 ♘d5 ♕d8 16 ♘xe7+ ♕xe7

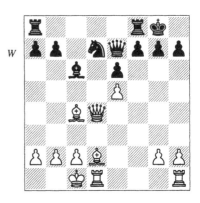

Plans and Counterplans:

White launches an attack against the enemy king while Black's targets are the white kingside pawns and he aims at invading the somewhat draughty white position. For example, 17 ♖he1 ♖fd8 18 ♕g4 ♘f8 and now 19 h4 ♕c5 20 ♗c3 ♕f2! messes up White's attack or 19 ♗f1 ♕c5 20 ♗c3 ♘g6 21 ♕g5!? (this is why the bishop on c4 had to be moved) 21...♖d5! 22 ♖xd5 ♗xd5 ∞.

C2b. 1 e4 c5 2 ♘f3 d6 3 d4 cxd4 4 ♘xd4 ♘f6 5 ♘c3 ♘c6 6 ♗g5 e6 7 ♕d2 a6

8 0-0-0

By parrying ♘db5 Black has prepared for two different plans:

C2b1. 8...h6 and
C2b2. 8...♗d7!?

The first plan drives the bishop back as after 9 ♗xf6 ♕xf6! Black has smooth equality, and the second makes use of the position of the bishop on g5 with a fine strategic motif!

C2b1. 1 e4 c5 2 ♘f3 d6 3 d4 cxd4 4 ♘xd4 ♘f6 5 ♘c3 ♘c6 6 ♗g5 e6 7 ♕d2 a6 0-0-0 h6

9 ♗e3!?

9 ♗xf6 ♕xf6 10 ♘b3 ♕d8! 11 f4 ♗d7 and then ...♕c7 and ...0-0-0 =. Attention! The queen first retreats via f6-d8-c7 to be near the king and avoid getting stuck on f6. Note that 9 ♗h4? drops a pawn: 9...♘xe4! 10 ♕f4 ♘g5! ∓. A serious alternative is 9 ♗f4 and on 9...♗d7 (not 9...♘xd4? 10 ♕xd4 e5? 11 ♗xe5! +−) 10 ♘xc6 ♗xc6 and now 11 ♕e1 ♕c7 12 e5 d5! or 11 f3 d5 12 ♕e1 ♗b4! with a lively game.

9...♗d7

Other tries are:

a) 9...♕c7 10 f3 ♖b8 11 ♔b1 ♗e7 12 g4 and ♗d3, h2-h4.

b) 9...♘xd4 10 ♗xd4 b5 11 f3 ♕a5 12 a3 e5 13 ♗f2! ♗e6 14 ♗h4 g5 15 ♗e1! b4? 16 ♘d5! ♗xd5 17 exd5 ♖b8 18 ♔b1 and the pawn on b4 falls.

c) 9...♗e7!? 10 f3 ♘xd4 11 ♗xd4 e5 12 ♗e3 ♗e6 13 g4 ♖c8 14 ♘d5 ♗xd5 15 exd5 e4!? and this time Black has managed to stay in the game.

10 f4!?

Weaker is 10 f3 b5 11 ♘xc6 ♗xc6 12 ♔b1 ♕c7 and White has no concrete threats.

10...b5 11 ♗d3 ♗e7 12 ♔b1 0-0

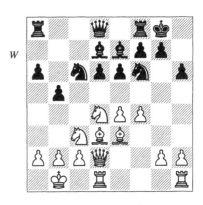

W

Plans and Counterplans:
White has play in the centre. He can thwart the threat of ...♘f6-g4 with h2-h3, and then play ♖he1 and e4-e5 or even play ♖he1 at once (answering ...♘g4 with ♗g1 followed by h2-h3). Black can get going on the queenside with ...♕c7, ...♘a5-c4 or after ...♘xd4 play ...♗c6, ready to meet e4-e5 with ...d6xe5 and ...♘d7.

C2b2. 1 e4 c5 2 ♘f3 d6 3 d4 cxd4 4 ♘xd4 ♘f6 5 ♘c3 ♘c6 6 ♗g5 e6 7 ♕d2 a6 8 0-0-0 ♗d7

9 f4

9 f3!? is a far from harmless move: 9...♖c8 10 ♔b1!? ♗e7 (on 10...b5 11 ♗xb5!? axb5 12 ♘dxb5 White takes on d6: three pawns and the initiative outweigh Black's extra piece) 11 h4 ♘e5 12 g4 b5 13 ♗d3! followed by ♗e3, h4-h5, g4-g5 with a promising attack for White. 13 ♗d3! is a good move as after 13...b4 14 ♘ce2 White has switched his knight and bishop, thus gaining further control over

the c4-square. Instead of 9...♖c8, Black is recommended to play the immediate 9...♗e7 and then 10 h4 b5 11 g4 (after the sacrifice 11 ♗xb5 axb5 12 ♘dxb5 Black can castle, leading to an unclear game) 11...0-0 12 ♗e3 ♘xd4 13 ♕xd4 ♕a5 with the attack ...b5-b4.

9...h6!?

Other possibilities for Black are 9...♕c7 10 ♗xf6 gxf6 11 ♗e2 h5! (to stop White from playing ♗h5!) and ...0-0-0 or 9...b5 10 ♗xf6 gxf6 (10...♕xf6? 11 e5 dxe5 12 ♘dxb5! +−) 11 ♘xc6 ♗xc6 12 ♕e1 ♗e7 13 ♗d3 ♕b6 and ...b5-b4, ...a7-a5-a4.

10 ♗h4

Or 10 ♗xf6 ♕xf6 11 ♘f3 ♕d8 and Black can continue with ...♕c7 and ...0-0-0.

10...g5!

Black wants to get hold of the e5-square!

11 fxg5 ♘g4! 12 ♘f3 hxg5 13 ♗g3

13 ♗xg5?? f6 14 ♗f4 e5 15 ♗e3 ♘xe3 16 ♕xe3 ♗h6! wins the queen!

13...♗e7 14 ♗e2

After the bishop swap, the pawn on d6 is indirectly protected by the fork ...♘f2.

14...♘ge5 ∞

Plans and Counterplans:
Black stands beautifully in the centre but his king has nowhere to go. An example from a World Championship match: 15 ♔b1 b5 16 ♖df1! (making room for the

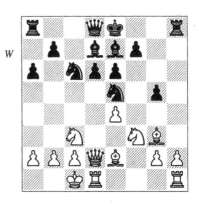

W

withdrawal of the knight from c3) 16...♖c8 17 ♘xe5 ♘xe5 18 ♖f2 f6 19 ♖hf1 ♗c6 20 a3 ♗b7 with chances for both sides. The strategic motif 9...h6!? 10 ♗h4 g5! 11 fxg5 ♘g4! must be present in one's repertoire!

V. Sveshnikov Variation

1 e4 c5 2 ♘f3 ♘c6 3 d4

On 2...♘c6 White sometimes changes his mind and, instead of entering the Open Variation, deviates with 3 ♗b5!? Then Black has two main ways to construct his game:

a) 3...e6 4 ♗xc6 (on 4 0-0, ♘ge7 and ...a7-a6 is Black's plan) 4...bxc6 5 b3 (or 5 d3 ♘e7 followed by ...♘g6, ...d7-d6, ...♗e7, ...0-0 and ...e6-e5 with the idea of a future ...f7-f5) 5...f6!? (Such super-modern ideas – the plan is a later ...♘h6-f7 – had been considered by traditional chess theory to be the privilege of street players) 6 0-0 ♘h6! 7 d4 ♘f7 8 ♗a3 cxd4 9 ♗xf8 ♔xf8 10 ♘xd4 ♗b7 11 ♘c3 c5 12 ♘de2 g6 intending ...♗g7 and ...♗c6, when Black has a solid game.

b) 3...g6!? 4 0-0 ♗g7 5 c3 (or 5 ♗xc6 bxc6 – the general principle is that pawns should capture towards the centre – 6 ♖e1 e5!? 7 c3 ♘e7 8 d4 cxd4 9 cxd4 exd4 10 ♘xd4 0-0 11 ♘c3 ♖b8) 5...♘f6 6 ♖e1 (6 e5 ♘d5 7 d4 cxd4 8 cxd4 0-0 9 ♘c3 ♘c7! – 9...♘xc3 10 bxc3 would only strengthen the white centre – 10 ♗a4 d6! =) 6...0-0 7 d4 d5! (after 7...cxd4 8 cxd4 d5 9 e5 ♘e4 White has the chance to play 10 ♘c3! ±) 8 exd5 ♕xd5 9 c4 ♕d6 10 dxc5 (10 d5 ♘d4!? 11 ♘xd4 cxd4 12 ♕xd4 ♘g4! 13 ♕f4 ♗e5 ∓) 10...♕xd1 11 ♖xd1 ♘e4 =.

3...cxd4 4 ♘xd4 ♘f6

Tournament practice has also seen the immediate 4...e5 5 ♘b5 d6!? (after 5...a6?! 6 ♘d6+ ♗xd6 7 ♕xd6 ♕f6 wherever White goes with the queen he is better. Black painfully misses the bishop from f8, e.g. 8 ♕a3!? ♕g6 9 ♗e3! ♕xe4 10 ♘c3 ♕b4 11 ♕xb4 ♘xb4 12 0-0-0 followed by ♗c5 and f2-f4 with an attack on Black's king in the middle) 6 ♘1c3 (White cannot draw any profit from the differences to the normal Sveshnikov with 6 c4 since 6...♗e7 7 ♘1c3 a6 8 ♘a3 ♗e6 9 ♘c2 ♖c8 10 ♗d2 ♗g5! equalizes) 6...a6 7 ♘a3 ♗e6!? 8 ♘c4 b5 9 ♘e3 ♘f6 10 g3!? (the fight revolves around the square d5) 10...b4 11 ♘cd5 ♘xe4 12 ♗g2 f5 13 0-0 ♖c8 14 ♗xe4 fxe4 15 f3! with an unclear position.

Black, however, does not obtain equality with 4...d5?!: 5 ♘c3 dxe4 6 ♘xc6 ♕xd1+ 7 ♔xd1 bxc6 9 ♘xe4 ♗f5 9, ♗d3 and ♔e2, ♗f4, ♖ad1 is better for White. Also slightly better is 5 ♗b5 dxe4 6 ♘xc6 ♕xd1+ 7 ♔xd1 a6 8 ♗a4 ♗d7 9 ♘c3 ♗xc6 10 ♗xc6+ bxc6 11 ♘xe4 ±, and 5 ♘b5!? deserves attention as well: 5...e6? 6 exd5 exd5 7 ♕xd5! ±; 5...d4 6 c3 e5 7 cxd4 exd4? 8 ♗f4 ±; 5...a6 6 exd5 axb5 7 ♗xb5; and finally 5...dxe4 6 ♕xd8+ ♔xd8 7 ♗e3 followed by ♘1c3, 0-0-0.

5 ♘c3

5 f3? d5! does not come into consideration, just as after 5 ♘xc6 bxc6 6 ♗d3 e5! 7 0-0 ♗c5! Black takes control.

5...e5!?

And this is the Sveshnikov. Black provides White with a serious strategic target: the d5-square. But to reach this target the white knights will have to wander around a lot, and Black's quick development will grant unique ways of equality.

6 ♘db5

6 ♘f3 ♗b4 7 ♗c4 0-0 (and not 7...♗xc3+ 8 bxc3 ♘xe4?? 9 ♕d5 +−) 8 0-0 d6 = 9 ♗g5?! ♗xc3! (the bishop can no longer go to a3!) 10 bxc3 h6 11 ♗h4 ♗e6 ∓. On 6 ♘b3 Black again plays 6...♗b4 7 ♗d3 d5. 6 ♘f5 d5! 7 exd5 ♗xf5 8 dxc6 bxc6 =.

6...d6

Black must not allow 7 ♘d6+ since this knight would have to be captured, weakening Black's dark squares and giving White the bishop pair.

7 ♗g5!?

White's threat is to take on f6 and then entrench his knight on d5. The other line is 7 ♘d5 ♘xd5 (the threat was check and rook on c7!) 8 exd5 ♘e7 9 c3 ♘f5! (9...a6? 10 ♕a4! +– ♗d7?? 11 ♘xd6 mate) and Black completes his development with ...♗e7, ...0-0 and ...a7-a6.

7...a6

The last moment to disperse the white cavalry.

8 ♘a3 b5!

Winning space and limiting the freedom of the knight on a3.

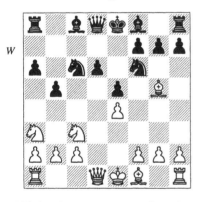

White faces a serious decision: he can immediately jump in to d5
A. 9 ♘d5,

after which Black becomes a little passive but does not have as many strategic weaknesses as he does if White first captures the knight on f6 by
B. 9 ♗xf6

But in the latter case Black also draws profit from the distorted pawn structure.

A. 1 e4 c5 2 ♘f3 ♘c6 3 d4 cxd4 4 ♘xd4 ♘f6 5 ♘c3 e5 6 ♘db5 d6 7 ♗g5 a6 8 ♘a3 b5 9 ♘d5

9...♗e7

9...♕a5+ 10 ♗d2 ♕d8 is sufficient only for a draw (11 ♗g5 ♕a5+), but White can sidestep this with 11 ♗d3!? ♘xd5 12 cxd5 ♘e7 13 c4!. Also 11 c4!? deserves attention.

10 ♗xf6

10 ♘xe7 ♘xe7 (10...♕xe7 11 c4 ♘d4 12 ♘c2 ±) 11 ♗xf6 gxf6 12 c4 (12 ♕f3 f5) 12...♗b7 13 cxb5 ♗xe4 14 bxa6 d5! 15 ♗b5+ ♔f8 16 0-0 ♕b6 and Black is active enough after ...♖g8, ...♘f5 and ...d5-d4.

10...♗xf6 11 c3

11 g3 0-0 12 ♗g2 ♗g5 13 0-0 ♘e7 14 ♘xe7+ ♕xe7 is equal; White will opt for c3, ♘c2-♘e3 while Black has ...♗e6, ...♖b8 and ...a6-a5.

11...0-0 12 ♘c2!

The knight must be brought back into play.

12...♖b8!?

12...♗g5 13 a4! bears down on Black's pawns on b5 and a6.

13 ♗e2

13 ♗d3 ♗g5 14 0-0 ♘e7 15 ♘xe7+ ♗xe7!? (on 15...♕xe7, 16 a4! is again uncomfortable, as after axb5 the white knight springs to b4) 16 a4 d5! 17 exd5 f5! and

Black has a splendid game: the pawn on d5 is hanging and the black pieces can get moving (...♗c5, ...e5-e4, ...f5-f4, ...♕g5/♕h4).

13...♗g5 14 0-0 a5 15 ♘ce3 ♗e6 16 ♕d3 ♘e7

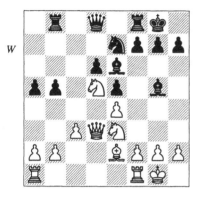

Plans and Counterplans:
First of all, White wishes to maintain his control over the d5-square. There is nothing Black can do about this, but he can swap on d5 to decrease the pressure on f5: 17 ♖fd1 ♘xd5 18 ♘xd5 ♕d7 19 ♕g3 ♗d8 20 b3!? ♔h8 21 c4 bxc4 (21...b4 22 c5!) 22 ♗xc4 g6 23 f4 exf4 24 ♕xf4 f5! =, when both 25 ♔h1 g5 and ...f5-f4, and 25 exf5 ♖xf5 26 ♕d4+ ♖e5! produce a balanced fight.

B. 1 e4 c5 2 ♘f3 ♘c6 3 d4 cxd4 4 ♘xd4 ♘f6 5 ♘c3 e5 6 ♘db5 d6 7 ♗g5 a6 8 ♘a3 b5 9 ♗xf6

9...gxf6
On 9...♕xf6 10 ♘d5 ♕d8 11 c4! (the piece sacrifice 11 ♗xb5!? axb5 12 ♘xb5 ♕a5+ 13 c3! is exciting,

because besides ♘c7 White is also threatening is the avalanche a2-a4, b2-b4) 11...b4 12 ♕a4! ♗d7 13 ♘b5! axb5 14 ♕xa8! +−.

10 ♘d5 ♗g7!?
A completely new discovery, the main point being the neutralization of the knight on d5. Let us see a titbit of the classical 10...f5:
a) 11 ♗xb5!? axb5 12 ♘xb5 ♕a5+!? 13 c3 ♕a4! 14 ♘bc7+ ♔d8 15 ♘xa8 ♕xa8 ∞.
b) 11 g3 fxe4 12 ♗g2 ♗e6! 13 ♗xe4 ♗g7 14 ♘f6+ ♗xf6 15 ♗xc6+ ♔e7 16 ♗xa8 ♕xa8 ∞.
c) 11 ♗d3! ♗e6 12 ♕h5 and Black can continue with either 12...♗g7 13 0-0 f4 14 c4!? or 12...♖g8!? 13 g3!? ♘d4 14 c3 fxe4 15 ♗xe4 ♗g4 16 ♕xh7 ♖g7 17 ♕h6 ♘f3+ 18 ♔e2!? (18 ♔f1). The latter is a fantastic position as both the white king and the queen are in the open, but nothing is certain: 18...♘g5+ 19 f3 ♘xe4 20 fxg4. All in all, 11 ♗d3 is the strongest answer to 10...f5.

The tactics of 10...♗g7!? is: if not 11 ♗d3, then ...f7-f5, while on 11 ♗d3 – let us just see ... !

11 ♗d3
11 c3 f5 12 exf5 ♗xf5 13 ♘c2 ♗e6! (the precise move-order, as on 13...♘e7, 14 ♗d3! is very powerful, for example 14...e4 15 ♘xe7 ♕xe7 16 ♗xb5+ axb5 17 ♕d5, or 14...♘xd5 15 ♗xf5 ♘e7 16 ♕g4 0-0 17 ♖d1 with a serious advantage for White) 14 ♘ce3 ♘e7 15 g3 ♘xd5 16 ♘xd5 0-0 17 ♗g2 ♖b8 18 0-0 a5 =.

11...♘e7! 12 ♘xe7

Not 12 c4? ♘xd5 13 cxd5 f5! 14 exf5 e4! 15 ♗xe4 ♗xb2 –+.

12...♕xe7

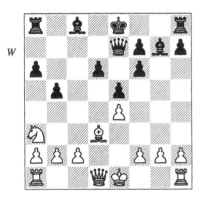

Plans and Counterplans:

White would like to activate his knight on a3, while Black would like to revitalize his bishop on g7 with ...f6-f5. For example: **13 c3** f5! 14 ♘c2 (on 14 exf5 e4, and besides ...♗xf5, Black is also threatening ...b5-b4!) 14...♕b7! 15 ♕f3 0-0 16 ♘e3 (not 16 exf5? e4! 17 ♕xe4 ♕xe4+ 18 ♗xe4 ♖e8 19 f3 d5 –+) 16...f4 17 ♘d5 ♗e6 18 g4! (the threat was 18...f5!) 18...b4! 19 c4 ♗xd5 20 cxd5 (20 exd5 e4! 21 ♗xe4 ♗xb2) = or **13 0-0** 0-0 14 c4 f5 15 ♕f3 bxc4 16 ♘xc4 d5 17 exd5 e4 18 ♕e3 ♗b7 19 d6 ♕f6 20 ♗c2 and now after either 20...f4!? or 20...♖ac8!? Black's compensation for the pawn is clear.

Postscript

The Sveshnikov Variation can also be reached via the Paulsen in the following move-order and via various sidelines:

1 e4 c5 2 ♘f3 e6 3 d4 cxd4 4 ♘xd4 ♘c6 5 ♘c3 ♘f6 6 ♘db5

Black was threatening 6...♗b4, so White has good reason to start something in the centre. The other option is 6 ♘xc6 bxc6 7 e5!? (7 ♗d3 d5) 7...♘d5 8 ♘e4!? (8 ♘xd5 cxd5 9 ♗d3 ♗a6! 10 0-0 ♗xd3 11 ♕xd3 ♕c7 12 ♖e1 ♖c8 13 c3 g6 followed by ...♗g7 and ...0-0 =) 8...♕c7 (8...♗a6!?) 9 f4 ♕a5+ 10 ♗d2 ♕b6 (Black has loosened up the defence of the squares e3 and b2) 11 ♗d3 ♗e7 12 ♕e2 f5! 13 exf6 ♘xf6 ∞. Black should not capture on b2 as then White gets a tremendous attack with 0-0 and f4-f5

6...d6

After 6...♗b4 7 a3! ♗xc3+ 8 ♘xc3 d5 9 exd5 exd5 (9...♘xd5 10 ♗d2 ±) 10 ♗d3 0-0 11 0-0 d4 12 ♘e2 ♕d5 13 ♘f4 ♕d6 14 ♘h5! Black has no compensation for White's bishop pair (±).

7 ♗f4

On 7 ♗g5? a6 8 ♗xf6 gxf6 9 ♘d4 ♗d7 White would get a Rauzer two tempi down (see section IV)

7...e5 8 ♗g5

8 ♘d5 ♘xd5 9 exd5 exf4 10 dxc6 bxc6 11 ♕f3! d5 12 0-0-0 ♗e7 ∞.

8...a6 9 ♘a3 b5

and we have reached the critical position of the Sveshnikov. Black can choose this move-order if for instance he wants to prevent White from playing 1 e4 c5 2 ♘f3 ♘c6 3 ♗b5.

VI. Dragon Variation

It obviously makes sense for Black to fianchetto his bishop in the Sicilian, particularly in the Open Variation when this bishop has dangerous scope along the diagonal a1-h8.

1 e4 c5 2 ♘f3

Aside from the standard 2...d6 and 2...♘c6, tournament practice has also seen the immediate advance **2...g6?!**, but this is premature at this moment as after 3 d4 ♗g7 White can transpose into a Benoni or a King's Indian (both identified as a Closed Game) with 4 d5 or after 4 ♘c3 ♘c6 5 ♗e3 he can force Black to go for a well-known Dragon line with 5...cxd4 6 ♘xd4. White can also go his own way on 2...g6 3 d4 cxd4 with 4 ♕xd4!? ♘f6 5 ♗b5!? ♘c6 (5...a6 6 e5!, 5...♕a5+ 6 ♕c3! ♕xc3+ 7 ♘xc3 and the threat is 8 e5) 6 ♕a4!? (6 ♗xc6!? bxc6 7 e5 ♘d5 8 0-0 ♗g7 9 ♕h4 and ♗h6 is again clearly better for White) 6...♗g7 7 0-0 0-0 8 e5 ♘e8 9 ♗f4 ± and White has only to centralize his rooks with ♘c3, ♖ad1, ♖fe1.

Before playing ...g7-g6 Black should make sure that the white queen cannot get to d4 too early. Therefore the two viable lines in the Dragon are:

A. The Standard Dragon: 1 e4 c5 2 ♘f3 d6 3 d4 cxd4 4 ♘xd4 ♘f6 5 ♘c3 g6

B. The Accelerated Dragon: 1 e4 c5 2 ♘f3 ♘c6 3 d4 cxd4 4 ♘xd4 g6.

A. 1 e4 c5 2 ♘f3 d6 2 d4 cxd4 4 ♘xd4 ♘f6 5 ♘c3 g6 (The Standard Dragon)

White can choose to continue according to his style:
A1. Positionally with kingside castling or
A2. Castling queenside with an attack.

A1. Positionally with kingside castling

1 e4 c5 2 ♘f3 d6 3 d4 cxd4 4 ♘xd4 ♘f6 5 ♘c3 g6 6 ♗e2

Some original ideas:

a) 6 ♗g5 ♗g7 7 ♗b5+ ♗d7 8 ♕e2 0-0 9 0-0-0 ♕a5 (Black is advised to vacate the d-file which may be opened by e4-e5) 10 ♖he1 ♖c8 11 ♘b3 ♗xb5 12 ♕xb5 ♕xb5 13 ♘xb5 =.

b) 6 h3 ♗g7 7 ♗c4 0-0 8 0-0 a6!? 9 ♗b3 b5 10 ♖e1 ♗b7 11 a4 bxa4 12 ♗xa4 ♕c7 13 ♗g5 ♘bd7 =.

c) 6 g3 ♗g7 (6...♘c6 7 ♗g2 ♘xd4 8 ♕xd4 ♗g7 followed by ...0-0, ...♕a5 and ...♗e6 is also reasonable) 7 ♗g2 ♘c6 8 0-0 ♗g4! 9 ♘de2 ♕c8 10 f3 ♗h3 =.

d) 6 f4 ♘c6! (6...♗g7 7 e5 dxe5 8 dxe5 ♘fd7 – after 8...♘d5 or 8...♘g4, then 9 ♗b5+! – 9 e6!?) 7 ♘xc6 bxc6 8 e5 ♘d7 9 exd6 exd6 10 ♗e3 ♗e7! 11 ♕d2 0-0 12 0-0-0 ♘b6 13 ♗e2 d5.

6...♗g7 7 0-0 0-0 8 ♘b3

White has not yet committed himself and this move is essential in order to stop Black from liberating himself with ...d6-d5. For example, 8 ♗e3 ♘c6 9 ♕d2 d5! 10 ♘xc6 (10 exd5 ♘xd5 11 ♘xd5 ♘xd4 12 c4 e5 =) 10...bxc6 11 e5 ♘e8 (11...♘d7? 12 f4 e6 13 ♘a4!) 12 f4 f6! 13 exf6 exf6 14 ♗f3 ♗e6! =. Nevertheless at the end 15 ♘xd5 cxd5 16 ♕xd5+ had to be stopped.

8...♘c6 9 ♗g5!?

This move has become fashionable lately. More traditional paths are:

a) **9 ♔h1** (preparing f4, which is not possible at once: 9 f4? b5! 10 ♗xb5 ♘xe4 11 ♗xc6 ♕b6+ and 12...♕xc6 is favourable for Black) 9...a6!? (9...a5 10 a4 ♗e6 11 f4 ♕c8 12 ♗f3 ♘b4 − 12...♖d8 13 ♘d5 − 13 ♘d4 ♗c4 14 ♖e1 ±) 10 a4 (White's plan is f2-f4, ♗f3, ♘d5 and when Black captures, then the e-pawn takes on d5 followed by c2-c4, ♘d4 and b2-b4 with a dream position. This dream could be cruelly disrupted by Black's b5 pawn; by possessing the c4-square Black would even have the chance of counterplay with ...♘c6-a5-c4. This is why White does not allow the move ...b7-b5, but this way it is the c4 and b3 squares that become weak) 10...♗e6! 11 f4 ♘a5 12 ♘xa5 (12 f5 ♗c4 13 e5 ♗xe2 14 ♘xe2 ♘e8) 12...♕xa5 13 ♗d3 ♖ac8 14 f5 ♗c4 15 ♕e2 ♗xd3 16 cxd3 e6! 17 ♗d2 exf5 18 exf5 ♖fe8 =.

b) **9 ♗e3 ♗e6 10 f4** and now besides the plan 10...♘a5 11 f5 ♗c4 Black can try 10...♕c8!? 11 ♔h1 (11 ♕e1 a5!? 12 a4 ♘b4 13 ♘d4 ♗c4 =) 11...♖d8 12 ♗g1 (12 ♗f3 ♗c4 13 ♖f2 e5) 12...d5!? 13 e5 ♘e4! with unclear complications.

c) **9 ♖e1 ♗e6 10 ♗f1 d5!** 11 ♘c5 (11 e5? ♘g4 12 f4 ♕b6+ −+) 11...♗g4 12 f3 d4! 13 ♘e2 ♗c8 followed by ...e7-e5 and ...b7-b6, when the initiative is in Black's hands.

9...a5!?

9...a6!? deserves attention: 10 f4 (10 a4 ♗e6 11 f4 ♘a5 12 ♔h1 ♖c8 13 f5 ♗xb3 14 cxb3 ♖xc3! 15 bxc3 ♘xe4 and Black has made a good trade. In this position the pawn on e4 is usually worth an exchange on c3!) 10...b5 11 ♗f3 b4 12 ♘a4 (not 12 ♘d5 ♘xd5 13 exd5 ♘a5 14 ♘d4 ♘c4 ∓; there is a large gap on e3 and the pawn on b2 is hanging) 12...♕c7! and Black is threatening ...a6-a5, ...♗a6.

10 a4 ♗e6 11 ♔h1

11 ♕d2?! ♖c8 12 ♖ad1 ♘e5 is not very attractive but 11 f4!? ♕c8 12 ♕e1 ♘b4 13 ♖c1 ♘xc2 14 ♖xc2 ♗xb3 15 ♖c1 ♕d8 16 ♕h4 with the idea of e4-e5 or f4-f5 may turn out to be a profitable investment.

11...♕c8! 12 f4 ♖d8 13 ♗f3 ♘b4

Plans and Counterplans:

Black is splendidly developed, so opening the centre seems like the reasonable goal. White has to look

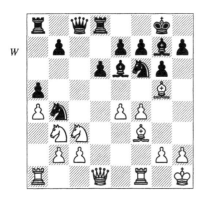

out since both **14 ♕d2 d5!** 15 e5 ♘e4 and **14 ♘d4 ♗c4** 15 ♖f2 h6 16 ♗h4 e5! 17 ♘bd5 exf4 18 ♗xf6 ♗xf6 19 ♘xd6 ♕c5! 20 ♖d2 ♗a6 are impossible. Perhaps best is the cautious **14 ♗h4!?** Now after 14...d5?! 15 e5 ♘e4 White can take on e7 or after 14...♗c4 15 ♖f2! e5!? the follow-up may be 16 ♕d2 with a tough fight. Perhaps 9 ♗g5 will only be a passing craze?!

A2. Castling queenside with an attack

1 e4 c5 2 ♘f3 d6 3 d4 cxd4 4 ♘xd4 ♘f6 5 ♘c3 g6 6 ♗e3 ♗g7

The bishop on e3 is worth its salt, but Black should exercise self-restraint as 6...♘g4? 7 ♗b5+ ♗d7 8 ♕xg4! would cost him the knight.

7 f3

7 ♕d2? ♘g4!

7...0-0

Black can also try 7...♘c6! Then on 8 ♗c4 exciting variations arise after 8...♕b6!?: 9 ♗b5 (9 ♕d2? ♘xe4! and the d4-knight hangs or

9 0-0? ♕xb2 ∓) 9...♕c7 10 ♘d5 ♘xd5 11 exd5 a6 12 ♗xc6+ bxc6 13 ♘xc6 ♗b7 14 ♗d4 ♗xd4 15 ♕xd4 0-0 and Black regains the pawn (16 ♘b4 a5!) or 9 ♘f5!? ♕xb2 10 ♘xg7+ ♔f8 11 ♘d5 ♘xd5 12 ♗xd5 ♔xg7 and of course White can attack with 13 ♖b1 or 13 0-0 (13 ♗xc6? ♕c3+ and ♕xc6), but Black's position can still be held. So on 7...♘c6, 8 ♕d2 is more precise and castling should no longer be delayed as on 8...♗d7 9 ♗c4 ♖c8 10 ♗b3 ♘e5 11 ♗h6! ± and now 11...♗xh6 12 ♕xh6 ♕a5 13 ♘e2 ♘c4 14 0-0-0 threatening g2-g4-g5, ♕g7 or 11...0-0 12 ♗xg7 ♔xg7 13 h4! ♘c4 14 ♗xc4 ♖xc4 15 h5 with a strong attack for White.

8 ♕d2 ♘c6

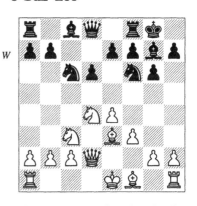

White can now decide whether he wants to continue with

A2a. 9 0-0-0,
A2b. 9 ♗c4.

The first grants quick development but allows ...d6-d5.

Against 9 g4, Black has to know that 9...e6!? is correct, for example 10 0-0-0 d5! 11 g5 ♘h5 12 h4 ♘g3 13 ♖g1 ♘xf1 14 ♖gxf1 ♘e5!? 15 b3 ♕a5.

A2a. 1 e4 c5 2 ♘f3 d6 3 d4 cxd4 4 ♘xd4 ♘f6 5 ♘c3 g6 6 ♗e3 ♗g7 7 f3 0-0 8 ♕d2 ♘c6 9 0-0-0

9...d5!?
It is logical to clear the centre so that the attacking potential of the g7-bishop can evolve, and in this position this concept involves the sacrifice of the exchange or a pawn! Black cannot meet 9...♘e5? with ...♗d7, ...♖c8, ...♘c4 to follow as White quickly penetrates with the typical attack ♗h6, h2-h4-h5-hxg6, ♗xg7, ♕h6+. This is no wonder as Black's knight on c4 is captured by the white bishop from its home square while for example in line b) the bishop first makes the route f1-c4-b3 and White's attack is still dangerous, even two moves slower. But Black should consider 9...♘xd4 10 ♗xd4 ♗e6 11 ♔b1! ♕c7! (as long as the rook is on f8, 11...♕a5 is impossible in view of 12 ♘d5! ♕xd2 and now 13 ♘xe7+ wins as the black king cannot attack the knight because of his own rook!) 12 h4 ♖fc8 13 h5 ♕a5 14 hxg6 hxg6 15 a3 (the threat was 15...♖xc3 and then ♕xa2+) 15...♖ab8! (the odd horizontal pin 15...b5 16 ♕g5! is unpleasant) 16 ♗d3 ♗c4!? with an unclear position. White's only

'advantage' is that he can draw with 17 ♗xc4 ♖xc4 18 ♗xf6 ♗xf6 19 ♘d5, when everything has disappeared from the board.
10 exd5
White cannot allow ...d5xe4, and it is not worth sidestepping this with 10 ♘xc6 bxc6 11 exd5 cxd5 12 ♘xd5 ♘xd5 13 ♕xd5 ♕c7! 14 ♕c5 ♕b7! 15 ♕a3 (15 b4 ♗f5 16 ♗d3 ♖ac8 17 ♕a5 ♖c3! 18 ♗xf5 ♖xe3 and White faces a deadly attack on the dark squares) 15...♗f5 16 ♗a6 ♕c7 17 ♕c5 ♕b6!? 18 ♕xb6 axb6 19 ♗c4 ♖fc8 20 ♗b3 ♖xa2! 21 ♖d8+! ♖xd8 22 ♗xa2 with a drawish endgame. Much more inventive is 10 ♕e1!? and on 10...dxe4?, of course 11 ♘xc6 +–. Therefore Black faces a choice between 10...e5 11 ♘xc6 bxc6 12 exd5 ♘xd5 13 ♗c4 ♗e6 14 ♘e4 ♕c7 15 ♗c5 ♖fd8 and 10...e6!? 11 g4! ♕e7! 12 ♘b3 (12 g5 ♘h5 13 exd5 ♘xd4 and the pawn on g5 will be hanging) 12...b6 13 g5?! ♘h5 14 exd5 exd5 15 ♘xd5 ♕e5!
10...♘xd5 11 ♘xc6 bxc6 12 ♗d4
We have already seen 12 ♘xd5 cxd5 13 ♕xd5 ♕c7! at the sideline 10 ♘xc6.
12...♘xc3!?
More beautiful lines are reached via 12...e5!? 13 ♗c5. It is a pity that Black does not equalize after 13...♖e8 14 ♘e4 f5 15 ♘d6 ♗f8 16 ♗b5!! (16 ♘xe8 ♗xc5) 16...♗d7 17 ♖fe1!, nor after 13...♗e6!? 14 ♘e4!? (14 ♗xf8 ♕xf8 followed by ...♖b8 and Black attacks with

...f7-f5, ...♗h6 and ...♘b4) 14...♖e8
(14...f5 would transpose into the
above variation) 15 h4 h6 16 g4!
♘f4 17 ♕c3 ♗d5 18 g5! ♘e6
(18...h5 19 ♕a3! ♕c7 20 ♘f6+ and
Black has to part with bishop on
g7) 19 gxh6 (19 ♗e3!?) 19...♗xh6+
20 ♗e3 and h4-h5. 12...♗xd4!? is
also playable: 13 ♕xd4 ♕b6 14
♘a4 (14 ♘xd5 cxd5 15 ♕xd5?!
♗e6 16 ♕d4 ♕a5 17 ♗c4 ♖ad8! 18
♕h4 ♗xc4 19 ♕xc4 ♕g5+ and
...♕xg2 ∓) 14...♕a5 15 b3 ♗f5 16
♕c5 ♕xc5 17 ♘xc5 ♘b4 ∞.
    13 ♕xc3 ♗h6+! 14 ♗e3
14 ♔b1?? e5!
    **14...♗xe3+ 15 ♕xe3 ♕b6 16
♕xe7**
Otherwise White has nothing.
    16...♗e6!

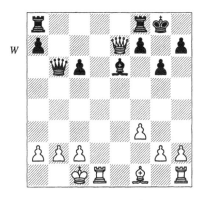

Plans and Counterplans:
Black has a tangible initiative for
the pawn but he still has to be inventive! White would like to develop and maintain his extra pawn
or turn it into a quick attack with
h2-h4-h5. His possible attempts
are:

a) 17 ♗d3 ♕e3+! 18 ♖d2 (18
♔b1 ♗xa2+! wins the white queen)
18...c5 19 ♖d1 ♖ad8 20 ♕h4 c4 21
♖e1 ♕b6 22 ♖xe6!? fxe6 23 ♕xc4
♖d4 and ♖fd8 ∞.
    b) 17 ♕a3 ♕f2! 18 ♕a5! ♗f5
19 ♕d2 ♕c5 20 ♕c3 ♕f2 = (or
20...♕xc3!? 21 bxc3 ♖b8) threatening 21...♖fd8.
    c) 17 ♕f6!? ♗xa2! 18 b3 a5 19
♗c4 (19 ♕b2 a4! 20 ♕xa2 ♕e3+
followed by ...axb3 is winning for
Black!) 19...♖a7! 20 h4 a4 21 h5
axb3 22 cxb3! (22 h6 b2+ 23 ♔d2
♖d8+ 24 ♗d3 ♕b4+ and ...♕f8!
and Black wins with his pawn on
b2!) 22...♕e3+ and the mating
nets around both kings can be dissolved with 23 ♔b2 ♕f2+ 24 ♔c1
(24 ♔c3 ♗xb3! 25 ♗xb3 ♖b7!
threatening both 26...♖xb3+ and
26...♕e3+) 24...♕e3+.

**A2b. 1 e4 c5 2 ♘f3 d6 3 d4 cxd4 4
♘xd4 ♘f6 5 ♘c3 g6 6 ♗e3 ♗g7 7
f3 0-0 8 ♕d2 ♘c6 9 ♗c4**

In this line White's attacking plan
is h2-h4-h5, ♗h6, hxg6, ♗xg7,
♕h6+. This concept is supported
by the bishop on c4 – later on b3 –
which is pinning the pawn on f7
and thus weakening the g6-pawn
as well. Naturally Black cannot
opt for ...d6-d5 in the centre, so he
has to mount his own attack on
the queenside, most violently
along the c-file. By attacking the
bishop on c4 he gains a tempo for
his mobilization and often he will
remove the knight on c3 – one of

the strongest defenders – with an exchange sacrifice. Meanwhile he has to obstruct or at least to delay the white assault.

9...♗d7

Black develops and makes room for the rook on the c-file. Other ideas are:

a) 9...♘a5 10 ♗b3 ♘xb3 11 axb3 a6 12 h4 d5 13 e5 ♘h5 14 g4 ♘g3 15 ♖g1 ♗xe5 16 0-0-0, threatening to win the knight. White can choose between the moves ♕e1, ♗f2, ♗f4, f4.

b) 9...a6 10 ♗b3 ♘a5 11 h4 b5 12 h5 ♘xb3 13 axb3 ♗d7 (not 13...♗b7? 14 hxg6 hxg6 15 ♗h6 +–) 14 ♗h6 and White can continue 15 hxg6 fxg6 16 ♗xg7 ♔xg7 17 ♕h6+ ♔g8 18 ♘d5!

c) 9...a5 10 ♗b3! ♗d7 11 a4! and Black's action is stopped, so White can calmly attack with h4-h5, ♗h6.

d) 9...♘d7 (Black directs both of his knights to c4) 10 ♗b3 ♘b6! (10...♘a5? 11 ♗h6! ♘b6 12 ♗xg7! ♔xg7 13 0-0-0 and after White has rescued the bishop on e3 from the threatened knight fork on c4 he can consider h2-h4-h5 or ♘c3-d5) 11 ♘xc6!? (11 0-0-0!? ♘a5 12 ♗h6?? ♘bc4 13 ♕g5 e5! 14 ♘de2 ♗f6 15 ♕g3 ♗h4 wins White's queen) 11...bxc6 12 0-0-0!? (on 12 ♗h6 c5 followed by c4 is dangerous) 12...a5 (12...c5? 13 ♗xc5) 13 a4 ♗e6 14 ♗h6 and it is difficult to find counterplay for Black.

e) 9...♘xd4 10 ♗xd4 ♗e6 11 ♗b3!? ♕a5 12 0-0-0 ♗xb3 13 cxb3

♖fc8 14 ♔b1 (after this move the white king finds a bomb-proof shelter) 14...♖c6 15 g4! (15 h4 h5!) 15...♖ac8 16 h4 h5! 17 g5 ♘e8 18 ♗xg7 ♘xg7 19 f4! ± and besides f4-f5 White can aim at the regrouping ♖f1-f3-d3-d4 as well as b3-b4.

10 0-0-0

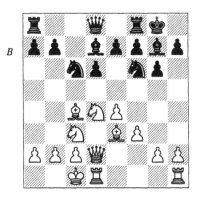

Black's two different continuations are:

A2b1. 10...♕a5 and then...♖fc8
A2b2. 10...♖c8.

These most fashionable setups are based on the strength of the rook on the c-file with the help of ...♘c6-e5-c4 or ...♕a5; and the exchange sacrifice on c3 is also on the cards. Black's attack is less energetic after **10...♕c7** 11 ♗b3 ♖fc8 12 h4 ♘e5 13 h5 ♘c4 14 ♗xc4 ♕xc4 15 hxg6 fxg6 (15...hxg6? 16 ♗h6 ♗h8 and now a beautiful decisive motif is 17 ♗f8! ♖xf8 18 ♖xh8+! ♔xh8 19 ♕h6+ ♔g8 20 ♘d5!! ♘xd5 21 ♖h1 and Black is inevitably mated!) 16 ♗h6 ♗h8 17 ♗g5 threatening ♗xf6 and ♘d5, ♕h6. The two black heavy pieces on the c-file bump into each other when for example attacking the knight on c3.

On **10...♕b8!?** it is wrong for White to play 11 g4?! b5 12 ♘dxb5? ♘e5 13 ♗e2 ♗xb5 14 ♘xb5 ♘xf3! and the white position has fallen apart. So recommended is 10...♕b8 11 h4 b5 12 ♗d5!? ♖c8 13 ♔b1 b4! 14 ♘ce2, although 14...h5! 15 ♘xc6 ♗xc6 16 ♘f4 and now 16...♕b7, parrying the threat 17 ♘xg6 ♗xd5 18 ♘xe7+, is playable with Black as well.

A2b1. 1 e4 c5 2 ♘f3 d6 3 d4 cxd4 4 ♘xd4 ♘f6 5 ♘c3 g6 6 ♗e3 ♗g7 7 f3 0-0 8 ♕d2 ♘c6 9 ♗c4 ♗d7 10 0-0-0 ♕a5

11 ♗b3 ♖fc8 12 ♔b1!?

The king stands better on b1 and occasionally it is handy that after ♘c3-d5, ...♕a5xd2 is not a check so the knight on d5 can itself capture something with a check. After 12 h4 ♘e5 Black often employs an exchange sacrifice on c3, e.g. 13 g4 ♘c4 14 ♗xc4 ♖xc4 15 h5 ♖xc3!? 16 ♕xc3 ♕xa2 or 13 h5 ♘xh5 14 g4 ♘f6 15 ♗h6 ♖xc3 16 bxc3 (16 ♗xg7 ♖xc2+ 17 ♗xc2 ♕xd2+ and ...♔xg7 with compensation for the exchange) 16...♗xh6 17 ♖xh6 (17 ♕xh6 ♕xc3 18 ♔b1 ♘c4 19 ♗xc4 ♕xc4 ±) 17...♖c8 with mutual chances. Black's compensation for the exchange comprises

a pawn, the destruction of White's queenside pawn structure, and the fact that there is little difference in scope between the white rook and Black's minor piece.

12...♘e5 13 h4

On 13 ♗h6 again the thematic 13...♗xh6 14 ♕xh6 ♖xc3! with the future mobilization of the a- and b-pawns.

13...♘c4 14 ♗xc4 ♖xc4 15 ♘b3!?

15 h5 ♖xc3!? 16 bxc3 ♘xh5 17 g4 ♘f6. The purpose of 15 ♘b3!? is to avoid a sacrifice on c3.

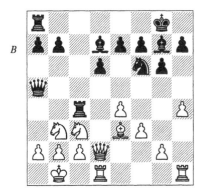

Plans and Counterplans:

If Black should aim at capturing the knight on c3 with **15...♕e5?!**, then after 16 ♗d4! ♕e6 17 g4! his queen is uncomfortably jammed in while White is threatening ♖he1, e4-e5 or ♘a5. On **15...♕a6** White utilizes the unprotected state of the d7-bishop with 16 e5! followed by 16...dxe5 17 ♘c5. Best is **15...♕c7!?**, aiming at the knight on c3. Now on 16 h5 ♖xc3! 17 ♕xc3 ♕xc3 18 bxc3 ♘xh5 followed by

...♗e6 and ...♖c8 is a fair trade. More complicated is 16 ♗d4! when 16...♗c6!? 17 h5 a5! 18 hxg6 hxg6 19 a4 ♗xa4 and now 20 ♗xf6 exf6 (and not 20...♗xf6? 21 ♘d5 with ♘xf6+ and ♕h6 mate to follow) or 20 ♘d5!? ♕d8!? leads to an open fight.

A2b2. 1 e4 c5 2 ♘f3 d6 3 d4 cxd4 4 ♘xd4 ♘f6 5 ♘c3 g6 6 ♗e3 ♗g7 7 f3 0-0 8 ♕d2 ♘c6 9 ♗c4 ♗d7 10 0-0-0 ♖c8

11 ♗b3 ♘e5 12 h4 h5!?
Black wants to nip White's attack in the bud. The classical continuation is 12...♘c4 13 ♗xc4 ♖xc4 and now the line 14 g4!? ♕c7 (14...h5!?) 15 h5 ♖c8 16 hxg6 fxg6 17 ♔b1 b5 18 ♘d5! ♘xd5 19 exd5 ♗e5 is not yet fully resolved but Black does not have much in the way of winning chances. White attacks with ♕d2-f2-h4 and then f3-f4-f5 while Black defends via ...♖c8-f8-f7. Also possible is 14 e5!? dxe5 15 ♘de2 ♖c7 16 ♘b5 ♗f5! 17 ♘xc7 ♕xc7 ∞, but White usually deviates after 14 h5 ♘xh5 15 g4 ♘f6. Here are some sample lines: 16 e5!? ♘xg4! (16...dxe5 17 ♘b3 threatening 18 g5) 17 fxg4 ♗xg4 18 ♖dg1 dxe5 19 ♖xg4 h5 or 16 ♗h6 ♘xe4! 17 ♕e3! (17 ♘xe4?! ♖xd4 18 ♕h2 ♗e5 19 f4 ♖xd1+ 20 ♖xd1 ♗h8) 17...♖xc3 18 bxc3 ♘f6 19 ♗xg7 ♔xg7 20 ♕h6+ ♔h8 21 ♘e2 ♖g8. It would be much too bold an act to evaluate these everchanging variations.

13 ♗g5!?
If Black now plays 13...♘c4 then White no longer surrenders his bishop but plays 14 ♕e2 and then g2-g4. The alternatives are:
a) 13 ♗h6 ♘c4 14 ♗xc4 ♖xc4 15 ♗xg7 ♔xg7 16 g4 hxg4 17 h5 ♖h8 and Black holds.
b) 13 g4 hxg4 14 h5 ♘xh5 15 ♗h6 e6 16 ♖dg1 ♕f6, threatening 17...♗xh6 and then 18...♕f4+.
c) 13 ♔b1 ♘c4 14 ♗xc4 ♖xc4 15 ♘b3 ♕c7 16 ♗d4 ♗c6 17 ♕e2 b5 ∞.

13...♖c5!?
Things will soon be happening on the fifth rank, *inter alia* ...a7-a5 or ...b7-b5.

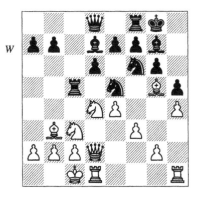

Plans and Counterplans:
Black is preparing for ...b7-b5, while White would like to break through in the centre with f3-f4 and e4-e5 or on the king's flank with g2-g4. The position yields even chances to both players, according to practice as well as theory. Here are a few typical examples:

a) 14 ♖he1 b5 15 f4 ♘c4 16 ♗xc4 ♖xc4 17 e5 b4 18 exf6 bxc3 19 ♕e2 ♖xd4 20 fxe7 ♕a5!

b) 14 ♔b1 a5!? (14...b5!?) 15 g4 (15 a4!?) 15...♖xc3! 16 ♕xc3 a4 17 ♗c4 ♕b6! threatening 18...♖c8.

c) 14 g4 hxg4 15 f4 ♘c4 16 ♕e2 ♕c8!? (16...b5) 17 f5 e5! 18 ♘db5 ♗xb5 19 ♘xb5 ♖xb5 20 ♗xf6 ♗xf6 21 ♗xc4 ♖b4! 22 ♗d5 gxf5 23 ♖df1 f4 24 ♖hg1 ♖e8 (24...g3 25 ♖xg3+ fxg3 26 ♖xf6 and the threat is 27 ♖g6+ and ♕h5 mate) 25 ♖xg4+ ♔f8 ∞. From time to time long analysis is published on the breathtaking excitement of the Dragon with queenside castling, which is then usually quickly revised or completely refuted by tournament practice. Therefore it is considered foolhardiness to enter this anything but clear-cut variation without serious theoretical inquiry and home preparation.

B. 1 e4 c5 2 ♘f3 ♘c6 3 d4 cxd4 4 ♘xd4 g6 (Accelerated Dragon)

The two major lines for White are:

B1. 5 ♘c3
with which White aims to transpose into the Standard Dragon. But by utilizing the differences Black can prevent White from castling queenside!

B2. 5 c4!?
with which, according to the recipe of Geza Maroczy, White grabs the opportunity to get a grip on the centre, thus taming the dragon. It is important to know that if instead of 4...g6 Black tries to sidestep the Maróczy with 4...♘f6 5 ♘c3 g6 his attempt fails to 6 ♘xc6! bxc6 7 e5 ♘d5 (7...♘g8 8 ♗c4 and ♕f3, ♗f4, 0-0-0 ±) 8 ♘xd5 cxd5 9 ♕xd5 ♖b8 10 e6! dxe6 11 ♕e5! attacking both black rooks and winning!

B1. 1 e4 c5 2 ♘f3 ♘c6 3 d4 cxd4 4 ♘xd4 g6 5 ♘c3

Nothing is gained by 5 ♘xc6?! bxc6 6 ♕d4 ♘f6 7 e5 ♘d5 8 e6 f6 9 exd7+ ♗xd7 followed by ...e7-e5, ...♗g7, ...0-0 and Black is on top. However, with 5 ♘b3 and ♗e2, ♘c3, 0-0 White can transpose into the 0-0 line of section A.

5...♗g7 6 ♗e3
After 6 ♘b3 ♗xc3+!? 7 bxc3 ♘f6 8 ♗d3 d5! 9 exd5 ♕xd5 a balance is created between the various positional factors.

6...♘f6 7 ♗c4!
White's move-order is very important: he should only play f2-f3 when ...♘f6-g4 is already threatened but then he absolutely must play it! 7 ♘xc6 bxc6 8 e5 ♘d5! 9 ♘xd5 cxd5 10 ♕xd5 ♖b8 yields good play for Black, for example 11 ♗xa7 ♖xb2 12 ♗d4 ♖xc2 13 ♗d3 e6 14 ♕a8 ♖c6 15 0-0 ♗a6 and after the exchanges the endgame is even, or 11 ♗c4 0-0 12 0-0 ♕c7 13 ♗f4 (13 f4 d6! 14 exd6 exd6 and b2-pawn is lost) 13...♗b7

14 ♕d4 d6! =. After 7 ♗e2 0-0 8
0-0 Black makes use of not yet
having played ...d7-d6 and that he
can play 8...d5!? in one move: 9
exd5 ♘xd5 10 ♘xd5 ♕xd5 11 ♗f3
♕c4!? ∞.

7...0-0!?

The following moves are weaker:

a) 7...♘a5? 8 ♗xf7+! ♔xf7 9
e5 ♘e8? 10 ♘e6! ♔xe6 11 ♕d5+
♔f5 12 g4+ and a quick mate.

b) 7...♕a5?! 8 0-0! (8 ♕d2?
♘xe4 9 ♘xc6 ♕xc3! 10 bxc3 ♘xd2
followed by ...dxc6 −+, or 8 f3?
♕b4 9 ♗b3 ♘xe4! and the knight
on d4 is again *en prise*) 8...0-0 9
♘b3 ♕c7 10 f4 d6 11 ♗e2 and
with the plan of ♗f3 and ♘d5!,
typical of this position, White is
better since the black queen is
misplaced on c7.

8 ♗b3!

All other moves can be answered by tactical possibilities:

a) 8 f3 ♕b6! (with the threats
9...♘xe4, 9...♘g4 and 9...♕xb2) 9
♗b3! ♘xe4 10 ♘d5! ♕a5+ 11 c3
♘c5 12 ♘xc6 dxc6 13 ♘xe7+ =.

b) 8 ♕d2? ♘g4! 9 ♘xc6 bxc6
10 ♗d4 ♗xd4! 11 ♕xd4 ♕b6! ∓.

c) 8 0-0 ♘xe4 9 ♘xe4 d5 10
♘xc6 bxc6 11 ♗d3 dxe4 12 ♗xe4
♕c7 with a slight, only theoretical
plus for White.

8...a5!?

After 8...d6 9 f3 ♗d7 10 ♕d2,
Black can exploit the fact that,
compared to the Standard Dragon,
♗c4-b3 has been played instead of
0-0-0 to continue 10...♘xd4!? 11
♗xd4 b5!. Then the position is by

no means simple: 12 h4 a5 13 a4
(13 h5? e5! 14 ♗e3 a4 15 ♗d5 b4
16 ♘e2 ♘xd5 17 ♕xd5 ♗e6 18
♕d2 d5! and Black is better)
13...bxa4 14 ♘xa4 e5 15 ♗e3 ♗e6!
is unclear.

9 a4

The pawn sacrifice 9 f3 d5!?
leads to unclear complications. A
few characteristic lines:

a) 10 ♘xd5? ♘xd5 11 exd5 (11
♗xd5? ♘xd4 12 ♗xd4 ♗xd4 13
♕xd4 e6 −+) 11...♘b4 12 c4 a4!
13 ♗c2 (13 ♗xa4 ♕a5!) 13...e5!! ∓
14 ♘e2 (14 dxe6?? ♗xd4 17 ♗xd4
♕xd4! −+) 14...♕h4+ and then
...♕xc4.

b) 10 exd5 ♘b4 11 ♘de2 a4!
12 ♘xa4 ♘fxd5 13 ♗f2 (13 ♗d4
♗xd4 14 ♘xd4?? ♘e3 followed by
...♕xd4 −+) 13...♗f5 14 0-0 b5 15
♘ac3 ♘xc3 and Black proceeds
with ...♕xd1 and ...♗xc2 =.

c) 10 ♗xd5 ♘xd5 11 exd5
♘b4 12 ♘de2 ♗f5 13 ♖c1 b5! 14
0-0 ♖c8 15 ♘d4 ♖xc3!? 16 bxc3
♘xa2 and ♘xc3 with good compensation for the exchange.

9...♘g4

A typical simplifying move in
this variation.

10 ♕xg4 ♘xd4 *(D)*

Plans and Counterplans:

The white queen has to step out
of the discovered attack ...d7-d5.
11 ♕d1?! ♘xb3 12 cxb3 d6 and
...♗e6 can only be better for Black
owing to his bishop pair and the
favourable pawn configuration.
But rich in ideas is **11 ♕h4!** ♘xb3

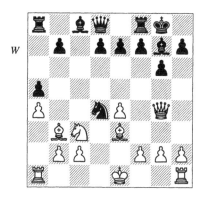

W

12 cxb3 and now White is threatening ♘d5 followed by ♗b6 or ♗g5. Against this,. Black has the interesting 12...♖a6 13 ♘d5 ♖e6!?, but it seems even better to either wait with 11...♘xb3 or defend with 11...d6 12 ♘d5!? ♖e8 13 ♗g5 ♗f8!? with the plan of ...♗e6, ...♘xb3 and ...♗xd5 working off the pressure.

B2. 1 e4 c5 2 ♘f3 ♘c6 3 d4 cxd4 4 ♘xd4 g6 5 c4!?

With the help of the pawns at c4 and e4 White take possession of the centre. Moreover, he often uses his control over the d5-square to jump in with ♘c3-d5. With precise play Black can hold things together.

5...♗g7

It is fashionable to play an early ♘c6xd4, prepared by 5...♘f6 6 ♘c3 d6. Then White has to refrain from 7 ♗e3 in view of 7...♘g4, so 7 f3 ♘xd4 8 ♕xd4 ♗g7 9 ♗e3 0-0 10 ♕d2 ♕a5 11 ♖c1 ♗e6 12 ♘d5! (on White's quiet play Black

creates counter-chances on the queenside via ...♖fc8, ...a7-a6 and ...b7-b5) 12...♕xd2+ (12...♕xa2 13 ♘xe7+ and ♗e2, 0-0 ±) 13 ♔xd2 ♗xd5 14 cxd5 ± and the white bishop pair attacks Black's queenside, or 7 ♗e2 ♘xd4 8 ♕xd4 ♗g7 9 ♗e3 0-0 10 ♕d2 ♗e6 11 ♖c1 ♕a5 12 b3 a6 13 f3 ♖fc8! (it is very important that the f-rook goes to c8 as, for example, on 13...♖ac8? 14 0-0 b5 15 ♘d5! ♕xd2 16 ♘xe7+ the king cannot attack the knight on e7 from f8. 13...♖fc8 makes possible 14 0-0 b5! since after 15 ♘d5 ♕xd2 followed by ...♘xd5 and ...♗d7 the position is even) 14 ♘d5 ♕xd2+ 15 ♔xd2 ♘xd5 (the bishop pair must be maintained) 16 cxd5 ♗d7 and although White has spatial advantage it is still hard to imagine that he can win. Black is threatening to occupy the c-file with ♗b2 or to upset the white pawn chain with ...f7-f5 and f5xe4. Instead of 9 ♗e3 White is advised to play 9 ♗g5!? 0-0 (9...h6 10 ♗e3 0-0 11 ♕d2 ♔h7 12 0-0 ♗e6 13 f4 ± and f4-f5 with a weakened black king position) 10 ♕d2 ♗e6 11 ♖c1 ♕a5 12 f3 ♖ac8 13 b3 a6 14 ♘a4!? (preventing ...b7-b5) 14...♕xd2+ 15 ♔xd2 ♖c6 16 ♘c3 followed by ♘d5 and Black's position is massive but passive (±).

6 ♗e3

6 ♘c2?! does not make much sense in view of 6...d6 7 ♗e2 ♘f6 8 ♘c3 ♘d7 9 ♗d2 0-0 10 0-0 ♘c5 11 b4!? ♘e6 (no good is 11...♘xe4

due to 12 ♘xe4 ♗xa1 13 ♘xa1 ±)
12 ♖b1 a5! 13 a3 axb4 14 axb4
♘cd4 ∞ or instead of 11 b4, 11 f3
a5 12 ♔h1 f5!? ∞ with active play
for Black.

6...♘f6 7 ♘c3 0-0

The liquidating combination
7...♘g4 8 ♕xg4 ♘xd4 does not
equalize: after 9 ♕d1 ♘e6 (9...e5
10 ♕d2 0-0 11 ♘b5! ♘xb5 12 cxb5
and Black will have problems on
the d-file) 10 ♖c1 Black's options
are:

a) 10...b6 11 ♗d3 ♗b7 12 0-0
0-0 13 ♗b1 ♖c8 14 b3 d6 15 ♕d2 ±.

b) 10...d6 11 ♕d2 ♗d7 12 ♗e2
0-0 13 0-0 ♘c5 14 f3 a5 15 ♖fd1
♗c6 16 b3 b6 17 ♗d4! ♗xd4 18
♕xd4 ♕b8 19 f4 ♕b7 20 ♘d5!
♖ad8 21 ♗f3 ♗xd5 22 cxd5 and
Black has no counterplay against
White's plans of e4-e5 or h2-h4-
h5.

c) 10...♕a5!? 11 ♗e2 b6 12 0-0
♗b7 13 f3 g5 14 ♖f2 h5 15 ♗f1
♕e5! 16 ♖d2! d6 17 ♘d5 ♔f8 18
b4! and Black has constructed an
interesting blockade but has no
active plan. White is threatening to
seize the initiative on the queenside with a4-a5 or ♕a4-d7.

8 ♗e2 d6

On 8...b6 9 0-0 ♗b7, not 10 ♖c1?
♘xd4 11 ♗xd4 ♗h6! (11...♘xe4??
12 ♘xe4 ♗xe4 13 ♗xg7 and ♕d4+
+−) and the rook on c1 and pawn
on e4 are simultaneously hanging, but 10 f3 d6 11 ♕d2, followed
by ♖fd1 and a2-a4-a5, is the correct reply.

9 0-0 ♗d7 10 ♕d2

A different piece constellation
is reached after 10 ♖c1 ♘xd4 11
♗xd4 ♗c6 12 f3 a5 13 b3 ♘d7 14
♗e3 ♘c5 15 a3 and now with
15...h5!? 16 b4 axb4 17 axb4 ♖a3!
18 bxc5 ♗xc3 19 cxd6 ♕xd6 with
equality as Black gets play along
the a-file.

**10...♘xd4 11 ♗xd4 ♗c6 12 f3
a5!**

Impeding b2-b4 and thus securing the c5 square for his knight.

13 b3

The only move-order that takes
White forward is b2-b3, a2-a3 and
b3-b4 since 13 a3? a4! allows Black
an everlasting blockade.

13...♘d7!?

Black is fully aware of the slight
plus White would have after 14
♗xg7 ♔xg7 15 f4 and ♗f3 but still
White's control over the d4-square
and other dark squares would
cease.

14 ♗e3!?

Trying for just a little more!

**14...♘c5 15 ♖ab1! ♕b6 16
♖fc1 ♖fc8**

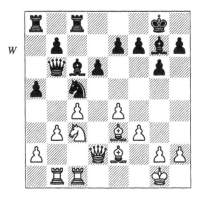

Plans and Counterplans:
Black holds two different dreams. He would like to play either ...a5-a4 after ...♕b4 or ...f7-f5 after the preparatory ...♕b6-d8-f8. White of course can think about a2-a3, b3-b4 or ♘d5. For example, **17 ♖c2! ♕d8** 18 a3 b6 (18...e6 19 ♗f1 ♗e5 20 b4 axb4 21 axb4 ♘a4 22 ♘e2 and ♘d4 ±, as all the black light-squared pieces are vulnerable) 19 b4 axb4 20 axb4 ♘a4 21 ♘d5! ± and it is hard for Black to do anything. On **17 ♖c2! ♕b4** 18 ♕c1! (threatening a2-a3 and b2-b4) 18...♕b6 19 a3 ♕d8 20 ♕d2 forces Black into the previous position with 17...♕d8. With the heavy piece manoeuvre ♕d2, ♖ab1, ♖fc1 and ♖c2 White can upset Black's queenside plan, and this even enables him to play b3-b4, after which he stands somewhat better. Of course with this he has only won the battle, not the whole war!

Alekhine Defence

1 e4 ♘f6

Black lures the white pawns ahead in order to later attack them or create counterplay around them.

2 e5

It is foolish to refuse Black's invitation:

2 ♘c3 d5 (2...e5 leads to the Vienna Game) 3 exd5 (or 3 e5 ♘e4!? 4 ♘ce2!? d4 5 c3 ♘c6 6 ♘xd4 ♘xd4 7 ♕a4+ c6 8 ♕xd4 ♕xd4 9 cxd4 ♘g5 followed by ...♗f5, ...♘e6, and ...0-0-0) 3...♘xd5 4 ♗c4 ♘b6 6 ♗b3 ♘c6 7 ♘f3 ♗f5 8 0-0 e6 followed by ...♗e7, ...0-0, ...♘a5 and ...♘xb3 with easy equality; or

2 d3 d5!? 3 e5 (3 ♘d2 e5 and then ...♘c6, ...♗c5, ...0-0) 3...♘fd7 4 f4 c5 and after ...e7-e6, ...♘c6, ...♗e7 Black will castle and either play ...b7-b5, ...a7-a5 or start picking on the white centre with ...f7-f6.

2...♘d5

2...♘g8 is senseless while 2...♘e4 is bad due to 3 d3 ♘c5 4 d4.

3 d4

Here are a few other options:

a) 3 ♗c4 ♘b6 4 ♗b3 c5! 5 d3 ♘c6 6 ♘f3 e6, and then Black proceeds with ...d7-d6 and stands a little better as White did not get to play d2-d4 (∓).

b) 3 ♘c3!? ♘xc3 4 dxc3 (4 bxc3 c5 5 f4 ♘c6 6 d4 d5 7 ♘f3 ♗g4) 4...d6 5 ♘f3 (5 ♗c4 ♘c6 6 ♘f3 dxe5 7 ♕xd8+ ♘xd8 8 ♘xe5

f6 9 ♘f3 e5 =) 5...♘c6 6 ♗b5 ♗d7 7 ♕e2 a6 8 ♗c4 e6 and Black can develop via ...d6xe5 and ...♗d6.

c) 3 c4 ♘b6 4 c5 ♘d5 5 ♗c4 (5 ♘c3 e6 6 ♘xd5 exd5 7 d4 d6 is equal) 5...e6 6 d4 b6 7 cxb6 axb6 (7...♘xb6!? followed by ...d6-d5, ...c7-c5 is also a good plan) 8 ♘f3 ♗a6 =.

3...d6

This opens up the diagonal of c8-bishop while allowing ...d6xe5 or ...c7-c5 to weaken the white centre. The two major lines for White are:

I. Four Pawns Attack: 4 c4 ♘b6 5 f4 and
II. Positional Variation: 4 ♘f3.

The first attempts to construct a large centre while the second concentrates on development.

Other choices are: 4 ♗c4 c6 (after 4...♘b6 5 ♗b3 dxe5 6 ♕h5!? e6 7 dxe5 Black needs to play actively) 5 ♕e2 dxe5 6 dxe5 ♗f5 7 ♘f3 e6 8 0-0 ♘d7 (8...♗g4!?) 9 a3 ♗e7 =; and the interesting 4 f4!?, e.g. 4...♗f5 5 ♘f3 e6 6 ♗d3 ♗xd3 7 ♕xd3 ♗e7, when a possible plan for Black is ...0-0 followed by ...dxe5 and ...c5, or 4...dxe5 5 fxe5 c5 6 ♘f3 cxd4 7 ♕xd4 ♘c6 8 ♕e4!? g6!? 9 ♗c4 ♘b6 10 ♗b3 ♗g7 11 0-0 ♗f5 12 ♕f4 0-0 with a complicated game.

I. 1 e4 ♘f6 2 e5 ♘d5 3 d4 d6 4 c4 ♘b6 5 f4 (Four Pawns Attack)

It is important to know that on 5 exd6 Black should transpose into the 4 ♘f3 g6 line with 5...cxd6 5 ♘f3 g6 and not play 5...exd6?! 6 ♘c3 ♗e7 owing to 7 ♕f3! ♘c6 8 ♗e3 0-0 9 0-0-0 ±.

5...dxe5

Black wants to continue ...♗f5, ...♘c6, ...e7-e6, but first he prevents White from recapturing with the d-pawn after, for instance, ♘c3 and ♗e3, or from playing e5xd6. A logical way to maintain the tension is 5...g6!?, since the bishop can be useful on g7 in the fight against the enemy centre. For example, 6 ♘c3 ♗g7 7 ♗e3 0-0 8 ♘f3 ♗e6!! and now 9 b3 c5! 10 dxc5 ♘6d7! 11 cxd6 exd6 12 ♕xd6 ♘xe5!! ∓; 9 ♕b3 a5! 10 ♘g5 a4 11 ♘xe6 axb3 12 ♘xd8 ♖xd8 13 a3 ♘c6 14 0-0-0 ♘a5 ∓; and of course 9 d5 is also not good due to 9...♗g4. Instead of 6 ♘c3 White can play 6 ♘f3 and then ♗e3, ♗e2 0-0 with d6xe5 to follow, and on ...♗e6 he may answer ♘bd2 with a level game.

6 fxe5 ♘c6

On 6...c5 7 d5 e6 8 ♘c3 White's centre appears frightening, although Black can try to undermine it with 8...exd5 9 cxd5 c4 followed by ...♗b4.

7 ♗e3

7 ♘f3 ♗g4 would only increase White's troubles.

7...♗f5 8 ♘c3

Not 8 e6?! fxe6 9 ♘c3 e5 10 d5 ♘b4 11 ♖c1 e6 12 a3 exd5! 13 axb4 d4 ∓.

8...e6 9 ♘f3 ♗e7

Or 9...♗g4 10 ♕d2!? ♕d7 11 ♗e2 0-0-0 12 c5!? ♘d5 13 ♘xd5 ♕xd5 14 b4 a6 15 a4 with a promising attack for White.

10 d5!?

After 10 ♗e2 0-0 11 0-0 f6 12 exf6 ♗xf6 Black obtains an equal game with ...♕e7 and ...♖ad8.

10...exd5

Precise; this way White's pawn on d5 will be hanging later on.

11 cxd5 ♘b4 12 ♘d4 ♗d7

On 12...♗g6 White replies 13 ♗b5+, while the line 12...♕d7 13 ♗b5 c6 14 0-0 ♗g6 15 dxc6 bxc6 16 ♘xc6! ♘xc6 17 ♕xd7+ ♔xd7 18 ♖fd1+ ♔c7 19 ♖ac1 is clearly better for White.

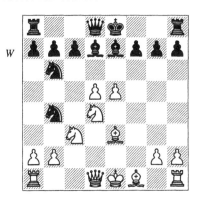

Plans and Counterplans:
Black has ...c7-c5 in mind. For example, **13 ♕b3 c5! 14 dxc6 (14 ♘f3 c4!) 14...bxc6 15 0-0-0 ♘6d5 16 ♗c4 ♖b8**. White should therefore

play more vigorously: **13 e6** fxe6 14 dxe6 ♗c6 15 ♕g4 (15 ♕h5+ g6 16 ♗e2? ♗f6!, but not 16...gxh5?? 17 ♗xh5+ ♔f8 18 ♗h6+ ♔g8 19 ♗f7 mate!) 15...♗h4+ 16 g3 ♗xh1 17 0-0-0 ♕f6 (17...♗f6? 18 ♘f5, threatening ♘xg7+ and ♕h5+) 18 gxh4 0-0. Now on, for example, 19 ♗b5 ♕e5 20 ♗g5 c5 21 e7 Black has the fantastic sequence 21...cxd4 22 exf8♕+ ♖xf8 23 ♖xh1 a5! 24 ♕e4 ♘xa2+ 25 ♔c2 ♖f2+ 26.. ♔b3 ♖xb2+! 27 ♔a3 ♖xb5 28 ♕xe5 ♖xe5 29 ♘xa2 ♘c4+ 30 ♔b3 b5 and Black stands better. On 19 ♗b5 the relatively untested 19...c6!? is also interesting. This would also be the reply if White first forces ...g7-g6 with 15 ♕h5+. Here Black could not play ...♕e5 in the end owing to ♗h6. Of course these long variations offer the possibility of novelties on nearly every move, but in such a tactical position one gets the feeling that the two sides have approximately even chances.

II. 1 e4 ♘f6 2 e5 ♘d5 3 d4 d6 4 ♘f3 (Positional Variation)

Black's main lines are:

A. 4...g6 and
B. 4...♗g4,

He has various other possibilities:

a) 4...♘b6 5 ♘c3 ♗g4 6 h3 ♗h5?! 7 g4 ♗g6 8 e6! fxe6 9 ♘g5 and White has the initiative.

b) 4...♘c6 5 c4 ♘b6 6 e6! fxe6 7 ♘g5 e5 8 d5 ♘d4 9 ♗d3 and besides ♕h5+, White is also threatening ♗e3, aiming to exploit the e6-square.

c) 4...c6 5 c4 ♘c7 6 exd6 exd6 7 ♗d3 ♗g4 8 0-0 ♗e7 9 ♘bd2 ♘d7 10 ♕c2 ♘f6 11 h3 ♗h5 12 ♘h4 ♗g6 13 ♘f5! ±.

d) 4...dxe5 (the most fashionable sideline) 5 ♘xe5 g6 (5...♘d7?! is suicidal: 6 ♘xf7! ♔xf7 7 ♕h5+ ♔e6 8 c4 ♘5f6 9 d5+ ♔d6 10 ♕f7 ♘e5 11 ♗f4 with a tremendous attack; instead of 8 c4 White can even play 8 g3!? and ♗h3) 6 ♗c4 c6 7 0-0 ♗g7 8 ♘d2! 0-0 9 ♘df3 ♘d7 10 ♘d3 a5 11 a4 ♘7b6 12 ♗b3 ♗g4 13 c3 ♘d7 14 h3 ♗xf3 15 ♕xf3 with a clear plus for White on account of his slight central advantage and the bishop pair (±).

A. 1 e4 ♘f6 2 e5 ♘d5 3 d4 d6 4 ♘f3 g6

5 ♗c4

5 ♘g5 is premature: 5...c6! 6 c4 ♘c7 7 ♕f3 f6 8 exf6 exf6 9 ♘e4 f5 10 ♘ec3 ♗g7 and ...0-0 =. Neither is anything gained by 5 c4 ♘b6 6 exd6 cxd6 7 ♗e2 ♗g7 8 0-0 0-0 9 h3 ♘c6 10 ♘c3 as Black obtains counterplay with either 10...e5 or 10...♗f5 11 ♗e3 d5 12 c5 ♘c4.

5...♘b6

5...c6 6 0-0 ♗g7 7 exd6 ♕xd6 8 h3 0-0 9 ♘bd2 ♗f5 10 ♗b3 and ♖e1, c2-c4, ♗g5 ♘e4 ±.

6 ♗b3 ♗g7

Not 6...♗g4?? 7 ♗xf7+.

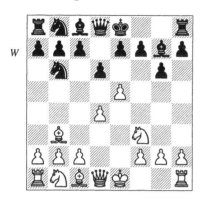

W

Plans and Counterplans:

White stands somewhat better, and has a pleasant choice between two plans. The positional one is **7 ♕e2 ♘c6 8 0-0 0-0 9 h3 a5 10 a4 dxe5 11 dxe5 ♘d4 12 ♘xd4 ♕xd4 13 ♖e1**, and with ♘b1-d2-f3 White repels the enemy queen. The tactical way is **7 ♘g5!?** e6 (not 7...0-0? 8 e6! fxe6 9 ♗xe6+ ♔h8 10 h4! ♘c6 11 h5 ♘xd4 12 hxg6 ♘xe6 13 ♖xh7+ ♔g8 14 ♕h5 +–, since White is threatening ♖h8+ and ♕h7 mate, while 7...d5 8 f4 f6 9 ♘f3 allows White a strong centre and freezes the bishop on g7) **8 ♕f3 ♕d7** (8...♕e7? 9 ♘e4 with the threat of ♗g5 or 8...0-0?! 9 ♕h3 h6 10 ♘f3 and Black's king position is weakened) **9 ♘e4 dxe5** and now White can further complicate matters with both **10 ♗h6** and **10 ♘f6+**. Apart from these two lines a very simple alternative is **7 a4!? a5 8 0-0 0-0 9 h3** with a spatial advantage for White – although Black's position is secure.

B.1 e4 ♘f6 2 e5 ♘d5 3 d4 d6 4 ♘f3 ♗g4

The most consistent move, undermining the centre.
5 ♗e2 e6 6 0-0 ♗e7
Not 6...♘c6?! 7 c4 ♘b6 8 exd6 cxd6 9 d5! exd5 10 cxd5 ♗xf3 11 gxf3! ♘e5 12 ♗b5+ ♘ed7 13 ♕d4 and the threat is 14 ♖e1+.
7 c4 ♘b6 8 h3 ♗h5 9 ♘c3 0-0 10 ♗e3

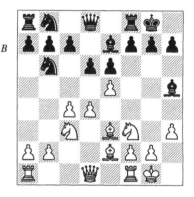

B

Plans and Counterplans:

Up to this point both sides have developed in simple fashion. Now it is down to Black to find a plan. **10...♘c6** does not seem good as after 11 exd6 cxd6 12 d5 the knight has to go. But **10...d5!?** is not hopeless: 11 c5 ♗xf3 (not 11...♘c4? 12 ♗xc4 and ♕e2 wins a pawn or 11...♘6d7 12 ♖c1 b6 13 c6! ♘xc6 14 ♘b5 +–) 12 gxf3! ♘c8 13 f4 ♘c6 and Black can follow the plan ...♗h4, ...♘8e7 and ...♘f5. And there is even a brand new idea: **10...a6!?**, threatening 11...♗xf3 12 ♗xf3 ♘xc4 as now on 13 ♗xb7 the rook on a8 has gained a place on a7! Play might therefore continue 10...a6!? 11 b3 d5 12 c5 ♘c8 13 b4 ♘c6 14 a3 f6! 15 exf6 ♗xf6 with equality; Black can try to continue either with ...♗xf3 and ...♘8e7, or ...♗f7 and ...e6-e5!? 10...a6!? has fitted perfectly into future developments – it has obstructed White's queenside pawns while White has played b4 in two moves rather than one and has not been able to strangle Black's equalizing action ...f7-f6.

In the Alekhine Defence Black has good reason to hope for equality. He should patiently but optimistically tolerate his permanent spatial handicap in order to be able to act at the right moment.

Pirc Defence

The plan of ...d7-d6, ...♘f6 and ...g7-g6 employed against 1 e4 is linked in chess literature to the name of grandmaster Pirc, who was very active in the 1930s. But in Hungary it is also associated with Aladar Antal, who had already written a monograph on the 'd6 opening' in the 1920s.

1 e4 d6

It is important to start this way so that White does not attack the knight that will soon appear on f6 with e4-e5. On 1...g6 White can play what he usually plays against 1...d6 or after 2 d4 ♗g7 he can choose between two lines which would not work under different conditions: 3 ♘f3 followed by c2-c3, ♗d3 or 3 ♘f3 d6 4 ♗c4 and then ♕e2. 1...g6 yields an additional considerable option to White: 2 c4!?, when 2...c5 3 ♘f3 ♗g7 4 d4 cxd4 5 ♘xd4 transposes into the Maróczy Bind or after 2...d6 3 d4 ♗g7 4 ♘c3 Black has the choice of the Modern Defence (4...♘c6) or the King's Indian (4...♘f6). These are really 1 d4 openings(!) and if one's opponent has not included them in his repertoire then this diversion can indeed be unpleasant!

2 d4

But now on 2 ♘f3 Black has the extra option of 2...♗g4!? 3 d4 ♘f6 4 ♘c3 e6 5 h3 ♗h5 6 g4 ♗g6 7

♕e2 c6! 8 h4 h6 9 h5 ♗h7 10 g5 hxg5 11 ♗xg5 ♕b6 12 0-0-0 ♘bd7 with a surprisingly solid game for Black. This line can also be reached via 1 d4 d6 2 ♘f3 ♗g4 3 e4.

2...♘f6 3 ♘c3 g6

White's most typical continuations are:

I. 4 ♘f3 followed by ♗e2 and 0-0,
II. 4 f4 and
III. 4 f3, ♗e3 and ♕d2.

Here are a few rare lines:

a) 4 g3 ♗g7 5 ♗g2 0-0 6 ♘ge2 e5 7 0-0 ♘c6 8 dxe5 (the threat was 8...exd4 9 ♘xd4 ♘xe4) 8...dxe5 is equal.

b) 4 ♗e2 ♗g7 5 h4 ♘c6 (or 5...h5 6 ♘f3 and White proceeds with ♘g5, f2-f3, ♗e3, ♕d2, 0-0-0, and with the constant threat g2-g4 White builds a strong attacking game) 6 h5 gxh5 7 ♗e3 ♘g4.

c) 4 ♗g5!? ♗g7 (4...h6 5 ♗e3 ♘g4 6 ♗c1 and after 7 f3 the bishop returns to e3 and the queen comes to d2 to attack the pawn on h6) 5 ♕d2 c6 6 f4 (after 6 ♗h6 ♗xh6 7 ♕xh6 ♕a5 the e4-pawn is hanging and Black is also threatening ...b7-b5) 6...0-0 7 ♘f3 b5.

As demonstrated by these variations, Black's play is almost identical to that of the King's Indian Defence. He can opt for either ...e7-e5 or ...c7-c6 (...a7-a6) and

...b7-b5 or perhaps ...c7-c5. The difference between these two openings is the placement of the white c-pawn. In the Pirc this pawn is on c2 rather than c4, which makes the centre weaker but White can more often castle queenside and the d4-square does not become a permanent hole. As we shall see, the advantages and disadvantages are roughly balanced.

I. 1 e4 d6 2 d4 ♘f6 3 ♘c3 g6 4 ♘f3

4...♗g7 5 ♗e2

On 5 ♗g5 Black can again go 5...c6 and then ...b7-b5 with counterplay. Also fine for Black is 5 ♗c4 0-0 6 ♕e2 (6 0-0? ♘xe4! 7 ♗xf7+ ♖xf7 8 ♘xe4 h6! and Black is somewhat better. He is threatening ...♗g4 and can also play ...♕f8!, ...♘c6 and then ...e7-e5) 6...c6 (with the idea again of ...♘xe4) 7 e5 ♘d5 ∞. On 5 h3 0-0 6 ♗e3 Black has the instructive 6...a6! (with the idea of ...b7-b5) 7 a4 b6! 8 ♗c4 e6 9 0-0 ♗b7 10 e5 dxe5 11 ♘xe5 ♘c6! 12 ♘xc6 ♗xc6 13 ♕e2 ♕c8!! 14 ♖ad1 ♕b7 and Black has the initiative.

5...0-0 6 0-0

6 h3 e5 (also possible is 6...b6 and ...♗b7) 7 0-0 exd4 8 ♘xd4 ♖e8 9 ♗f3 ♘bd7 followed by ...♘e5 yields Black good chances.

Black can now play

A. 6...c6 and
B. 6...♗g4,

but he also has several other alternatives. For example:

a) 6...♘c6?! 7 d5 ♘b4 8 ♖e1 e6 9 a3 ♘a6 10 dxe6 ♗xe6 11 ♘d4 ♗d7 12 ♗g5 ±.

b) 6...♘bd7 7 e5 ♘e8 8 ♗g5!? f6 9 exf6 exf6 10 ♗e3 ±.

c) 6...a6!? 7 ♖e1 e6!? 8 ♗g5 h6 9 ♗f4 b5! 10 e5 b4!! 11 ♘b1 (not 11 exf6 ♕xf6 and two pieces are hanging) 11...♘d5 12 ♗d2 ♘d7 and Black is already more developed and is threatening to gain more space with ...g6-g5. On 6...a6!? White can consider 7 a4 or 7 e5 dxe5 8 ♘xe5!?

A. 1 e4 d6 2 d4 ♘f6 3 ♘c3 g6 4 ♘f3 ♗g7 5 ♗e2 0-0 6 0-0 c6

7 a4

Impeding ...b7-b5. On 7 ♖e1 ♘bd7 8 ♗f4 (8 e5 dxe5 9 dxe5 ♘g4 10 e6 fxe6 and now the otherwise winning 11 ♘g5 fails as the pawn on f2 is hanging!) 8...♕c7 9 e5 ♘h5 10 ♗g5 dxe5 11 ♗xe7 ♖e8 12 d5 ♕b6 13 dxc6 bxc6 14 ♗a3 e4! with a double-edged fight or 7 h3 ♘bd7 8 e5 ♘e8 9 ♖e1 dxe5 10 dxe5 ♘c7 11 ♗f4 ♘e6 12 ♗g3 ♕b6 with yet another complicated game.

7...♕c7

Also good is 7...a5 with the manoeuvre ...♘b8-a6-b4.

8 a5 ♖d8 9 ♗e3 d5! *(D)*

Plans and Counterplans:
On **10 e5 ♘e4 11 ♘xe4 dxe4 12 ♘g5 c5 13 c3 ♘c6** White's centre has exploded, while after **10 exd5**

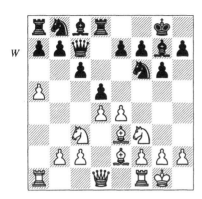

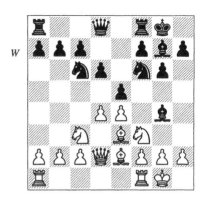

♘xd5 11 ♘xd5 cxd5 White can play for ♕d2 and ♗f4 and Black has the option of ...♗f5 and ...♘c6.

B. 1 e4 d6 2 d4 ♘f6 3 ♘c3 g6 4 ♘f3 ♗g7 5 ♗e2 0-0 6 0-0 ♗g4

7 ♗e3
7 h3 ♗xf3 8 ♗xf3 ♘c6 9 d5 ♘e5 10 ♗e2 c6 11 f4 ♘ed7 12 ♗f3 ♕a5 grants Black promising queenside counterplay.
7...♘c6!? 8 ♕d2
8 d5 ♗xf3!? 9 ♗xf3 ♘e5 10 ♗e2 c6 11 f4 ♘ed7 12 dxc6 bxc6 and White's bishop pair counterbalances Black's play on the b-file.
8...e5

Plans and Counterplans:
Here White can close the position with **9 d5** ♘e7 10 ♖ad1, but then Black surprisingly changes the nature of the game with 10...♗d7 11 ♘e1 b5! (11...♘g4!?) 12 a3 a5 13 ♘d3 ♕b8 14 f3 c6! 15 dxc6 ♗xc6 ±. Besides 16...b4, Black is also threatening 16...d5. Alternatively, White can open things up

with **9 dxe5** dxe5 10 ♖ad1, when the game is even after 10...♕c8 and ...♖d8.

II. 1 e4 d6 2 d4 ♘f6 3 ♘c3 g6 4 f4

4...♗g7 5 ♘f3
The premature 5 e5? leads to the dismemberment of White's own centre: 5...♘fd7 6 ♘f3 c5!? 7 exd6 0-0 (7...exd6 8 ♕e2+) 8 dxe7 ♕xe7+ 9 ♕e2 ♕d8 10 ♗e3 ♖e8 11 0-0-0 ♕a5 with a dangerous queenside initiative for Black (...♘c6, ...♘f6). After 5 ♘f3 Black's choices are:

A. 5...c5!? and
B. 5...0-0

A. 1 e4 d6 2 d4 ♘f6 3 ♘c3 g6 4 f4 ♗g7 5 ♘f3 c5!?

Tempting White to enter some incredibly sharp lines.
6 ♗b5+!?
Black has nothing to fear after both 6 e5 ♘fd7 and 6 d5 0-0 7 ♗e2

e6! 8 dxe6 ♗xe6, as in both cases White central plus has evaporated. 6 dxc5 ♕a5 7 ♗d3 ♕xc5 8 ♕e2 0-0 9 ♗e3 ♕a5 10 0-0 ♗g4 11 h3 ♗xf3 12 ♕xf3 ♘c6 13 a3 ♘d7! again leads to a balanced game.

6...♗d7

The only move, since 6...♘bd7? 7 e5 ♘g4 8 e6! fxe6 9 ♘g5 wins outright and after 6...♘fd7 7 ♗e3 0-0 8 ♕d2 the black pieces are entangled on the d7-square.

7 e5!?

This is more testing than 7 ♗xd7+ ♘bxd7!? 8 e5 ♘h5! 9 g4? ♘xf4 10 ♗xf4 cxd4 11 ♕xd4 dxe5 12 ♗xe5 ♘xe5 −+.

7...♘g4 8 e6

White has picked up speed. 8 ♗xd7+ ♕xd7 9 d5 dxe5 10 h3 e4! 11 ♘xe4 ♘f6 is without thrills, but the same cannot be said about 8 h3!? cxd4 9 ♕xd4 ♘h6 10 ♗d2!? (10 g4 ♗xb5 11 ♘xb5 ♘c6 12 ♕e4 0-0! is unclear) 10...♗xb5 11 ♘xb5 ♘c6 12 ♕f2 dxe5 13 fxe5 0-0 14 0-0-0 ♕b6!? In this line, instead of 9...♘h6 another feasible path is 9...dxe5 10 ♕d5 e4! 11 ♘g5 ♘h6 12 ♕xb7 ♗xc3+ 13 bxc3 0-0! 14 ♕xa8 ♕c7 and besides 15...♕xc3+ Black is also threatening to net the queen with 15...♘c6.

8...♗xb5

In the past few years another line has caught fire: 8...fxe6 9 ♘g5 ♗xb5, when White has a choice between two ways to capture:

a) 10 ♘xe6 ♗xd4! 11 ♘xb5 (11 ♘xd8 ♗f2+ 12 ♔d2 ♗e3+ followed by a perpetual on e3 and

f2!) 11...♕a5+ 12 ♕d2 ♗f2+ 13 ♔d1 ♕xd2+! 14 ♔xd2 ♔d7! ∞.

b) 10 ♘xb5 ♕a5+ 11 c3 ♕xb5 12 ♘xe6 and now both 12...♘a6 13 ♘xg7+ ♔f7 14 ♕xg4 ♔xg7 and 12...♕c4!? 13 ♕xg4 cxd4 14 ♘xg7+ ♔f7 15 f5 ♔xg7 16 ♕h4 ♘c6 have both stood up to the test of tournament practice.

9 exf7+ ♔d7!

Active, indeed!

10 ♘xb5

Not 10 ♘g5? h5 11 ♘xb5 ♕a5+ 12 ♘c3 cxd4 −+.

10...♕a5+ 11 ♘c3 cxd4 12 ♘xd4

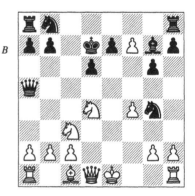

Plans and Counterplans:
What a crazy position! Black's king is floating around in the middle but he is the more developed side. Here are two examples from tournament practice:

a) 12...♗xd4 13 ♕xd4 (or 13 ♕xg4+ ♕f5) 13...♘c6 14 ♕c4 ♕b6 15 ♕e2 h5 16 h3 ♘h6 and the knight will return on f5.

b) 12...h5!? 13 h3 ♘c6! 14 ♘e2 ♘h6 15 ♗e3 ♘f5 16 ♗f2 ♖ac8 17

0-0 h4 and the black king dances to c7 and b8 whilst he will also round up the pawn on f7.

B. 1 e4 d6 2 d4 ♘f6 3 ♘c3 g6 4 f4 ♗g7 5 ♘f3 0-0

6 ♗d3

Other possibilities are:

a) 6 e5 ♘fd7 **7 h4** c5! **8 h5?!** cxd4 **9 hxg6?!** dxc3 **10 gxf7+** (10 gxh7+ ♔h8 and the white pawn protects the black king from attack!) **10...♖xf7 11 ♗c4** e6! **12 ♘g5** (12 ♗xe6 ♘xe5 13 ♗xf7+ ♘xf7 ∓) **12...♘f8! 13 ♘xf7 ♔xf7 14 ♕h5+ ♔g8 15 f5 ♕a5 16 fxe6 cxb2+ 17 ♔e2 ♕c7!** and Black wins. As it is demonstrated by this nearly twenty-year-old example, if one is undeveloped one should not play for mate!

b) 6 ♗e3 b6!? (Black does not give up on the plan of ...c7-c5) **7 ♗d3** (7 e5 ♘g4 8 ♗g1 c5 9 h3 ♘h6 10 d5 ♘d7 11 ♕e2 b5! and on 12 ♘xb5 ♗a6, while on 12 ♕xb5 ♖b8, and on 12 0-0-0 b4 13 ♘e4 ♘b6 followed by ...♗b7) **7...c5 8 ♕e2** ♘c6 **9 e5** ♘g4 **10 ♗e4** ♘b4!! **11 ♗xa8?!** ♗a6 **12 ♕d2** ♘xe3 **13 ♗e4** cxd4, and after d6xe5 Black has a tremendous game. Of course in these examples White's play was poor, but they serve to demonstrate that White must take care.

6...♘c6!?

White is on top after both 6...c5 7 dxc5 dxc5 8 ♕e2 ♘c6 9 e5 ♘d5 10 ♘xd5 ♕xd5 11 ♗c4 ♕d7 12 c3! and 6...♘a6 7 0-0 ♘b4 8 d5! with

a2-a4, ♕e1 and ♕h4 to follow. 6...♗g4 7 h3 ♗xf3 8 ♕xf3 ♘c6 9 ♗e3 e5 10 dxe5 dxe5 11 f5! ♘d4 12 ♕f2 is also better for White on account of his bishop pair and active chances on the kingside.

7 e5

On 7 0-0, Black can play 7...e5!? 8 fxe5 dxe5 9 d5 ♘d4 10 ♘xe5 ♘xe4 11 ♗xe4 ♗xe5 12 ♗f4 ♗g7! (after 12...♗xf4 the king position is left exposed) 13 ♕d2 ♘f5 14 ♘b5 ♘d6 15 ♘xd6 cxd6 with an even game. Another possible line is 7...♗g4!? 8 e5 dxe5 9 dxe5 ♘d5 10 h3 ♘xc3 11 bxc3 ♗f5!?

7...dxe5 8 fxe5

After 8 dxe5 ♘d5 9 ♗d2 ♗g4 Black is threatening to invade on d4 with his knight.

8...♘h5!

Black's plan is ...♗g4 and ...f7-f6, and for this the knight is best placed on h5.

9 ♘e2!?

9 ♗e2 ♗g4 10 ♗e3 f6 11 exf6 exf6 12 0-0 f5! 13 h3 ♗xf3 14 ♗xf3 f4 and ...♘g3 with active play.

9...♗g4 10 c3

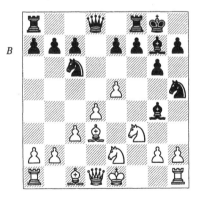

Plans and Counterplans:
Black must not take on f3 as then the f-pawn will strengthen White's centre. There is only one way to attack the pawn chain, and this is ...f7-f6. However, it is risky to play this immediately as on 10...f6 White can play 11 ♕b3+ and ♕xb7. So Black should first play 10...♔h8 and on 11 0-0 f6! 12 exf6 ♗xf6 and ...e7-e5 when he has obtained equal chances.

III. 1 e4 d6 2 d4 ♘f6 3 ♘c3 g6 4 ♗e3

This a common way to begin since 4...♘g4 5 ♗g5 h6 6 ♗c1 ♗g7 provides no cause for worry in view of 7 f3 ♘f6 8 ♗e3. With his surplus move Black has only 'gained' a weakling on h6.

4...♗g7
Perhaps this move can be spared as well: 4...c6!? 5 ♕d2! (the most precise, as after 5 f3 ♕b6! 6 b3 White can no longer carry out the plan of ♕d2, 0-0-0 because the move b2-b3 is too weakening) 5...b5 6 f3 ♘bd7 7 g4 ♘b6!? 8 b3 ♗b7 9 h4 h5 10 g5 ♘fd7 11 f4 ♗g7 12 f5 0-0!? with chances for both sides.

5 f3 c6 6 ♕d2 b5!?
More consistent than 6...♘bd7 7 g4 e5 8 h4 0-0 9 h5 exd4 10 ♗xd4 ♘e5 11 hxg6 fxg6 12 ♗xe5! dxe5 13 ♗c4+ ♔h8 14 ♕xd8 ♖xd8 15 ♘h3 and the knight hurries towards g5 (±).

7 0-0-0

Or 7 ♗h6 ♗xh6!? 8 ♕xh6 ♘bd7 9 ♗d3 (9 0-0-0 b4 10 ♘ce2 ♕b6 and Black's plan is ...a7-a5-a4 and ...b4-b3) 9...e5 10 dxe5 dxe5 11 0-0-0 ♕e7 =.

7...♕a5
The threat is 8...b4, when the a2-pawn is hanging.

8 ♔b1 ♘bd7!
Not 8...b4? 9 ♘ce2, with ♘c1 to follow, when Black has no attack.

9 ♗h6!
Stepping out in advance of the threatened ...♘b6-c4.

9...♗xh6 10 ♕xh6 ♘b6

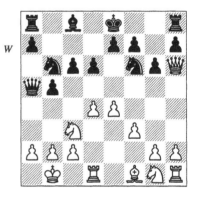

Plans and Counterplans:
Black wants to build up an attack with ...♖b8, ...♘c4, ...♗e6 and ...b5-b4, but White can parry this with ♘c3-e2-c1 or by capturing the knight on c4 and playing ♔a1 and ♖b1. Meanwhile, after ♘h3-f4 White can play for e4-e5 while controlling the d5-square. The latter plan is so strong that on 11 ♘h3 Black has to play 11...♗xh3! 12 ♕xh3 0-0 with equal chances in the middlegame.

Nimzowitsch Defence And Other Eccentricities

Those eccentrics who dislike theoretical lines and prefer to make their opponents think for themselves from the first move can answer 1 e4 with 1...a6, 1...b6 or 1...♘c6. Although these moves are rather dubious, they should not be underestimated as they do have strategic purpose. These three openings may also arise from 1 d4 if White follows up with 2 e4.

I. 1 e4 a6

2 d4

As a general principle one should reply to a suspicious move by developing, occupying the centre.

2...b5 3 ♘f3 ♗b7 4 ♗d3 ♘f6 5 ♕e2

Not 5 e5?! as after 5...♘d5 the central knight is active and cannot be driven away.

5...e6 6 0-0 c5 7 c3 ±

White is clearly better as he dominates the centre. Later he will threaten to attack the enemy king with e4-e5 or to annoy the pawn on b5 with a2-a4. On 7...d5 he can play 8 e5 ♘fd7 (8...♘e4 9 ♘bd2) 9 ♘g5!? The f-pawn is threatening to advance and the knight cannot be chased away with 9...h6? due to 10 ♕h5! ♕e7 11 ♘f7!

II. 1 e4 b6

2 d4 ♗b7 3 ♗d3 e6

Not 3...f5? 4 exf5 ♗xg2 5 ♕h5+ and wins.

4 ♘f3 c5 5 c3 ♘f6 6 ♕e2 ♗e7 7 0-0 ♘c6 8 e5 ♘d5 9 dxc5!? bxc5 10 ♘a3

10 a3!? followed by 11 c4 is also not bad.

10...0-0 11 ♘c4 ±

In view of the pawn on e5.

III. 1 e4 ♘c6

This is the Nimzowitsch Defence.

2 d4

2 ♘f3 forces Black to enter some other opening, for example 2...e5 transposes into one of the Open Games and 2...d5 3 exd5 ♕xd5 4 ♘c3 to the Centre-Counter.

2...d5

2...d6? 3 d5 ♘b8 (3...♘e5 4 f4 ♘d7 5 ♘c3 c5 6 ♘f3 threatening e4-e5-e6 and then ♗b5+). 4 c4 followed by ♘c3 ± with an immense advantage in development. On 2...e5, 3 d5?! is a slight mistake as after 3...♘ce7 with the setup ...d7-d6, ...f7-f5, ...♘f6, ...g7-g6, ...♗g7 and 0-0 Black achieves good play. White has the simple 3 dxe5 ♘xe5 4 ♘f3! (4 f4 would weaken the white king position to a great extent) 4...♕f6 (4...♘xf3+ 5 ♕xf3 ♕f6 6 ♕g3 ± or 4...d6 5 ♘d4!? and ♘c3, ♗e2, 0-0, f2-f4 ±) 5 ♘xe5 ♕xe5 6 ♗d3 followed by ♕e2, ♘c3, ♗d2, 0-0-0, f2-f4 is White's plan.

3 ♘c3

After 3 exd5?! ♕xd5 4 ♘f3 ♗g4 5 ♗e2 0-0-0 Black's has rapid development. An interesting alternative is 3 e5 ♗f5 4 c3 e6 5 ♘f3 followed by ♗e2, ♗e3, ♘bd2 and 0-0.

3...dxe4

3...e6 is quite a bad French Defence. 3...♘f6 4 e5 ♘d7 5 f4 is perhaps even worse.

4 d5 ♘e5

4...♘b8 5 ♗c4 (5 ♘xe4? e6) 5...♘f6 6 ♗f4 and ♕e2, 0-0-0 ±.

5 ♕d4!? ♘g6 6 ♕xd4

6 ♘xe4? e5!

6...a6 7 ♘f3 ♘f6 8 ♕a4+ ♗d7

9 ♕b3 ♕c8 10 ♗d3 ± and Black's development is sickly.

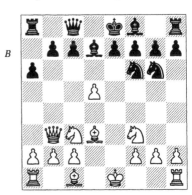

Plans and Counterplans:
White can now play 0-0 and ♖e1, and since Black's plan of ...c7-c5 and ...b7-b5 can be neutralized by a2-a4 Black has to settle for ...e7-e6, ...♗e7 and ...0-0. With his knight on g6, Black may even have to face an attack with h2-h4-h5!